DIRECTORY OF SCOTS
Banished to the
American Plantations

1650-1775

Map of Scotland, 1618.

DIRECTORY OF SCOTS
Banished to the
American Plantations

1650-1775

By

David Dobson

GENEALOGICAL PUBLISHING CO., INC.
Baltimore 1984

Introduction

During the seventeenth and eighteenth centuries thousands of Scots men, women, and children immigrated to the British colonies or plantations in the Americas. The impact of this on the demographic structure of the time varied considerably from colony to colony. According to an article by Forrest and Ellen S. McDonald entitled "The Ethnic Origins of the American People, 1790," in the April 1980 issue of *The William and Mary Quarterly,* based on an analysis of surnames, the proportion of the population of Scottish origin varied from as high as 32.9% in North Carolina to 8.7% in Connecticut. Though no similar research has been done on the West Indian colonies there is evidence to suggest that a similar pattern existed there also; for example, H. E. Egerton in his book *British Colonial Policy* reckoned that in 1762 about one-third of the European inhabitants were Scots or of Scottish origin.

Scottish immigration to the Americas during the seventeenth and eighteenth centuries tended to be spasmodic and generally small-scale, with certain notable exceptions. These exceptions consisted of several attempts to establish independent Scottish colonies and, on several occasions, the mass transportation of political prisoners. During the seventeenth century attempts were made to establish Scottish colonies in places as diverse as Nova Scotia, east New Jersey, South Carolina, and at Darien, but these had little success and were soon merged into nearby English settlements—with the exception of Darien, which failed, the surviving colonists returning to Scotland or moving to the English plantations in Jamaica or mainland America.

From the 1650s to 1830, when it was declared illegal, banishment and transportation to the colonies was a traditional punishment for certain serious crimes such as rebellion, adultery or forgery, though latterly it was used for what would now be considered petty crimes. Originally only the Scottish Privy Council could banish a person from Scotland, but in 1671 the Court of Justiciary was established and it also had such power. Though there was a steady trickle of criminals being transported to the plantations there were periods when the addition of political prisoners turned the trickle into a torrent. These periods included the Civil

War, the Covenanter Risings, and the Jacobite Rebellions. In the aftermath of the Civil War, Cromwell transported thousands of Scots soldiers as prisoners to Virginia, New England, and the West Indies; for example, 1,200 were shipped from Knockfergus and Port Patrick in May 1656. These were supplemented by a number of Scots seamen and pirates held in English jails. The Covenanter Risings of the later seventeenth century led to around 1,700 Scots men and women being banished to the plantations. The failure of the Jacobite Rebellions of 1715 and 1745 resulted in around 1,600 men, women, and children being shipped to the colonies in America.

Though demographical and historical evidence does indicate a strong Scottish element within the colonial population, genealogists require quite specific data. Very often the link between the original settler and his Scottish origins is missing. This link, ideally, comes in the form of a ship's passenger list which identifies the emigrant, his occupation, age, place of origin, and possibly the reason for emigration. Such lists do exist intermittently from the 1770s but are practically non-existent prior to that date. However, although data referring to the emigration of voluntary emigrants is virtually non-existent, bureaucratic necessity has resulted in records of many involuntary emigrants surviving. From the records of the Privy Council of Scotland, the High Court of Justiciary, Treasury and State Papers, prison records, and a contemporary journal, *The Scots Magazine,* in conjunction with miscellaneous published works, especially regarding the 1745 Rebellion, it has been possible to compile a directory of Scots banished to the American plantations, 1650-1775. While the directory does not claim to be a comprehensive source of reference to banished Scots, largely due to the fact that certain records, notably those pertaining to the Cromwellian transportees, have not survived, it does bring together in a concise form the overwhelming bulk of information referring to the Scots who were banished to the colonies prior to 1775.

I should like to express my appreciation for the help given me by the staff of the Public Record Office, London, the Scottish Record Office, Edinburgh, and the Library of the University of St. Andrews.

David Dobson

References

AC   Register of the Criminal Court of the Admiralty

CTB   Calendar of Treasury Books

CTP   Calendar of Treasury Papers

DNY   Documents Illustrative of the Colonial History of the State of New York

ETR   Edinburgh Tolbooth Records

GR   Glasgow Records

HM   History of Maryland

JAB   Jacobites of Aberdeen and Banff in the Rising of 1715
Jacobites of Aberdeen and Banff in the '45

JC   Records of the High Court of Justiciary

LC   Lamond Clan

NER   The New England Historical and Genealogical Register

OR   The Forfarshire or Lord Ogilvy's Regiment, 1745/46

P   Prisoners of the '45

PC   Register of the Privy Council of Scotland

PRO   Public Record Office

RM   B. Ransom McBride, "Lists of Scottish Rebel Prisoners . . . 1746," The North Carolina Genealogical Society Journal (May 1980)

SM   Scots Magazine

SP/C   State Papers (Colonial)

VSP   Virginia State Papers, Calendar of

For

Sean, Melanie, Matthew, and Nigel

DIRECTORY OF SCOTS
Banished to the
American Plantations

1650-1775

The Canongate Tolbooth.

ABERCROMBY JOHN
Skeith, Banffshire. Lieu-
tenant and ADC to Lachlan
Macintosh. Macintosh Regiment
Jacobite Army 1715. Captured
at Preston. Transported on
Elizabeth and Anne, master
Edward Trafford, from Liver-
pool 29 June 1716 to
Virginia or Jamaica. Landed
in Virginia - unindentured
(SP/C)(JAB)

ABERNETHY JANET
Daughter of William Abernethy
deceased, in Old Manse of
Foveran. Petty thief, Banished
at Aberdeen. Transported on
Betsy, master James Ramsay.
Landed Port of James River
Upper District 29 April 1772
(SM)(JC)

ABBOTT FREDERICK
Jacobite captured at Preston.
Transported on Elizabeth and
Anne, master Edward Trafford,
from Liverpool 29 June 1716
to Virginia or Jamaica. Land-
ed in Virginia - unindentured
(SP/C)

ADAM JOHN
Ormadale. Covenanter in Arg-
ll's rebellion. Prisoner in
Canongate Tolbooth. Banished
to Plantations 30 July 1685.
Transported from Leith by
John Ewing to Jamaica
7 August 1685
(PC)

ADAM ROBERT
Labourer, 18, Stirling. Jac-
obite captured at Carlisle.
Imprisoned at Carlisle and
York. Transported on Veteran
master John Ricky, from Liver-
pool 5 May 1747 for Leeward
Islands. Liberated by French
privateer and landed on
Martinique June 1747
(P)(RM)

ADAM WILLIAM
Merchant in Culross.
Covenanter prisoner.
Banished to America
16 August 1670
(PC)

ADAMSON WILLIAM
Smith. Williamstoun.
Covenanter. Transported
from Leith by James Curry
baillie in Edinburgh to
Virginia on Convertin,
master Captain Lightfoot
September 1668
(PC)

AITKEN THOMAS
Son of James Aitken,
needlemaker in Glasgow.
Pickpocket. Prisoner in
Edinburgh Tolbooth.
Banished to Plantations
in America for 14 years
at Edinburgh 4 August 1766
(JC)

AITKEN WILLIAM
Impost waiter, 20, Edin-
burgh. Jacobite in Elcho's
Life Guards. Imprisoned in
Edinburgh, Canongate and
Carlisle. Transported on
Gildart, master Richard
Holmes, from Liverpool
24 February 1747. Landed
Port North Potomack, Mary-
land 5 August 1747
(P)(PRO)

AITOUN JOHN
Heuchheid, Avendale.
Covenanter prisoner.
Banished to America
October 1684
(PC)

ALEXANDER DAVID
Transported on Rainbow
master William Gordon,
from Greenock. Landed
Port Hampton, Virginia
3 May 1775
(JC)

1

ALDCORN MR ADAM
Chaplain to Lady Cavers.
Covenanter prisoner in
Edinburgh Tolbooth. Ban-
ished on St Michael of
Scarborough, master
Edward Johnston, from
Leith 12 December 1678
(PC)

ALEXANDER DUNCAN
Covenanter in Argyll's
rebellion. Prisoner in
Canongate Tolbooth. Ban-
ished to Plantations
24 July 1685. Transport-
ed from Leith by John
Ewing to Jamaica
7 August 1685
(PC)

ALEXANDER GEORGE
Covenanter. Newburgh.
Prisoner in Edinburgh
Tolbooth. Banished to
Plantations 1 August
1678. Transported on
St Michael of Scar-
borough, master Edward
Johnston from Leith
12 December 1678
(PC)

ALISON COLIN
Prisoner in Leith
Tolbooth. Banished to
America 11 October 1684.
Transported from Leith
by George Scott of Pit-
lochie to East New Jersey
August 1685
(PC)

ALISON PATRICK
Carnwath. Covenanter
Prisoner in Edinburgh
Tolbooth. Banished to
Carolina 2 July 1684.
Transported by Robert
Malloch 1 August 1684
(PC)(ETR)

ALLAN ALEXANDER
24, shoemaker. Edinburgh
Jacobite in Duke of Perth
regiment. Prisoner in Dalkeith, Edinburgh, Carlisle.
Transported 24 Feb. 1747(P)

ALLAN CHARLES
19, cooper's servant.
Son of Harry Allan, Leith.
Jacobite in Elcho's Life
Guards. Prisoner in Perth,
Montrose, Inverness, ships,
Tilbury. Transported by
Samuel Smith to Jamaica or
Barbados 31 March 1747
(P)(RM)

ALLAN JOHN
Cumnock. Covenanter.
Prisoner in Edinburgh Tolbooth. Banished to Plantations 24 July 1685. Trans-
ported from Leith by John
Ewing to Jamaica 7 August
1685
(ETR)(PC)

ALLAN JOHN
Journeyman wright. Pollock-
shaws. Thief and housebreaker. Banished to Plantations
for life 1774
(SM)

ALLAN ROBERT
Thief. Prisoner in Edin-
burgh Tolbooth. Banished to
Plantations in America for
life at Edinburgh 17 July
1749
(JC)

ALLEN JAMES
Jacobite. Captured at Preston. Transported on Friendship, master Michael Mankin
from Liverpool 24 May 1716
to Maryland. Sold to Elizabeth Brown, Maryland,
20 August 1716
(SP/C)(HM)

ALLEN JAMES
Town caddy or labourer, 60.
Aberdeen. Jacobite in Stony-
wood's regiment. Prisoner in
Aberdeen, Canongate, Carlisle
Transported on Johnson master
William Pemberton, from
Liverpool 24 February 1747.
Landed Port Oxford, Maryland
5 August 1747
(P)(JAB)(PRO)

2

SCOTS BANISHED TO THE AMERICAN PLANTATIONS

ALSTON MARY alias YORSTOUN
Thief and vagabond.
Prisoner in Jedburgh Tol-
booth. Banished to Plant-
ations in America for life
at Jedburgh 10 May 1732
(JC)

ALTON JOHN
22, servant. Jacobite.
Prisoner in Canongate and
Carlisle. Transported 24
February 1747
(P)

ANDERSON AGNES
Banished to Barbados or
Virginia 28 February 1667
(PC)

ANDERSON ALASTAIR
Royalist soldier captured
at Worcester. Transported
on John and Sarah, master
John Greene, from Graves-
end 13 May 1652 to Boston
(NER)

ANDERSON ALEXANDER
Servant to George Anderson
in Kirkliston. Covenanter.
Prisoner in Canongate Tolbooth. Banished to Plant-
ations 13 June 1678.
Transported from Leith on
St Michael of Scarborough,
master Edward Johnston,
12 December 1678
(PC)

ANDERSON ALEXANDER
Upper Dalachie, Banff.
Jacobite sergeant in
Glenbucket"s regiment.
Prisoner in Carlisle and
Lancaster. Transported
21 September 1748
(P)

ANDERSON DAVID
Royalist soldier captured
at Worcester. Transported
on John and Sarah, master
John Greene, from Graves-
end 13 May 1652 to Boston
(NER)

ANDERSON DAVID
Sailor. Leith. Housebreaker.
Banished to Plantations for
life at Stirling 28 April
1774
(SM)

ANDERSON JAMES
Covenanter. Prisoner in
Edinburgh Tolbooth. Banished
to Virginia 4 August 1668.
Transported on Convertin,
master Captain Lightfoot,
from Leith September 1668
to Virginia
(PC)

ANDERSON JAMES
Tailor, 25. Ross-shire.
Jacobite. Captured at Carlisle. Prisoner in Carlisle
and Lancaster. Transported
on Veteran, master John
Ricky, from Liverpool
5 May 1747 for Leeward Islands. Liberated by French
privateer and landed on
Martinique June 1747
(P)(PRO)

ANDERSON JAMES
Bellie, Speyside. Farmer.
Jacobite in Ogilvy's regi-
ment. Prisoner in Aberdeen
and Carlisle. Transported
April 1747
(P)

ANDERSON JAMES alias PAIP
A youth. Banished for 14
years to Plantations in
America or British West
Indies at Aberdeen
September 1775
(SM)

3

ANDERSON JOHN
Royalist soldier captured
at Worcester. Transported
on John and Sarah, master
John Greene, from Graves-
end 13 May 1652 to Boston
(NER)

ANDERSON JOHN
Servant to George Winget,
maltman in Glasgow. Cove-
nanter. Prisoner in Canongate Tolbooth. Banished to
Plantations 13 June 1678.
Transported from Leith on
St Michael of Scarborough,
master Edward Johnston,
12 December 1678
(PC)

ANDERSON JOHN
Covenanter prisoner.
Banished to Plantations in
Indies or elsewhere. Trans-
ported by a Leith skipper
11 October 1681
(PC)

ANDERSON JOHN
Lanark. Covenanter. Pris-
oner in Edinburgh Tolbooth.
Escapee from Lanark Tolbooth.
Banished to Plantations
10 December 1685. Transported from Leith on Alexander
Fearne's ship John and Nicholas
master Edward Barnes,
17 December 1685
(ETR)(PC)

ANDERSON JOHN
Gardener, 18. Aberdeenshire.
Jacobite in Duke of Perth"s
regiment. Captured at Carlisle.
Prisoner in Carlisle and
Lancaster. Transported on
Veteran, master John Ricky,
from Liverpool 5 May 1747 for
Leeward Islands. Liberated by
French privateer and landed
on Martinique June 1747
(P)(JAB)(PRO)

ANDERSON MARGARET
Wife of John Copland,
tenant in Upper Mains of
Allardyce. Thief. Banished
to Plantations for 7 years
1770
(SM)

ANDERSON ROBERT
Jacobite captured at
Preston. Transported on
Elizabeth and Anne, master
Edward Trafford, from
Liverpool 29 June 1716
to Virginia or Jamaica.
Landed in Virginia -
unindentured
(SP/C)

ANDERSON THOMAS
Servant to John McKenzie of
Balmaduthie, Ross-shire.
Jacobite in Cromarty's
regiment. Prisoner in
Inverness and Tilbury.
Transported by Samuel Smith
to Jamaica or Barbados
31 March 1747
(P)(RM)

ANDERSON WALTER
Portsoy. Thief. Banished
to Plantations for 14 years
1770
(SM)

ANDERSON WILLIAM
Royalist soldier captured
at Worcester. Transported
on John and Sarah, master
John Greene, from Gravesend
13 May 1652 to Boston
(NER)

ANDREW DAVID
Thief. Banished to Barbados
Transported from Ayr 1653
(JC)

ANDREW WILLIAM
Covenanter. Prisoner in
Edinburgh Tolbooth. From
Linlithgow. Banished to
Plantations 27 May 1684.
Transported by Robert Malloch
to Carolina 1684 (PC)

ANGUS MARY
Parish of Torryburn.
Spirits thief. Banished
for life in 1772
(SM)

ANGUS MARY
Child murder. Banished
for life at Glasgow 1753
(SM)

ANGUS WILLIAM
Abercorn. Covenanter.
Prisoner in Edinburgh
Tolbooth. Banished to the
Plantations 1 August 1678.
Transported from Leith on
St Michael of Scarborough,
master Edward Johnston,
12 December 1678
(PC)

ANNAN ALEXANDER
Butcher, 19. Aberdeen.
Jacobite in Stonywood's
regiment. Prisoner in
Aberdeen, Canongate and
Carlisle. Transported on
Gildart, master Richard
Holmes, from Liverpool
24 February 1747. Landed
at Port North Potomack,
Maryland, 5 August 1747
(P)(JAB)(PRO)

ANNAND WALTER
Prisoner in Canongate
Tolbooth. Transported
from Leith by George
Scott of Pitlochie to
East New Jersey
7 August 1685
(PC)

ANTON JEAN
Child murder. Prisoner
in Perth Tolbooth.
Banished from Scotland
for 5 years at Perth
20 May 1728
(JC)

ARBUCKLE JOHN
Covenanter. Prisoner in
Edinburgh and Canongate
Tolbooths. Banished to the
Plantations in America
10 December 1685. Transported
from Leith by Alexander
Fearne on John and Nicholas,(?)
master Edward Barnes,
17 December 1685
(ETR)(PC)

ARBUTHNOTT JOHN
Tailor, 63. Aberdeen. Jacobite
in Duke of Perth's regiment.
Captured at Carlisle. Prisoner
in Carlisle, York and Lincoln.
Transported on Johnson,
master William Pemberton,
from Liverpool 22 April 1747.
Landed at Port Oxford, Maryland 5 August 1747
(P)(JAB)(PRO)

ARMOR JAMES
Merchant. Prisoner in
Hutcheson's Hospital and
Glasgow Tolbooth. Released
to go to America 27 March
1685
(PC)

ARMSTRONG EDWARD
Drummer, 17th Regiment of
Foot Thief. Banished for life
to America 25 February 1772.
Transported on Matty, master
Robert Peacock, from Port
Glasgow. Landed Port Oxford,
Maryland 16 May 1772
(JC)

ARMSTRONG ROBERT
alias HETHERSGILL
Prisoner in Jedburgh Tolbooth.
Transported to Barbados
17 April 1666
(ETR)

ARNOTT DAVID
Jacobite captured at Preston.
Transported from Liverpool on
Elizabeth and Anne, master
Edward Trafford, 29 June 1716
to Virginia or Jamaica.
Landed in Virginia - unindent-
ured (SP/C)

ARNOT JOHN
Covenanter. Tenant in
Balgedy. Prisoner in
Canongate Tolbooth.
Banished to Plantations
13 June 1678. Transported
on St Michael of Scar-
borough, master Edward
Johnston, from Leith
12 December 1678
(PC)

ASKING JOSEPH
Jacobite captured at
Preston. Transported
on Scipio from Liver-
pool 30 March 1716
(SP/C)

AUCHENLECK JOSEPH
Jacobite captured at
Preston. Transported
on Scipio from Liver-
pool 30 March 1716
(SP/C)

AULD JOHN
Drummerboy, 14. Falkirk.
Jacobite in Kilmarnock's
Horse. Prisoner in
Stirling, Edinburgh and
Carlisle. Transported
1747(?)
(P)

AUSTIE ROBERT
Forres. Thief. Banished
to Plantations for life
at Inverness 9 May 1770.
Transported on Crawford,
master James McLean,
from Port Glasgow. Landed
at Port Oxford, Maryland
23 July 1771
(SM)(JC)

AYRE WILLIAM
Jacobite captured at
Preston. Transported on
Friendship, master Michael
Mankin, from Liverpool
24 May 1716 to Maryland.
Sold to Aaron Rawlings,
Maryland, 20 August 1716
(SP/C)(HM)

AYSTON JAMES
Jacobite captured at
Preston. Transported on
Elizabeth and Anne, master
Edward Trafford, from Liver-
pool 15 July 1716 for
Virginia
(SP/C)

BAILLIE GEORGE
Bonnetmaker, 44. Dundee.
Jacobite captain. Prisoner
in Stirling and Carlisle.
Transported on Gildart,
master Richard Holmes, from
Liverpool 24 February 1747.
Landed at Port North Potomack
Maryland, 5 August 1747
(P)(PRO)

BAILLIE GILBERT
Gypsy. Prisoner in Edinburgh
Tolbooth. Transported from
Greenock to New York
21 October 1682
(ETR)

BAILLIE HUGH
Gypsy. Prisoner in Edinburgh
Tolbooth. Transported from
Greenock to New York
21 October 1682
(ETR)

BAILLIE JAMES the younger
Gypsy. Prisoner in Edinburgh
Tolbooth. Transported from
Greenock to New York
21 October 1682
(ETR)

BAILLIE JAMES
Forger. Transported to
America for life 16 July
1765
(SM)

BAILLIE or McDONALD JEAN
Banished for life. Trans-
ported on Brilliant, master
Robert Bennet, from Glasgow.
Landed at Port Hampton,
Virginia 7 October 1772
(JC)

BAILLIE JOHN
Gypsy. Prisoner in Edin-
burgh Tolbooth. Trans-
ported from Greenock to
New York 21 October 1682
(ETR)

BAILLIE MARGARET
Gypsy. Prisoner in Edin-
burgh Tolbooth. Trans-
ported from Greenock to
New York 21 October 1682
(ETR)

BAILLIE ROBERT
Gypsy and thief. Prisoner
in Dumfries Tolbooth.
Banished to Plantations
in America for life at
Dumfries 1 May 1739
(JC)

BAIN DONALD alias MCLEOD
Servant. Borrowstoun,
Caithness. Housebreaker
and thief. Transported
for life 1772
(SM)

BAIN DUNCAN
Farmer, 30. Glastollaigh
Ross-shire. Jacobite in
Cromarty's regiment.
Prisoner in Inverness
and ships. Transported
from London by Samuel
Smith 31 March 1747 to
Jamaica or Barbados
(P)(RM)

BAIN GEORGE
Labourer, 25. Aberdeen-
shire. Jacobite in
Ogilvy's regiment.
Captured at Carlisle.
Prisoner at Carlisle and
York. Transported on the
Veteran, master John
Ricky, from Liverpool
5 May 1747 for Leeward
Islands. Liberated by
French privateer and
landed on Martinique
June 1747
(P)(JAB)(RM)

BAIN JOHN
Corimonie, Glenurquhart.
Jacobite in Glengarry's
regiment. Prisoner in
Inverness and Tilbury.
Transported 1747(?)
(P)

BAIN KENNETH
24, servant to Daniel McLeod.
Ross-shire. Jacobite in
Cromarty's regiment.
Prisoner at Inverness and
Tilbury. Transported from
London by Samuel Smith to
Jamaica or Barbados 31 March
1747
(P)(RM)

BAIN WILLIAM
Elgin. Cattle thief.
Transported for life at
Inverness 1752
(SM)

BAIRD JAMES
Calderwater. Covenanter.
Prisoner in Canongate or
Edinburgh Tolbooth. Banished
2 July 1684. Transported from
Leith by Robert Malloch,
merchant in Edinburgh, to
Carolina August 1684
(PC)

BAIRD JAMES
Kirkhousell, Kintyre.
Covenanter in Argyll's
rebellion. Captured at
Dunbarton. Prisoner in
Edinburgh Tolbooth. Banished
to Plantations 31 July 1685.
Transported from Leith by
John Ewing to Jamaica August
1685
(PC)

BAIRD WILLIAM
Silk dyer. Aberdeen. Jacobite
in Stonywood's regiment.
Prisoner at Aberdeen and Carlisle. Transported on Gildart
master Richard Holmes, from
Liverpool. Landed at Port
North Potomack, Maryland
5 August 1747 (P)(JAB)(PRO)

BALFOUR ALEXANDER
Fife. Covenanter. Prisoner
in Canongate Tolbooth. Banished to the Plantations
June 1684. Transported by
George Lockhart, merchant
in New York, James Glen,
stationer burgess of Edinburgh, and Thomas Gordon,
burgess of Edinburgh
June 1684
(PC)

BALFOUR DAVID
Leith. Sailor. House-
breaker. Banished to the
Plantations for life at
Stirling 28 April 1774
(SM)

BALFOUR JAMES
Fife. Covenanter.Prisoner
in Canongate Tolbooth. Banished to the Plantations
June 1684. Transported by
George Lockhart, merchant
in New York, James Glen,
stationer burgess of Edinburgh, and Thomas Gordon,
burgess of Edinburgh 1684
(PC)

BALLINTINE WILLIAM
Jacobite captured at
Preston. Transported on
Scipio from Liverpool
30 March 1716
(SP/C)

BARCLAY DAVID
Courquhally. Covenanter.
Prisoner in Edinburgh
Tolbooth. Banished to
the Plantations in the
Indies 1 August 1678.
Transported from Leith
on St Michael of Scar-
borough, master Edward
Johnston, 12 December
1678
(PC)

BARCLAY JANET
Wife of William Crighead.
Rioter at Mylnefield.
Banished to the Plantations
for life at Perth 1773
(SM)

BARNET JOHN
Servant to John Innes of
Muirfold Esq. Banished to
the Plantations at Aberdeen
21 September 1764. Rapist.
(SM)

BARRON JANET
Thief. Banished to the
Plantations for life at
Aberdeen 1753
(SM)

BARRY THOMAS
Jacobite captured at Preston.
Transported on Godspeed,
master Arthur Smith, from
Liverpool 28 July 1716 for
Virginia. Sold to Randall
Garland in Maryland
17 October 1716
(SP/C)(HM)

BAXTER AGNES
Daughter of William Baxter in
Cardean, parish of Airlie.
Child murder. Transported to
the Plantations for life 1760
(SM)

BAXTER DAVID
Weaver in Murray of Nivilands
Factory in Crieff, Cupar,Fife.
Jacobite in Duke of Perth's
regiment. Prisoner at Tilbury
Transported 20 March 1747
(P)

BAXTER ISABEL
Child murder. Banished at
Dumfries 12 June 1758
(SM)

BAYNE WILLIAM
alias MACILVONE
Rieneclash, Ross-shire.
Thief. Banished to
America at Inverness
1755
(SM)

BEAN DUNCAN
Jacobite captured at
Preston. Transported
on Two Brothers, master
Edward Rathbone, from
Liverpool 26 April 1716
for Jamaica. Landed on
Montserrat June 1716
(SP/C)(CTP)

BEAN DUNCAN
Jacobite. Prisoner at
Inverness and Tilbury.
Transported 20 March
1747
(P)

BEAN GEORGE
Jacobite. Prisoner at
York. Transported to
Antigua 6 May 1747
(P)

BEAN KENNETH
Cromarty. Jacobite in
Cromarty's regiment.
Prisoner at Inverness,
ship, Tilbury. Trans-
ported by Samuel Smith
from London 20 March
1747 to Jamaica or
Barbados
(P)(RM)

BEATON ANGUS
48, miller to the laird
of Ardglogh, Little
Laids, Caithness. Jac-
obite in Cromarty's
regiment. Prisoner at
Inverness, ships, Til-
bury. Transported by
Samuel Smith from
London 31 March 1747
to Jamaica or Barbados
(P)(RM)

BEATTIE JAMES
Edinburgh. Thief.
Transported on the
Merchant of Glasgow
to the Plantations
December 1670
(PC)

BEATTY FRANCIS
Jacobite captured at
Preston. Transported on the
Elizabeth and Anne, master
Edward Trafford, from Liver-
pool to Virginia or Jamaica
29 June 1716. Landed in
Virginia - unindentured
(SP/C)(VSP)

BEGG MILES
Jacobite captured at Preston.
Transported on the Godspeed,
master Arthur Smith, from
Liverpool 28 July 1716 for
Virginia. Sold to Michael
Martin in Maryland
17 October 1716
(SP/C)(HM)

BELCHES ALISON
Servant to Thomas Purves,
tenant in Lintlaws. Child
murder. Prisoner in Edin-
burgh Tolbooth. Banished
from Scotland at Edinburgh
30 July 1744
(JC)

BELL ALISON
Prisoner in Edinburgh
Tolbooth. Transported from
Greenock to New York
21 October 1682
(ETR)

BELL JOHN
Ropemaker. Stirling. Thief.
Banished to Plantations for
life 1770
(SM)

9

BELL WILLIAM
46, bookseller.
Berwickshire. Jacobite
in the Manchester regiment
captured at Carlisle. Trans
ported on the Veteran,
master John Ricky, from
Liverpool 5 May 1747 for
Leeward Islands. Liberated
by French privateer and
landed on Martinique
June 1747
(P)(RM)

BENNET WILLIAM
Forger, aged over 80.
Banished at Jedburgh 1751
(SM)

BENNE JAMES
Royalist soldier capt-
ured at Worcester.
Transported on the John
and Sarah, master John
Greene, from Gravesend
13 May 1652 for Boston
(NER)

BEVERIDGE JOHN
Islay. Covenanter in
Argyll's rebellion.
Prisoner in Canongate
Tolbooth. Banished
30 July 1685. Trans-
ported from Leith by
George Scott of Pitlochie
to East New Jersey
August 1685
(PC)

BEVERLEY JOHN or WILLIAM
Jacobite captured at
Culloden. Prisoner at
Inverness. Transported
on the Johnson, master
William Pemberton, from
Liverpool 21 March 1747.
Landed at Port Oxford,
Maryland 5 August 1747
(P)(PRO)

BISHOP PETER
Hosier. Paisley. Reset.
Transported to America for
14 years in 1767
(JRR)

BLACK DANIEL
Royalist soldier captured at
Worcester. Transported on the
John and Sarah, master John
Greene, from Gravesend to
Boston 13 May 1652
(NER)

BLACK ELIZABETH
Servant to John Aitken,
grocer, Edinburgh. Child
murder. Prisoner in Edin-
burgh Tolbooth. Ban ished to
the Plantations for life at
Edinburgh 22 December 1774
(JC)

BLACK GAVIN
Monkland. Prisoner in Glasgow
Tolbooth. Banished to the
Plantations at Glasgow June
1684. Transported from the
Clyde on the Pelican by
Walter Gibson, merchant in
Glasgow, to America June 1684
(PC)

BLACK JAMES
Labourer, 18. Jacobite.
Prisoner at Canongate and
Carlisle. Transported on the
Gildart, master Richard
Holmes, from Liverpool.
Landed at Port North Potomack
Maryland 5 August 1747
(P)(PRO)

BLACK JANET
Servant girl. Airth. Child
murder. Banished to the
Plantations for life 1770.
Transported on the Crawford,
master James McLean, from
Port Glasgow. Landed at Port
Oxford, Maryland 23 July 1771
(SM)(JC)

BLACK JOHN
Covenanter. Prisoner in
Leith Tolbooth. Trans-
ported from Leith by
George Scott of Pitlochie
to East New Jersey
August 1685
(PC)

BLACK MALCOLM
Achahoish. Tenant of the
laird of Cragintyrey,
Argyll. Covenanter in
Argyll's rebellion.
Prisoner in Canongate
Tolbooth and Paul's
Hospital, Edinburgh.
Banished to the Plant-
ations 30 July 1685.
Transported from Leith
by John Ewing to
Jamaica August 1685
(LC)(PC)

BLACK NEIL
Melford, Glenbeg.
Covenanter in Argyll's
rebellion. Prisoner in
Paul's Work, Edinburgh.
Banished to the Plant-
ations 24 July 1685.
Transported from Leith
by John Ewing to Jamaica
August 1685
(PC)

BLACK PETER
Son of Hugh Black in
Portavaidue. Assault on
a Revenue Officer.
Transported to Grenada
13 July 1765
(AC)(LC)

BLACK THOMAS
Vagabond and robber.
Prisonerin Edinburgh
Tolbooth. Transported
on the Convertin, master
Captain Lightfoot, from
Leith or Burntisland to
Virginia 3 September 1668
(PC)

BLACKWOOD JAMES
Carmannock. Covenanter.
Prisoner in Edinburgh
Tolbooth. Transported from
Leith on the St Michael of
Scarborough, master Edward
Johnston, 12 December 1678
(PC)

BLACKWOOD JAMES
Jacobite captured at Preston
Transported on the Elizabeth
and Anne from Liverpool to
Virginia or Jamaica 29 June
1716. Landed in Virginia -
indentured
(SP/C)(VSP)

BLACKWOOD JAMES
Thief. Banished for 7 years
at Glasgow 1753
(SM)

BLAIR ARCHIBALD
Prisoner banished to America
Transported on the Concord,
master James Butchart, from
Glasgow. Landed Charles
County, Maryland 24 May 1728
Sold there by David Cochrane
merchant in Maryland
(JC)

BLAIR JAMES
Jacobite captured at Preston
Transported from Liverpool
on the Scipio 30 March 1716
(SP/C)

BLAIR JOHN
Thief. Banished to Barbados.
Transported from Ayr 1653
(JC)

BLAIR THOMAS
Feuar in Gartmore. Jacobite.
Prisoner at Stirling and
Carlisle. Transported
21 March 1747
(P)

BOGIE ROBERT
Prisoner in Edinburgh
Tolbooth. Transported
from Leith to the
Plantations 15 Novem-
ber 1679
(ETR)

BONE JANET
Child murder. Banished
to the Plantations at
Ayr 1751
(SM)

BOW JAMES
Jacobite captured at
Preston. Transported
on the Godspeed, master
Arthur Smith, from
Liverpool 29 July 1716
for Virginia. Sold to
John Philpott in Mary-
land 17 October 1716
(SP/C)(HM)

BOWER JOHN
Tailor. Glasgow. Jac-
obite. Prisoner at
Pathfoot and Stirling.
Transported on the
Gildart, master Richard
Holmes, from Liverpool.
Landed Port North Poto-
mack, Maryland 5 August
1747
(P)(PRO)

BOWIE ANGUS
Craskie, Glenmoriston.
Jacobite in Glengarry's
regiment. Prisoner at
Inverness and London.
Transported 1747(?)
(P)

BOWIE JOHN
Glasgow. Covenanter.
Prisoner in Edinburgh
Tolbooth. Banished to the
Plantations in the Indies
1 August 1678. Transported
from Leith on the St Michael
of Scarborough, master
Edward Johnston, 12 December
1678
(PC)

BOWIE JOHN
Servant, 14. Aberdeen.
Jacobite captured at Carlisle
Prisoner at Carlisle. Trans-
ported on the Veteran,master
John Ricky, from Liverpool
5 May 1757 for Leeward
Islands. Liberated by a
French privateer and landed
on Martinique June 1747
(P)(JAB)(RM)

BOWIE ROBERT
Servant, 14. Aberdeenshire.
Strathbogie. Jacobite in
Lord Lewis Gordon's regiment.
Prisoner at Carlisle, Chester
and York. Transported on the
Johnson, master William
Pemberton , from Liverpool.
Landed Port Oxford, Maryland
5 August 1747
(P)(JAB)(PRO)

BOWIE WILLIAM
Thief. Ballindrum, Glen
Moriston. Jacobite in Glen-
garry's regiment. Prisoner
at Inverness and Tilbury.
Transported 1747(?)
(P)

BOWMAN JAMES
Thief. Banished to the
Plantations for life at Ayr
24 May 1775
(SM)

BOWYER FRANCIS
Catholic schoolmaster, 63.
Morar. Jacobite. Prisoner at
Inverness and Tilbury. Trans-
ported 20 March 1747
(P)

BOY GEORGE
Jacobite. Prisoner at York.
Transported to Antigua
8 May 1747
(P)

BOYE JOHN
Royalist soldier captured
at Worcester. Transported
on the John and Sarah,
master John Green from
Gravesend 13 May 1652 to
Boston
(NER)

BOY ROBERT
Royalist soldier captured
at Worcester. Transported
on the John and Sarah,
master John Greene, from
Gravesend 13 May 1652 to
Boston
(NER)

BOYD HUGH
Son of Robert Boyd,
weaver in Glasgow. Pick-
pocket. Prisoner in Edin
burgh Tolbooth. Banished
to the Plantations in
America for 14 years at
Edinburgh 4 August 1766
(JC)

BOYD ROBERT
Son of Robert Boyd,
weaver in Glasgow. Pick-
pocket. Prisoner in Edin
burgh Tolbooth. Banished
to the Plantations in
America for 14 years at
Edinburgh 4 August 1766
(JC)

BOYLE ALEXANDER
Jacobite captured at
Preston. Transported
from Liverpool on the
Anne, master Robert
Wallace, 31 July 1716
to Virginia
(SP/C)

BOYLE ANDREW
Former executioner in
Edinburgh. Thief. Ban-
ished to the Plantations
for life at Stirling
12 May 1768
(SM)

BOYNE MARGARET
Elgin. Child murder.
Banished to the Plantations
for life at Inverness
10 May 1768
(SM)

BRADLEY CHARLES
Sailor. Greenock. Rioter.
Banished to the Plantations
for 5 years at Glasgow 1773
(SM)

BRADSHAW THOMAS
Counterfeiter. Prisoner in
Edinburgh Tolbooth. Banished
to the Plantations in America
for life at Edinburgh
17 July 1749
(JC)

BRAIDWOOD JAMES
Carmannock. Covenanter.
Prisoner in Edinburgh Tolbooth
Banished to the Plantations
in the Indies 1 August 1678.
Transported from Leith on the
St Michael of Scarborough,
master Edward Johnston,
12 December 1678
(PC)

DRAND JAMES
Jacobite. Transported on the
Gildart, master Richard Holmes
from Liverpool. Landed Port
North Potomac, Maryland
5 August 1747
(PRO)

BRENDAN JOHN
Jacobite captured at Preston.
Transported from Liverpool on
the Friendship, master Michael
Mankin, 24 May 1716 for Maryland. Landed in Maryland and
sold to Ben Whartfield
20 August 1716
(SP/C)(HM)

BRIGGS PAUL
Jacobite captured at Preston.
Transported from Liverpool on
the Scipio 30 March 1716
(SP/C)

BRISBANE MATTHEW
Son of the laird of Ros-
land. Parental assault.
Transported on the St John
of Leith, by William Binnie
and William Dunbar, merchants in Edinburgh
1 May 1674
(PC)

BRODIE JOHN
Servant, 20. Jacobite.
Prisoner at Canongate and
Carlisle. Transported on
the Gildart, master Rich-
ard Holmes, from Liverpool.
Landed at Port North Poto-
mack, Maryland 5 August
1747
(P)(PRO)

BROWN ALEXANDER
Prisoner in Edinburgh
Tolbooth. Transported
from Greenock to New York
21 October 1682
(ETR)

BROWN ANDREW
Farmer, 20. Dunnichen.
Jacobite. Prisoner at
Arbroath,Dundee, Canon-
gate, Carlisle. Trans-
ported on the Gildart,
master Richard Holmes,
from Liverpool. Landed
at Port North Potomack,
Maryland 5 August 1747
(P)(PRO)

BROWN ARCHIBALD
Covenanter in Argyll's
rebellion. Banished to
the Plantations 30 July
1685. Prisoner in Edin-
burgh Tolbooth. Trans-
ported from Leith by
John Ewing to Jamaica
August 1685
(PC)

BROWN CHARLES
Transported on the Rainbow,
master William Gordon, from
Greenock. Landed Port Hampton
Virginia 3 May 1775
(JC)

BROWN GEORGE
Covenanter. Prisoner at Glas-
gow, Dunnottar and Leith.
Banished at Leith to East New
Jersey 18 August 1685. Trans-
ported from Leith by George
Scott of Pitlochie to East
New Jersey August 1685
(PC)

BROWN JAMES
Frosk. Covenanter. Prisoner
in Canongate Tolbooth. Banished to the Plantations in
the Indies 7 November 1678.
Transported from Leith on the
St Michael of Scarborough,
master Edward Johnston,
12 December 1678
(PC)

BROWN JAMES
Carter. Glasgow. Horsethief.
Banished to the Plantations
for life 1774
(SM)

BROWN JANET
Vagabond. Banished to the
Plantations for life at
Aberdeen 11 May 1717
(JC)

BROWN JANET
Child murder. Prisoner in
Banff Tolbooth. Banished to
the Plantations in America
for life at Edinburgh 7 July
1740
(JC)

BROWN JEAN
Prisoner in Edinburgh
Tolbooth. Transported on
The Ewe and Lamb, master
John Guthrie, by Laurence
Trent, merchant, to the
Plantations in America
2 May 1672
(PC)

BROWN JEAN
Gypsy and thief. Prisoner
in Dumfries Tolbooth. Banished to the Plantations
in America for life at
Dumfries 1 May 1739
(JC)

BROWN JEAN
Thief. Banished for life
at Aberdeen 1753
(SM)

BROWN JOHN
Buchlivie. Covenanter.
Prisoner in Canongate
Tolbooth. Transported
from Leith on the St
Michael of Scarborough,
master Edward Johnston,
to the Plantations
12 December 1678
(PC)

BROWN JOHN
Tailor. Covenanter.
Prisoner in Kirkcud-
bright Tolbooth.
Banished to the
Plantations at Kirk-
cudbright 13 October
1684
(PC)

BROWN JOHN
Jacobite captured at
Preston. Transported
from Liverpool on the
Elizabeth and Anne,
master Edward Trafford,
29 June 1716 for
Virginia or Jamaica
(SP/C)

BROWNE JOHN
Jacobite captured at Preston.
Transported from Liverpool
on the Anne, master Robert
Wallace, 31 July 1716 for
Virginia
(SP/C)

BROWN JOSEPH
Tailor, 16. Banff. Jacobite
captured at Carlisle.
Prisoner at Carlisle, York and
Lincoln. Transported on the
Veteran, master John Ricky
from Liverpool 5 May 1747 for
Leeward Islands. Liberated by
a French privateer and landed
on Martinique June 1747
(P)(JAB)(PRO)

BROWN LILLEAS
Daughter of Robert Brown,
deceased, flesher, Kilmarnock
Child murder. Banished from
Scotland for life. Prisoner
in Edinburgh Tolbooth
13 August 1741
(JC)

BROWN MARION
Daughter of John Brown, Loch-
rutten Parish, Kirkcudbright.
Prisoner in Edinburgh Tolbooth
Child murder. Banished to
America for 14 years at
Edinburgh 9 March 1767
(SM)(JC)

BROWNE MARK
Jacobite captured at Preston.
Transported from Liverpool on
the Anne, master Robert
Wallace 31 July 1716 for
Virginia
(SP/C)

BROWN ROBERT
Vagabond. Banished to the
Plantations for life at
Aberdeen 11 May 1717
(JC)

BROWN NINIAN
Jacobite captured at
Preston. Transported
on the Godspeed, master
Arthur Smith,from Liver-
pool 28 July 1716 for
Virginia. Sold to Thomas
Jameson in Maryland
17 October 1716
(SP/C)(HM)

BROWN THOMAS
Covenanter. Prisoner
in Edinburgh Tolbooth.
Banished to the Plant-
ations 24 July 1685
(PC)

BROWN WILLIAM
Prisoner in Edinburgh
Tolbooth. Transported
from Leith to the
Plantations 15 November
1679
(ETR)

BROWN WILLIAM
Former servant to Alex.
Littlejohn, Old Manse
of Fintry. Soldier in
the 49th Foot. Fraud.
Banished at Aberdeen.
Transported on the
Betsy, master James
Ramsay,landed at Port
of James River Upper
District. 29 April 1772
(SM)(JC)

BROWNHILLS THOMAS
Labourer, 22. Kinnaird,
Inchture. Jacobite in
Ogilvy's regiment. Trans-
ported on the Veteran,
master John Ricky, from
Liverpool 5 May 1747 for
the Leeward Islands.
Liberated by a French
privateer and landed on
Martinique June 1747
(P)(OR)(RM)

BROWNLEE ALEXANDER
Watchmaker, 20. Edinburgh.
Jacobite artilleryman.
Captured at Carlisle. Prisoner
at Carlisle, York and Lincoln.
Transported on the Veteran,
master John Ricky, from
Liverpool 5 May 1747 for the
Leeward Islands. Liberated
by a French privateer and
landed on Martinique June 1747
(P)(RM)

BRUCE ....
Servitour to John Hamilton,
mason, Edinburgh. Rioter.
Transported to Virginia or
Barbados 13 September 1666
(PC)

BRUCE ALEXANDER
Jacobite captured at Preston.
Transported to Virginia or
Jamaica on the Elizabeth
and Anne, master Edward
Trafford, from Liverpool
29 June 1716. Landed in
Virginia - unindentured
(SP/C)(VSP)

BRUCE ROBERT
Jacobite captured at Preston.
Transported on the Elizabeth
and Anne, master Edward
Trafford, from Liverpool for
Virginia or Jamaica 29 June
1716. Landed in Virginia -
indentured
(SP/C)(VSP)

BRUCE ROBERT
Jacobite captured at Preston.
Transported from Liverpool on
the Anne, master Robert
Wallace, 31 July 1716 for
Virginia
(SP/C)

BRUCE WILLIAM
Husbandman, 20. Dun-
beath, Caithness.
Jacobite in Cromarty's
regiment. Prisoner at
Inverness, ships, and
Tilbury. Transported
by Samuel Smith to
Jamaica or Barbados
31 March 1747
(P)(RM)

BRUNTOUN JANET
Prisoner in Edinburgh
Tolbooth. Transported
from Greenock to New
York 21 October 1682
(ETR)

BRYCE JOHN
Mealmaker. Cambusnethan.
Covenanter. Transported
from Leith by James
Curry, baillie of Edin-
burgh, on the Convertin,
master Captain Lightfoot,
to Virginia 18 June 1668
(PC)

BRYCE MALCOLM
Covenanter. Prisoner in
Canongate Tolbooth. Ban-
ished to the Plantations
30 July 1685. Stigmatised
4 August 1685
(PC)

BRYCE THOMAS
Maltman. Covenanter.
Irvine, then Glasgow.
Prisoner in Glasgow Tol-
booth. Banished to the
Plantations at Glasgow
June 1684. Transported
from the Clyde on the
Pelican by Walter Gibson,
merchant in Glasgow, to
America June 1684
(PC)

BRYDIE CHARLES
Thief. Banished to the
Plantations at Aberdeen
1752
(SM)

BUCHANAN ALEXANDER
Buchlivie. Covenanter.
Prisoner in Canongate Tol-
booth. Transported from
Leith on the St Michael of
Scarborough, master Edward
Johnston, to the Plantations
12 December 1678
(PC)

BUCHANAN ALEXANDER
19. Son of the laird of
Auchleishie, Callander,
Perthshire. Jacobite
captain in Duke of Perth's
regiment. Prisoner at Perth
Canongate, Carlisle, ship,
and London. Transported on
the Johnson, master William
Pemberton, from Liverpool.
Landed at Port Oxford, Mary
land 5 August 1747
(P)(PRO)

BUCHANAN ANDREW
Kippen. Prisoner in Canon-
gate Tolbooth. Transported
from Glasgow by Walter
Gibson, merchant in Glasgow,
to the Plantations in
America June 1684
(PC)

BUCHANAN ANDREW
Shirgarton. Covenanter.
Prisoner in Canongate Tol-
booth. Transported from
Leith on the St Michael of
Scarborough, master Edward
Johnston, 12 December 1678
(PC)

BUCHANAN DAVID
Royalist soldier captured
at Worcester. Transported
on the John and Sarah,
master John Greene, from
Gravesend 13 May 1652 to
Boston
(NER)

BUCHANAN GEORGE
Kippen. Prisoner in Canongate Tolbooth. Transported
from Glasgow by Walter Gibson, merchant in Glasgow, to
Plantations in America
June 1684 (PC)

BUCHANAN GILBERT
Baker. Glasgow.
Covenanter. Banished
to the Plantations in
the Indies 13 June 1678
(PC)

BUCHANAN GRISEL
Westfield of Cathcart.
Prisoner in Glasgow.
Banished to the Plant-
ations for 14 years at
Glasgow 11 September
1766. Thief
(SM)

BUCHANAN JOHN
Royalist soldier cap-
tured at Worcester.
Transported on ship
John and Sarah, master
John Greene, from
Gravesend 13 May 1652
to Boston
(NER)

BUCHANAN JOHN
Son of John Buchanan,
cooper in Glasgow.
Prisoner in Glasgow
Tolbooth. Banished at
Glasgow June 1684.
Transported from the
Clyde on the Pelican,
by Walter Gibson, mer-
chant in Glasgow, to
America June 1684
(PC)

BUCHANAN JOHN
Servant to Captain Alex.
Buchanan, 22. Auchter-
arder. Jacobite in the
Duke of Perth's regiment.
Prisoner at Auchterarder,
Stirling and Carlisle.
Transported on the Gil-
dart, master Richard
Holmes, from Liverpool.
Landed at Port North
Potomack, Maryland
5 August 1747
(P)(PRO)

BUCHANAN MARION
Prisoner in Edinburgh
Tolbooth. Transported
from Greenock to New York
21 October 1682
(ETR)

BUCHANAN of BALQUHAN WALTER
Thief. Banished to the
Plantations in America for
life at Stirling 21 May 1729
(JC)

BURCH RICHARD
Jacobite captured at Preston.
Transported on the Godspeed,
master Arthur Smith, from
Liverpool 28 July 1716 for
Virginia. Sold to Benjamin
Tasker in Maryland 17 Oct-
ober 1716
(SP/C)(HM)

BURNE JOHN
Jacobite captured at Preston.
Transported on the Elizabeth
and Anne, master Edward
Trafford, from Liverpool
29 June 1716 for Virginia or
Jamaica 29 June 1716. Landed
in Virginia - unindentured
(SP/C)(VSP)

BURNETT JOHN
Miller, 28. Ballindarg.
Jacobite in Ogilvy's regiment
Prisoner at Airlie, Montrose,
Dundee, Canongate and Carlisle
Transported on the Johnson,
master William Pemberton,
from Liverpool. Landed at
Port Oxford, Maryland
5 August 1747
(P)(OR)(PRO)

BUTTER THOMAS
Jacobite captured at Preston.
Transported on the Friendship, master Michael Hankin,
from Liverpool 24 May 1716
to Maryland. Sold toFrancis
Bullock in Maryland 20 August
1716
(SP/C)(HM)

CAIRG JOHN
Pedlar, 25. Jacobite
Prisoner at Carlisle.
Transported 1747(?)
(P)

CALDERWOOD JOHN
Thief. Prisoner in
Edinburgh Tolbooth.
Banished to Virginia
7 November 1667
(PC)

CALLEND JAMES
Glover. Covenanter.
Prisoner in Canongate
Tolbooth. Transported
from Glasgow by Walter
Gibson, merchant in
Glasgow, to the Plant-
ations in America May
1684
(PC)

CALLENDAR DAVID
Royalist soldier capt-
ured at Worcester. Trans-
lated on the John and
Sarah, master John Greene,
from Gravesend to Boston
13 May 1652
(NER)

CALLENDAR JAMES
Royalist soldier capt-
ured at Worcester. Trans-
ported on the John and
Sarah, master John Greene,
from Gravesend to Boston
13 May 1652
(NER)

CAMERON ALEXANDER
20. Nairn. Jacobite in
McIntosh's regiment. Prisoner at Inverness, ships,
and Tilbury. Transported
by Samuel Smith 31 March
1747 to Jamaica or Barb-
ados
(P)(RM)

CAMERON ALEXANDER
Labourer, 16. Lochaber.
Jacobite in Lochiel's regiment.
Prisoner at Edinburgh, Car-
lisle, Chester and York.
Transported to Antigua 8 May
1747
(P)

CAMERON ALEXANDER
Labourer, 19. Lochaber.
Jacobite in Lochiel's regiment.
Captured at Carlisle. Prisoner
at Carlisle and York. Trans-
ported by Samuel Smith to
Jamaica or Barbados 31 March
1747
(P)(RM)

CAMERON ALEXANDER
Cartwright at Lord Murray's,
Dunmaglass, Inverness, 19.
Jacobite in McIntosh's regi-
ment. Prisoner at Inverness
and Tilbury. Transported on
the Veteran, master John
Ricky, from Liverpool 5 May
1747 for the Leeward Islands.
Liberated by a French privateer
and landed on Martinique
June 1747
(P)(RM)

CAMERON ALLAN
Sheepstealer. Banished at
Stirling 1752
(SM)

CAMERON ANNE
Spinner, 28. Lochaber. Jacobite
captured at Carlisle. Prisoner
at Carlisle and Lancaster.
Transported on the Veteran,
master John Ricky, from Liverpool 5 May 1747 for Leeward
Islands. Liberated by a French
privateer and landed on Martinique June 1747
(P)(RM)

CAMERON DANIEL or DONALD
40. Ardnamurchan. Jacobite
in Lochiel's regiment.
Prisoner at Prestonpans,
Edinburgh, Carlisle, and
York. Transported by
Samuel Smith to Jamaica
or Barbados 31 March 1747
(P)(RM)

CAMERON DONALD
Farmer, 30. Glen Urquhart.
Jacobite in Glengarry's
regiment. Prisoner at
Inverness and Tilsbury.
Transported by Samuel Smith
to Jamaica or Barbados
31 March 1747
(P)(RM)

CAMERON DONALD
Husbandman, 48. Fort William
Jacobite in Lochiel's regiment. Prisoner at Inverness,
ships, Medway. Transported
by Samuel Smith 31 March
1747 to Jamaica or Barbados
(P)(RM)

CAMERON DONALD
Pedlar, 20. Rahoy, Morven.
Jacobite in Lochiel's regiment. Prisoner at Inverness
ships, Tilbury. Transported
by Samuel Smith 31 March
1747 to Jamaica or Barbados
(P)(RM)

CAMERON DONALD
Thief. Transported for life
at Inverness May 1753
(SM)

CAMERON DOUGALL
Inverness. Jacobite in
Lochiel's regiment. Prisoner
at Carlisle, York and
Chester. Captured at Car-
lisle. Transported on the
Gildart, master Richard
Holmes, from Liverpool.
Landed at Port North Poto-
mack, Maryland 5 August
1747
(P)(PRO)

CAMERON DUNCAN
Servitor to Robert Farquharson
of Achriachen. Thief. Prisoner in Aberdeen Tolbooth.
Banished to the Plantations
for life at Aberdeen May 1726
(JC)

CAMERON DUNCAN
Servant to Aeneas MacDonald,
70. Moidart. Jacobite.
Prisoner at Cranston, Edin-
burgh and Carlisle. Trans-
ported by Samuel Smith 21
March 1747 to Jamaica or
Barbados
(P)(RM)

CAMERON DUNCAN
Husbandman, 32. Glenmoriston.
Jacobite in Glengarry's regiment. Prisoner at Inverness,
ship and Tilbury. Transported
by Samuel Smith 31 March 1747
to Jamaica or Barbados
(RM)(P)

CAMERON EFFIE
Spinner,28. Lochaber. Jacobite.
Captured at Carlisle. Prisoner
at Carlisle and Lancaster.
Transported on the Veteran,
master John Ricky, from Liver-
pool 5 May 1747 for Leeward
Islands. Liberated by a French
privateer and landed on
Martinique June 1747
(P)(RM)

CAMERON EWAN
Husbandman, 30. Hillhouses,
Ross. Jacobite in Lord Lovat's
regiment. Prisoner at Inver-
ness, ships, Tilbury. Trans-
ported by Samuel Smith 19
March 1747 to Jamaica or
Barbados
(P)(RM)

CAMERON EWAN MORE
Aleseller, 52. Mary-
burgh, Fort William.
Jacobite in Lochiel's
regiment. Prisoner at
Inverness, ship, Tilbury.
Transported by Samuel
Smith 19 March 1747 to
Jamaica or Barbados
(RM)(P)

CAMERON FINLAY
Jacobite captured at
Preston. Transported on
the Friendship, master
Michael Mankin, from
Liverpool 24 May 1716
Sold to William Elbert
in Maryland 20 August
1716
(SP/C)(HM)

CAMERON FLORAand child
Spinner, 40. Lochaber.
Jacobite captured at
Carlisle. Prisoner at
Carlisleand Lancaster.
Transported on the
Veteran, master John
Ricky, from Liverpool
5 May 1747 for the Lee-
ward Islands. Liberated
by a French privateer
and landed on Martin-
ique June 1747

CAMERON JOHN
Jacobite captured at
Preston. Transported
on the Godspeed, master
Arthur Smith, from Liver-
pool 28 July 1716 for
Virginia. Sold to William
Penn in Maryland
17 October 1716
(SP/C)(HM)

CAMERON JOHN
Labourer, 33. Jacobite
in Lochiel's regiment.
Prisoner at Edinburgh,
Canongate and Carlisle.
Transported by Samuel
Smith 31 March 1747 to
Jamaica or Barbados
(P)(RM)

CAMERON JOHN
Weaver, 22. Aigus, Ross-shire.
Jacobite in Lord Lovat's
regiment. Prisoner at Inver-
ness, ships, and Tilbury.
Transported by Samuel Smith
31 March 1747 to Jamaica or
Barbados
(P)

CAMERON JOHN
Labourer, 60. Lochaber.
Jacobite in Lochiel's regiment
Captured at Carlisle. Prisoner
at Carlisle and York. Trans-
ported by Samuel Smith 31 March
1747 to Jamaica or Barbados
(P)

CAMERON JOHN
Labourer, 70. Jacobite in
Lochiel's regiment. Captured
at Carlisle. Prisoner at Car-
lisle and Lancaster. Trans-
ported by Samuel Smith to
Jamaica or Barbados
(P)(RM)

CAMERON JOHN
Horsethief. Banished to the
Plantations for 14 years at
Inverness 20 May 1775
(SM)

CAMERON KENNETH
Husbandman, 21. Lochmallin ,
Ross. Jacobite in Cromarty's
regiment. Prisoner at Inverness
ships and Medway. Transported
by Samuel Smith 31 March 1747
to Jamaica or Barbados
(P)(RM)

CAMERON MALCOLM
Fort William. Jacobite in
Lochiel's regiment. Prisoner
at Prestonpans, Edinburgh,
Canongate and Carlisle. Trans-
ported on the Gildart, master
Richard Holmes, from Liverpool.
Landed at Port North Potomack
Maryland 5 August 1747
(P)(PRO)

CAMERON ROBERT
West Teviotdale. Covenanter.
Prisoner in Canongate Tol-
booth. Banished to the
Plantations 24 July 1685.
Transported from Leith by
John Ewing to Jamaica
August 1685
(PC)

CAMERON WILLIAM
Farmer, 35. Glen Urquhart.
Jacobite in Glengarry's
regiment. Prisoner at
Inverness, ship, Tilbury.
Transported by Samuel
Smith 31 March 1747 to
Jamaica or Barbados
(P)(RM)

CAMPBELL ALEXANDER
Weaver. Argyll. Jacobite.
Prisoner at Carlisle and
York. Transported on the
Veteran, master John Ricky,
from Liverpool 5 May 1747
for the Leeward Islands.
Liberated by a French
privateer and landed on
Martinique June 1747
(P)(RM)

CAMPBELL ANGUS
Lochaber. Jacobite. Pris-
oner at Dalkeith, Edinburgh
Carlisle and York.Transport
ed 4 September 1748
(P)

CAMPBELL ARCHIBALD
Mondrige, Kintyre. Cov-
nanter. Prisoner in Paul's
Work, Edinburgh. Banished
to the Plantations 24 July
1685. Stigmatised 4 August
1685
(PC)

CAMPBELL BARBARA
Spinner, 19. Perthshire.
Jacobite captured at Carlisle.
Prisoner at Carlisle and
Chester. Transported on the
Veteran, master John Ricky,
from Liverpool 5 May 1747 for
Leeward Islands. Liberated by
French privateer and landed
on Martinique June 1747
(P)(RM)

CAMPBELL CHARLES
Airth. Covenanter. Banished
to the Plantations in America
18 August 1670
(PC)

CAMPBELL COLIN
Covenanter in Argyll's
rebellion. Prisoner in Leith
Tolbooth. Transported from
Leith by Robert Barclay of
Urie July 1685. Banished to
the Plantations 30 July 1685.
Stigmatised
(PC)

CAMPBELL DANIEL
Jacobite captured at Preston.
Transported from Liverpool
30 March 1716 on the Scipio
(SP/C)

CAMPBELL DANIEL
19. Jacobite in Lord George
Murray's regiment. Prisoner
at Inverness, ship, Tilbury.
Transported 1747(?)
(P)

CAMPBELL DANIEL
20. Barrisdale's regiment.
Prisoner at Inverness, ship,
Tilbury. Transported by
Samuel Smith 31 March 1747
to Jamaica or Barbados
(P)(RM)

CAMPBELL DAVID
Falkirk. Covenanter.
Prisoner in Canongate Tol-
booth. Banished to the
Plantations 11 August 1685
Transported from Leith by
George Scott of Pitlochie
to East New Jersey August
1685
(PC)

CAMPBELL DONALD
Covenanter. Prisoner in
Paul's Work, Edinburgh.
Banished to the Plant-
ations August 1685.
Transported from Leith
by John Ewing August
1685
(PC)

CAMPBELL DONALD
28, cattleherd to Alex
McDonald of Dalchosnie,
Perth. Jacobite. Prison-
er at Inverness, ship,
Medway, Tilbury. Trans-
ported by Samuel Smith
31 March 1747 to Jam-
aica or Barbados
(P)(RM)

CAMPBELL DOUGALL
Servant, 18. Lochaber.
Jacobite. Prisoner at
Whitehaven, Carlisle,
and York. Transported
on the Veteran, master
John Ricky, from Liver
pool 5 May 1747 for the
Leeward Islands. Lib-
erated by a French
privateer and landed on
Martinique June 1747
(P)(RM)

CAMPBELL DUNCAN
24. Ross. Jacobite in
Cromarty's regiment.
Prisoner at Inverness,
ship and Tilbury.
Transported 20 March
1747 from London by
Samuel Smith to Jam-
aica or Barbados
(P)(RM)

CAMPBELL DUNCAN
Labourer, 16. Argyll.
Jacobite. Captured at Carlisle
Prisoner at Carlisle, York
and Lincoln. Transported on
the Veteran, master John
Ricky, from Liverpool 5 May
1747 for the Leeward Islands.
Liberated by a French
privateer and landed on
Martinique June 1747
(P)(RM)

CAMPBELL ELISABETH
Wife of Robert Campbell,
soldier in the Argyll
Fencibles. Pickpocket. Banished to the Plantations for
7 years 1 September 1763
(SM)

CAMPBELL EWAN
20. Ross. Jacobite in Cromarty's regiment. Prisoner
at Inverness, ships and Tilbury. Transported 31 March
1747 by Samuel Smith to
Jamaica or Barbados
(P)(RM)

CAMPBELL GILBERT
18, servant to Janet Gordon.
Sutherland. Jacobite in Lord
Lewis Gordon's regiment.
Prisoner at Inverness, ship,
and Tilbury. Transported by
Samuel Smith 31 March 1747
to Jamaica or Barbados
(P)(RM)

CAMPBELL JAMES
Royalist soldier captured at
Worcester. Transported on the
John and Sarah, master John
Greene, from Gravesend 13 May
1652 for Boston
(NER)

CAMPBELL JAMES
Jacobite captured at Preston.
Transported from Liverpool on
the Scipio 30 March 1716
(SP/C)

CAMPBELL JAMES or MCGREGOR
Piper. Crieff. Jacobite
in Glengyle's regiment.
Prisoner at Carlisle.
Transported 21 November
1748
(P)

CAMPBELL JANET
Prisoner in Edinburgh
Tolbooth. Transported
from Greenock to New
York 21 October 1682
(ETR)

CAMPBELL JOHN
Son of Donald Campbell.
Auchenchrydie, Cowal.
Covenanter. Prisoner
in Paul's Work, Edin-
burgh. Banished to the
Plantations 24 July
1685. Transported
from Leith by John
Ewing to Jamaica
7 August 1685
(PC)

CAMPBELL JOHN
Son of Walter Campbell.
Dunalter, Kintyre. Cov-
enanter. Prisoner in
Paul's Work, Edinburgh.
Banished to the Plant-
ations 24 July 1685.
Transported from Leith
by John Ewing to Jamaica
7 August 1685
(PC)

CAMPBELL JOHN
Son of Robert Campbell.
Lochwoar, Lorne. Coven-
anter. Prisoner in Paul's
Work, Edinburgh. Banish-
ed to the Plantations
24 July 1685. Transport-
ed from Leith by John
Ewing to Jamaica 7 Aug-
ust 1685
(PC)

CAMPBELL JOHN
Carrisk, Lochfyneside.
Covenanter. Prisoner in Paull's
Work, Edinburgh. Banished to
the Plantations 24 July 1685
(PC)

CAMPBELL JOHN
Prisoner in Canongate Tolbooth
Transported from Leith by
Robert Barclay of Urie to
East New Jersey July 1685
(PC)

CAMPBELL JOHN
Jacobite. Transported on the
Gildart, master Richard Holmes,
from Liverpool. Landed at
Port North Potomack, Maryland
5 August 1747
(PRO)

CAMPBELL JOHN
Fisherman. Mull. Jacobite.
Prisoner at Stirling and Car-
lisle. Transported 21 March
1747
(P)

CAMPBELL JOHN
Labourer, 20. Inverness.
Jacobite. Prisoner at Perth,
Edinburgh, Canongate, Carlisle,
Lancaster and York. Trans-
ported on the Veteran, master
John Ricky, from Liverpool
5 May 1747 for Leeward Islands.
Liberated by a French privateer
and landed on Martinique June
1747
(P)(RM)

CAMPBELL JOHN
Blacksmith, 21. Skerhiese.
Jacobite in Cromarty's regiment
Prisoner at Inverness, ships
and Medway. Transported 21
September 1748
(P)

CAMPBELL JOHN
Jacobite. Prisoner at Carlisle
and Lancaster. Transported
9 November 1748
(P)

CAMPBELL JOHN
Servant, 15. Rannoch,
Argyllshire. Jacobite in
Glengarry's regiment.
Prisoner at Perth, Edin-
burgh, Canongate, Carlisle
Lancaster and York. Trans-
ported on the Veteran,
master John Ricky, from
Liverpool 5 May 1747 for
the Leeward Islands. Lib-
erated by a French priv-
ateer and landed on
Martinique June 1747
(P)(RM)

CAMPBELL NEIL
Royalist soldier captured
at Worcester. Transported
on the John and Sarah,
master John Greene, from
Gravesend to Boston 13
May 1652
(NER)

CAMPBELL PATRICK
Son of Duncan Campbell
Meikletoun of Edinaple.
Thief. Prisoner in Stir-
ling Tolbooth.Banished
to the Plantations in
America at Stirling
20 May 1726
(JC)

CAMPBELL ROBERT
Covenanter. Prisoner
in Canongate and Leith
Tolbooths. Transported
from Leith by George
Scott of Pitlochie to
East New Jersey August
1685. Banished to the
Plantations 11 August
1685
(PC)

CAMPBELL THOMAS
Assault. Banished to
the Plantations at Ayr
1751
(SM)

CAMPBELL WILLIAM
Covenanter. Prisoner in Leith
Tolbooth. Transported by George
Scott of Pitlochie from Leith
to East New Jersey August 1685
(PC)

CAMPBELL WILLIAM
Tailor, 18. Rea, Caithness.
Jacobite in Cromarty's regiment.
Prisoner at Inverness, ships,
Tilbury. Transported by Samuel
Smith 31 March 1747 to Jamaica
or Barbados
(P)(RM)

CAMPBELL WILLIAM
Weaver, 21. Grandtully, Perth.
Jacobite in Roy Stuart's regiment. Captured at Carlisle.
Prisoner at Carlisle and Lancaster. Transported on the
Veteran, master John Ricky,
from Liverpool 5 May 1747 for
the Leeward Islands. Liberated
by a French privateer and landed on Martinique June 1747
(P)(RM)

CAMPBELL WILLIAM
alias MACLEAN NEIL
Son of Gillian Campbell, deceas-
ed, Kilmichael. Horsethief.
Banished to the Plantations.
Transported on the Rainbow,
master William Gordon, from
Greenock. Landed at Port
Hampton, Virginia 3 May 1775
(SM)(JC)

CANE HUGH
Jacobite captured at Preston.
Transported on the Elizabeth
and Anne, master Edward Trafford
from Liverpool 29 June 1716
for Virginia or Jamaica.
Landed on Virginia - unindentured
(SP/C)(VSP)

CANNON JOHN
Jacobite captured at
Preston. Transported on
the Two Brothers,master
Edward Rathbone, from
Liverpool 26 April 1716
to Jamaica. Landed on
Montserrat June 1716
(SP/C)(CTP)

CANNON SAMUEL
Banscalloch. Covenanter.
Prisoner in Kirkcudbright
Tolbooth. Banished to the
Plantations at Kirkcud-
bright 13 October 1684.
Taken from Dumfries to
Edinburgh. Prisoner in
Canongate Tolbooth 16
February 1685
(PC)

CARGILL WILLIAM
Tobacconist, 20. Mont-
rose. Jacobite in Ogilvy's
regiment. Prisoner at
Perth, Edinburgh and
Carlisle. Transported on
the Gildart, master Rich-
ard Holmes, from Liver-
pool. Landed at Port
North Potomack, Maryland
5 August 1747
(PRO)

CARMELL JAMES
Jacobite captured at
Preston. Transported on
the Two Brothers, master
Edward Rathbone, from
Liverpool 26 April 1716
for Jamaica. Landed on
Montserrat June 1716
(SP/C)(CTP)

CARMICHAEL JAMES
Workman. Leadhills.
Assault. Prisoner in
Edinburgh Tolbooth.
Banished 27 April 1725
(ETR)

CARMICHAEL JOHN
Royalist soldier captured at
Worcester. Transported on the
John and Sarah, master John
Greene, from Gravesend 13 May
1652 for Boston
(NER)

CARMICHAEL WILLIAM
Royalist soldier captured at
Worcester. Transported on the
John and Sarah, master John
Greene, from Gravesend 13 May
1652 for Boston
(NER)

CARNEGIE ALEXANDER
Labourer, 40. Brechin. Jacobite
in Ogilvy's regiment. Captured
at Carlisle. Prisoner at Carlisle. Transported on the
Johnson, master William Pemberton, from Liverpool. Landed at
Port Oxford, Maryland 5 August
1747
(P)(OR)(PRO)

CARNOCHAN EDMOND
Prisoner in Canongate Tolbooth.
Banished to the Plantations
10 December 1685. Transferred
from Canongate Tolbooth to
Leith 17 December 1685. Trans-
ported from Leith by Alexander
Fearne on his ship, master
Edward Barnes to America
17 December 1685
(PC)(ETR)

CARR ALEXANDER
Jacobite captured at Preston.
Transported on the Elizabeth
and Anne, master Edward Trafford
from Liverpool 29 June 1716 for
Virginia or Jamaica. Landed in
Virginia - unindentured
(SP/C)(VSP)

CARR ALEXANDER
Thief. Banished to
America 14 February 1764.
Transported on the ship
Boyd, master William Dunlop
Landed at Norfolk,Virginia
24 August 1764
(JC)

CARRIE JOHN
Pedlar. Arbroath. Jac-
obite in Ogilvy's regi-
ment. Prisoner at Perth
Edinburgh, Canongate,
Carlisle. Transported
on the Gildart, master
Richard Holmes, from
Liverpool. Landed at
Port North Potomack,
Maryland 5 August 1747
(P)(OR)(PRO)

CARRON RICHARD
Jacobite. Prisoner at
Carlisle. Transported
to Antigua 8 May 1747
(P)

CARTER NEIL
Royalist soldier capt-
ured at Worcester.
Transported on the John
and Sarah,master John
Greene, from Gravesend
13 May 1652 to Boston
(NER)

CARUS CHRISTOPHER
Jacobite captured at
Preston. Transported
on the Elizabeth and
Anne, master Edward
Trafford, from Liver-
pool 29 June 1716 for
Virginia or Jamaica.
Landed in Virginia
- indentured
(SP/C)(VSP)

CASSILLS JEAN
Servant to John Russell in
Easter Lenzie. Covenanter.
Banished to the Plantations
in America at Glasgow
6 October 1684. Prisoner in
Dunnottar Castle June 1685
(PC)

CATTENACH ALEXANDER
Miller, 17. Badenoch.
Jacobite. Prisoner at Carlisle
and York. Transported on the
Veteran, master John Ricky,
from Liverpool 5 May 1747 for
the Leeward Islands. Liberated
by a French privateer and land
ed on Martinique June 1747
(P)(RM)

CAVERS JOHN
Covenanter. Prisoner in Edinburgh Tolbooth. Transported
from Leith on the St Michael
of Scarborough, master Edward
Johnston, to the Plantations
12 December 1678
(PC)

CAVIE CHRISTIAN
Covenanter. Prisoner in Dunn-
ottar Castle and Leith Tolbooth
Taken to Edinburgh Tolbooth
31 October 1684. Banished to
the Plantations 11 October 1684
Transported from Leith by George
Scott of Pitlochie to East New
Jersey August 1685
(PC)

CAW JOHN
Writer. Edinburgh. Jacobite in
Roy Stuart's regiment. Prisoner
at Inverness, ship, Tilbury,
Southwark. Transported 1747(?)
(P)

27

CHALMERS CHARLES
Merchant, 30.Edinburgh.
Jacobite in Elcho's Life
Guards. Prisoner at Perth
Montrose, Inverness, ship
Medway. Transported from
London by Samuel Smith
31 March 1747 to Jamaica
or Barbados
(P)(RM)

CHALMERS ISABEL
Knitter, 25. Mearns.
Jacobite in Glengarry's
regiment. Captured at
Carlisle. Prisoner at
York, Carlisle and
Chester. Transported on
the Veteran, master John
Ricky, from Liverpool
5 May 1747 for the Lee-
ward Islands. Liberated
by a French privateer and
landed on Martinique June
1747
(P)(RM)

CHALMERS JOHN
Kinneil Jacobite in
Dillon's French Service.
Prisoner at Arbroath and
Carlisle. Transported
21 March 1747
(P)

CHALMERS JOHN
Labourer, 21. Perthshire.
Jacobite captured at Car-
lisle. Prisoner at Carlisle
and Lancaster. Transported
on the Veteran, master John
Ricky, from Liverpool 5 May
1747 for the Leeward Islands
Liberated by a French privateer and landed on Martinique June 1747
(P)(RM)

CHALMERS PATRICK
Jacobite captured at Preston.
Transported from Liverpool
on the Anne,master Robert
Wallace, 31 July 1716 for
Virginia.
(SP/C)

CHALMERS WILLIAM
Gardener. Mearns. Jacobite
in Duke of Perth's regiment.
Captured at Carlisle. Prisoner
at Carlisle and Chester.
Transported on the Johnson,
master William Pemberton,
from Liverpool. Landed at
Port Oxford, Maryland
5 August 1747
(P)(PRO)

CHAMBERS JOHN
Jacobite captured at Preston.
Transported on the Godspeed,
master Arthur Smith, from
Liverpool 28 July 1716 for
Virginia. Sold to Charles
Digges in Maryland 17 October
1716
(SP/C)(HM)

CHAPMAN JAMES
Gardener. Durn, Banffshire.
Jacobite in Glenbucket's
regiment. Captured at Carlisle
Prisoner at Carlisle and
Chester. Transported on the
Johnson, master William
Pemberton, from Liverpool.
Landed at Port Oxford, Mary-
land 5 August 1747
(P)(PRO)

CHAPMAN WILLIAM
Pedlar, 32. Aberdeenshire.
Jacobite in Grant's regiment.
Captured at Carlisle. Pris-
oner at Carlisle and Lincoln.
Transported on the Veteran,
master John Ricky, from
Liverpool for the Leeward
Islands 5 May 1747. Liberated
by a French privateer and
landed on Martinique June 1747
(P)(JAB)(RM)

28

CHAPP JAMES
21, Smith. St Marnoch's
Church, Banffshire. Jac-
obite in Roy Stuart's
regiment. Prisoner at
Edinburgh, Stirling and
Carlisle. Transported on
the Gildart, master
Richard Holmes, from
Liverpool 21 February
1747(?). Landed at Port
North Potomack, Maryland
5 August 1747
(P)(PRO)

CHATTO WILLIAM
Saddler. Kelso. Attempt-
ed murder. Banished to
the Plantations for life
at Jedburgh 25 May 1769
(SM)

CHEYNE JOHN
Royalist soldier capt-
ured at Worcester. Trans-
ported on the John and
Sarah, master John
Greene, from Gravesend
13 May 1652 for Boston
(NER)

CHISHOLM ADAM
Jacobite captured at
Preston. Transported on
the Elizabeth and Anne,
master Edward Trafford,
from Liverpool 29 June
1716 for Virginia or
Jamaica
(SP/C)(VSP)

CHISHOLM DONALD
26. Blairy, Glen Urqu-
hart. Jacobite in Glen-
garry's regiment. Pris-
oner at Inverness, ships
Tilbury. Transported by
Samuel Smith 21 March
1747 from London to
Jamaica or Barbados
(P)(RM)

CHISHOLM DONALD
27, Farmer. Glenmoriston.
Jacobite in Glengarry's regiment
Prisoner at Inverness, ship, Til-
bury. Transported 21 March 1747
(P)

CHISHOLM JOHN
40, Weaver. Invercannich, Inver
ness. Jacobite in Chisholm's
regiment. Transported by Samuel
Smith from London 31 March 1747
to Jamaica or Barbados
(P)(RM)

CHRISTIE ADAM
Prisoner in Edinburgh Tolbooth.
Warded 26 January 1721. Released
for transportation by John
Chalmers, merchant in Edinburgh,
to Virginia 9 February 1721
(ETR)

CHRISTIE ALEXANDER
Howmill. Adulterer. Banished to
the Plantations for life at
Aberdeen 12 May 1775
(SM)

CHRISTIE GEORGE
Apprentice to Neil Stewart,
musician, Edinburgh. Forger.
Prisoner in Edinburgh Tolbooth.
Banished to the Plantations in
America for life at Edinburgh
21 January 1765
(JC)

CHRISTIE JAMES
33, Linen weaver. Jacobite in
the Duke of Perth's regiment.
Prisoner at Midcalder, Edinburgh
and Carlisle. Transported on the
Gildart, master Richard Holmes,
from Liverpool. Landed at Port
North Potomack, Maryland
5 August 1747
(P)(PRO)

CLANNY MR HUGH
Prisoner in Dumfries Tolbooth.
Banished from Scotland for life
at Dumfries 2 May 1717
(JC)

CLAPERTON THOMAS
Weaver. Fochabers, Banff.
Jacobite in Glenbucket's
regiment. Captured at
Carlisle. Prisoner at
Carlisle, and Chester.
Transported on the John-
son, master William
Pemberton, from Liverpool
Landed at Port Oxford,
Maryland 5 August 1747
(P)(PRO)

CLAPERTON WILLIAM
Ploughboy, 13. Son of
Thomas Claperton (above).
Jacobite in Glenbucket's
regiment. Banff. Captured
at Carlisle. Transported
on the Veteran, master
John Ricky, from Liverpool
to the Leeward Islands
5 May 1747. Liberated by a
French privateer and landed
on Martinique June 1747
(P)(JAB)(RM)

CLARK DUNCAN
Jacobite captured at
Preston. Transported on the
Elizabeth and Anne, master
Edward Trafford, from Liver
pool 29 June 1716 for
Virginia or Jamaica
(SP/C)(VSP)

CLARKSON JAMES
Linlithgow. Covenanter.
Prisoner in Edinburgh Tol-
booth. Transported from
Leith by Robert Malloch,
merchant in Edinburgh, to
Carolina May 1684
(PC)

CLARK JOHN
Writer. Edinburgh. Pris-
oner in Edinburgh Tolbooth
Banished to the Plantations
12 December 1678. Trans-
ported from Leith on the
St Michael of Scarborough,
master Edward Johnston
(PC)

CLARK JOHN
Banished for 10 years.
Transported on the Brilliant,
master Robert Bennet, from
Glasgow. Landed at Port
Hampton, Virginia 7 October
1772
(JC)

CLAVERING MRS ELIZABETH
(NEE HAMILTON)
Seamstress, 22. Banff.
Jacobite captured at Carlisle
Prisoner at Carlisle and York.
Transported from Liverpool on
the Veteran, master John Ricky,
for the Leeward Islands.
Liberated by a French privateer
and landed on Martinique June
1747. (Her husband, Edward
Clavering was from Northumber-
land, and had served with the
Jacobite Manchester regiment
- he was executed in York
1 November 1746)
(P)(RM)

CLERK DOUGAL
in Otter, tenant of the laird
of Gallachie. Covenanter in
Argyll's rebellion. Prisoner
in Edinburgh Tolbooth. Transported from Leith by John Ewing
to Jamaica 12 August 1685.
Banished to the Plantations
31 July 1635
(ETR)(PC)

CLERK JOHN
Covenanter in Argyll's rebellion
Transported from Leith by William
Arbuckle, merchant in Glasgow, to
New England 9 July 1685
(PC)

CLERK MARY
Covenanter. Banished to the
Plantations 28 July 1685. Stigmatised. Transported from Leith
by John Ewing to Jamaica August
1685
(PC)

CLYDESDALE RICHARD
Chapman. Covenanter. Pris-
oner in Edinburgh Tolbooth
Banished to the Plantations
in the Indies 7 November
1678. Transported from
Leith on the St Michael of
Scarborough,master Edward
Johnston, 12 December 1678
(PC)

COATS WILLIAM
Labourer, 55. Aberdeenshire
Jacobite. Prisoner at Car-
lisle, and Lancaster. Trans-
ported from Liverpool on the
Veteran, master John Ricky,
5 May 1747 for the Leeward
Islands. Liberated by a
French privateer and landed
on Martinique June 1747
(P)(JAB)(RM)

COCHRAN MUNGO
Glasgow. Covenanter. Prisoner in Edinburgh Tolbooth.
Transported on the St Michael
of Scarborough, master
Edward Johnston, from Leith
to the Plantations 12 December, 1678
(PC)

COFFIE JAMES
Banished for life. Trans-
ported on the Brilliant,
master Robert Bennet, from
Glasgow. Landed at Port
Hampton, Virginia
7 October 1772
(JC)

COLFORD MARGARET
Banished to America.
Transported on the Concord,
of Glasgow, master James
Butchart, from Glasgow.
Landed at Charles County,
Maryland 24 May 1728. Sold
there by David Cochrane,
merchant in Maryland
(JC)

COLLEY JAMES
Horsehirer. Attempted rape.
Banished to the Plantations
at Aberdeen 8 September 1763
(SM)

COLQUHOUN ARCHIBALD
32, Farmer. Appin. Jacobite
in Stewart of Ardshiel's
regiment. Prisoner at Inverness, ship, Tilbury. Transported by Samuel Smith from
London to Jamaica or Barbados
20 March 1747
(P)(RM)

CONAHER JOHN
Jacobite captured at Preston.
Transported on the Friendship,
master Michael Mankin, from
Liverpool to Maryland 24 May
1716. Sold to Philip Kersey
in Maryland 20 August 1716
(SP/C)(HM)

CONNELL WILLIAM
Jacobite. Transported on the
Johnson, master William
Pemberton, from Liverpool
Landed at Port Oxford, Mary-
land 5 August 1747
(P)(PRO)

COOK THOMAS
Tenant of David Lumsden of
Cushnie, Aberdeenshire.
Jacobite captured at Preston
1715. Transported to Virginia
(JAB)

COOPER PATRICK
Jacobite captured at Preston.
Transported on the Friendship,
master Michael Mankin, from
Liverpool to Maryland 24 May
1716. Sold to Albertus
Greening in Maryland 20 August
1716
(SP/C)(HM)

COPLAND ROBERT
Jacobite captured at Preston
Transported from Liverpool
on the Elizabeth and Anne,
master Edward Trafford, for
Virginia or Jamaica 29 June
1716. Landed in Virginia -
unindentured
(SP/C)

COPLAND WILLIAM
Thief. Banished to the
Plantations for 7 years at
Aberdeen 12 May 1775
(SM)

CORBETT ANDREW
Covenanter. Prisoner in
Leith and Dunnottar. Banish
ed to the Plantations, at
Leith 18 August 1685. Trans
ported from Leith by George
Scott of Pitlochie to East
New Jersey August 1685
(PC)

CORBETT JOHN
Covenanter. Prisoner in
Dunnottar and Canongate.
Banished to the Plantat-
ions, at Burntisland 20
May 1685. Transported
from Leith by George
Scott of Pitlochie to
East New Jersey August
1685
(PC)

CORHEAD AGNES
Covenanter. Prisoner in
Dumfries, Dunnottar and
Leith. Banished to the
Plantations, at Leith 18
August 1685. Transported
from Leith by George
Scott of Pitlochie to East
New Jersey August 1685
(PC)

CORSAN JOHN
Covenanter. Prisoner in Leith.
Banished to the Plantations,
at Leith 18 August 1685. Trans-
ported from Leith by George
Scott of Pitlochie to East New
Jersey August 1685
(PC)

CORSE ELIZABETH
Covenanter. Prisoner in
Dunnottar and Leith. Banished
to the Plantations 11 October
1684. Transported from Leith
by George Scott of Pitlochie
to East New Jersey August 1685
(PC)

COUTTS JAMES
Blackmailer. Transported to
America, at Aberdeen May 1749
(SM)

COWAN BARBARA
Covenanter. Prisoner in Dumfries
Burntisland, Dunnottar and Leith
Banished to the Plantations, at
Leith 18 August 1685. Transport
ed from Leith by George Scott
of Pitlochie to East New Jersey
August 1685
(PC)

COWAN MARJORY
Covenanter. Prisoner in Burnt-
island, Dunnottar and Leith.
Banished to the Plantations, at
Leith 18 August 1685. Transported
from Leith by George Scott of
Pitlochie to East New Jersey
August 1685
(PC)

COWAN WILLIAM
Tailor, 52. Prestonpans. Jac-
obite in the Duke of Perth's
regiment. Captured at Carlisle
Prisoner at Carlisle, York and
Lincoln. Transported on the
Johnson, master William Pember-
ton, from Liverpool. Landed at
Port Oxford, Maryland 5 August
1747
(P)(PRO)

CRAIG JOHN
Thief. Banished to the
Plantations for life, at
Aberdeen May 1753
(SM)

CRAIGHEAD GEORGE
For conducting a clandes-
tine marriage. Prisoner
in Edinburgh Tolbooth.
Banished from Scotland
at Edinburgh 6 February
1750
(JC)

CRAIGIN ROBERT
Tailor, 21. Jacobite.
Prisoner in Edinburgh,
and Carlisle. Transport-
ed on the Johnson, master
William Pemberton, from
Liverpool. Landed at Port
Oxford, Maryland 5 August
1747
(P)(PRO)

CRAIGOW JANET
Childmurder. Banished at
Ayr September 1749
(SM)

CRAMPTON JAMES
Jacobite captured at
Preston. Transported on
the Godspeed,master
Arthur Smith, from Liver
pool 28 July 1716 for
Virginia. Sold to Francis
Clavo in Maryland 17 Oct-
ober, 1716
(SP/C)(HM)

CRANE PETER
19, Hardwareman. Perth-
shire. Jacobite. Prison-
er in Carlisle and Lan-
caster. Transported 21
February 1747
(P)

CRASTER WILLIAM
Jacobite. Captured at Preston.
Transported from Liverpool on
the Elizabeth and Anne, master
Edward Trafford, 29 June 1716
to Virginia or Jamaica. Landed
in Virginia - unindentured
(SP/C)(VSP)

CRAWFORD DUNCAN
Prisoner in Edinburgh Tolbooth
Banished to the Plantations
11 August 1685. Transported by
John Ewing from Leith 12 August
1685 to Jamaica
(ETR)(PC)

CRAWFORD GIDEON
Lanark. Covenanter. Prisoner in
Edinburgh Tolbooth. Warded
20 June 1684. Banished to the
Plantations 2 July 1684. Trans-
ported to Carolina by Robert
Malloch, merchant in Edinburgh,
1 August 1684
(ETR)(PC)

CRAWFORD JOHN
Otter, Argyll. Covenanter in
Argyll's rebellion. Prisoner
in Edinburgh Tolbooth. Banished to the Plantations
31 July 1685. Transported from
Leith by John Ewing to Jamaica
12 August 1685
(ETR)(PC)

CRICHTON DAVID
Dundee. Jacobite. Prisoner in
Stirling and Carlisle. Trans-
ported 21 March 1747
(P)

CRICHTOUN JOHN
Kilpatrick on the Muir. Covenanter. Prisoner in Canongate
Tolbooth. Banished to Carolina
19 June 1684. Transported from
Leith by Robert Malloch, merchant
burgess of Edinburgh, to Carolina August 1684
(PC)

CRICHTON JOHN
Dalry. Covenanter. Pris-
oner in Dumfries, Burnt-
island, Dunnottar and
Leith. Banished to the
Plantations, at Leith
18 August 1685. Trans-
ported from Leith by
George Scott of Pitlochie
to East New Jersey
August 1685
(PC)

CRIGHTON JAMES
Arbroath. Jacobite in
Ogilvy's regiment. Pris-
oner in Arbroath, Dundee
and Canongate. Transport-
ed on the Gildart, master
Richard Holmes, from
Liverpool. Landed at Port
North Potomack, Maryland
5 August 1747
(P)(OR)(PRO)

CRIGHTON JOHN
Labourer. Cablen, Perth-
shire. Jacobite in Roy
Stuart's regiment. Capt-
ured at Carlisle. Prisoner
at Carlisle and Chester.
Transported on the Gil-
dart, master Richard Holmes
from Liverpool. Landed at
Port North Potomack, Maryland 5 August 1747
(P)(PRO)

CROSBIE DAVID
Carmannock. Covenanter.
Prisoner in Edinburgh
Tolbooth. Transported on
the St Michael of Scar-
borough, master Edward
Johnston, from Leith to
the Plantations 12 Dec-
ember, 1678
(PC)

CRUIKSHANK JOHN
Herdsman, 14. Aberdeen. Jac-
obite in Ogilvy's regiment.
Transported or the Veteran,
master John Ricky, from
Liverpool 5 May 1747 for the
Leeward Islands. Liberated by
a French privateer and landed
on Martinique June 1747
(P)(OR)(RM)

CUMIN JOHN
Weaver. Bridgend of Glasgow.
Covenanter. Prisoner in Canon-
gate Tolbooth. Banished to the
Plantations 1 August 1678. Trans
ported from Leith on the
St Michael of Scarborough, master
Edward Johnston, 12 December 1678
(PC)

CUMMIN ALEXANDER
Jacobite captured at Preston.
Transported from Liverpool on
the Anne, master Robert Wallace,
to Virginia 31 July 1716
(SP/C)

CUMMING DUNCAN
65. Auchtuie, Glen Urquhart.
Jacobite in Glengarry's regiment
Prisoner at Inverness. Transport
ed 21 March 1747
(P)

CUMMING JANE
Alvie, Morayshire. Jacobite.
Prisoner at Carlisle and Lan-
caster. Transported on the
Johnson, master William Pember-
ton, from Liverpool. Landed at
Port Oxford, Maryland 5 August
1747
(P)(PRO)

CUMMIN PETER
Jacobite captured at Preston.
Transported from Liverpool on
the Scipio 30 March 1716
(SP/C)

CUMMIN PETER
Jacobite captured at
Preston. Transported from
Liverpool on the Scipio,
30 March 1716
(SP/C)

CUMMINS WILLIAM
Jacobite captured at
Preston. Transported from
Liverpool on the Friendship
master Michael Mankin, to
Maryland 24 May 1716. Sold
to Thomas McNemara in Mary
land 20 August 1716
(SP/C)(HM)

CUNNINGHAM ALEXANDER
Cook to the Earl of Strath
more. Fireraiser. Trans-
ported from the Clyde on
the Swallow of Westchester
by John Leckie and partners
merchants in Glasgow, to
the Plantations in America
probably Virginia, 10 August 1677
(PC)

CUNNINGHAM ARCHIBALD
Thief. Prisoner in Edin-
burgh Tolbooth. Transport-
ed on William Johnston's
The Blossom to the
Plantations 23 December
1680
(ETR)

CUNNINGHAM ARTHUR
Paisley. Prisoner in
Glasgow Tolbooth. Ban-
ished to the Plantations
at Glasgow June 1684.
Transported from the
Clyde on the Pelican
by Walter Gibson,
merchant in Glasgow,
to America June 1684
(PC)

CUNNINGHAM JOHN
Prisoner in Edinburgh Tolbooth
Banished to the Plantations 29
July 1685. Stigmatised 4 August
1685. Transported from Leith by
John Ewing to Jamaica 11 August
1685
(ETR)(PC)

CUNNINGHAM JOHN
Labourer, 32. Argyll. Jacobite
in the Duke of Perth's regiment
Captured at Carlisle. Prisoner
at Carlisle and Lancaster.
Transported from Liverpool
on the Veteran, master John
Ricky, for the Leeward Islands
Liberated by a French privateer
and landed on Martinique June
1747
(P)(RM)

CUNNINGHAM PATRICK
Covenanter. Prisoner at Burntisland, Dunnottar, Leith and
Edinburgh. Banished to the
Plantations, at Leith 18 August
1685. Transported from Leith
by George Scott of Pitlochie
to East New Jersey August 1685
(PC)

CUNNINGHAM WILLIAM
Covenanter. Prisoner in Edin-
burgh Tolbooth. Banished to
East New Jersey 21 August 1685.
Transported from Leith by George
Scott of Pitlochie to East New
Jersey 22 August 1685.
(Possibly the William Cunningham
of Ashinyards who was brought to
Edinburgh Tolbooth from Ayr Tol-
booth 25 October 1684)
(ETR)(PC)

DALGETTY JOHN
Jacobite captured at Preston.
Transported on the Friendship,
master Michael Mankin, from
Liverpool to Maryland 24 May
1716. Sold to Phile. Lloyd in
Maryland 20 August 1716
(HM)(SP/C)

DALGLEISH ALEXANDER
Kilkryde. Covenanter.
Prisoner at Burntisland,
Dunnottar, and Leith.
Banished to the Plant-
ations, at Leith 18 Aug-
ust 1685. Transported
from Leith by George
Scott of Pitlochie to
East New Jersey August
1685
(PC)

DALGLEISH ELIZABETH
Child murder. Banished
for life. 16 March 1768
(JC)

DALZIELL ELIZABETH
Vagabond. Banished to
the Plantations for life,
at Aberdeen 11 May 1717
(JC)

DAVIDSON ALEXANDER
Shoemaker. Canongate.
Jacobite. Prisoner at
Gask, Canongate and Car-
lisle. Transported March
1747
(P)

DAVÍDSON ALEXANDER
27. Charlton, Aberdeen.
Jacobite in Farquharson's
regiment. Prisoner at
Inverness, ship, Tilbury.
Transported from London
by Samuel Smith 31 March
1747 to Jamaica or Bar-
bados
(P)

DAVIDSON ALEXANDER
Herdsman, 17. Badenoch.
Jacobite. Prisoner at
Stirling, Canongate,
Carlisle and York. Trans-
ported from Liverpool on
the Veteran, master John
Ricky, for the Leeward
Islands. Liberated by a
French privateer and
landed on Martinique June
1747
(P)(RM)

DAVIDSON ANDREW
Jacobite captured at Preston.
Transported on the Friendship,
master Michael Mankin, from
Liverpool to Maryland 24 May
1716. Sold to Francis Bullock
in Maryland 20 August 1716
(SP/C)(HM)

DAVIDSON BENJAMIN
Thief. Banished at Perth for
life September 1750
(SM)

DAVIDSON CHARLES
Thief. Prisoner in Edinburgh
Tolbooth. Transported on the
Phoenix of Leith, master James
Gibson, by Robert Learmonth,
merchant in Edinburgh, to
Virginia from Leith 4 May 1666
(ETR)

DAVIDSON CHARLES
Servant to Alexander Gordon,
Aberzeldie. Jacobite in Stony-
wood's regiment. Transported on
the Johnson, master William
Pemberton, from Liverpool.
Landed at Port Oxford, Maryland
5 August 1747
(P)(PRO)

DAVIDSON JOHN
Upper Old Garth. Thief. Prisoner
in Dumfries Tolbooth. Banished
to the Plantations in the East
or West Indies, at Dumfries
May 1720
(JC)

DAVIDSON JOHN
Jacobite in the Duke of Perth's
regiment. Prisoner in Carlisle.
Transported 1747(?)
(P)

DAVIDSON JOHN
Undermiller. Gordon's Mill.
Banished to the Plantations for
7 years, at Aberdeen 14 Sept-
ember, 1765. Wifebeater
(SM)

DAVIDSON PETER
Strathmiglo. Thief.
Banished to the Plant-
ations for 14 years,1769
(SM)

DAVIDSON WILLIAM
Tenant of David Lumsden
of Cushnie, Aberdeenshire.
Jacobite captured at
Preston. Transported from
Liverpool by Michael Man-
kin on the Friendship to
Maryland or Virginia 24
May 1716. Sold to Mor-
decai Moor in Maryland
20 August 1716
(SP/C)(JAB)(HM)

DAVIDSON WILLIAM
Robber. Banished to the
Plantations for life, at
Perth 1773
(SM)

DAVIE MARION or MARY
Servant to John Boston
at Wester Grange. Child
Murder. Banished to the
Plantations in America
for life, at Edinburgh
1 December 1766. Prisoner
in Edinburgh Tolbooth
(JC)

DAVIE ROBERT
Jacobite. Transported
from Liverpool on the
Johnson, master William
Pemberton. Landed at
Port Oxford, Maryland
5 August 1747
(PRO)

DAW ANDREW
Jacobite captured at
Preston. Transported on
the Friendship, master
Michael Mankin, from
Liverpool 24 May 1716.
Sold to Roger Woolforde
in Maryland 20 August
1716
(SP/C)(HM)

DELL WILLIAM
Royalist soldier captured at
Worcester. Transported on the
John and Sarah, master John
Greene, from Gravesend 13 May
1652 for Boston
(NER)

DENHAM JAMES
Jacobite captured at Preston.
Transported on the Friendship,
master Michael Mankin, from
Liverpool 24 May 1716 for Mary-
land. Sold to John Clark in
Maryland 20 August 1716
(SP/C)(HM)

DENOVAN JAMES
Foulshiels, Whitburn, Linlithgow.
Horsethief. Prisoner in Edinburgh
Tolbooth. Banished to the Plant-
ations in America for 14 years,
at Edinburgh 22 March 1763
(JC)

DEWARS ALEXANDER
Banished to the Plantations in
America. Bail bond by Robert
Paterson 2 October 1728. Trans-
ported from Glasgow on the
brigantine John and Robert, master
Thomas Clark, to South Carolina.
Landed in America 22 July 1730.
Indentured
(JC)

DICK DAVID
Shoemaker, 22. Jacobite. Prisoner
at Edinburgh and Carlisle. Trans-
ported on the Gildart, master
Richard Holmes, from Liverpool
Landed at Port North Potomac,
Maryland 5 August 1747
(P)(PRO)

DICK JOHN alias KIDD
Livingstone. Covenanter. Prisoner
in Glasgow Tolbooth. Banished at
Glasgow June 1684. Transported
from the Clyde on the Pelican by
Walter Gibson, merchant in Glasgow,
to America June 1684
(PC)

DICK QUENTIN
Covenanter. Prisoner at
Edinburgh and Dunnottar.
Banished to the Plantat-
ions, at Burntisland 20
May 1685
(PC)

DICKENSON GEORGE
Jacobite captured at
Preston. Transported from
Liverpool on the Elizabeth
and Anne, master Edward
Trafford, to Virginia or
Jamaica 29 June 1716.
Landed in Virginia -
indentured
(SP/C)(VSP)

DICKS ROBERT
Prisoner in Edinburgh Tolbooth. Banished to the
Plantations. Transported
on the St Michael of Scarborough, master Edward
Johnston, from Leith
12 December 1678
(PC)

DICKSON JAMES
Ropemaker. Stirling. Thief.
Banished to the Plantations
for 7 years in 1770
(SM)

DICKSON THOMAS
Servant to Mrs Drummond,
Meadowhope. Rape.Prisoner
in Edinburgh Tolbooth.
Banished to the Plantat-
ions in America for 7
years, at Edinburgh
4 August 1744
(JC)

DIN JOHN alias KEELLY
Branshog. Thief. Banish-
ed to the Plantations in
America, at Stirling
21 May 1729
(JC)

DINGWALL DANIEL
Glover, 31. Inverness. Jacobite captured at Carlisle.
Prisoner at Carlisle and Lancaster. Transported from Liverpool on the Veteran, master
John Ricky, 5 May 1747 for the
Leeward Islands. Liberated by
a French privateer and landed
on Martinique June 1747
(P)(RM)

DINGWALL DONALD
24, servant to Farquhar McCrae.
Ross-shire. Jacobite in
Cromarty's regiment. Prisoner
at Inverness and Tilbury. Transported from London by Samuel
Smith to Jamaica or Barbados
31 March 1747
(P)(RM)

DIXON JAMES
Jacobite captured at Preston.
Transported on the Godspeed,
master Arthur Smith, from
Liverpool 28 July 1716 for
Virginia. Sold to John Bruce
in Maryland 18 October 1716
(SP/C)(HM)

DODDS JAMES
Farmer, 29. Setonhill Mains,
Belton, Haddington. Jacobite
in Belmerino's Life Guards.
Prisoner at Inverness, ship
and Tilbury. Transported from
London by Samuel Smith 31 March
1747 to Jamaica or Barbados
(P)(RM)

DONALD WILLIAM
Stampmaster at Greenock. Forger.
Prisoner in Renfrew Tolbooth.
Banished to the Plantations in
America for life, at Edinburgh
27 February 1744
(JC)

DONALD JAMES
Tailor, 20. Mearns. Jac-
obite in Lord George
Murray's regiment. Capt-
ured at Carlisle. Pris-
oner at Carlisle and
Lincoln. Transported on
the Veteran, master John
Ricky, from Liverpool to
the Leeward Islands 5
May 1747. Liberated by a
French privateer and
landed on Martinique
June 1747
(P)(RM)

DONALDSON ALEXANDER
Labourer, 40. Banff.
Jacobite. Prisoner at
Whitehaven and Carlisle
Transported 1747(?)
(P)

DONALDSON CHARLES
Jacobite captured at
Preston. Transported on
the Friendship, master
Michael Mankin, from
Liverpool 24 May 1716.
Landed in Maryland and
sold to Aaron Rawlings
20 August 1716
(SP/C)(HM)

DONALDSON JAMES
25, servant to Andrew
Hay of Ranass, Banff.
Jacobite in Pitsligo's
Horse. Prisoner at
Inverness, ships, and
Tilbury. Transported
1747(?)
(P)

DONALDSON JAMES
Wright, 50. Edinburgh.
Jacobite in Ogilvy's
regiment. Prisoner at
Dunblane, Montrose,
Dundee, canongate and
Carlisle. Transported
on the Gildart, master
Richard Holmes, from
Liverpool. Landed at
Port North Potomack,
Maryland 5 August 1747
(P)(PRO)

DONALDSON JOHN
Jacobite captured at Preston.
Transported from Liverpool on
the Elizabeth and Anne, master
Edward Trafford, for Virginia
or Jamaica 29 June 1716. Landed
Virginia - inindentured
(SP/C)(VSP)

DONALDSON THOMAS
Jacobite captured at Preston.
Transported from Liverpool on
the Friendship, master Michael
Mankin, to Maryland 24 May 1716.
Sold to John Cheney in Maryland
20 August 1716
(SP/C)(HM)

DONALDSON WILLIAM
Jacobite captured at Preston.
Transported from Liverpool on
the Elizabeth and Anne, master
Edward Trafford, to Virginia
or Jamaica 29 June 1716. Landed
in Virginia - unindentured
(SP/C)(VSP)

DOUGALL ARTHUR
Wright. Glasgow. Covenanter.
Prisoner in Canongate Tolbooth
Banished to the Plantations in
the Indies 13 June 1678. Transported on the St Michael of Scar
borough, from Leith 12 December
1678, master Edward Johnston
(PC)

DOUGLAS CHARLES
Covenanter. Prisoner in Canongate
Tolbooth, Dunnottar Castle, and
Leith Tolbooth. Banished to the
Plantations, at Leith 18 August
1685. Transported from Leith by
George Scott of Pitlochie to
East New Jersey August 1685
(PC)

DOUGLAS THOMAS
Prisoner in Edinburgh Tolbooth.
Transported by Alexander Fearne
and Edward Barnes, his shipmaster
to America from Leith 17 December
1685
(ETR)

DOUGLAS THOMAS
  Tinker. Bannockburn.
  Thief. Banished at Stir-
  ling 1754
  (SM)

DOUGLAS WILLIAM
  Bridge of Ken. Covenanter.
  Prisoner at Dumfries,
  Burntisland, Dunnottar
  and Leith. Banished to
  the Plantations, at Leith
  18 August 1685. Transport
  ed from Leith by George
  Scott of Pitlochie to
  East New Jersey August
  1685
  (PC)

DOW JOHN
  Servant to Lord Nairn, 30.
  Atholl. Jacobite. Prisoner
  at Perth, Canongate and
  Carlisle. Transported on
  the Gildart,master Richard
  Holmes, from Liverpool.
  Landed at Port North Poto-
  mack, Maryland 5 August
  1747
  (P)(PRO)

DOWNIE JOHN
  Covenanter in Argyll's
  rebellion. Prisoner in
  Laigh Parliament House,
  Edinburgh. Banished to
  the Plantations 7 August
  1685. Stigmatised. Trans
  ported from Leith by
  John Ewing to Jamaica
  August 1685
  (PC)

DRENAN WILLIAM
  Covenanter. Prisoner in
  Edinburgh Tolbooth. Banished to the Plantations
  29 July 1685. Stigmatised
  4 August 1685. Transported from Leith by John
  Ewing to Jamaica 11 August 1685
  (ETR)(PC)

DRUMMOND GEORGE
  Tinker. Pathhead. Horsethief.
  Banished to the Plantations
  for life, at Perth 28 April
  1773
  (SM)

DRUMMOND GILBERT
  Servant to Mrs Robert Mercer
  of Aldie, 33. Meiklour, Caputh
  Perthshire. Jacobite in the
  Atholl Brigade. Prisoner at
  Canongate and Carlisle. Trans-
  ported on the Johnson, master
  William Pemberton, from
  Liverpool. Died aboard ship
  7 June 1747
  (P)(PRO)

DRUMMOND JOHN or MCGREGOR
  Balquhidder. Jacobite in
  Glengyle's regiment. Prisoner
  at Canongate and Carlisle.
  Transported 1747(?)
  (P)

DRYSDALE JOHN
  Covenanter. Banished to the
  Plantations in the Indies
  11 October 1681
  (PC)

DUFF DANIEL
  Labourer, 26. Perthshire.
  Jacobite captured at Carlisle
  Prisoner at Carlisle and
  Lincoln. Transported on the
  Veteran, master John Ricky,
  from Liverpool 5 May 1747 for
  the Leeward Islands. Liberated
  by a French privateer and
  landed on Martinique June 1747
  (P)(PRO)

DUFF DANIEL
  Atholl. Jacobite in Ogilvy's
  regiment. Captured at Carlisle
  Prisoner at Carlisle and York.
  Transported by Samuel Smith
  21 April 1747 to Jamaica or
  Barbados
  (P)(RM)

40

DUFF DONALD
Jacobite captured at
Preston. Transported from
Liverpool on the Susannah,
master Thomas Bromhall, to
South Carolina 7 May 1716
(SP/C)

DUFF JAMES
Strathbraan. Jacobite in
Roy Stuart's regiment.
Captured at Carlisle.
Prisoner at Carlisle.
Transported from Liverpool
(P)

DUFF JOHN
Labourer. Kirkton, Perth-
shire. Jacobite in Roy
Stuart's regiment. Capt-
ured at Carlisle. Pris-
oner at Carlisle and
Chester. Transported on
the Johnson, master William
Pemberton, from Liverpool.
Landed at Port Oxford in
Maryland 5 August 1747
(P)(PRO)

DUFF ROBERT
Painter, 25. Glasgow.
Jacobite. Prisoner at
Canongate and Carlisle.
Transported on the Gil-
dart, master Richard
Holmes, from Liverpool.
Landed at Port North
Potomack, Maryland
5 August 1747
(P)(PRO)

DUFFUS ANDREW
Horsethief. Banished to
the Plantations for 14
years, at Inverness
20 May 1775
(SM)

DUNBAR ELIZABETH
Banff. Child murder.
Transported, at Aber-
deen. September 1750
(SM)

DUNBAR JAMES
Prisoner in Edinburgh Tolbooth.
For wounding by shooting.
Banished to Virginia
16 July 1668
(PC)

DUNBAR JAMES
Labourer, 17. Morayshire.
Jacobite. Prisoner at Carlisle,
York and Lincoln. Transported
on the Veteran, master John
Ricky, from Liverpool 5 May 1747
for the Leeward Islands. Liber-
ated by a French privateer and
landed on Martinique June 1747
(P)(RM)

DUNBAR JOHN
Jacobite captured at Preston.
Transported from Liverpool on the
Elizabeth and Anne, masterEdward
Trafford, to Virginia or Jamaica
29 June 1716. Landed in Virginia
- indentured
(SP/C)(VSP)

DUNBAR JEREMY
Tenant of David Lumsden of Cushnie
Aberdeenshire. Jacobite captured
at Preston. Transported on the
Friendship, master Michael Mankin,
from Liverpool 24 May 1716 to
Maryland or Virginia. Sold to
Hugh Kennedy in Maryland 20
August 1716. Returned to Scotland
(P)(JAB)(SP/C)

DUNCAN ALEXANDER
Jacobite captured at Preston.
Transported from Liverpool on the
Two Brothers, master Edward Rath-
bone, 26 April 1716 for Jamaica.
Landed on Montserrat June 1716
(SP/C)(CTP)

DUNCAN CHRISTIAN
St Ninian's, Stirling. Child
murder. Banished to the Plantations for life, at Stirling
5 September 1765
(SM)

DUNCAN GRIZELL
Wife of George Gray,
tailor, Kirkness. Forger.
Prisoner in Edinburgh Tol
booth. Banished to the
Plantations in America
for life, at Edinburgh
20 December 1743
(JC)

DUNCAN GRISEL
Thief. Banished to the
Plantations for life, at
Perth September 1750
(SM)

DUNCAN JAMES
Grange. Covenanter. Ban-
ished to the Plantations
in America 16 August 1670
(PC)

DUNCAN JAMES
Balquhan. Thief. Banish-
ed to the Plantations in
America, at Stirling 21
May 1729
(JC)

DUNCAN JAMES or DAVIDSON
Shoemaker, Cairngressie,
Kincardineshire. Deserter
from Colonel Morris's
Highland regiment. Cattle
thief. Banished to the
Plantations for 7 years,
at Aberdeen 8 September
1763
(SM)

DUNCAN JOHN
Jacobite captured at
Preston. Transported on
the Two Brothers, master
Edward Rathbone, from
Liverpool 26 April 1716
for Jamaica. Landed on
Montserrat June 1716
(SP/C)(CTP)

DUNCAN JOHN
14, apprentice carpenter. Dundee
Jacobite in Ogilvy's regiment.
Prisoner at Carlisle and York.
Transported 1747(?)
(P)

DUNCAN JOHN
Servant to Captain John Kinloch.
Perthshire. Jacobite in Ogilvy's
regiment. Prisoner at Canongate
and Carlisle. Transported 1747(?)
(P)

DUNCAN JOHN
Fisherman, 42. Montrose. Jacobite.
Drummer in Ogilvy's regiment.
Captured at Carlisle. Prisoner
at Carlisle and York. Transported
1747(?)
(P)

DUNCAN JOHN
Jacobite. Transported on the
Johnson, master William Pemberton,
from Liverpool. Landed at Port
Oxford, Maryland 5 August 1747
(PRO)

DUNCAN JOHN
Jacobite. Transported on the
Gildart, master Richard Holmes,
from Liverpool. Landed at Port
North Potomack, Maryland
5 August 1747
(PRO)

DUNCAN PETER
Labourer, 32. Dundee. Jacobite
in Ogilvy's regiment. Prisoner
at Canongate and Carlisle. Trans-
ported on the Gildart, master
Richard Holmes, from Liverpool.
Landed at Port North Potomack,
Maryland 5 August 1747
(P)(OR)(PRO)

DUNCAN ROBERT
Jacobite captured at Preston.
Transported from Liverpool on the
Elizabeth and Anne, master Edward
Trafford,to Virginia or Jamaica
29 June 1716
(SP/C)(VSP)

DUNCAN WILLIAM
15, gardener. Edinburgh.
Jacobite in Duke of Perth's
regiment. Prisoner at Carlisle, Chester, Whitehaven
and Liverpool. Transported
1747(?)
(P)

DUNDAS MR JAMES
Son of the laird of Dundas.
Covenanter. Transported to
the Plantations in America
11 August 1670
(PC)

DUNLOP JANET
Transported on the Polly,
master James McArthur,
from Port Glasgow. Landed
at Port Oxford, Maryland
16 September 1771
(JC)

DUNN QUENTIN
Goal thief. Kirkcudbright.
To be scourged or sent to
Barbados 25 January 1666
(PC)

DUNN QUENTIN
Covenanter. Prisoner in
Edinburgh Tolbooth. Ban-
ished to the Plantations
29 July 1685. Stigmatised
4 August 1685. Transport-
ed from Leith by John
Ewing to Jamaica 11 Aug-
ust 1685
(ETR)(PC)

DUNN WILLIAM
Jacobite captured at
Preston. Transported on
the Elizabeth and Anne,
master Edward Trafford,
from Liverpool to Virg-
inia or Jamaica 29 June
1716. Landed on Virgin-
ia - unindentured
(SP/C)

DURIE ISOBEL
Covenanter. Prisoner in
Leith Tolbooth. Banished to the
Plantations, at Leith 18 August
1685. Transported from Leith by
George Scott of Pitlochie to
East New Jersey August 1685
(PC)

DURRAR WILLIAM
30, servant to Alexander Durran.
Ashdale, Aberdeen. Jacobite in
Farquharson's. Prisoner at Inverness and Tilbury. Transported
20 March 1747
(P)

DURY MARGARET
Widow of James Kello, merchant in
Edinburgh. Covenanter. Banished
to the Plantations 29 July 1663
(PC)

DUTT ALEXANDER
Jacobite captured at Preston.
Transported from Liverpool on the
Scipio 30 March 1716
(SP/C)

DYKES ANDREW
St Bride's Chapel. Covenanter.
Banished to the Plantations in
America 17 October 1684
(PC)

DYKES MARGARET
22. Linlithgow. Jacobite. Prisoner
at Carlisle and Lancaster. Transported on the Veteran, master John
Ricky, from Liverpool 5 May 1747
for the Leeward Islands. Liberated
by a French privateer and landed
on Martinique June 1747
(P)(RM)

EARLE ANN
Child murder. Banished for life,
at Ayr 1753
(SM)

EDWARD ANDREW
Servant, 24. Angus.
Jacobite in Ogilvy's regiment. Transported on the
Veteran, master John Ricky,
from Liverpool 5 May 1747
for the Leeward Islands.
Liberated by a French privateer and landed on Martinique June 1747
(P)(OR)(RM)

EDWARD JAMES
Greenock. Covenanter. Prisoner in Edinburgh Tolbooth.
Banished to the Plantations
2 July 1684. Transported to
Carolina by Robert Malloch,
merchant in Edinburgh 1 August 1684
(ETR)(PC)

EDWARD JOHN
Dalgaine. Covenanter. Prisoner in Glasgow Tolbooth.
Banished to the Plantations
at Glasgow June 1684. Trans
ported from the Clyde on
the Pelican by Walter Gibson, merchant in Glasgow,
to America June 1684
(PC)

EDWARD ROBERT
Cumnock. Covenanter in
Argyll's rebellion. Prisoner in Laigh Parliament
House, Edinburgh. Banished
to the Plantations 30 July
1685. Stigmatised 4 August
1685. Transported from
Leith by John Ewing to Jam
aica August 1685
(PC)

EDWARDS JAMES
Earl of Airlie's land, Lin-
trathen. Jacobite in the
Duke of Perth's regiment.
Prisoner at Stirling. Trans
ported 1747(?)
(P)

EGLINTON WILLIAM
Rioter. Banished, at Glas-
gow May 1749
(SM)

ELDER DONALD
Son of William Elder, tenant in
Ifauld, Parish of Reay, Caithness
Shipwreck looter. Banished to the
Plantations 1772. Transported on
the Donald,master Thomas Ramsay,
and landed in Port James, Upper
District, Virginia 13 March 1773
(SM)(JC)

ELDER WILLIAM
18, servant to William McKenzie.
Kilcoy, Ross. Jacobite in Crom-
arty's regiment. Prisoner at
Inverness, ships and Tilbury.
Transported from London by
Samuel Smith to Jamaica or Bar-
bados 31 March 1747
(P)(RM)

ELDER WILLIAM
Tenant in Ifauld, Parish of Reay,
Caithness. Shipwreck looter. Ban-
ished to the Plantations for life
1772
(SM)

ELDER WILLIAM
Soldier. Robber. Prisoner in
Edinburgh Tolbooth. Banished to
the Plantations in America for
life, at Edinburgh 3 March 1747
(JC)

ELLIOT JOHN
Covenanter. Prisoner in Canongate
Tolbooth. Banished to the Plant-
ations 24 July 1685. Stigmatised
4 August 1685. Transported by
John Ewing from Leith to Jamaica
August 1685
(PC)

ELLIOT ROBERT
Earlside. Thief. Prisoner in Jed-
burgh Tolbooth. Banished from
Scotland for life, at Jedburgh
11 May 1726
(JC)

EWAN JOHN
Waterside of Montrose, Angus.
Thief. Banished to the Plantat-
ions for life 1773
(SM)

EWART JEAN
Coal bearer. Edinburgh.
Child murder. Banished
to America for life 6
March 1771. Transported
on the Crawford, master
James McLean, from Port
Glasgow. Landed at Port
Oxford, Maryland 23 July
1771
(JC)

EWART WILLIAM
Shoemaker. Dumfries.
Rioter in Dumfries 1759.
Prisoner in Edinburgh
Tolbooth. Transported
to the Plantations for
7 years in 1760. Banish-
ed at Edinburgh 15 Dec-
ember 1760
(SM)(JC)

FAA MARY
Gypsy. Prisoner in Jed-
burgh Tolbooth. Banished
at Jedburgh 30 November
1714. Transported via
Glasgow on a Greenock
ship, master James Wat-
son, by merchants Robert
Buntine of Airdoch, James
Lees and Charles Crawford
to Virginia 1 January
1715
(GR)

FAA PETER
Gypsy. Prisoner in Jed-
burgh Tolbooth. Banished
at Jedburgh 30 November
1714. Transported via
Glasgow on a Greenock
ship, master James Wat-
son, by merchants Robert
Buntine of Airdoch, James
Lees and Charles Crawford
to Virginia 1 January
1715
(GR)

FAIRBAIRN JOHN
Kirkliston. Covenanter.
Prisoner in Edinburgh
Tolbooth. Transported
from Leith on the St
Michael of Scarborough
12 December 1678 (PC)

FALA JOHN
Shoemaker. Kelso. Covenanter.
Prisoner in Edinburgh Tolbooth.
Transported to the Plantations
16 October 1684
(PC)

FALCONER JAMES
Rioter. Glasgow. Banished to
Barbados. Transported from
England January 1726
(PRO)

FALCONER ROBERT
Smith. Elgin. Thief. Banished
to the Plantations in America
26 January 1767, at Edinburgh
(SM)(JC)

FERGUSON ALEXANDER
30, Farmer. Glenmoriston.
Jacobite in Glengarry's regiment.
Prisoner at Inverness, ship and
Tilbury. Transported 1747(?)
(P)

FARQUHARSON ALEXANDER
Jacobite in Farquharson's regiment
Prisoner at Inverness and Tilbury.
Transported from London by Samuel
Smith 31 March 1747 to Jamaica or
Barbados
(P)(RM)

FARQUHARSON ALEXANDER
40, Farmer. Achenriachen, Glenmoriston. Jacobite in Glengarry's
regiment. Prisoner at Inverness,
ship and Tilbury. Transported
from London by Samuel Smith to
Jamaica or Barbados 31 March 1747
Escaped and returned to Scotland
(P)(RM)

FARQUHARSON DONALD
32. Achnagoren, Glenmoriston.
Jacobite in Glengarry's regiment.
Prisoner at Inverness and Tilbury.
Transported from London by Samuel
Smith to Jamaica or Barbados
31 March 1747
(P)(RM)

FARQUHARSON DONALD
48, Farmer. Balquhidder.
Jacobite in the Duke of
Perth's regiment. Prisoner
at Inverness, ship, Medway.
Transported from London by
Samuel Smith to Barbados
or Jamaica 31 March 1747
(P)(RM)

FARQUHARSON DUNCAN
23. Glenmoriston. Jacobite
in Farquharson's regiment.
Prisoner at Inverness and
Tilbury. Transported from
London by Samuel Smith to
Barbados or Jamaica 31
March 1747
(P)(RM)

FARQUHARSON OF CULTS HARRY
Son of Arthur Farquharson
of Cults, Glengairn. Served in Spanish army for two
years. Returned to Scotland
prior to 1715. Jacobite
captured at Preston. Transported to Virginia. Married
Elizabeth Morgan, heiress
of Torgalter
(JAB)

FARQUHARSON HUGH WILLIAM
Jacobite. Prisoner at
Inverness and Tilbury.
Transported 1747(?)
(P)

FARQUHARSON LAWRENCE
Cobletown of Tulloch,
Aberdeenshire. Son of
Donald Farquharson, the
eldest son of Donald
Farquharson, 2nd of
Allanaquoich, by his
second wife Helen
Garden. Jacobite captured
at Preston. Transported on
the Godspeed,master Arthur
Smith, to Virginia from
Liverpool 28 July 1716.
Sold to John Bruce in Mary
land 17 October 1716
(JAB)(SP/C)(HM)

FARQUHARSON PETER
40. Achnagoren, Glenmoriston.
Jacobite in Glengarry's regiment.
Prisoner at Inverness and Tilbury.
Transported from London by Samuel
Smith to Barbados or Jamaica 31
March 1747
(P)(RM)

FARQUHARSON OF ALLANAQUOICH ROBERT
Second son of Donald Farquharson
of Allanaquoich, Aberdeenshire
and Helen Garden. Gentleman.
Roman Catholic. Husband of
Mary Gordon. Jacobite captured
at Preston. Transported on the
Anne,master Robert Wallace, from
Liverpool 31 July 1716 for
Virginia. Returned to Scotland
(JAB)(SP/C)

FARQUHARSON WILLIAM
Farmer. Tarland, Aberdeenshire.
Jacobite in Farquharson's regi-
ment. Prisoner at Inverness and
Tilbury. Transported from London
by Samuel Smith 31 March 1747 to
Jamaica or Barbados
(P)(RM)

FENWICK BARBARA
Prisoner in Edinburgh Tolbooth.
Transported by Laurence Trent,
merchant, on the Ewe and Lamb,
master John Guthrie 2 May 1672
to the Plantations in America
(PC)

FENWICK JAMES
Covenanter. Prisoner in Leith
Tolbooth. Banished to the Plant-
ations, at Leith 18 August 1685.
Transported from Leith by George
Scott of Pitlochie to East New
Jersey August 1685
(PC)

FENWICK JOHN
Gypsy. Prisoner in Jedburgh Tol-
booth. Banished at Jedburgh 30
November 1714. Transported via
Glasgow on a Greenock ship, master
James Watson, by merchants Robert
Buntine of Airdoch, James Lees and
Charles Crawford to Virginia 1 Jan-
uary 1715
(GR)

FERGUSON ALEXANDER
Forger. Prisoner in Edin-
burgh Tolbooth. Banished
to the Plantations 3 Feb-
ruary 1670. Transported
from Leith by James John-
ston, James Currie and
Patrick Fyfe , merchants
in Edinburgh, on the
Ewe and Lamb, master
James Guthrie, to Vir-
ginia
(PC)

FERGUSON ALEXANDER
Jacobite captured at
Preston. Transported on
the Elizabeth and Anne,
master Edward Trafford,
from Liverpool 29 June
1716 for Virginia or Jam-
aica. Landed in Virginia
- unindentured
(SP/C)(VSP)

FERGUSON DAVID
Bridgend, Glasgow. Cove-
nanter. Prisoner in Edin
burgh Tolbooth. Transported from Leith on the St
Michael of Scarborough,
master Edward Johnston
12 December 1678
(PC)

FERGUSON DONALD
Ruchoard. Covenanter in
Argyll's rebellion. Pris-
oner in Laigh Parliament
House, Edinburgh. Banish
ed to the Plantations 24
July 1685. Transported
from Leith by John Ewing
to Jamaica August 1685
(PC)

FERGUSON DONALD
Jacobite captured at Preston
Transported from Liverpool
on the Elizabeth and Anne,
master Edward Trafford, to
Virginia or Jamaica 29 June
1716
(SP/C)(VSP)

FERGUSON DUNCAN
Tenant of Polmaes, Parish of
St Ninian's. Covenanter. Pris-
oner in Edinburgh Tolbooth.
Banished to the Plantations 5
February 1685, at Edinburgh.
Transported from Leith by George
Scott of Pitlochie to Jamaica
August 1685
(ETR)(PC)

FERGUSON DUNCAN
Covenanter. Prisoner in Edinburgh
Tolbooth. Banished to the Plantations in Carolina. To be transported by Robert Malloch, merchant in Edinburgh, 5 August 1684
(PC)(ETR)

FERGUSON DUNCAN
Jacobite captured at Preston.
Transported on the Godspeed,
master Arthur Smith, from Liver-
pool 28 July 1716 for Virginia.
Sold to John Fendall in Maryland
17 October 1716
(SP/C)(HM)

FERGUSON DONALD
Servant to McDonald of Gartmore,
Skye. Jacobite sergeant in the
Duke of Perth's regiment.
Prisoner at Culloden, Inverness,
ship and Tilbury. Transported
1747(?)

FERGUSON DUNCAN
Farmer, 34. Perthshire. Jacobite
in the Duke of Perth's regiment.
Prisoner at Perth, Canongate,
Carlisle and Lancaster. Trans-
ported on the Johnson, master
William Pemberton, from Liver-
pool. Landed at Port Oxford,
Maryland 5 August 1747
(P)(PRO)

FERGUSON FRANCIS
Tenant of David Lumsden of Cushnie
Aberdeenshire. Jacobite captured
at Preston. Transported from
Liverpool on the Scipio,
30 March 1716
(JAB)(SP/C)

SCOTS BANISHED TO THE AMERICAN PLANTATIONS

FERGUSON ELSPETH
Covenanter. Prisoner at
Dunnottar and Leith. Ban-
ished to the Plantations,
at Leith 18 August 1685.
Transported from Leith by
George Scott of Pitlochie
to East New Jersey August
1685
(PC)

FERGUSON GILBERT
Covenanter in Argyll's
rebellion. Prisoner in
Canongate Tolbooth. Ban-
ished to the Plantations
30 July 1685. Transport-
ed from Leith by John
Ewing to Jamaica August
1685
(PC)

FERGUSON HENRY
Jacobite captured at
Preston. Transported
from Liverpool on the
Friendship,master Michael
Mankin, for Maryland 24
May 1716. Landed in Mary-
land and sold to Darley
Dullany 20 August 1716
(HM)(SP/C)

FERGUSON JAMES
Jacobite captured at
Preston. Transported on
the Elizabeth and Anne,
master Edward Trafford,
from Liverpool 29 June
1716 for Virginia or Jam-
aica. Landed in Virginia
- unindentured
(SP/C)(VSP)

FERGUSON JANET
Covenanter. Prisoner at
Burntisland, Dunnottar,
and Leith. Banished to the
Plantations, at Leith 18
August 1685. Transported
from Leith by George Scott
of Pitlochie to East New
Jersey August 1685
(PC)

FERGUSON LAWRENCE
Jacobite captured at Preston.
Transported from Liverpool on
the Elizabeth and Anne, master
Edward Trafford, to Virginia or
Jamaica 29 June 1716. Landed in
Virginia - unindentured
(SP/C)(VSP)

FERGUSON PATRICK
Jacobite captured at Preston.
Transported from Liverpool on the
Elizabeth and Anne, master Edward
Trafford, to Virginia or Jamaica.
Landed in Virginia - unindentured
(SP/C)(VSP)

FERGUSON PATRICK
Labourer. Perthshire. Jacobite
in the Duke of Perth's regiment.
Captured at Carlisle. Prisoner
at Carlisle and Lancaster. Trans-
ported from Liverpool on the
Johnson, master William Pemberton
Landed at Port Oxford, Maryland
5 August 1747
(P)(PRO)

FERGUSON PETER
Jacobite captured at Preston.
Transported from Liverpool on
the Two Brothers, master Edward
Rathbone, 26 April 1716 for
Jamaica. Landed in Montserrat
June 1716
(SP/C)(CTP)

FERGUSON WILLIAM
Weaver. Lanark. Covenanter.
Transported from Leith on the
Convertin, Captain Lightfoot,
by James Currie, baillie of
Edinburgh, to Virginia September
1668
(PC)

FERGUSON WILLIAM
Jacobite captured at Preston.
Transported on the Godspeed,
master Arthur Smith, from Liver-
pool to Virginia 28 July 1716.
Sold to John Bruce in Maryland
17 October 1716
(SP/C)(HM)

FERGUSON WILLIAM
55, farmer. Glenmoriston.
Jacobite in Glengarry's
regiment. Prisoner at
Inverness, ship,Tilbury.
Transported 1747(?)
(P)

FERGUSON WILLIAM
Rioter. Galloway.
Transported for 7 years,
at Ayr 1752
(SM)

FIDDES DAVID
18. Farnell, Angus.
Jacobite in Ogilvy's
regiment. Prisoner at
Lethnot, Montrose, Inver-
ness, ship and Tilbury.
Transported from London
by Samuel Smith to Bar-
bados or Jamaica 31
March 1747
(P)(RM)

FINLAY JEAN
Thief. Banished to the
Plantations for life, at
Aberdeen May 1753
(SM)

FINDLAY ALEXANDER
Buchlyvie. Covenanter.
Prisoner in Canongate
Tolbooth. Transported
from Leith on the St
Michael of Scarborough,
master Edward Johnston
12 December 1678
(PC)

FINLAY WILLIAM
Jacobite captured at
Preston. Transported on
the Elizabeth and Anne,
master Edward Trafford,
from Liverpool 29 June
1716 for Virginia or
Jamaica. Landed in
Virginia - unindentured
(SP/C)(VSP)

FINLAYSON ALEXANDER
30, servant to John McInivire,
Lochcarron, Ross-shire. Jacobite
in Cromarty's regiment. Prisoner
at Inverness and Tilbury, Transported 20 March 1747
(P)

FINLAYSON JOHN
24, servant to Donald McLeod.
Ballygower, Skye. Jacobite in
Cromarty's regiment. Prisoner
at Inverness and Tilbury.
Transported 20 March 1747
(P)

FINNEY JEAN
Paisley. Child murder. Banished
to the Plantations, at Glasgow
1758
(SM)

FINNEY ROBERT
Jacobite captured at Preston.
Transported from Liverpool on
the Elizabeth and Anne, master
Edward Trafford, to Virginia or
Jamaica 29 June 1716
(SP/C)(VSP)

FINNIE JOHN
Tenant of David Lumsden of
Cushnie, Aberdeenshire. Jacobite
captured at Preston. Transported
to Virginia 1715
(JAB)

FINNISON JOHN
Covenanter. Prisoner in Canongate
Tolbooth. Banished to the Plant-
ations 28 July 1685. Stigmatised
4 August 1685. Transported from
Leith by John Ewing to Jamaica
August 1685
(PC)

FINNISON PETER
Covenanter. Banished to the
Plantations in America, at
Glasgow 11 October 1684
(PC)

FISHER JAMES
Weaver. Bridgend, Glasgow.
Covenanter. Banished to the
Plantations in the Indies
13 June 1678
(PC)

FISHER PATRICK
Thief. Banished to America,
at Stirling 1752
(SM)

FLEMING ALEXANDER
Horsehirer, 20. Aberdeen.
Jacobite in Crichton of
Auchengoul's regiment.
Prisoner at Aberdeen, Can-
ongate and Carlisle. Trans
ported on the Gildart,master
Richard Hughes, from Liver-
pool. Landed at Port North
Potomack, Maryland 5 Aug-
ust 1747
(P)(JAB)(PRO)

FLEMING JOHN
Stenhouse. Covenanter.
Prisoner in Canongate or
Edinburgh Tolbooth. Ban-
ished to the Plantations
2 July 1684. Transported
from Leith by Robert
Malloch, merchant in Edinburgh, to Carolina August
1684
(PC)

FLETCHER DUNCAN
Covenanter in Argyll's
rebellion. Prisoner in
Paul's Work, Edinburgh.
Banished to the Plantat-
ions 30 July 1685. Trans-
ported from Leith by John
Ewing to Jamaica August
1685
(PC)

FLETCHER JOHN
Rumcadle, Kintyre. Cov-
enanter. Prisoner in
Paul's Work, Edinburgh.
Banished to the Plant-
ations 24 July 1685.
Transported from Leith
by John Ewing to Jamaica
August 1685 (PC)

FLOOD DANIEL
Sailor. Greenock. Rioter.
Banished to the Plantations
for 5 years, at Glasgow 1773
(SM)

FORBES ALEXANDER
20, servant to the Pretender.
Wemyss. Jacobite in the Duke
of Perth's regiment. Prisoner
at Larbert, Stirling, ship
and Medway. Transported from
London by Samuel Smith to
Jamaica or Barbados 31 March
1747
(P)(RM)

FORBES DONALD
43, farmer. Strathnairn.
Jacobite in McIntosh's regiment.
Prisoner at Inverness, ship and
Tilbury. Transported from
London by Samuel Smith to Jam-
aica or Barbados 20 March 1747
(P)(RM)

FORBES MARGARET
Child murder. Banished to
America, at Aberdeen 1755
(SM)

FORBES THOMAS
Tenant of David Lumsden of
Cushnie, Aberdeenshire. Jacobite
captured at Preston. Transported
from Liverpool on the Friendship,
master Michael Mankin, to Maryland or Virginia 24 May 1716.
Sold to William Bladen esq. in
Maryland 20 August 1716. Returned to Scotland
(SP/C)(JAB)(HM)

FORBES WILLIAM
20, Husbandman. Fochabers. Jacobite in Lord Lewis Gordon's
regiment. Fought at Culloden.
Prisoner at Inverness, ship and
Tilbury. Transported 20 March
1747
(P)(JAB)

FORD JOHN
Covenanter. Prisoner at
Canongate, Dunnotter and
Leith. Banished to the
Plantations, at Leith
18 August 1685. Trans-
ported from Leith by
George Scott of Pitlochie
to East New Jersey August
1685
(PC)

FORMAN JOHN
Covenanter. Prisoner at
Burntisland, Dunnottar
and Leith. Banished to
the Plantations, at Leith
18 August 1685. Transported from Leith by George
Scott of Pitlochie to
East New Jersey August
1685
(PC)

FORREST JAMES
Covenanter. Cambusnethan.
Son of Marion Forrest, and
brother of Margaret Forrest
Prisoner at Stirling and
Canongate. Banished to the
Plantations 24 July 1685.
Transported from Leith by
George Scott of Pitlochie
to East New Jersey August
1685
(PC)

FORREST MARGARET
Covenanter. Sister of
James Forrest, and daugh-
ter of Marion Forrest.
Prisoner in Glasgow, Dun-
nottar and Leith. Banish-
ed to the Plantations 11
October 1684. Transported
from Leith by George Scott
of Pitlochie to East New
Jersey August 1685
(PC)

FORSYTH JAMES
Annandale. Covenanter.
Prisoner at Glasgow, Dun-
nottar and Leith. Banish-
ed to the Plantations, at
Leith 18 August 1685.
Transported to East New
Jersey by Pitlochie 1685
(PC)

FOSTER JOHN
70, husbandman. Jacobite.
Prisoner at Carlisle. Transported
on the Johnson, master William
Pemberton, from Liverpool.
Landed at Port Oxford, Maryland
5 August 1747
(P)(PRO)

FOSTER THOMAS
Jacobite captured at Preston.
Transported from Liverpool on the
Elizabeth and Anne, master Ed-
ward Trafford, to Virginia or
Jamaica 29 June 1716. Landed in
Virginia - indentured
(SP/C)(VSP)

FOWLER JOHN
Transported on the Rainbow,
master William Gordon, from
Greenock. Landed at Port Hamp-
ton, Virginia 3 May 1775
(JC)

FRAZER ALEXANDER alias BAYNE
Thief. Banished at Perth.
Warded in Edinburgh Tolbooth
13 September 1720. Released
for transportation to the
Plantations 15 December 1720
(ETR)

FRASER ALEXANDER
22, weaver. Inverness. Jacobite
in Lord Lovat's regiment.
Prisoner at Inverness, ship
and Tilbury. Transported from
London by Samuel Smith to
Jamaica or Barbados 31 March
1747
(P)(RM)

FRASER ALEXANDER
22. Moray. Jacobite in the
Duke of Perth's regiment.
Prisoner at Edinburgh, ship
and Tilbury. Transported from
London by Samuel Smith to
Jamaica or Barbados 20 March
1747
(P)(RM)

FRASER ALEXANDER
Miller. Hamesucken. Banished
to the Plantations, at Inverness September 1750 (SM)

FRASER ALLAN
Prisoner in Edinburgh
Tolbooth. Transported
to the Plantations in
America by Alexander
Fearne 17 December
1685
(ETR)

FRASER ANNE
Child murder. Transport-
ed, at Inverness Septem-
ber 1750
(SM)

FRASER DAVID
22. "Deaf and Dumb".
Glen Urquhart. Jacobite
in Lord Lovat's regiment
Prisoner at Tilbury.
Transported from London
by Samuel Smith to Jam-
aica or Barbados 20
March 1747
(P)(RM)

FRASER DAVID
27, servant to the
Master of Lovat. Inver
ness. Jacobite sergeant
in Lord Lovat's regi-
ment. Prisoner at
Culloden, Inverness,
ship and Tilbury. Trans-
ported from London by
Samuel Smithto Jamaica
or Barbados 31 March
1747
(P)(RM)

FRASER DONALD
19, tailor. Logie, Ross.
Jacobite in Cromarty's
regiment. Prisoner at
Inverness, ships, Til-
bury. Transported from
London by Samuel Smith
to Jamaica or Barbados
31 March 1747
(P)(RM)

FRASER DONALD
22, husbandman. Fort Augustus.
Jacobite in Lovat's regiment.
Prisoner at Culloden, Inverness,
ships and Medway.Transported
from London by Samuel Smith to
Jamaica or Barbados 20 March
1747
(P)(RM)

FRASER DONALD the elder
Thief. Banished to the Plantations, at Inverness October
1749
(SM)

FRASER HELEN
Child murder. Banished to the
Plantations, at Perth 1 Sept-
ember 1763
(SM)

FRASER HUGH
28, blacksmith. Montrose.
Jacobite in Ogilvy's regiment.
Prisoner at Montrose, Inverness,
ship and Tilbury. Transported
from London by Samuel Smith to
Jamaica or Barbados 31 March
1747
(P)(RM)

FRASER HUGH
26, husbandman. Innermurie,
Inverness. Jacobite in Lovat's
regiment. Prisoner at Inverness
ship and Tilbury. Transported
from London by Samuel Smith to
Barbados or Jamaica 31 March
1747
(P)(RM)

FRASER HUGH
26, husbandman. Drumhardinich,
Inverness. Jacobite in Lovat's
regiment. Prisoner at Inverness
ships and Tilbury. Transported
from London by Samuel Smith to
Barbados or Jamaica 31 March
1747
(P)(RM)

FRASER HUGH or EWAN
32, tailor. Colwoolen,
Inverness. Jacobite in
Lovat's regiment. Pris-
oner at Inverness, ship
and Tilbury. Transported
from London by Samuel
Smith to Barbados or
Jamaica 31 March 1747
(P)

FRASER HUGH
27, Husbandman. Auch-
indach, Inverness.
Jacobite in Drummond's.
Prisoner at Inverness,
ships and Tilbury.
Transported from London
by Samuel Smith to Bar-
bados or Jamaica 31
March 1747
(P)(RM)

FRASER JAMES
Labourer, 68. Inverness.
Jacobite in Lovat's regi
ment. Prisoner at Inver-
ness, ship and Tilbury.
Transported from London
by Samuel Smith to Bar-
bados or Jamaica 31
March 1747
(P)(RM)

FRASER MR JOHN
Covenanter. Prisoner at
Edinburgh, Burntisland,
Dunnottar and Leith.
Banished to the Plant-
ations, at Leith 18 Aug-
ust 1685. Transported
from Leith by George
Scott of Pitlochie to
East New Jersey August
1685. Returned to Scot-
land February 1691.
Minister of parish of
Hassenden
(ETR)(PC)

FRASER JOHN
Jacobite captured at
Preston. Transported on
the Scipio from Liver-
pool 30 March 1716
(SP/C)

FRASER JOHN
22, farmer. Delcaitack, Glenmoriston. Jacobite in Glengarry's
regiment. Prisoner at Inverness,
ship and Tilbury. Transported
from London by Samuel Smith to
Barbados or Jamaica 31 March 1747
(P)(RM)

FRASER JOHN
40. Inverwick, Glenmoriston.
Jacobite in Glengarry's regiment
Prisoner at Inverness, ship and
Tilbury. Transported from London
by Samuel Smith to Barbados or
Jamaica 20 March 1747
(P)(RM)

FRASER JOHN
50, farmer. Craigscory, Inverness
Jacobite in Lovat's regiment.
Prisoner at Inverness, ship and
Tilbury. Transported from London
by Samuel Smith to Barbados or
Jamaica 31 March 1747
(P)(RM)

FRASER JOHN
34, weaver. Inverness. Jacobite
in Lovat's regiment. Prisoner at
Inverness and Tilbury. Transport
ed from London by Samuel Smith
to Jamaica or Barbados 31 March
1747
(P)(RM)

FRASER JOHN
22, servant to an Edinburgh
lawyer. From Inverness. Jacobite
in Lovat's regiment. Prisoner at
Inverness, ship and Tilbury.
Transported from London by Samuel
Smith to Barbados or Jamaica 31
March 1747
(P)(RM)

FRASER JOHN
30, farmer. Crochill, Inverness.
Jacobite in Lovat's regiment.
Prisoner at Inverness, ships and
Medway. Transported from London
by Samuel Smith to Barbados or
Jamaica 31 March 1747
(P)(RM)

FRASER OWEN
Inverness. Jacobite.
Prisoner at Inverness
and Tilbury. Transported
20 March 1747
(P)

FRASER PETER
36. Inverness. Jacobite
in Lovat's regiment.
Prisoner at Inverness
and on ships. Transport-
ed 20 March 1747
(P)

FRASER RODERICK
28, Farmer. Dingwall.
Jacobite in Cromarty's
regiment. Prisoner at
Inverness, ship and
Tilbury. Transported
from London by Samuel
Smith to Barbados or
Jamaica 31 March 1747
(P)(RM)

FRASER SIMON
20. Aird, Inverness.
Jacobite in Lovat's
regiment. Prisoner at
Inverness, ship and
Tilbury. Transported
from London by Samuel
Smith to Barbados or
Jamaica 31 March 1747
(P)(RM)

FRAZER WILLIAM
Jacobite captured at
Preston. Transported on
the Susannah, master
Thomas Bromhall, from
Liverpool to South
Carolina 7 May 1716
(SP/C)

FRAZER WILLIAM alias OIG
Thief. Banished at Perth
Warded in Edinburgh Tol-
booth 13 September 1720.
Released for transport-
ation to the Plantations
15 December 1720
(ETR)

FRASER WILLIAM
26, husbandman. Kirkton, Aird,
Inverness. Jacobite in Lovat's
regiment. Prisoner on ships and
at Tilbury. Transported from
London by Samuel Smith to Jamaica or Barbados 31 March 1747
(P)(RM)

FRENCH ANDREW
Covenanter. Prisoner in Edinburgh
Tolbooth. Transported from Leith
by Alexander Fearne to America
December 1685
(PC)(ETR)

FRENCH WILLIAM
Cambusnethan. Covenanter.
Prisoner in Edinburgh Tolbooth.
Transported from Leith on the
John and Nicholas by Alexander
Fearne to America December 1685
(ETR)(PC)

FRISSELL EDWARD
Royalist soldier captured at
Worcester. Transported on the
John and Sarah, master John Greene
from Gravesend 13 May 1652 for
Boston
(NER)

FRISSELL WILLIAM
Royalist soldier captured at
Worcester. Transported on the
John and Sarah, master John
Greene, from Gravesend 13 May
1652 for Boston
(NER)

FYFE ALEXANDER
Weaver. Wardend of Turfbegg,
Forfar. Assault. Prisoner at
Forfar and Perth. Banished to
the Plantations in America for
7 years, at Perth 20 May 1726
(JC)

GADDIE GEORGE
Thief. Banished to America for
life, at Aberdeen 1752
(SM)

GARDINER CHRISTINE
Child murder. Prisoner in
Edinburgh Tolbooth. Ban-
ished to the Plantations,
and stigmatised, 30 July
1685. Transported from
Leith by John Ewing to
Jamaica August 1685
(ETR)(PC)

GAIRDNER JOHN
Monkland. Covenanter.
Prisoner in Edinburgh
Tolbooth. Banished to
the Plantations 5 May
1684. Transported to
America by George Lock-
hart, merchant in New
York, James Glen, stat-
ioner burgess of Edin-
burgh, and Thomas Gordon
burgess of Edinburgh
16 May 1684
(PC)

GAIRDNER JOHN
Servant to James Ralston
in Wester Harieburn.
Covenanter. Warded in
Edinburgh Tolbooth 2
July 1684. Banished to
the Plantations 2 July
1684. Transported to
Carolina by Robert
Malloch 1 August 1684
(ETR)(PC)

GALL ALEXANDER
Sheepstealer. Banished
to America, at Aberdeen
1755
(SM)

GALT JOHN
Thatcher. Glasgow. Coven-
anter. Prisoner in Glas-
gow Tolbooth. Banished to
the Plantations, at Glas-
gow June 1684. Transport-
ed from the Clyde on the
Pelican by Walter Gibson,
merchant in Glasgow, to
America June 1684
(PC)

GARDNER ARCHIBALD
Jacobite. Transported from Liver-
pool on the Gildart, master
Richard Holmes. Landed at Port
North Potomack, Maryland 5 August
1747
(PRO)

GARDNER PATRICK
Jacobite. Transported on the
Hockenhill, master Hockenhill
Short, from Liverpool 25 June
1716 for South Carolina
(SP/C)

GARDNER PETER
Tailor, 18. Jacobite captured at
Carlisle. Transported on the
Johnson, master William Pemberton
from Liverpool. Landed at Port
Oxford, Maryland 5 August 1747
(P)(PRO)

GARVIE WILLIAM
Farmer. Inchrory, Ross. Jacobite
in Cromarty's regiment. Prisoner
at Inverness, ship and Tilbury.
Transported from London by Samuel
Smith to Jamaica or Barbados 20
March 1747
(P)

GAVINE JAMES
Covenanter. Prisoner in Edinburgh
Tolbooth. Banished to the Plant-
ations 30 July 1685. Stigmatised
4 August 1685. Transported from
Leith by John Ewing to Jamaica
11 August 1685
(ETR)(PC)

GAVIN JOHN
Banished to the Plantations.
Transported from Leith by John
Ewing to Jamaica August 1685
(PC)

GAY EDWARD
Bridgend, Glasgow. Covenanter.
Prisoner in Edinburgh Tolbooth.
Transported from Leith on the
St Michael of Scarborough,
master Edward Johnston
(PC)

GEDDES ALEXANDER
Labourer. Sanston, Aberdeenshire. Jacobite in
Glenbucket's regiment.
Captured at Carlisle.
Prisoner at Carlisle and
Chester. Transported on
the Gildart, master Richard Holmes, from Liverpool. Landed at Port
North Potomack, Maryland
5 August 1747
(JAB)(P)(PRO)

GEMMILL GRISSELL
Covenanter. Prisoner in
Leith Tolbooth. Banished
to the Plantations, at
Leith 18 August 1685.
Transported from Leith
on the Henry and Francis,
master Richard Hutton, by
George Scott of Pitlochie
to East New Jersey 5 September, 1685
(PC)

GEMMILL JOHN
Covenanter. Prisoner in
Canongate Tolbooth. Banished to the Plantations
in America 26 November
1685. Transported from
Leith on the John and
Nicholas, master Edward
Barnes, by Alexander
Fearne 17 December 1685
(ETR)(PC)

GENTLE ....
Carter. Falkirk. Robber.
Banished to the Plantations for 14 years 1773
(SM)

GIBB JOHN
"Sweetsinger" (a cult).
Transported from Leith
to America by George
Lockhart, merchant in New
York, James Glen, stationer burgess of Edinburgh,
and Thomas Gordon, burgess of Edinburgh 16 May
1684
(PC)

GIBB JOHN
Prisoner in Canongate Tolbooth. Transported from
Leith to East New Jersey
by Robert Barclay of Urie
30 July 1685
(PC)

GIBB JOHN
Covenanter. Prisoner in
Edinburgh. Banished to the
Plantations 24 August 1685.
Transported from Leith by
John Ewing to Jamaica August
1685
(PC)

GIBBON FRANCIS
Jacobite in Balmerino's Horse
Prisoner at Tilbury and
Southwark. Transported 1747(?)
(P)

GIBSON JOHN
Dalgain. Covenanter. Prisoner
in Glasgow Tolbooth. Banished
to the Plantations, at Glasgow June 1684. Transported
from the Clyde on the Pelican
by Walter Gibson, merchant in
Glasgow, to America June 1684
(PC)

GIBSON JOHN
Weaver, 20. Dundee. Jacobite
in Ogilvy's regiment. Prisoner at Arbroath, Stirling
and Carlisle. Transported on
the Gildart, master Richard
Holmes, from Liverpool. Landed at Port North Potomack,
Maryland 5 August 1747
(P)(OR)(PRO)

GIBBON ARTHUR
Sheepstealer. Banished to the
Plantations, at Aberdeen May
1749
(SM)

GIBBONS JOHN
Banished for life. Transported on the Brilliant, master Robert Bennet, from Glasgow. Landed at Port Hampton, Virginia 7 October 1772
(JC)

GILCHRIST BESSIE
Kilroy. Covenanter. Prisoner at Dumfries, later taken to Edinburgh. Banished to the Plantations, at Dumfries 24 October 1684
(PC)

GILCHRIST ROBERT
Dalgarnock, Nithsdale. Covenanter. Prisoner at Dumfries, Burntisland, Dunnottar and Leith. Banished to the Plantations, at Leith 18 August 1685. Transported from Leith on the Henry and Francis, master Richard Hutton, by George Scott of Pitlochie to East New Jersey 5 September 1685
(PC)

GILCHRIST WILLIAM
Blacksmith. West Kirk Parish, Edinburgh. Thief and rioter at Charles Sawer's mill. Banished to America for 7 years at Edinburgh 6 March 1741
(SM)

GILFILLAN JOHN
Covenanter. Prisoner at Glasgow, Burntisland, Dunnottar and Leith. Banished to the Plantations, at Leith 18 August 1685. Transported from Leith on the Henry and Francis, master Richard Hutton, by George Scott of Pitlochie to East New Jersey 5 September 1685
(PC)

GILKERSON GAVIN
Monkland. Covenanter. Prisoner in Edinburgh Tolbooth. Banished to the Plantations 5 May 1684. Transported to America by George Lockhart, merchant in New York, James Glen, stationer burgess in Edinburgh, and Thomas Gordon, burgess of Edinburgh 16 May 1684
(PC)

GILL HENRY
Jacobite captured at Preston. Transported from Liverpool on the Susannah, master Thomas Bromhall, to South Carolina 7 May 1716
(SP/C) (CTB)

GILLILAND JOHN
Covenanter. Prisoner in Edinburgh Tolbooth. Banished to the Plantations 24 July 1685. Transported from Leith by Robert Barclay of Urie to East New Jersey 30 July 1685
(ETR)(PC)

GIRVAN CATHERINE
Covenanter. Prisoner in Leith Tolbooth. Banished to the Plantations, at Leith 18 August 1685. Transported from Leith on the Henry and Francis by George Scott of Pitlochie to East New Jersey 5 September 1685. Richard Hutton, shipmaster
(PC)

GLANDY JOHN
Jacobite. Captured at Preston. Transported from Liverpool on the Friendship, master Michael Mankin, to Maryland 24 May 1716. Sold to Hugh Speddon in Maryland 20 August 1716
(SP/C)(CTB)(HM)

GLASS JOHN
Jacobite captured at
Preston. Transported on
the Scipio, master John
Scaisbrick, from Liver-
pool to Antigua 30 March
1716
(CTB)(SP/C)

GLASS JOHN
40, "Brogmaker". Milton
of Redcastle, Ross. Jac-
obite in Cromarty's regi-
ment. Prisoner at Inver-
ness, ships and Medway.
Transported from London
to Jamaica or Barbados by
Samuel Smith 31 March 1747
(P)(RM)

GLEN ROBERT
Rioter. Prisoner in Ayr
Tolbooth and Glasgow Tol-
booth. Banished to the
Plantations in America
for 7 years, at Ayr
2 May 1726
(JC)

GLENDINNING JOHN
Jacobite captured at
Preston. Transported on
the Elizabeth and Anne,
master Edward Trafford,
from Liverpool to Jam-
aica or Virginia 29 June
1716. Landed in Virginia
- unindentured
(CTB)(SP/C)(VSP)

GLESSEN JOHN
Jacobite captured at
Preston. Transported on
the Scipio, master John
Scaisbrick, from Liver-
pool to Antigua 30 March
1716
(CTB)(SP/C)

GOLDER JOHN
Jacobite. Prisoner at
Carlisle and Liverpool.
Transported from Liver-
pool on the Gildart, mas-
ter Richard Holmes. Lan-
ded Port North Potomack,
Maryland 5 August 1747
(PRO)(P)

GOLLAN DONALD
Avoch, Ross. Jacobite.
Transported 1747(?)
(P)

GOODBRAND ALEXANDER
Carpenter, 30. Banff. Jacobite
Prisoner at Carlisle, York and
Liverpool. Transported on the
Veteran, master John Ricky,
from Liverpool 5 May 1747.
Liberated by a French privateer
and landed on Martinique June
1747 while en route for the
Leeward Islands
(JAB)(P)(RM)

GOODWILLIE DAVID
Thief. Banished to America, at
Edinburgh 1752
(SM)

GOODWIN ROBERT
Covenanter. Glasgow. Prisoner
in Leith Tolbooth. Transported
from Leith on the Henry and
Francis, master Richard Hutton,
by George Scott of Pitlochie
to East New Jersey 5 September
1685
(PC)

GORDON ALEXANDER
Tenant of David Lumsden of
Cushnie, Aberdeenshire. Jacobite
captured at Preston. Transported
from Liverpool on the Friendship,
master Michael Mankin, 24 May
1716, for Virginia or Maryland.
Sold to John Gresham in Maryland
20 August 1716
(JAB)(SP/C)(HM)(CTB)

GORDON ALEXANDER
Kirkton of Cabrach, Aberdeen.
Thief. Banished for life to the
Plantations, at Aberdeen 30
April 1768
(SM)

GORDON ANNABELL
Covenanter. Prisoner at
Dunnottar and Leith.
Banished to the Plantat-
ions, at Leith 18 August
1685. Transported from
Leith on the Henry and
Francis, master Richard
Hutton, by George Scott
of Pitlochie to East New
Jersey 5 September 1685
(PC)

GORDON BESSIE
Covenanter. Prisoner at
Dumfries, Burntisland,
Dunnottar and Leith.
Banished to the Plantat-
ions, at Leith 18 August
1685. Transported from
Leith on the Henry and
Francis, master Richard
Hutton, by George Scott
of Pitlochie to East
New Jersey 5 September
1685
(PC)

GORDON OF BINHALL CHARLES
Aberdeen. 17, son of Pat-
rick Gordon of Binhall.
Jacobite paymaster in
Glenbucket's regiment.
Captured at Carlisle.
Prisoner at Carlisle and
Southwark. Transported
to Maryland 1747
(P)

GORDON DANIEL
Royalist soldier captured
at Worcester. Transported
on the John and Sarah,
master John Green, from
Gravesend to Boston
13 May 1652
(NER)

GORDON GEORGE
Forger. Banished to
America for life, at
Aberdeen 1752
(SM)

GORDON JAMES
Royalist soldier captured
at Worcester. Transported
on the John and Sarah, master
John Greene, from Gravesend
to Boston 13 May 1652

GORDON JAMES
28. Birkenbush, Cullen.
Jacobite Lieutenant in Grant's
regiment. Captured at Carlisle
Prisoner at Carlisle and
Southwark. Transported
1747(?)
(P)

GORDON JAMES
Orderettan. Horsethief. Banished to the Plantations
for life, at Aberdeen
18 May 1769
(SM)

GORDON JEAN
Thief. Prisoner in Jedburgh
Tolbooth. Banished from
Scotland, at Jedburgh 10
May 1732
(JC)

GORDON JOHN
Royalist soldier captured at
Worcester. Transported on the
John and Sarah, master John
Greene, from Gravesend to
Boston 13 May 1652
(NER)

GORDON JOHN
Weaver, 19. Loynavere, Elgin.
Jacobite in Glenbucket's
regiment. Captured at Carlisle. Prisoner at Carlisle
and York. Transported on the
Veteran, master John Ricky,
from Liverpool 5 May 1747
for the Leeward Islands.
Liberated by a French privateer and landed on Martinique June 1747
(P)(RM)

SCOTS BANISHED TO THE AMERICAN PLANTATIONS

GORDON JOHN
Tailor. Dumfries. Rioter
in Dumfries 1759. Pris-
oner in Edinburgh Tol-
booth. Transported to
the Plantations for 14
years, at Edinburgh
15 December 1760
(SM)(JC)

GORDON MARGARET
Goodwife of Arioland.
Covenanter. Banished to
the Plantations
17 October 1684
(PC)

GORDON ROBERT
Prisoner in Edinburgh or
Canongate Tolbooth. Ban-
ished to the Plantations
in Carolina. Transported
from Leith by Robert
Malloch 1684
(PC)

GORDON THOMAS
58. "Farms lands of the
Duke of Gordon". Strath-
bogie. Jacobite in Lord
Lewis Gordon's regiment.
Prisoner at Inverness,
ship and Tilbury. Trans-
ported from London to
Jamaica or Barbados by
Samuel Smith 31 March 1747
(P)(RM)

GORDON WILLIAM
Thief. Banished to the
Plantations for life, at
Aberdeen 1753
(SM)

GORTIE GEORGE
Jacobite captured at Preston. Transported from Liverpool on the Scipio, master
John Scaisbrick, to Antigua
30 March 1716
(CTB)

GOUK DAVID
20. Servant to James Histies.
Near Montrose. Jacobite in
Ogilvy's regiment. Prisoner
at Inverness and Tilbury.
Transported from London to
Jamaica or Barbados 31 March
1747 by Samuel Smith
(P)(RM)

GOUSSE CAPRAISE
Servant to George Leslie Esq.,
Nelfield, Edinburgh. Assault.
Prisoner in Edinburgh Tolbooth.
Banished to the Plantations in
America for life, at Edinburgh
20 December 1765
(JC)

GOVAN JOHN
Prisoner in Edinburgh Tolbooth.
Transported from Leith to the
Plantations November 1679
(ETR)

GOVAN THOMAS
Servant to John Bell in Craig-
prie. Covenanter. Prisoner in
Edinburgh Tolbooth. Banished
to the Plantations 7 November
1678. Transported from Leith on
the St Michael of Scarborough,
master Edward Johnston
12 December 1678
(PC)

GOVAN WILLIAM
Servant to Helen Fountain, tenant
in Puncheonlaw. Covenanter.
Prisoner in Canongate Tolbooth.
Banished to the Plantations 7
November 1678. Transported from
Leith on the St Michael of Scar-
borough, master Edward Johnston,
12 December 1678
(PC)

GOWAN DONALD
40. Farmer. Aich, Ross. Jacobite
in Cromarty's regiment. Prisoner
at Inverness and Tilbury. Transported from London to Barbados or
Jamaica 31 March 1747
(P)(RM)

SCOTS BANISHED TO THE AMERICAN PLANTATIONS

GRAEME or OGILVIE JANET
Spouse to Andrew Wilson,
founder. Aberfoyle. Thief.
Banished to the Plantat-
ions for life, at Perth
May 1770. Transported on
the Crawford, master
James McLean from Port
Glasgow. Landed at Port
Oxford, Maryland
23 July 1771
(SM)(JC)

GRAHAM ALEXANDER
Covenanter. Prisoner in
Paul's Work, Edinburgh.
Transported from Leith
to East New Jersey by
Robert Barclay of Urie
August 1685
(PC)

GRAHAM CHARLES
22. Son of John Graham
of Airth. Jacobite in
Glengarry's regiment.
Prisoner at Inverness,
ships and Medway. Trans-
ported 20 March 1747
(P)

GRAHAM CHARLES
Tain. Jacobite in Crom-
arty's regiment. Prison-
er at Dunrobin, Inverness
ship and Tilbury. Trans-
ported 31 March 1747
(P)

GRAHAM DAVID
Jacobite captured at Pres-
ton. Transported from
Liverpool on the Godspeed,
master Arthur Smith, 28
July 1716. Sold to John
Fendall in Maryland
18 October 1716
(SP/C)(CTB)(HM)

GRAHAM FERGUS
Jacobite captured at Pres-
ton. Transported from Liver-
pool on the Elizabeth and
Anne, master Edward Trafford.
Landed at York Virginia
(CTB)(SP/C)(VSP)

GRAHAME GEORGE
Edinburgh. Thief. Transported
on the Merchant of Glasgow
to the Plantations December
1670
(PC)

GRAHAM IVOR
Innerneil, Argyll. Covenanter.
Prisoner in Paul's Work, Edinburgh. Banished to the Plantations 24 July 1685. Transported from Leith to Jamaica
7 August 1685 by John Ewing
(PC)

GRAHAM JAMES
Jacobite captured at Preston.
Transported from Liverpool on
the Anne, master Robert
Wallace, to Virginia 31 July
1716
(SP/C)(CTB)

GRAHAM JOHN
Prisoner in Canongate Tolbooth.
Transported from Leith to the
Plantations 12 December 1678
on the St Michael of Scarborough
master Edward Johnston
(PC)

GRAHAM SAMUEL
Prisoner in Edinburgh and Canon-
gate Tolbooths. Banished to the
Plantations 11 August 1685
(ETR)(PC)

GRAHAM THOMAS
Skirling. Covenanter. Banished
to the Plantations in America
27 October 1684. Possibly the
Thomas Graham, prisoner in
Leith Tolbooth, who was trans-
ported from Leith to East New
Jersey 5 September 1685 by
George Scott of Pitlochie on the
Henry and Francis, master Richard
Hutton
(PC)

GRAHAM WILLIAM
Covenanter. Prisoner in
Linlithgow Tolbooth.
Transported to the Plant-
ations in America by
Walter Gibson, merchant
in Glasgow 27 May 1684
(PC)

GRAHAM WILLIAM
Prisoner in Edinburgh
Tolbooth. Transported
from Leith to America
by Alexander Fearne
and his shipmaster
Edward Barnes December
1685
(ETR)

GRAINGER MARGARET
Transported on the
Polly, master James McArthur
from Port Glasgow. Landed
at Port Oxford, Maryland
16 September 1771
(JC)

GRANT ALASTAIR
Royalist soldier captured
at Worcester. Transported
from Gravesend on the
John and Sarah, master
John Greene, to Boston
13 May 1652
(NER)

GRANT ALEXANDER
Royalist soldier captured
at Worcester. Transported
from Gravesend on the
John and Sarah, master
John Greene, to Boston
13 May 1652
(NER)

GRANT ALEXANDER
57, farmer. Delcaitack,
Glenmoriston. Jacobite
in Glengarry's regiment
Prisoner at Inverness,
ship, Tilbury and South
wark. Transported from
London by Samuel Smith
to Jamaica or Barbados
20 March 1747
(P)(RM)

GRANT ALEXANDER
25, carpenter. Aberdeen.
Jacobite in Lord Lewis Gordon's
regiment. Captured at Carlisle.
Prisoner at Carlisle and York.
Transported from Liverpool on
the Veteran, master John Ricky,
to the Leeward Islands 5 May
1747. Liberated by a French
privateer and landed on
Martinique June 1747
(P)(JAB)(RM)

GRANT ALEXANDER
48, boatman. West Innerwick,
Glenmoriston. Jacobite in Glen-
garry's regiment. Prisoner at
Inverness, ship and Tilbury.
Transported from London to
Barbados by Samuel Smith 29
March 1747. Returned to Scot-
land 1748
(P)

GRANT ALEXANDER
31, farmer. Glenmoriston.
Jacobite in Glengarry's regiment. Prisoner at Inverness,
ship and Tilbury. Transported
from London to Barbados or
Jamaica by Samuel Smith 31
March 1747
(P)(RM)

GRANT ALEXANDER
35. Glenmoriston. Jacobite in
Glengarry's regiment. Prisoner
at Inverness and Tilbury.
Transported from London to
Barbados or Jamaica by Samuel
Smith 31 March 1747
(P)(RM)

GRANT ALEXANDER
55, farmer. Wester Innerwick,
Glenmoriston. Jacobite in
Glengarry's regiment. Prisoner
at Inverness, ship and Tilbury
Transported from London to
Jamaica or Barbados by Samuel
Smith 31 March 1747
(P)

GRANT ALLAN
60, labourer. Strathspey.
Jacobite in Roy Stuart's
regiment. Prisoner at
Edinburgh. Transported
on the Johnson, master
William Pemberton, from
Liverpool 5 May 1747.
Landed at Port Oxford,
Maryland 5 August 1747
(P)(PRO)

GRANT ANGUS
50, farmer. Glenmoriston.
Jacobite in Glengarry's
regiment. Prisoner at
Inverness, ship and Til-
bury. Transported from
London to Jamaica or
Barbados by Samuel Smith
31 March 1747
(P)(RM)

GRANT ANGUS
Wester Dundreggan, Glen-
moriston. 54, farmer.
Jacobite in Glengarry's
regiment. Prisoner at
Inverness, ship and Til-
bury. Transported 31
March 1747
(P)

GRANT ANGUS
22, labourer. Glengarry.
Jacobite in Glengarry's
regiment. Prisoner at
Carlisle, Whitehaven and
York. Transported from
Liverpool on the Johnson,
master William Pemberton,
5 May 1747. Landed at
Port Oxford, Maryland
5 August 1747
(P)(PRO)

GRANT ANGUS
31, farmer. Glenmoriston.
Jacobite in Glengarry's
regiment. Prisoner at
Inverness, ship and Til-
bury. Transported from
London to Barbados or
Jamaica by Samuel Smith
30 March 1747
(P)(RM)

GRANT ARCHIBALD
40, farmer. Glenurquhart. Jacobite in the Duke of Perth's
regiment. Prisoner at Inverness
and Tilbury. Transported from
London to Barbados or Jamaica
by Samuel Smith 31 March 1747
(P)(RM)

GRANT CHARLES
19, miller. Abernethy, Inverness
Jacobite in Roy Stuart's regiment
Captured at Carlisle. Prisoner at
Carlisle and Lincoln. Transported
from Liverpool on the Veteran,
master John Ricky, to the Leeward
Islands 5 May 1747. Liberated by
a French privateer and landed on
Martinique June 1747
(P)(RM)

GRANT CHARLES (alias JOHN THOMPSON)
Land labourer. Thief and house-
breaker. Banished for life 1772.
Transported on the Phoenix,
master John Lamont, from Port
Glasgow. Landed at Port Accomack,
Virginia 20 December 1773
(JC)(SM)

GRANT DANIEL
Royalist soldier captured at
Worcester. Transported on the
John and Sarah, master John
Greene, from Gravesend to Boston
13 May 1652
(NER)

GRANT DANIEL
Jacobite captured at Preston.
Transported on the Godspeed,
master Arthur Smith, from Liver-
pool for Virginia 28 July 1716.
Sold to William MacConnochie in
Maryland 18 October 1716
(SP/C)(HM)(CTB)

GRANT DONALD
36, farmer. Balnagarn, Glenmoriston
Jacobite in Glengarry's regiment.
Prisoner at Inverness, ship and
Tilbury. Transported from London
to Barbados or Jamaica by Samuel
Smith 31 March 1747
(P)(RM)

GRANT DONALD
32, farmer. Ballintombuy,
Glenmoriston. Jacobite in
Glengarry's regiment.
Prisoner at Inverness,
ship and Tilbury. Trans-
ported from London to
Jamaica or Barbados by
Samuel Smith 31 March
1747
(P)(RM)

GRANT DONALD
40, farmer. Wester Dun-
dreggan, Glenmoriston.
Jacobite in Glengarry's
regiment. Prisoner at
Inverness, ship and Til-
bury. Transported from
London to Barbados or
Jamaica by Samuel Smith
31 March 1747
(P)(RM)

GRANT DONALD
62, farmer. Glenmoriston
Jacobite in Glengarry's
regiment. Prisoner at
Inverness, ship and Til-
bury. Transported 20
March 1747
(P)

GRANT DONALD
60. Balry, Glenmoriston
Jacobite in Glengarry's
regiment. Prisoner at
Inverness, ship and Til-
bury. Transported to
Barbados 19 March 1747
(P)

GRANT DONALD
58, farmer. Glenmoriston
Jacobite in Glengarry's
regiment. Prisoner at
Inverness, ship and Til-
bury. Transported from
London to Barbados or
Jamaica by Samuel Smith
31 March 1747
(P)(RM)

GRANT DUGAL
50, farmer. Glenmoriston. Jacobite in Glengarry's regiment.
Prisoner at Inverness and Tilbury. Transported from London
to Barbados or Jamaica by Samuel
Smith 31 March 1747
(P)(RM)

GRANT DUNCAN
45, farmer. Wester Dundreggan,
Glenmoriston. Jacobite in Glen-
garry's regiment. Prisoner at
Inverness, ship and Tilbury.
Transported 20 March 1747
(P)

GRANT ELIZABETH
20, seamstress. Banff. Jacobite.
Captured at Carlisle. Prisoner
at Carlisle and York. Transported 20 March 1747
(P)

GRANT FARQUHAR
Jacobite in Glengarry's regiment
Prisoner at Inverness and Tilbury
Transported 31 March 1747
(P)

GRANT FARQUHAR
43, farmer. Glenmoriston.
Jacobite in Glengarry's regiment
Prisoner at Inverness, ship and
Tilbury. Transported 20 March
1747
(P)

GRANT GEORGE
40, farmer. Glenmoriston. Jac-
obite in Glengarry's regiment.
Prisoner at Inverness, ship and
Tilbury. Transported from London
to Barbados or Jamaica by Samuel
Smith 31 March 1747
(P)(RM)

GRANT HUGH
50, farmer. Glenmoriston. Jac-
obite in Glengarry's regiment.
Prisoner at Inverness, ship and
Tilbury. Transported from London
to Barbados or Jamaica by Samuel
Smith 31 March 1747
(P)(RM)

GRANT JAMES
Royalist soldier captured
at Worcester. Transported
on the John and Sarah,
master John Greene, from
Gravesend to Boston 13 May
1652
(NER)

GRANT JAMES
50, farmer. Blairy, Glen-
moriston. Jacobite in Glengarry's regiment. Prisoner
at Inverness, ship and Tilbury. Transported from London to Barbados or Jamaica
by Samuel Smith 31 March
1747
(P)(RM)

GRANT JAMES
61, farmer. Wester Innerwick
Glenmoriston. Jacobite in
Glengarry's regiment. Pris-
oner at Inverness, ship and
Tilbury. Transported 1747(?)
(P)

GRANT JOHN
Royalist soldier captured
at Worcester. Transported
on the John and Sarah,
master John Greene, from
Gravesend to Boston 13 May
1652
(NER)

GRANT JOHN
Royalist soldier captured
at Worcester. Transported
on the John and Sarah,
master John Greene, from
Gravesend to Boston 13 May
1652
(NER)

GRANT JOHN
34, weaver. Banff. Jacob-
ite in Roy Stuart's regi-
ment. Transported from
Liverpool on the Johnson,
master William Pemberton,
5 May 1747. Landed at
Port Oxford, Maryland
5 August 1747
(P)(PRO)

GRANT JOHN
'A boy'. Glenmoriston. Jacobite
in Glengarry's regiment. Pris-
oner at Edinburgh, Carlisle and
York. Transported
(P)

GRANT JOHN
55, farmer. Glen Urquhart. Jac-
obite in Glengarry's regiment.
Prisoner at Inverness, ship and
Tilbury. Transported from London
to Barbados or Jamaica by Samuel
Smith 31 March 1747
(P)(RM)

GRANT JOHN
45, farmer. Glenmoriston. Jac-
obite in Glengarry's regiment.
Prisoner at Inverness, ship and
Tilbury. Transported from London
to Barbados or Jamaica by Samuel
Smith 31 March 1747
(P)(RM)

GRANT JOHN
22. Glenmoriston. Jacobite in
Glengarry's regiment. Prisoner
at Inverness, ship and Tilbury.
Transported from London to Jamaica or Barbados by Samuel Smith
31 March 1747
(P)(RM)

GRANT JOHN
40, farmer. Craskie, Glenmoriston
Jacobite in Glengarry's regiment.
Prisoner at Inverness, ship and
Tilbury. Transported from London
to Barbados or Jamaica by Samuel
Smith 31 March 1747
(P)(RM)

GRANT JOHN
30, farmer. Glenmoriston. Jac-
obite in Glengarry's regiment.
Prisoner at Inverness, ship and
Tilbury. Transported from London
to Barbados or Jamaica by Samuel
Smith 31 March 1747
(P)(RM)

GRANT JOHN
40, farmer. Glenmoriston.
Jacobite in Glengarry's
regiment. Prisoner at
Inverness, ship and Til-
bury. Transported from
London to Barbados or
Jamaica by Samuel Smith
31 March 1747
(P)(RM)

GRANT JOHN
25, farmer. Glenmoriston.
Jacobite in Glengarry's
regiment. Prisoner at
Inverness, ship and Til-
bury. Transported from
London to Barbados or
Jamaica by Samuel Smith
31 March 1747
(P)(RM)

GRANT JOHN
40, farmer. Glenmoriston.
Jacobite in Glengarry's
regiment. Prisoner at
Inverness, ship and Til-
bury. Transported from
London to Barbados or
Jamaica b y Samuel Smith
31 March 1747
(P)(RM)

GRANT JOHN
26, farmer. Glenmoriston.
Jacobite in Glengarry's
regiment. Prisoner at
Inverness, ship and Til-
bury. Transported from
London to Barbados or
Jamaica by Samuel Smith
31 March 1747
(P)(RM)

GRANT JOHN
41, farmer. East Achlein,
Glenmoriston. Jacobite in
Glengarry's regiment. Prisoner at Inverness, ship
and Tilbury. Transported
from London to Barbados
or Jamaica by Samuel
Smith 31 March 1747
(P)(RM)

GRANT JOHN
45, farmer. Balnagarn, Glen-
moriston. Jacobite in Glen-
garry's regiment. Prisoner at
Inverness, ship and Tilbury.
Transported from London to
Barbados or Jamaica by Samuel
Smith 31 March 1747
(P)(RM)

GRANT JOHN
50, farmer. Glenmoriston. Jac-
obite in Glengarry's regiment.
Prisoner at Inverness, ship and
Tilbury. Transported from London
to Barbados or Jamaica by Samuel
Smith 31 March 1747
(P)(RM)

GRANT JOHN
38, farmer. Inverwick, Glenmoriston. Jacobite in Glengarry's
regiment. Prisoner at Inverness,
ship and Tilbury. Transported
from London to Barbados or Jamaica by Samuel Smith 31 March
1747
(P)(RM)

GRANT JOHN
40, labourer. Badenoch or Lochaber. Jacobite in Lochiel's
regiment. Captured at Carlisle.
Transported from Liverpool on the
Veteran, master John Ricky, to
the Leeward Islands 5 May 1747.
Liberated by a French privateer
and landed on Martinique June 1747
(P)(RM)

GRANT JOHN alias BRACHADER
Rictian. Horsethief. Banished to
the Plantations for 14 years, at
Inverness 10 May 1768
(SM)

GRANT LUDOVICK
Jacobite captured at Preston.
Transported from Liverpool to
South Carolina on the Susannah,
master Thomas Bromhall 7 May 1716
(SP/C)(CTB)

GRANT PATRICK
Royalist soldier captured
at Worcester. Transported
on the John and Sarah,
master John Greene, from
Gravesend to Boston 13 May
1652
(NER)

GRANT PATRICK
30, farmer. Glenmoriston.
Jacobite in Glengarry's
regiment. Prisoner at
Inverness and Tilbury.
Transported
(P)

GRANT PETER
46. East Achlein, Glen-
moriston. Jacobite in
Glengarry's regiment.
Prisoner at Inverness,
ship and Tilbury. Trans
ported 20 March 1747
(P)

GRANT PETER
24, fiddler. Glen
Urquhart. Jacobite in
Glengarry's regiment.
Prisoner at Inverness,
ship and Medway. Trans-
ported from London to
Barbados or Jamaica by
Samuel Smith 31 March 1747
(P)(RM)

GRANT PETER
50, farmer. Glenmoriston
Jacobite in Glengarry's
regiment. Prisoner at
Inverness, ship and Til-
bury. Transported from
London to Barbados or
Jamaica 31 March 1747
(P)(RM)

GRANT ROBERT
Tenant of David Lumsden of
Cushnie, Aberdeenshire.
Jacobite captured at Pres-
ton. Transported from
Liverpool on the Elizabeth
and Anne, master Edward

Trafford, to Virginia or Jamaica
29 June 1716. Landed in Virginia
- Unindentured
(JAB)(SP/C)(CTBⅩVSP)

GRANT THOMAS
Royalist soldier captured at
Worcester. Transported on the
John and Sarah, master John
Greene, from Gravesend to
Boston 13 May 1652
(NER)

GRANT WALTER
40, Barber in Edinburgh, from
Teviotdale. Jacobite in Strath-
allan's Horse. Prisoner at
Inverness, ship and Tilbury.
Transported from London to Jamaica or Barbados by Samuel Smith
20 March 1747
(P)(RM)

GRANT WILLIAM
Royalist soldier captured at
Worcester. Transported on the
John and Sarah, master John
Greene, from Gravesend to
Boston 13 May 1652
(NER)

GRANT WILLIAM
Jacobite captured at Preston.
Transported from Liverpool on
the Friendship, master Michael
Mankin, to Maryland 24 May 1716
Sold to Thomas Davis in Maryland
20 August 1716
(SP/C)(HM)(CTB)

GRANT WILLIAM
48, linen weaver. Aberdeen. Jacobite in Lord Lewis Gordon's
regiment. Transported from Liverpool on the Gildart, master Rich
ard Holmes,landed at Port North
Potomack, Maryland 5 August 1747
(P)(PRO)

GRAY GEORGE
Tailor. Kirkness. Forger. Pris-
oner in Edinburgh Tolbooth. Ban-
ished to the Plantations in
America for life, at Edinburgh1743
(JC)

GRAY JAMES
Prisoner in Edinburgh Tolbooth. Transported by
George Hutchison, merchant
in Edinburgh, to Barbados
7 December 1665
(ETR)

GRAY JAMES
Prisoner in Edinburgh Tol-
booth. Transported from
Leith to the Plantations
November 1679
(ETR)

GRAY JAMES
Covenanter. Prisoner in
Edinburgh Tolbooth. Ban-
ishedto the Plantations
in Carolina 6 August 1684
To be taken by Robert
Malloch, merchant in Edin
burgh. Transported from
Leith by John Ewing to
Jamaica August 1685
(ETR)(PC)

GRAY JAMES
Leith. Writer of threat-
ening letters. Prisoner
in Edinburgh Tolbooth.
Banished to the Plantat-
ions in America for life,
at Edinburgh 11 July 1737
(JC)

GRAY JOHN
Keith, Banffshire. Jac-
obite in Glenbucket's
regiment. Captured at
Carlisle. Transported
from Liverpool on the
Gildart, master Rich-
ard Holmes. Landed at
Port North Potomack,
Maryland 5 August 1747
(P)(JAB)(PRO)

GRAY JOHN
22, weaver. Liff, Angus. Jac-
obite in Ogilvy's regiment.
Prisoner at Perth and Carlisle.
Transported from Liverpool om
the Johnson, master William
Pemberton. Landed at Port Oxford
Maryland 5 August 1747
(PRO)(P)

GRAY WILLIAM
Soldier, 31st Regiment of Foot.
Banished to America for life,
at Jedburgh 12 October 1772.
Transported on the Phoenix,
master John Lamont, from Port
Glasgow. Landed at Port Accomack
Virginia 20 December 1772. Thief
and housebreaker
(SM)(JC)

GREIG MARY
Duns, Berwickshire. Cattlethief.
Banished to the Plantations 1768
(SM)

GREENHILL WILLIAM
Gardener. Lethenday, Perth.
Jacobite in Ogilvy's regiment.
Prisoner at Perth, Canongate
and Carlisle. Transported
(P)

GREWER GEORGE
Labourer. Angus. Jacobite in
Ogilvy's regiment. Prisoner at
Carlisle and Lincoln. Trans-
ported from Liverpool 22 April
1747
(P)

GRIER FERGUS
Covenanter. Prisoner in Leith
Tolbooth. Transported from Leith
by George Scott of Pitlochie on
the Henry and Francis, master
Richard Hutton, to East New
Jersey 5 September 1685
(PC)

GRIER JAMES
Covenanter. Prisoner in
Leith Tolbooth. Trans-
ported from Leith to
East New Jersey by George
Scott of Pitlochie on the
Henry and Francis, master
Richard Hutton, 5 Septem-
ber 1685
(PC)

GRIER JOHN
Brigmark. Covenanter.
Prisoner in Kirkcud-
bright Tolbooth. Banish
ed to the Plantations, at
Kirkcudbright 13 October
1684
(PC)

GRIER ROBERT
Covenanter. Prisoner in
Edinburgh Tolbooth. Ban-
ished to Virginia 4 Aug-
ust 1668. Transported
from Leith on the Con-
vertin, master Captain
Lightfoot, to Virginia
September 1668
(PC)

GRIER THOMAS
Cormilligan. Covenanter.
Banished to the Plantat-
ions 24 October 1684
(PC)

GRIEVE WALTER
Thief. Prisoner in Jed-
burgh Tolbooth. Banished
to the Plantations in
America, at Jedburgh
11 May 1726
(JC)

GREIVE WILLIAM
Linlithgow. Covenanter.
Prisoner in Canongate Tol-
booth. Banished to the
Plantations in America
27 May 1684. Transported
to Carolina by Robert Mall-
och, merchant in Edinburgh
June 1684
(PC)

GRINDLAY WILLIAM
Prisoner in Edinburgh Tolbooth.
Transported from Leith to the
Plantations November 1679
(ETR)

GROVES WILLIAM
Soldier in the 67th Regiment.
Rapist. Banished to the Plant-
ations for life, at Jedburgh
11 May 1775
(SM)

GUILD THOMAS
Jacobite captured at Preston.
Transported from Liverpool on
the Susannah, master Thomas
Bromhall, 7 May 1716
(CTB)(SP/C)

GUNN ANGUS
20, husbandman. Lairn, Caithness.
Jacobite in Cromarty's regiment.
Prisoner at Inverness, ship and
Tilbury. Transported from London
to Barbados or Jamaica by Samuel
Smith 20 March 1747
(P)(RM)

GUNN DANIEL
Royalist soldier captured at Worcester. Transported on the John
and Sarah, master John Greene,
from Gravesend to Boston 13 May
1652
(NER)

GUNN DANIEL
30. Caithness. Jacobite. Prisoner
at Inverness and ship. Transported
31 March 1747
(P)

GUNN DONALD
40, husbandman. Dunbeath, Caithness. Jacobite in Cromarty's regiment. Prisoner at Inverness, ship
and Medway. Transported from Lon
don to Barbados or Jamaica 31 March
1747
(P)(RM)

69

GUNN DONALD
30. Soldier. Caithness.
Jacobite in Cromarty's
regiment. Prisoner at
Inverness, ship and Med-
way. Transported from
London to Jamaica or Bar
bados by Samuel Smith 31
March 1747
(P)(RM)

GUNN JOHN
Vagabond. Banished to the
Plantations for life, at
Aberdeen 11 May 1721
(JC)

GUTHRIE JOHN
Jacobite captured at
Preston. Transported
from Liverpool to South
Carolina on the Susannah,
master Thomas Bromhall,
7 May 1716
(SP/C)(CTB)

GUTHRIE ROBERT
Jacobite captured at
Preston. Transported
from Liverpool to South
Carolina on the Wakefield,
master Thomas Beck, 21
April 1716
(CTB)(SP/C)

HADDEN .....
Banished to Barbados or
Virginia 27 February 1667
(PC)

HACKSTONE WILLIAM
Tailor. Edinburgh. Cov-
enanter. Prisoner in
Edinburgh Tolbooth.
Transported from Leith
on the St Michael of
Scarborough, master
Edward Johnston, to the
Plantations in the Indies
12 December 1678
(PC)

HADDOWAY ARCHIBALD
Glasgow. Covenanter. Prisoner in
Edinburgh Tolbooth. Transported
from Leith on the St Michael of
Scarborough, master Edward
Johnston, to the Plantations
12 December 1678
(PC)

HALDANE JAMES
Merchant. Thief. Prisoner in
Jedburgh and Edinburgh Tolbooths.
Banished to the Plantations in
America, at Jedburgh 10 May 1722.
Transferred to Glasgow 30 May
1722 for transportation to New
England
(ETR)(JC)

HALKET CHARLES
20, labourer. Aberdeen. Rebel
cess collector. Captured at
Carlisle. Transported on the
Veteran, master John Ricky,
from Liverpool 5 May 1747.
Liberated by a French privateer
and landed on Martinique June
1747
(P)(JAB)(RM)

HALL JAMES
Tenant of Colin MacEachen. Kin-
tyre. Covenanter in Argyll's
rebellion. Prisoner in Laigh
Parliament House, Edinburgh.
Banished to the Plantations
31 July 1685. Transported from
Leith by John Ewing to Jamaica
August 1685
(PC)

HALL WILLIAM
Jacobite captured at Preston.
Transported from Liverpool on
the Scipio, master John Scais-
brick, to Antigua 30 March 1716
(CTB)

70

HALTON JOHN
Jacobite. Prisoner at
Carlisle and Liverpool.
Transported from Liver-
pool on the Gildart,
master Richard Holmes,
landed at Port North
Potomack, Maryland
5 August 1747
(P)(PRO)

HAMILTON BESSIE
Prisoner in Edinburgh
Tolbooth. Transported
to Barbados by George
Hutchison, merchant in
Edinburgh 12 December
1665
(ETR)(PC)

HAMILTON DAVID
Royalist soldier capt-
ured at Worcester.
Transported on the John
and Sarah, master John
Greene, from Gravesend
to Boston 13 May 1652
(NER)

HAMILTON GEORGE
Portioner of Broun-
castle. Covenanter.
Banished to the Plant-
ations in America 24
December 1684. Prisoner
at Glasgow and Edinburgh
(PC)

HAMILTON ISOBEL
Prisoner in Edinburgh
Tolbooth. Transported
to Barbados by George
Hutchison, merchant in
Edinburgh 7 December
1665
(ETR)

HAMILTON JAMES
Prisoner in Canongate.
Transported to Carolina
by Walter Gibson, merch-
ant, Glasgow 19 August
1684
(PC)

HAMILTON ISABEL
50, knitter. Musselburgh. Jacobite. Transported on the
Veteran, master John Ricky,
from Liverpool 5 May 1747 for
the Leeward Islands. Liberated
by a French privateer and landed
on Martinique June 1747
(P)(RM)

HAMILTON JAMES
Royalist soldier captured at
Worcester. Transported on the
John and Sarah, master John
Greene, from Gravesend to
Boston 13 May 1652
(NER)

HAMILTON JAMES
Servant to James Balderstone,
skinner, Leith. Thief. Prisoner
in Edinburgh Tolbooth. Banished
to America for 7 years, 9 March
1767
(SM)(JC)

HAMILTON JOHN
Gypsy. Prisoner in Edinburgh
Tolbooth. Transported from
Greenock to New York 21 October
1682
(ETR)

HAMILTON MATTHEW
Servant to John Howie, husbandman. Kintyre. Covenanter in
Argyll's rebellion. Prisoner
in Edinburgh Tolbooth. Banished
to the Plantations 24 July 1685.
Stigmatised 30 July 1685. Trans
ported from Leith by John Ewing
to Jamaica August 1685
(PC)(ETR)

71

HAMILTON ROBERT
Gardener. Gorthie, Perth.
Jacobite in the Duke of
Perth's regiment. Prison-
er at Chester. Transport-
ed from Liverpool on the
Johnson, master William
Pemberton. Landed at Port
Oxford, Maryland 5 August
1747
(P)(PRO)

HAMILTON RORY
Royalist soldier captured
at Worcester. Transported
on the John and Sarah,
master John Greene, from
Gravesend to Boston 13
May 1652
(NER)

HAMMOND GEORGE
Jacobite captured at
Preston. Transported from
Liverpool to South Carol-
ina on the Susannah, mas-
ter Thomas Bromhall, 7
May 1716
(SP/C)(CTB)

HANDYSIDE ROBERT
Jacobite captured at
Preston. Transported on
the Two Brothers, master
Edward Rathbone, from
Liverpool for Jamaica
26 April 1716. Landed on
Montserrat June 1716
(SP/C)(CTB)(CTP)

HANNA WILLIAM
Covenanter from the Bor-
ders. Prisoner in Dum-
fries and Leith. Trans-
ported from Leith on the
Henry and Francis, mas-
ter Richard Hutton, to
East New Jersey by
George Scott of Pitlochie
5 September 1685
(PC)

HANNAWINKLE ALEXANDER
Forger. Prisoner in Edin-
burgh. Banished to the
Plantations 1775
(JC)

HANOMAN JOHN
Royalist soldier captured at
Worcester. Transported on the
John and Sarah, master John
Greene, from Gravesend to
Boston 13 May 1652
(NER)

HANTON JAMES
Brechin, Angus. Thief. Banish-
ed to America or the British West
Indies for 7 years, at Aberdeen
September 1775
(SM)

HARDWICK WILLIAM
Jacobite captured at Preston.
Transported from Liverpool to
St Kitts on the Hockenhill,
master H.Short, 25 June 1716
(SP/C)(CTB)

HARKNESS JOHN
Servant to Margaret Fraser in
Mitchellslacks. Covenanter.
Banished to the Plantations,
at Dumfries 24 October 1684
(PC)

HARPER JOHN
Fenwick. Covenanter. Prisoner
in Edinburgh Tolbooth. Banished
to the Plantations 5 May 1684.
Transported by George Lockhart,
merchant in New York, James Glen,
stationer burgess of Edinburgh,
and Thomas Gordon, merchant
burgess of Edinburgh, 19 May 1684
(PC)

HARRIS JOHN
Jacobite captured at Preston.
Transported from Liverpool to
Virginia or Jamaica on the
Elizabeth and Anne, master Edward
Trafford, 29 June 1716. Landed in
Virginia - unindentured
(CTB)(SP/C)(VSP)

HARROWAY MR JOHN
Prisoner in Edinburgh Tolbooth. Transported from
Leith to the Plantations
on the St Michael of Scarborough 12 December 1678
(PC)

HARVIE JOHN
Dalserf. Covenanter. Prisoner in Dunnottar and Leith
Banished to the Plantations
at Leith 18 August 1685.
Transported from Leith on
the Henry and Francis, master Richard Hutton, to East
New Jersey by George Scott
of Pitlochie 5 September
1685
(PC)

HASTIE ANN
Daughter of Robert Hastie,
town piper, Dunbar. Child
murder. Prisoner in Edin-
burgh Tolbooth. Banished
to the Plantations in
America for life, at Edin
burgh 8 August 1760
(JC)

HASTIE WILLIAM
Covenanter. Prisoner in
Edinburgh and Canongate
Tolbooths. Transported
from Leith to the Plant-
ations in Jamaica by
John Ewing 24 July 1685
(PC)

HAY JOHN
Covenanter. Prisoner in
Edinburgh Tolbooth. Ban-
ished to the Plantations
31 July 1685. Stigmatised
4 August 1685
(PC)

HAY JOHN
Thief. Banished to the
Plantations for life, at
Aberdeen 1753
(SM)

HAY JOHN
Jacobite captured at Preston.
Transported from Liverpool on
the Friendship, master Michael
Mankin, to Maryland 24 May 1716.
Sold to William Holmes, Maryland
24 August 1716
(SP/C)(CTB)(HM)

HAY WILLIAM
Prisoner in Edinburgh Tolbooth.
Transported from Leith on the
St Michael of Scarborough,
master Edward Johnston, to the
Plantations 12 December 1678
(PC)

HECTOR JOHN
Salmon fisher, 42. Cruives, Old
Machar, Aberdeenshire. Jacobite.
Prisoner at Canongate and Car-
lisle. Transported from Liver-
pool on the Johnson, master
William Pemberton. Landed at
Port Oxford, Maryland 5 August
1747
(P)(JAB)(PRO)

HEDERICK JAMES
Royalist soldier captured at
Worcester. Transported on the
John and Sarah, master John
Greene, from Gravesend to
Boston 13 May 1652
(NER)

HENDRY JAMES
Jacobite captured at Preston.
Transported on the Friendship,
master Michael Mankin, from
Liverpool to Maryland 24 May
1716. Sold to John Oldham in
Maryland 20 August 1716
(SP/C)(HM)

HENDERSON CHARLES
Jacobite captured at Preston.
Transported from Liverpool on
the Elizabeth and Anne, master
Edward Trafford, to Virginia or
Jamaica 29 June 1716. Landed in
Virginia - unindentured
(CTB)(SP/C)

HENDERSON COLIN
Torryburn. Spirits thief.
Banished to the Plantat-
ions for life in 1772
(SM)

HENDERSON JAMES
30, cook. Angus. Jacobite
in Ogilvy's regiment.
Captured at Carlisle.
Transported from Liverpool
on the Veteran, master
John Ricky, 15 May 1747
for the Leeward Islands.
Liberated by a French
privateer and landed on
Martinique June 1747
(P)(OR)(RM)

HENDERSON JOHN
Ruchoard.Covenanter. Prisoner
at Burntisland, Dunnottar,
Leith and Thieveshole, Edinburgh. Banished to the Plant
ations, at Leith 18 August
1685. Transported from Leith
on the Henry and Francis,
master Richard Hutton, by
George Scott of Pitlochie to
East New Jersey 5 September
1685
(PC)

HENDERSON JOHN
Writer in Edinburgh. Son of
Peter Henderson, writer in
Falkirk. Forger. Prisoner
in Edinburgh Tolbooth. Ban-
ished to the Plantations in
America for life, at Edin-
burgh 11 August 1775
(JC)

HENDERSON ROBERT
Tenant of David Lumsden of
Cushnie, Aberdeenshire. Jac-
obite captured at Preston.
Transported on the Friend-
ship, master Michael Mankin,
from Liverpool 24 May 1716.
Sold to Edward Penn, Mary-
land 20 August 1716
(JAB)(SP/C)(HM)(CTB)

HENDERSON WILLIAM
Jacobite captured at Preston.
Transported from Liverpool to
St Kitts on the Hockenhill,
master H. Short, 25 June 1716
(SP/C)(CTB)

HENDERSON WILLIAM
Jacobite captured at Preston.
Transported from Liverpool to
South Carolina on the Wakefield,
master Thomas Beck, 21 April
1716
(SP/C)(CTB)

HENRY ALEXANDER
Prisoner in Edinburgh Tolbooth.
Transported from Leith to the
Plantations in America by Alex-
ander Fearne 17 December 1685
(ETR)

HENSHAW WILLIAM
Merchant in Glasgow. Covenanter.
Transported to the Plantations
in the Indies 13 June 1678
(PC)

HEPBURN JANET
Daughter of Alexander Hepburn,
workman in Dumfries. Spouse to
Alexander Walker, chaisedriver
in Dumfries. Fireraiser. Banished
to the Plantations for life 1767
(SM)

HERD JOHN
Jacobite captured at Preston.
Transported from Liverpool on the
Susannah, master Thomas Bromhall,
to South Carolina 7 May 1716
(SP/C)(CTB)

HERIOT ALEXANDER
Covenanter. Prisoner in Edinburgh
Tolbooth. Banished to Carolina 6
August 1684. Transported from Leith
by Robert Malloch, merchant in Edin
burgh
(PC)

HERRIES ROBERT
Surgeon. Dunbarton. Coven-
anter. Banished to the
Plantations in the Indies
7 November 1678
(PC)

HERRING JANET
Washerwoman. East Lothian.
Jacobite captured at Car-
lisle. Prisoner at Carlisle
and Lancaster. Transported
from Liverpool on the Johnson, master William Pemberton. Landed at Port Oxford
Maryland 5 August 1747
(P)(PRO)

HERRON PATRICK
Royalist soldier captured
at Worcester. Transported
on the John and Sarah, master John Greene, from
Gravesend to Boston 13 May
1652
(NER)

HERSHELL DAVID
40, shoemaker. Brechin.
Jacobite in Ogilvy's regiment. Prisoner at Inver-
ness, ship and Tilbury.
Transported from London to
Barbados or Jamaica by Sam
uel Smith 31 March 1747
(P)(RM)

HEYS JAMES
Jacobite captured at Pres-
ton. Transported from
Liverpool to St Kitts on
the Hockenhill, master H.
Short, 25 June 1716
(SP/C)(CTB)

HIGBEN ROBERT
Royalist soldier captured
at Worcester. Transported
from Gravesend to Boston
on the John and Sarah,
master John Greene, 13
May 1652
(NER)

HIGGINS GEORGE
Linlithgow. Covenanter. Prisoner
in Canongate Tolbooth. Banished
to the Plantations in America
27 May 1684. Transported from
Leith by Robert Malloch to
Carolina 29 May 1684
(PC)

HILL JAMES
Jacobite captured at Preston.
Transported from Liverpool on the
Friendship, master Michael Mankin,
to Maryland 24 May 1716. Sold to
Humphrey Godman, Maryland 20 Aug-
ust 1716
(SP/C)(HM)(CTB)

HILL JANET
Rioter in Glasgow. Banished to
Barbados. Transported from England
January 1726
(PRO)

HILL SAMUEL
Soldier, 22nd Regiment of Foot.
Robber. Banished to America for
life 10 March 1772
(JC)

HODGE ARCHIBALD
Pedlar. Prisoner in Edinburgh Tol-
booth. Warded 26 January 1721.
Transported to Virginia 9 February
1721 by John Chalmers, merchant in
Edinburgh
(ETR)

HODGE JOHN
Armourer in Glasgow. Covenanter.
Prisoner in Canongate, Dunnottar
and Leith. Banished to the Plant
ations 9 October 1684. Transported
from Leith on the Henry and Fran-
cis, master Richard Hutton, by
George Scott of Pitlochie to East
New Jersey 5 September 1685
(PC)

HODGEON ADAM
Douglas. Covenanter. Prisoner in Glasgow Tolbooth. Banished at Glasgow June 1684. Transported from the Clyde on the Pelican, by Walter Gibson, merchant in Glasgow to America June 1684
(PC)

HODGSON GEORGE
Jacobite captured at Preston. Transported on the Godspeed, master Arthur Smith, from Liverpool to Virginia 28 July 1716. Sold to John Nelly in Maryland 18 October 1716
(SP/C)(CTB)(HM)

HOGG ANDREW
Gypsy. Prisoner in Edinburgh Tolbooth. Transported from Greenock to New York 21 October 1682
(ETR)

HOGG DANIEL
Royalist soldier captured at Worcester. Transported on the John and Sarah, master John Greene, from Gravesend to Boston 13 May 1652
(NER)

HOGG JAMES
Butcher. Falkirk. Cattle thief. Banished to the Plantations for 7 years 1767
(SM)

HOGG JOHN
Royalist soldier captured at Worcester. Transported on the John and Sarah, master John Greene, from Gravesend to Boston 13 May 1652
(NER)

HOGG JOHN
Covenanter. Prisoner in Canongate Tolbooth. Banished to the Plantations 3 December 1685. Transported from Leith by Alexander Fearne to the Plantations in America December 1685
(PC)(ETR)

HOGG NEIL
Royalist soldier captured at Worcester. Transported on the John and Sarah, master John Greene, from Gravesend to Boston 13 May 1652
(NER)

HOLLAND THOMAS
Jacobite captured at Preston. Transported from Liverpool on the Elizabeth and Anne, master Edward Trafford, to Virginia or Jamaica 29 June 1716
(SP/C)(CTB)(VSP)

HOLM LADY
Covenanter. Prisoner in Kirkcudbright Tolbooth. Transported to the Plantations 13 October 1684
(PC)

HOLMES MARGARET
Prisoner in Edinburgh Tolbooth. Banished to the Plantations 31 July 1685. Stigmatised. Transported from Leith by John Ewing to Jamaica August 1685
(ETR)(PC)

HOME GEORGE
Royalist soldier captured at Worcester. Transported on the John and Sarah, master John Greene from Gravesend to Boston 13 May 1652
(NER)

HOME FRANCIS
Wedderburn, Duns, Berwickshire. Jacobite captured at Preston. Transported from Liverpool on the Elizabeth and Anne, master Edward Trafford 29 June 1716. Lamded in Virginia - indentured
(CTB)(SP/C)(VSP)

HOME GEORGE
30, writer, Edinburgh.
Son of George Home of
Whitefield, Duns, Ber-
wickshire. Jacobite.
Prisoner at Carlisle and
Lancaster. Transported
on the Veteran, master
John Ricky, from Liver-
pool for the Leeward
Islands 5 May 1747.
Liberated by a French
privateer and landed
on Martinique June 1747
(P)(RM)

HOME JEAN
Daughter of Thomas Home,
wright in Carrington.
Thief and fireraiser.
Banished for 3 years,
17 July 1769
(JC)

HOOD ADAM
Covenanter. Prisoner in
Burntisland, Dunnottar
and Leith. Transported
from Leith on the Henry
and Francis, master
Richard Hutton, by George
Scott of Pitlochie to
East New Jersey 5 Sept-
ember 1685
(PC)

HOOD ANDREW
20, apprentice to John
Christopher, Tain, Ross.
Jacobite in Cromarty's
regiment. Prisoner at
Inverness and Tilbury.
Transported 19 March 1747
(P)

HORNE WILLIAM
Prisoner in Edinburgh
Tolbooth. Transported
from Leith by Alexander
Fearne to the Plantations
17 December 1685
(ETR)

HORN WILLIAM
Angus. Jacobite in Ogilvy's
regiment. Prisoner at Perth,
Canongate and Carlisle.
Transported 1747(?)
(P)

HORNER BARBARA
Wife of Thomas Hunter. Dinduff.
Covenanter. Banished to the
Plantations, at Dumfries 24
October 1684. Taken to Edinburgh
(PC)

HOSIE WILLIAM
Banished for 10 years. Trans-
ported on the Brilliant, master
Robert Bennet, from Glasgow.
Landed at Port Hampton, Virginia
7 October 1772
(JC)

HOW DANIEL
Royalist soldier captured at
Worcester. Transported on the
John and Sarah, master John
Greene, from Gravesend to
Boston 13 May 1652
(NER)

HOWARD WILLIAM
Jacobite captured at Preston.
Transported from Liverpool on the
Scipio, master John Scaisbrick,
to Antigua 30 March 1716
(CTB)(SP/C)

HOWATSON JAMES
Craigbuie. Covenanter. Banished
to the Plantations, at Dumfries
24 October 1684
(PC)

HOWIE JOHN
Prisoner in Edinburgh Tolbooth.
Transported from Leith on Edward
Bird's ship to Barbados 22 Decem-
ber 1665
(ETR)

HOWIE JOHN
Covenanter in Argyll's
rebellion. Prisoner in
Edinburgh Tolbooth.
Banished to the Plant-
ations 29 July 1685.
Transported from Leith
to Jamaica by John Ewing
11 August 1685
(ETR)(PC)

HOWIE SAMUEL
Covenanter in Argyll's
rebellion. Prisoner in
Edinburgh Tolbooth.
Banished to the Plant-
ations 29 July 1685.
Transported from Leith
to Jamaica by John Ewing
11 August 1685
(ETR)(PC)

HOWNAM JAMES
Son of Andrew Hownam,
weaver in Langholm.
Rioter. Banished to the
Plantations for life, at
Dumfries May 1750
(SM)

HOWNAME WALTER
Covenanter in Argyll's
rebellion. Prisoner in
Canongate Tolbooth.
Banished to the Plant-
ations 30 July 1685.
Stigmatised 4 August
1685. Transported from
Leith to Jamaica by John
Ewing August 1685
(PC)

HUDSON DANIEL
Royalist soldier captured
at Worcester. Transported
on the John and Sarah,
master John Greene, from
Gravesend to Boston 13
May 1652
(NER)

HUDSON JOHN
Royalist soldier captured at
Worcester. Transported on the
John and Sarah, master John
Greene, from Gravesend to Boston
13 May 1652
(NER)

HUGHES JOHN
Jacobite. Prisoner at Carlisle
and Whitehaven. Transported 1747
(P)

HUME ALASTAIR
Royalist soldier captured at
Worcester. Transported on the
John and Sarah, master John
Greene, from Gravesend to Boston
13 May 1652
(NER)

HUME DAVID
Royalist soldier captured at
Worcester. Transported on the
John and Sarah, master John
Greene, from Gravesend to
Boston 13 May 1652
(NER)

HUME THOMAS
Jacobite captured at Preston.
Transported from Liverpool on the
Godspeed, master Arthur Smith,
for Virginia 28 July 1716.
Landed in Maryland and sold to
Judith Bruce 18 October 1716
(CTB)(SP/C)(HM)

HUNT EDWARD
Jacobite captured at Preston.
Transported from Liverpool on
the Scipio, master John Scais-
brick, to Antigua 30 March 1716
(CTB)(SP/C)

HUNTER JOHN
Covenanter. Prisoner in
Canongate and Leith. Banished to the Plantations
in America 10 December
1685. Transported from
Leith by Alexander Fearne
December 1685
(ETR)(PC)

HUNTER JOHN
Jacobite captured at
Preston. Transported from
Liverpool on the Elizabeth and Anne, master
Edward Trafford, 29 June
1716 for Virginia or
Jamaica
(CTB)(SP/CχVSP)

HUNTER PATRICK
Jacobite captured at
Preston. Transported from
Liverpool on the Friendship, master Michael Mankin, 24 May 1716. Sold to
James Calston, Maryland
20 August 1716
(SP/C)(HM)(CTB)

HUNTER THOMAS the elder
Husband of Barbara Horner.
Dinduff. Covenanter. Banished to the Plantations,
at Dumfries 24 October
1684. Taken to Edinburgh
(PC)

HUTCHESON JOHN
Husband of Marion Weir.
Feuar in Hairlaw. Covenanter. Prisoner in Leith
Tolbooth. Transported
from Leith on the Henry
and Francis, master Richard Hutton, by George
Scott of Pitlochie to
East New Jersey 5 September 1685
(PC)

HUTCHESON ROBERT
Banished to Jamaica. Transported from Leith by John Ewing
7 August 1685
(PC)

HUTSON JEAN
Gypsy and thief. Prisoner in
Dumfries Tolbooth. Banished to
the Plantations in America for
life, at Dumfries 1 May 1739
(JC)

INGLIS ALISON
Scone, Perth. Adulterer. Banished for life, at Perth 1753
(SM)

INGLIS PATRICK
Royalist soldier captured at
Worcester. Transported on the
John and Sarah, master John
Greene, from Gravesend to
Boston 13 May 1652
(NER)

INGLIS PETER
Servant to John Hay, accountant
in Edinburgh. Housebreaker. Banished to America for 7 years, 21
January 1772. Transported on the
Matty, master Robert Peacock,
from Port Glasgow. Landed at
Port Oxford, Maryland 16 May 1772
(JC)

INGLIS WILLIAM
Mason. Glasgow. Covenanter. Prisoner in Glasgow Tolbooth. Banished at Glasgow June 1684.
Transported from the Clyde on the
Pelican by Walter Gibson, merchant
in Glasgow, to America June 1684
(PC)

INNES JAMES
Jacobite captured at
Preston. Transported on
the Africa, master Rich-
ard Cropper, from Liver-
pool to Barbados 15 July
1716
(SP/C)(CTB)

INNES WILLIAM
26, fiddler. Servant to
Charles Gordon of Buckie,
Banff. Jacobite in Lord
Lewis Gordon's regiment.
Prisoner at Inverness
and Tilbury. Transported
from London to Barbados
or Jamaica by Samuel
Smith 31 March 1747
(P)(RM)

INNES WILLIAM
Wigmaker. Fochabers.
Jacobite in Lord Lewis
Gordon's regiment. Pris-
oner at Inverness, ship
and Tilbury. Transported
from London to Jamaica
or Barbados by Samuel
Smith 31 March 1747
(P)(RM)

IRELAND JAMES
Son of James Ireland,
writer and notary public,
in Edinburgh. Housebreaker
Prisoner in Edinburgh Tolbooth. Banished to the
Plantations in America for
life, at Edinburgh 11 August 1764
(JC)

IRELAND JOHN
Covenanter. Warded in
Edinburgh Tolbooth by
order of the Privy Coun-
cil 10 July 1685. Ban-
ished to the Plantations
Transported from Leith
to Jamaica by John Ewing
11 August 1685
(ETR)(PC)

IRONSIDE CHRISTIAN
Child murder. Banished at Aber-
deen September 1749
(SM)

IRVINE JAMES
34, shoemaker. Gribton, Nithsdale
Jacobite. Prisoner at Aberdeen,
Canongate and Carlisle. Trans-
ported from Liverpool on the
Johnson, master William Pemberton
Landed at Port Oxford, Maryland
5 August 1747
(P)(PRO)

IRWIN GEORGE
Jacobite. Prisoner at Carlisle
and Liverpool. Transported on the
Johnson, master William Pemberton
from Liverpool 5 May 1747. Landed
at Port Oxford, Maryland 5 August
1747
(PRO)

IVAR JOHN
Banished to the Plantations.
Transported from Leith by John
Ewing to Jamaica August 1685
(PC)

IVAR MALCOLM
Covenanter in Argyll's rebellion.
Prisoner in Paul's Work, Edinburgh
Banished to the Plantations 30
July 1685
(PC)

JACK ALEXANDER
Gardener. Prisoner in Dumfries
Tolbooth. Banished from Scotland
at Dumfries 1 May 1746
(JC)

JACK ANDREW
30. Caithness. Jacobite in Cromarty's regiment. Prisoner at Inverness and Tilbury. Transported
from London to Barbados or Jamaica
by Samuel Smith 20 March 1747
(P)(RM)

JACK DUNCAN or DONALD
58, beggar. Ross. Jacobite
in Cromarty's regiment.
Prisoner at Inverness and
Tilbury. Transported 20
March 1747
(P)

JACK WILLIAM
36. Merchant and messenger.
Elgin. Jacobite in Strath-
allan's Horse. Prisoner at
Tilbury. Transported to
Barbados by Samuel Smith
31 March 1747
(P)(RM)

JACK WILLIAM
Thief. Transported to
America, Edinburgh 1752
(SM)

JACKSON ANNE
Forger. Banished for life,
at Inverness September
1754
(SM)

JACKSON ANNABEL
Covenanter. Prisoner at
Dunnottar and Leith. Ban-
ished to the Plantations
at Leith 18 August 1685
Transported from Leith by
George Scott of Pitlochie
to East New Jersey on the
Henry and Francis, master
Richard Hutton 5 September
1685
(PC)

JACKSON JAMES
Royalist soldier captured
at Worcester. Transported
on the John and Sarah,
master John Greene, from
Gravesend to Boston 13 May
1652
(NER)

JACKSON JOHN
Servant to Humphrey Colquhoun,
Braestob, Glasgow. Covenanter.
Prisoner at Glasgow, Canongate
and Dunnottar. Banished to the
Plantations 30 July 1685. Trans-
ported from Leith by John Ewing
to Jamaica August 1685
(PC)

JACKSON PATRICK
Royalist soldier captured at
Worcester. Transported on the
John and Sarah, master John
Greene, from Gravesend to
Boston 13 May 1652
(NER)

JACKSON RICHARD
Royalist soldier captured at
Worcester. Transported on the
John and Sarah, master John
Greene, from Gravesend to Boston
13 May 1652
(NER)

JACKSON THOMAS
Covenanter. Prisoner in Thieves'
Hole,Edinburgh. Banished to the
Plantations 24 July 1685. Trans-
ported from Leith to East New
Jersey by George Scott of Pit-
lochie on the Henry and Francis,
master Richard Hutton, 5 Sept-
ember, 1685
(PC)

JACKSON WALTER
Royalist soldier captured at
Worcester. Transported on the
John and Sarah, master John
Greene, from Gravesend to
Boston 13 May 1652
(NER)

JACKSON WILLIAM
19, labourer. Angus.
Jacobite in Ogilvy's
regiment. Captured at
Carlisle. Prisoner at
Carlisle and Lincoln.
Transported from Liver-
pool on the Veteran,
master John Ricky, for
the Leeward Islands.
Liberated by a French
privateer and landed
on Martinique June 1747
(P)(OR)(RM)

JACKSON WILLIAM
Covenanter. Prisoner
in Edinburgh and Can-
ongate. Banished to
the Plantations 31
July 1685. Transport-
ed from Leith on the
Henry and Francis,
master Richard Hutton,
by George Scott of
Pitlochie to East New
Jersey 5 September
1685
(ETR)(PC)

JAMESON DAVID
Royalist soldier capt-
ured at Worcester.
Transported on the John
and Sarah,master John
Greene, from Gravesend
to Boston 13 May 1652
(NER)

JAMIE ROBERT
Montrose. Thief. Banished
to America or the British
West Indies for 14 years,
at Perth September 1775
(SM)

JAMIESON ALEXANDER
Servant. Mauchline. Cov-
enanter in Argyll's reb-
ellion. Prisoner in Edin-
burgh Tolbooth. Banished
to the Plantations 29
July 1685. Stigmatised
4 August 1685. Transport
ed from Leith to Jamaica
by John Ewing August 1685
(ETR)(PC)

JAMIESON ANNE
Thief. Prisoner in Ayr Tolbooth.
Banished to the Plantations in
America for 7 years, at Ayr
29 August 1748
(JC)

JAMIESON ARCHIBALD
Prisoner in Edinburgh Tolbooth.
Transported from Leith to East
New Jersey by Robert Barclay of
Urie 31 July 1685
(PC)

JAMIESON DAVID
"Sweet singer"(a cult) Covenanter
Prisoner in Edinburgh Tolbooth.
Banished to the Plantations 5 May
1684. Transported from Leith by
George Lockhart, merchant in New
York, James Glen, stationer burg-
ess of Edinburgh, and Thomas Gor-
don, merchant burgess of Edinburgh
to the Plantations in America 19
May 1684
(DNY)(PC)

JAMIESON DAVID
Covenanter. Linlithgow. Prisoner
in Canongate Tolbooth. Banished
to the Plantations in America 27
May 1684. Transported from Leith
to Carolina by Robert Malloch,
merchant in Edinburgh, 29 May 1684
(PC)

JAMIESON NEIL
Royalist soldier captured at
Worcester. Transported on the John
and Sarah, master John Greene,
from Gravesend to Boston 13 May
1652
(NER)

JAMIESON PATRICK
Royalist soldier captured at
Worcester. Transported on the John
and Sarah, master John Greene,
from Gravesend to Boston 13 May
1652
(NER)

JAPP JOHN
16, carpenter. Banff.
Jacobite in the Duke of
Perth's regiment. Capt-
ured at Carlisle. Pris-
oner at Carlisle and
Lincoln. Transported
from Liverpool on the
Veteran, master John
Ricky, 5 May 1747 for
the Leeward Islands.
Liberated by a French
privateer and landed
on Martinique June 1747
(P)(JAB)(RM)

JARDINE ANDREW
Covenanter in Argyll's
rebellion. Prisoner in
Edinburgh Tolbooth.
Banished to the Plant-
ations 28 July 1685.
Stigmatised 4 August
1685
(PC)

JERVY JOHN
Wright. Falkirk. Pris-
oner in Canongate Tol-
booth. Banished to the
Plantations in the
Indies 7 November 1678.
Transported from Leith
on the St Michael of
Scarborough, master
Edward Johnston,
December 1678
(PC)

JOHNSON NEIL
Royalist soldier captured
at Worcester. Transported
on the John and Sarah,
master John Greene, from
Gravesend to Boston
13 May 1652
(NER)

JOHNSON JOHN
30, husbandman. Lancashire,
England. Jacobite. Transported
on the Veteran, master John
Ricky, from Liverpool 5 May 1747
for the Leeward Islands. Liberated by a French privateer and
landed on Martinique June 1747
(P)(RM)

JOHNSON RICHARD
England. Jacobite. Transported
from Liverpool on the Gildart,
master Richard Holmes. Landed
at Port North Potomack, Maryland
5 August 1747
(P)(PRO)

JOHNSON WILLIAM
Jacobite soldier captured at
Preston. Transported from Liver-
pool on the Godspeed, master
Arthur Smith, for Virginia 28
July 1716. Sold to Charles Digges
in Maryland 18 October 1716
(SP/C)(CTB)(HM)

JOHNSTON CECILIA
Widow of William Anderson,
merchant in Wick. Child murder.
Banished to America, at Inverness
14 September 1759
(SM)

JOHNSTON DONALD
Covenanter in Argyll's rebellion.
Prisoner in the Correction House,
Edinburgh. Banished to the Plant-
ations 30 July 1685. Transported
from Leith to Jamaica by John
Ewing August 1685
(PC)

JOHNSTON GEORGE
Covenanter. Prisoner in Leith.
Transported by George Scott of
Pitlochie to East New Jersey on the
Henry and Francis, master Richard
Hutton 5 September 1685
(PC)

JOHNSTON HELEN
Thief. Prisoner in Edinburgh Tolbooth. Banished to the Plantations for life, at Edinburgh 7 February 1775
(JC)

JOHNSTON JAMES
Jacobite captured at Preston. Transported from Liverpool on the Elizabeth and Anne, master Edward Trafford, to Jamaica or Virginia. Landed in Virginia - unindentured
(SP/C)(CTB)

JOHNSTON JOHN
Jacobite captured at Preston. Transported from Liverpool on the Susannah, master Thomas Bromhall, to South Carolina 7 May 1716
(CTB)

JOHNSTON JOHN
18. Banff. Jacobite in Kilmarnock's Horse. Prisoner at Inverness and Tilbury. Transported
(P)

JOHNSTON JOHN
Jacobite captured at Preston. Transported on the Elizabeth and Anne, master Edward Trafford, from Liverpool 29 June 1716 for Virginia or Jamaica. Landed in Virginia - unindentured
(CTB)(SP/C)

JOHNSTON ROBERT
Jacobite captured at Preston. Transported on the Elizabeth and Anne, master Edward Trafford from Liverpool 29 June 1716 for Virginia or Jamaica. Landed in Virginia - unindentured
(CTB)(SP/C)

JOHNSTON ROBERT
46, labourer. Stonehaven. Jacobite in Bannerman's regiment Prisoner at Inverness and Tilbury. Transported from London to Jamaica or Barbados by Samuel Smith 31 March 1747
(P)(RM)

JONES PATRICK
Royalist soldier captured at Worcester. Transported on the John and Sarah, master John Greene, from Gravesend to Boston 13 May 1652
(NER)

JOINER DAVID
20, labourer. Aberdeen. Jacobite in Grant's regiment. Captured at Carlisle. Prisoner at Carlisle and York. Transported on the Veteran, master John Ricky, for the Leeward Islands 5 May 1747. Liberated by a French privateer and landed on Martinique June 1747
(P)(JAB)(RM)

JOSS MARGARET
Banffshire. Child murder. Transported, at Aberdeen 1751
(SM)

JUNKEIN JAMES
Kilmacolm. Prisoner in Edinburgh Tolbooth. For assaulting the minister of Kilmacolm. Banished to the Plantations 9 June 1670. Transported by Sir George Maxwell of Newark
(PC)

KEIN PATRICK
Prisoner in Edinburgh
Tolbooth. Transported
from Leith to the Plant-
ations November 1679
(ETR)

KEITH ALEXANDER
Prisoner in Edinburgh
tolbooth. Transported
from Greenock to New
York 21 October 1682
(ETR)

KEITH ANDREW
Tenant in Gerth, Caith-
ness. Housebreaker. Ban-
ished to America for life
25 July 1769
(JC)

KEITH GEORGE
35, shoemaker, Aberdeen.
Jacobite in Glengarry's
regiment. Captured at
Carlisle. Prisoner at
Carlisle and York. Trans
ported from Liverpool on
the Veteran, master John
Ricky, 5 May 1747 for
the Leeward Islands. Lib
erated by a French priv-
ateer and landed on
Martinique June 1747
(P)(JAB)(RM)

KEITH JAMES
20, servant. Glenbervie.
Jacobite. Prisoner at
Stirling and Chester.
Transported from Liver-
pool on the Gildart,
master Richard Holmes
5 May 1747. Landed at
Port North Potomack,
Maryland 5 August 1747
(P)(PRO)

KEITH WILLIAM
Banished for theft August
1774. Transported on the
......., master John
Rankine. Landed at Port
North Potomack, Maryland
17 October 1775
(JC)

KELL NEIL
Transported from Leith to
Jamaica by John Ewing
7 August 1685
(PC)

KELLIE JOHN
Dunbar. Covenanter. Prisoner
in Edinburgh, Dunnottar and
Leith. Banished to the Plantations 5 February 1685. Transported from Leith on the Henry
and Francis, master Richard
Hutton, to East New Jersey by
George Scott of Pitlochie
5 September 1685
(PC)

KELLIE KATHERINE
Covenanter. Prisoner in Leith.
Transported from Leith on the
Henry and Francis, master Rich-
ard Hutton, to East New Jersey
by George Scott of Pitlochie
5 September 1685
(PC)

KELLO JOHN
Prisoner in Edinburgh or Canon-
gate. Transported from Leith
to Carolina by Robert Malloch
August 1684
(PC)

KEMLO JOSEPH
Blacksmith. Hardgate, Old Machar,
Aberdeen. Jacobite in Stonywood's
regiment. Prisoner at Aberdeen,
canongate and Carlisle. Trans-
ported from Liverpool on the
Gildart, master Richard Holmes.
Landed at Port North Potomack,
Maryland 5 August 1747
(P)(JAB)(PRO)

KEMPIE JOHN
40, servant to Lord Oliphant.
Gask. Jacobite. Prisoner at Perth
Canongate and Carlisle. Trans-
ported 1747(?)
(P)

KENNEDY ALEXANDER
Jacobite captured at
Preston. Transported on
the Two Brothers, master
Edward Rathbone, from
Liverpool for Jamaica
26 April 1716. Landed
in Montserrat June 1716
(SP/C)(CTB)(CTP)

KENNEDY BESSIE
Cockethill. Covenanter.
Banished to the Plant-
ations 23 October 1684
(PC)

KENNEDY DANIEL
Jacobite captured at
Preston. Transported on
the Godspeed, master
Arthur Smith, from
Liverpool 28 July 1716
for Virginia. Sold to
John Courts, Maryland
18 October 1716
(SP/C)(CTB)(HM)

KENNEDY DUNCAN DOW
alias MCGILESPICK BAAN
Kilinan, Glengarry.
Cattle thief. Trans-
ported for 14 years,
at Inverness 26 May
1764
(SM)

KENNEDY JOHN
Covenanter. Banished
to the Plantations 28
July 1685. Stigmatised
4 August 1685. Trans-
ported from Leith to
Jamaica by John Ewing
August 1685
(PC)

KENNEDY JOHN
Jacobite captured at
Preston. Transported
from Liverpool on the
Scipio, master John
Scaisbrick, 30 March
1716 to Antigua
(CTB)(SP/C)

KENNEDY JOHN
Jacobite captured at Preston.
Transported from Liverpool on
the Two Brothers, master Edward
Rathbone, 26 April 1716 for
Jamaica. Landed in Montserrat
June 1716
(SP/C)(CTB)(CTP)

KENNEDY JOHN
Jacobite captured at Preston.
Transported from Liverpool on
the Scipio, master John Scais-
brick, to Antigua 30 March 1716
(SP/C)(CTB)

KENNEDY JOHN
Jacobite captured at Preston.
Transported from Liverpool on
the Elizabeth and Anne, master
Edward Trafford, for Jamaica or
Virginia 29 June 1716. Landed in
Virginia - indentured
(SP/C)(CTB)(VSP)

KENNEDY JOHN
32, labourer. Perthshire. Jacobite. Prisoner in Edinburgh,
Carlisle and York. Transported
from Liverpool on the Veteran,
master John Ricky, 5 May 1747
for the Leeward Islands. Liberated by a French privateer and
landed on Martinique June 1747
(P)(RM)

KENNEDY JOHN
54. Perthshire. Jacobite in
Keppoch's regiment. Prisoner at
Inverness and Tilbury. Transported
from London to Barbados or Jamaica
by Samuel Smith 31 March 1747
(P)

KENNEDY JOHN
20. Cowherd. Dougin, Inverness.
Jacobite in Glengarry's regiment
Prisoner at Inverness, ship and
Tilbury. Transported from London
to Jamaica or Barbados by Samuel
Smith 31 March 1747
(P)(RM)

KENNEDY MALCOLM
Jacobite captured at
Preston. Transported on
the Wakefield, master
Thomas Beck, from Liver-
pool 21 April 1716 for
South Carolina
(SP/C)(CTB)

KENNEDY MARY
20, washerwoman. Glen-
garry. Jacobite in Glen-
garry's regiment. Capt-
ured at Carlisle. Pris-
oner at Carlisle, York
and Chester. Transported
on the Veteran, master
John Ricky, from Liver-
pool to the Leeward
Islands 5 May 1747. Lib-
erated by a French priv-
ateer and landed on
Martinique June 1747
(P)(RM)

KENNOUGH ALEXANDER
Jacobite. Prisoner at
Carlisle. Transported
1747(?)
(P)

KENNY JOHN (MCKENNY)
Jacobite captured at
Preston. Transported on
the Godspeed, master
Arthur Smith, from Liv-
erpool for Virginia 28
July 1716. Sold to
Marmaduke Simms in
Maryland 18 October 1716
(SP/C)(CTB)

KERR ANNA
Widow of Mr John Duncan,
minister at Dundrennan.
Covenanter. Banished to
the Plantations 29 July
1668
(PC)

KERR DANIEL
Covenanter. Prisoner in Laigh
Parliament Hall, Edinburgh.
Transported from Leith by
William Arbuckle, merchant in
Glasgow, to New England 9 July
1685
(PC)

KERR DONALD
35, farmer. Achnagaird, Ross.
Jacobite in Cromarty's regiment.
Prisoner at Inverness and Tilbury
Transported 20 March 1747
(P)

KERR JOHN
Jacobite captured at Preston.
Transported from Liverpool on the
Scipio, master John Scaisbrick,
to Antigua 30 March 1716
(SP/C)(CTB)

KERR JOHN
Jacobite captured at Preston.
Transported from Liverpool on the
Elizabeth and Anne, master
Edward Trafford, for Virginia or
Jamaica 29 June 1716. Landed in
Virginia - unindentured
(CTB)(SP/C)(VSP)

KERR ROBERT
Jacobite captured at Preston.
Transported from Liverpool on the
Elizabeth and Anne, master
Edward Trafford, for Virginia or
Jamaica 29 June 1716. Landed in
Virginia - unindentured
(CTB)(SP/C)(VSP)

KERR WALTER
Covenanter. Prisoner in Canon-
gate Tolbooth. Transported from
Leith on the Henry and Francis,
master Richard Hutton, to East
New Jersey by John Johnston,
druggist 5 September 1685
(PC)

KIDD ALEXANDER
Jacobite captured at
Preston. Transported from
Liverpool on the Elizabeth
and Anne, master Edward
Trafford, for Virginia or
Jamaica 29 June 1716.
Landed in Virginia -
unindentured
(SP/C)(CTB)(VSP)

KIDD DAVID
Weaver. Logie. Prisoner
in Canongate Tolbooth.
Transported from Leith
on the St Michael of
Scarborough, master
Edward Johnston, to the
Plantations 12 December
1678
(PC)

KILGOUR PETER
Ardoe, Banchory. Horse-
thief. Banished to the
Plantations for life,
at Aberdeen 18 May 1770
(SM)

KINCAID JOHN
Chalcarrock. Covenanter.
Prisoner at Wigton, Dum-
fries, Edinburgh and
Leith. Transported from
Leith on the Henry and
Francis, master Richard
Hutton, to East New Jer-
sey by George Scott of
Pitlochie 5 September
1685
(PC)

KING JAMES
21, labourer. Darrow,
Aberdeen. Jacobite.
Prisoner at Perth, Stir-
ling, Canongate and Car-
lisle. Transported on the
Johnson, master William
Pemberton, from Liverpool
Landed at Port Oxford,
Maryland 5 August 1747
(P)(PRO)

KING JOHN
Covenanter. Prisoner at Glasgow
Dûnnottar and Leith. Banished
to the Plantations, at Leith
18 August 1685. Transported
from Leith on the Henry and
Francis, master Richard Hutton,
to East New Jersey by George
Scott of Pitlochie 5 September
1685
(PC)

KIRK JOHN
Prisoner in Edinburgh Tolbooth.
Transported from Leith to the
Plantations November 1679
(ETR)

KIRK ROBERT
Prisoner in Edinburgh Tolbooth.
Transported from Leith to the
Plantations November 1679
(ETR)

KIRKWALL ELIZABETH
Prisoner in Edinburgh Tolbooth.
Banished to the Plantations 28
July 1685. Stigmatised. Trans-
ported from Leith to Jamaica by
John Ewing 7 August 1685
(PC)

KIRKWOOD JAMES
Covenanter. Prisoner at Ayr,
Edinburgh and Leith. Banished
to the Plantations 5 February
1685. Transported from Leith
to East New Jersey on the Henry
and Francis, master Richard
Hutton, by George Scott of
Pitlochie 5 September 1685
(PC)

KNOWLES WILLIAM
30, salmon fisher. Nether Banchory. Jacobite. Prisoner at Canongate and Carlisle. Transported
from Liverpool on the Gildart,
master Richard Holmes. Landed at
Port North Potomack. Maryland
5 August 1747
(P)(PRO)

KNOWLIN THOMAS
Jacobite. Prisoner at
Inverness and Tilbury.
Transported 20 March 1747
(P)

KNOX JANET
Glasgow. Thief. Banished
to the Plantations, at
Glasgow 1758
(SM)

KNOX THOMAS
Transported on the Rain-
bow, master William Gordon,
from Greenock. Landed at
Port Hampton, Virginia
3 May 1775
(JC)

KYNAH ALEXANDER
16, labourer. Prisoner
at Carlisle. Transported
1747(?)
(P)

LACKY JAMES
16, weaver. Edinburgh.
Jacobite. Prisoner at
Carlisle and York.
Transported on the
Veteran, master John
Ricky, from Liverpool
for the Leeward Islands
5 May 1747. Liberated
by a French privateer
and landed on Martin-
ique June 1747
(P)(RM)

LAING JAMES
Wright. Criminal.
Transported on the
St John of Leith to the
Plantations by William
Binnie and William Dun-
bar, merchants in Edin-
burgh 1 May 1674
(PC)

LAING JAMES
Renfrew. Horse and sheep
thief. Banished at Glas-
gow 1754
(SM)

LAING JEAN
Spouse to Andrew Meiklehose,
weaver, Walnuik of Paisley.
Thief. Transported for 14 years,
at Glasgow 11 May 1764
(SM)

LAING THOMAS
Workman at Lord Hopetoun's lead
mines. From Aberdeen. Jacobite
in Roy Stuart's regiment. Prisoner at Edinburgh and Carlisle.
Transported from Liverpool on
the Gildart, master Richard
Holmes., 5 May 1747. Landed at
Port North Potomack, Maryland
5 August 1747
(P)(JAB)(PRO)

LAING WILLIAM
Hawick. Covenanter. Prisoner in
Edinburgh Tolbooth. Banished to
the Plantations in America 5 May
1684. Transported from Leith by
George Lockhart, merchant in New
York, James Glen, stationer
burgess of Edinburgh, and Thomas
Gordon, merchant burgess of Edin-
burgh 19 May 1684
(PC)

LAIRD KATHERINE
Thief and whore. Prisoner in
Edinburgh Tolbooth. Banished
to Virginia 4 May 1666. Trans-
ported from Leith on the
Phoenix of Leith, master James
Gibson
(ETR)

LAIRD JAMES
26, servant to the laird of
Muirie, Errol. Jacobite in
Ogilvy's regiment. Captured at
Culloden. Prisoner at Culloden,
Inverness and Tilbury, Trans-
ported from London to Jamaica
or Barbados by Samuel Smith
31 March 1747
(P)(RM)

LAMB JAMES
25, watchmaker. Edinburgh.
Jacobite artilleryman.
Captured at Carlisle. Prisoner at Carlisle, York and
Lincoln. Transported on the
Veteran, master John Ricky,
from Liverpool 5 May 1747
for the Leeward Islands.
Liberated by a French privateer and landed on Martinique June 1747
(P)(RM)

LAMOND ARCHIBALD
Kilbride. Covenanter in
Argyll's rebellion. Pris-
oner in the Laigh Parlia-
ment House, Edinburgh.
Banished to the Plantat-
ions 31 August 1685.
Transported from Leith to
Jamaica by John Ewing
August 1685
(LC)(PC)

LAMOND JOHN or JOSEPH
Groom to the Duke of Perth.
26. Aberdeen. Jacobite.
Prisoner at Perth, Canon-
gate and Carlisle. Trans-
ported from Liverpool on
the Gildart, master Rich-
ard Holmes, 5 May 1747.
Landed Port North Poto-
mack, Maryland 5 August
1747
(P)(JAB)(PRO)

LAMOND SORLEY
Drum. Covenanter in
Argyll's rebellion. Pris-
oner in Paul's Work, Edin
burgh. Banished to the
Plantations 30 July 1685
Transported from Leith to
Jamaica by John Ewing
August 1685
(LC)(PC)

LAMPO SAMUEL
Libel. Banished to America
4 November 1751
(AC)

LANG JOHN
Thief. Prisoner in Edinburgh
Tolbooth. Banished to the
Plantations in America for life,
at Edinburgh 17 July 1749
(JC)

LAUCHLISON MARIE
Burnhead. Covenanter. Banished
to the Plantations 23 October
1684
(PC)

LAUDER DAVID
Jacobite captured at Preston.
Transported from Liverpool on the
Godspeed, master Arthur Smith
to Virginia 28 July 1716.
Sold to Francis Goodrich in
Maryland 17 October 1716
(CTB)(SP/C)(HM)

LAUDER GEORGE
Jacobite captured at Preston.
Transported from Liverpool on the
Elizabeth and Anne, master
Edward Trafford, to Virginia or
Jamaica 29 June 1716. Landed in
Virginia - unindentured
(CTB)(SP/C)

LAUDER WILLIAM
Ballykinian. Thief. Banished to
the Plantations in America, at
Stirling 21 May 1729
(JC)

LAW DAVID
Covenanter. Prisoner in Edinburgh
Tolbooth. Banished to the Plant-
ations 24 July 1685
(PC)

LAW JAMES
Kirkliston. Covenanter. Prisoner
in Edinburgh Tolbooth. Transported
to the Plantations in the Indies
1 August 1678
(PC)

LAWRY THOMAS
Jacobite captured at Preston
Transported from Liverpool
on the Friendship, master
Michael Mankin, to Maryland
24 May 1716. Sold to Phil.
Lloyd Esq., Maryland
20 August 1716
(SP/C)(HM)(CTB)

LAWSON JAMES
22, workman. Wester Coull,
Lintrathen, Angus. Jacob-
ite in Ogilvy's regiment.
Transported from Liverpool
on the Veteran, master
John Ricky, 5 May 1747 to
the Leeward Islands. Lib-
erated by a French priv-
ateer and landed on
Martinique June 1747
(P)(OR)(RM)

LAWSON MARION
Prisoner in Edinburgh Tol-
booth. Transported from
Greenock to New York
21 October 1682
(ETR)(PC)

LAWSON MARION
Covenanter. Prisoner in
Edinburgh Tolbooth. Ban-
ished to the Plantations
28 July 1685. Transported
from Leith to Jamaica by
John Ewing August 1685
(PC)

LAWSON MARY
Monymusk, Aberdeenshire.
Child murder. Banished to
the Plantations for life,
at Aberdeen 16 May 1766
(SM)

LAWSON PETER
Weaver in Torryburn. Spir-
its thief. Banished at
Perth 14 October 1772,
Transported on the Phoenix,
master John Lamont, from
Port Glasgow. Landed at
Port Accomack, Virginia
20 December 1773
(SM)(JC)

LAWSON WILLIAM
Prisoner in Edinburgh Tolbooth
Banished to the Plantations.
Transported from Leith by
Alexander Fearne 17 December
1685
(ETR)

LAWSON WILLIAM
England. Jacobite. Transported
from Liverpool on the Gildart,
master Richard Holmes. Landed
at Port North Potomack, Maryland 5 August 1747
(P)(PRO)

LAWTON ALEXANDER
Jacobite captured at Preston.
Transported from Liverpool to
St Kitts on the Hockenhill,
master H. Short 25 June 1716
(SP/C)(CTB)

LECKIE CATHERINE
Child murder. Prisoner in Edinburgh Tolbooth. Banished to the
Plantations 30 July 1685. Transported from Leith to Jamaica
by John Ewing August 1685
(PC)

LECKIE WILLIAM
Merchant in Glasgow. Covenanter.
Prisoner in Edinburgh Tolbooth.
Banished to the Plantations in
the Indies 13 June 1678
(PC)

LEMON JOHN
Jacobite captured at Preston.
Transported from Liverpool to
South Carolina 7 May 1716 on
the Susannah, master Thomas
Bromhall
(SP/C)(CTB)

LESLIE ALEXANDER
Jacobite captured at Preston.
Transported from Liverpool to
South Carolina 7 May 1716 on
the Susannah, master Thomas
Bromhall
(SP/C)(CTB)

LESLIE MARGARET
Covenanter. Prisoner at
Dunnottar and Leith. Ban-
ished to the Plantations,
at Leith 18 August 1685.
Transported from Leith
to East New Jersey on the
Henry and Francis,master
Richard Hutton, by George
Scott of Pitlochie
5 September 1685
(PC)

LICKPRIVICK JAMES
Cathcart. Covenanter.
Prisoner in Edinburgh
Tolbooth. Banished to the
Plantations in the Indies
7 November 1678. Transport-
ed from Leith on the St
Michael of Scarborough
12 December 1678
(PC)

LILBOURNE JAMES
Prisoner in Edinburgh
Tolbooth. Transported
from Leith to the
Plantations November
1679
(ETR)

LINDSAY BENJAMIN
Banished for 10 years.
Transported on the
Brilliant, master Robert
Bennet, from Glasgow.
Landed at Port Hampton,
Virginia 7 October 1772
(JC)

LINDSAY ELIZABETH
Gypsy. Prisoner in Jed-
burgh Tolbooth. Banished
at Jedburgh 30 November
1714. Transported from
Glasgow on a Greenock
ship, master James Watson,
by merchants Robert Bun-
tine of Airdoch, James
Lees and Charles Crauford
to Virginia 1 January 1715
(GR)

LINDSAY JAMES
Jacobite captured at Preston.
Transported from Liverpool on
the Elizabeth and Anne, master

Edward Trafford, to Virginia
or Jamaica 29 June 1716. Landed
at Virginia - unindentured
(CTB)(SP/C)(VSP)

LINDSAY JOHN
Jacobite captured at Preston.
Transported from Liverpool to
Antigua on the Scipio, master
John Scaisbrick, 30 March 1716
(CTB)(SP/C)

LINTRON JANET
Covenanter. Prisoner in Leith.
Banished to the Plantations, at
Leith 18 August 1685. Transported
from Leith to East New Jersey on
the Henry and Francis, master
Richard Hutton, by George Scott
of Pitlochie 5 September 1685
(PC)

LIVINGSTONE ALEXANDER
Falkirk. Murderer. Prisoner in
Edinburgh Tolbooth. Banished to
the Plantations in America for
life, at Edinburgh 6 December
1749
(JC)

LIVINGSTONE WILLIAM
Prisoner in Edinburgh Tolbooth.
Parental assault. Banished to
the Plantations 26 August 1685.
Transported from Leith to East
New Jersey on the Henry and
Francis, master Richard Hutton,
by George Scott of Pitlochie
5 September 1685
(ETR)(PC)

LOCKHART GAVIN
Covenanter. Prisoner in
Edinburgh Tolbooth. Ban-
ished to the Plantations
25 August 1685. Transport-
ed from Leith to East New
Jersey on the Henry and
Francis, master Richard
Hutton, by George Scott
of Pitlochie 5 September
1685
(PC)

LOWE ABRAHAM
Jacobite captured at
Preston. Transported
from Liverpool on the
Friendship, master
Michael Mankin, to Mary-
land 24 May 1716. Sold
to Thomas Larkin, Mary-
land 20 August 1716
(SP/C)(HM)(CTB)

LOWE ALASTAIR
Royalist soldier captured
at Worcester. Transported
on the John and Sarah,
master John Greene, from
Gravesend to Boston 13
May 1652
(NER)

LOWE JAMES
Jacobite captured at
Preston. Transported on
the Friendship, master
Michael Mankin, from
Liverpool to Maryland
24 May 1716. Sold to
Benjamin Tasker, Mary-
land 20 August 1716
(SP/C)(HM)(CTB)

LOW RODERICK
Servant to Lord Cromarty
Tarbat House, Ross. Jac-
obite in the Duke of
Perth's regiment. Pris-
oner at Inverness and Til-
bury. Transported from
London to Barbados or
Jamaica 30 March 1747 by
Samuel Smith
(P)(RM)

LUCKY JOHN
Servant to Moir of Stonywood, 19.
Son of William Lucky, shoemaker,
Aberdeen. Jacobite in Stonywood's
regiment. Prisoner at Aberdeen,
Canongate and Carlisle. Trans-
ported from Liverpool on the
Gildart, master Richard Holmes,
5 May 1747. Landed at Port North
Potomack, Maryland 5 August 1747
(P)(JAB)(PRO)

LUGTON SIMON
Tailor. Edinburgh. Jacobite.
Prisoner at Edinburgh, Carlisle
and Liverpool. Transported
November 1748
(P)

LUMSDEN HENRY
Jacobite captured at Preston.
Transported from Liverpool on the
Friendship, master Michael
Mankin, to Maryland 24 May 1716.
Sold to Jacob Henderson, Maryland
20 August 1716
(SP/C)(HM)(CTB)

LUNDY CHARLES
Jacobite captured at Preston.
Transported from Liverpool on the
Scipio, master John Scaisbrick,
to Antigua 30 March 1716
(CTB)(SP/C)

LYON PHILIP
Jacobite captured at Preston.
Transported from Liverpool to
South Carolina on the Wakefield,
master Thomas Beck, 21 April
1716
(SP/C)(CTB)

LYON WALTER
Formerly in Barbados. Prisoner
in Edinburgh Tolbooth. Transported to the Plantations
23 September 1662
(ETR)

LYON WILLIAM
Jacobite captured at
Preston. Transported on
the Elizabeth and Anne,
master Edward Trafford,
from Liverpool for Jam
aica or Virginia 29
June 1716. Landed in
Virginia - unindentured
(CTB)(SP/C)(VSP)

MCADAM ARCHIBALD
Covenanter in Argyll's
rebellion. Prisoner in
Laigh Parliament House
Edinburgh. Transported
from Leith to New Eng-
land by William Arbuc-
kle, merchant in Glas-
gow, July 1685
(PC)

MCADAM GILBERT
Dalmellington. Coven-
anter. Prisoner in
Glasgow Tolbooth. Ban-
ished at Glasgow June
1684. Transported from
the Clyde on the Pelican,
by Walter Gibson, merch-
ant in Glasgow, to
America June 1684
(PC)

MACALASTAIR JOHN
Royalist soldier captured
at Worcester. Transported
on the John and Sarah,
master John Greene, from
Gravesend to Boston 23
May 1652
(NER)

MACANDREW WILLIAM
Royalist soldier captured
at Worcester. Transported
on the John and Sarah,
master John Greene, from
Gravesend to Boston 13
May 1652
(NER)

MCARRAN JANET or MCKINNON
16, spinner. Perth. Jacobite
captured at Carlisle. Prisoner
at Carlisle and Lancaster.
Transported 1747(?)
(P)

MCARTHUR DUNCAN
Son of Charles McArthur, work-
man in Inveraray. Banished to
America for life, at Inveraray
September 1772. Transported
from Port Glasgow on the
Phoenix, master John Lamont.
Shoplifter. Landed at Port
Accomack, Virginia 20 December
1772
(JC)

MCARTHUR GILBERT
Drover. Islay. Covenanter.
Prisoner at Paul's Work. Edin-
burgh. Banished to the Plant-
ations 24 July 1685. Transport-
ed from Leith to Jamaica by
John Ewing August 1685
(PC)

MCAULAY JAMES
Jacobite in Roy Stuart's
regiment. Prisoner at Carlisle
and York. Captured at Carlisle
Transported 1747(?)
(P)

MCAULAY MALCOLM
Covennater in Argyll's rebelliom
Prisoner in Laigh Parliament House
Edinburgh. Banished to the Plant-
ations 31 July 1685. Transported
from Leith to Jamaica by John
Ewing August 1685
(PC)

MACAULAY WILLIAM
Rioter. Banished at Glasgow.
May 1749
(SM)

MCBAIN DUNCAN or DONALD
30, husbandman by the
river Nairn, Inverness.
Jacobite in Cromarty's
or the McIntosh regiment.
Prisoner at Inverness,
ship and Medway. Trans-
ported 1747(?)
(P)

MCBAIN JAMES
48, parochial catechist.
Petty, Inverness. Jacob-
ite. Prisoner at Inver-
ness, ship and Tilbury.
Transported 20 March
1747
(P)

MCBAIN JOHN
48, servant to David
Michie near Dunkeld. Jac-
obite in the McIntosh
regiment. Prisoner at
Inverness and Tilbury.
Transported 1747(?)
(P)

MCBEAN ANGUS
Jacobite captured at
Preston. Transported from
Liverpool to Virginia on
the Anne, master Robert
Wallace 31 July 1716
(CTB)(SP/C)

MCBEAN DANIEL
Jacobite captured at
Preston. Transported from
Liverpool to Virginia on
the Anne, master Robert
Wallace 31 July 1716
(CTB)(SP/C)

MCBEAN ELIAS
Jacobite captured at
Preston. Transported from
Liverpool to South Carolina
on the Susannah, master
Thomas Bromhall 7 May 1716
(CTB)(SP/C)

MCBEAN FRANCIS
Jacobite captured at Preston.
Transported from Liverpool on the
Godspeed, master Arthur Smith
for Virginia 28 July 1716.
Sold to Charles Born, Maryland
17 October 1716
(SP/C)(CTB)(HM)

MCBEAN JOHN
Jacobite captured at Preston.
Transported from Liverpool on the
Friendship, master Michael Mankin
to Maryland 24 May 1716.
Sold to John Ford, Maryland
20 August 1716
(SP/C)(CTB)(HM)

MCBEAN JOHN
Jacobite captured at Preston.
Transported from Liverpool on the
Elizabeth and Anne, master Edward
Trafford for Virginia or Jamaica
29 June 1716
(CTB)(SP/C)

MCBEAN JOHN
Jacobite captured at Preston.
Transported from Liverpool on the
Anne, master Robert Wallace, for
Virginia 31 July 1716
(CTB)(SP/C)

MCBEAN LACHLAN
Jacobite captured at Preston.
Transported from Liverpool on the
Wakefield, master Thomas Beck, for
South Carolina 21 April 1716
(CTB)

MCBEAN WILLIAM
Jacobite captured at Preston.
Transported from Liverpool on the
Friendship, master Michael Mankin
for Maryland 24 May 1716.
Sold to Phil. Lloyd Esq., Mary-
land 20 August 1716
(SP/C)(HM)

MCBRIDE JOHN
Covenanter in Argyll's
rebellion. Prisoner in
Edinburgh Tolbooth.
Transported from Leith to
New England by William
Arbuckle, merchant in
Glasgow, 6 July 1685
(PC)

MCCALL WILLIAM
Covenanter. Prisoner in
Edinburgh Tolbooth. Ban-
ished to the Plantations
31 July 1685. Stigmatised
Transported from Leith to
Jamaica by John Ewing
August 1685
(PC)

MCCALLUM ARCHIBALD
Covenanter in Argyll's
rebellion. Prisoner in
Laigh Parliament House,
Edinburgh. Banished to
the Plantations 31 July
1685. Transported from
Leith to Jamaica by
John Ewing August 1685
(PC)

MCCALLUM DONALD
Jacobite captured at
Preston. Transported
from Liverpool to South
Carolina on the Susannah
master Thomas Bromhall
7 May 1716
(SP/C)(CTB)

MCCALLUM DUNCAN
Tenant of the laird of
Otter. Covenanter in
Argyll's rebellion. Pris-
oner in the Laigh Parlia-
ment House, Edinburgh.
Banished to the Plantat-
ions 30 July 1685. Trans
ported from Leith to New
England by William Arb-
uckle, merchant in Glas-
gow July 1685
(PC)

MCCALLUM DUNCAN
Jacobite captured at Preston.
Transported from Liverpool to
South Carolina on the Susannah,
master Thomas Bromhall, 7 May
1716
(CTB)(SP/C)

MCCALLUM GILBERT
Jacobite. Prisoner at Carlisle,
York and Lincoln. Transported
on the Johnson, master William
Pemberton, from Liverpool 22
April 1747. Landed at Port
Oxford, Maryland 5 August 1747
(P)(PRO)

MCCALLUM JOHN
Covenanter in Argyll's rebellion.
Prisoner in Edinburgh Tolbooth.
Banished to the Plantations 30
July 1685. Transported from Leith
to East New Jersey by Robert
Barclay of Urie August 1685
(PC)

MCCALLUM JOHN
Jacobite captured at Preston.
Transported from Liverpool to
Jamaica on the Two Brothers,
master Edward Rathbone, 26 April
1716. Landed in Montserrat June
1716
(SP/C)(CTB)(CTP)

MCCALLUM JOHN
Jacobite captured at Preston.
Transported from Liverpool to
South Carolina on the Susannah,
master Thomas Bromhall, 7 May
1716
(CTB)(SP/C)

MCCALLUM JOHN
Jacobite captured at Preston.
Transported from Liverpool for
Virginia on the Godspeed, master
Arthur Smith, 28 July 1716. Sold
to John Hawkins, Maryland, 17
October 1716
(SP/C)(CTB)(HM)

MCCALLUM MALCOLM
Jacobite captured at
Preston. Transported from
Liverpool for Virginia on
the Godspeed, master Arth-
ur Smith, 28 July 1716.
Sold to John Wilder, Mary-
land 17 October 1716
(SP/C)(CTB)(HM)

MCCALLUM NEIL
Covenanter in Argyll's
rebellion. Prisoner in the
Laigh Parliament House,
Edinburgh. Banished to the
Plantations 31 July 1685.
Transported from Leith to
Jamaica by John Ewing
August 1685
(PC)

MACCALINDEN ALISTAIR
Royalist soldier captured
at Worcester. Transported
on the John and Sarah,
master John Greene, from
Gravesend to Boston
13 May 1652
(NER)

MCCALMAN WILLIAM
Culbrattoun. Covenanter.
Prisoner in Leith Tolbooth
Bansished to the Plantat-
ions 17 October 1684.
Transported from Leith to
East New Jersey by George
Scott of Pitlochie on the
Henry and Francis, master
Richard Hutton, 5 Septem-
ber 1685
(PC)

MACCANN DANIEL
Royalist soldier captured
at Worcester. Transported
from Gravesend to Boston
on the John and Sarah,
master John Greene, 13
May 1652
(NER)

MCCANN EDWARD
Jacobite captured at Preston.
Transported from Liverpool to
Jamaica on the Two Brothers,
master Edward Rathbone, 26
April 1716. Landed in Mont-
serrat June 1716
(SP/C)(CTP)

MACCAULAY JAMES
Royalist soldier captured at
Worcester. Transported from
Gravesend to Boston on the
John and Sarah, master John
Greene, 13 May 1652
(NER)

MACCAULAY MALCOLM
Transported from Leith to
Jamaica by John Ewing August
1685
(PC)

MCCHARLARTIE JOHN
Covenanter in Argyll's rebellion
Prisoner in the Laigh Parlia-
ment House, Edinburgh. Banished
to the Plantations 31 July 1685
Transported from Leith to Jam-
aica by John Ewing August 1685
(PC)

MCCHISHOLM JOHN
Spittal. Covenanter. Prisoner in
Canongate Tolbooth. Banished to
Carolina 19 June 1684. Trans-
ported from Leith by Robert
Malloch, merchant in Edinburgh,
19 October 1684
(PC)

MCCLASER ALEXANDER
Jacobite captured at Preston.
Transported from Liverpool for
Jamaica on the Two Brothers,
master Edward Rathbone,
26 April 1716. Landed in Mont-
serrat 1716
(SP/C)(CTB)(CTP)

MCCLEIKERAYE JOHN
Prisoner in Edinburgh
Tolbooth. Transported
from Leith to the Plant-
ations 15 November 1679
(ETR)

MCCLELLAND ANDREW
Covenanter. Prisoner in
Leith Tolbooth. Banished
to the Plantations, at
Leith 18 August 1685.
Transported from Leith to
East New Jersey by George
Scott of Pitlochie on the
Henry and Francis, master
Richard Hutton, 5 Septem-
ber 1685
(PC)

MCCLELAND ROBERT
Covenanter. Prisoner at
Dunnottar and Leith.
Banished to the Plant-
ations, at Leith 18 Aug-
ust 1685. Transported
from Leith to East New
Jersey by George Scott of
Pitlochie on the Henry
and Francis, Richard Hut
ton 5 September 1685
(PC)

MCCLINTOCK JAMES
Merchant. Glasgow. Cov-
enanter. Prisoner in
Glasgow Tolbooth. Banish
ed at Glasgow June 1684.
Transported from the Clyde
on the Pelican by Walter
Gibson, merchant in Glas-
gow, to America June 1684
(PC)

MCCLOUTHEN HUGH
Jacobite. Prisoner at Inv-
erness, Chester and Tilbury.
Transported 1747(?)

MCCLURE ELISABETH
Barley. Covenanter. Prisoner
at Kirkcudbright, Dumfries and
Edinburgh. Banished to the
Plantations, at Kirkcudbright
13 October 1684
(PC)

MCCLURE MARY
Barley. Covenanter. Prisoner
at Kirkcudbright. Banished to
the Plantations, at Kirkcudbright 13 October 1684
(PC)

MCCLURG MARGARET
Spouse to Alexander Milligan,
Covenanter. Banished to the
Plantations 17 October 1684
(PC)

MACCOLM DAVID
Royalist soldier captured at
Worcester. Transported from
Gravesend to Boston on the
John and Sarah, master John
Greene, 13 May 1652
(NER)

MACCOLM JOHN
Royalist soldier captured at
Worcester. Transported from
Gravesend to Boston on the
John and Sarah, master John
Greene, 13 May 1652
(NER)

MCCOMB GILBERT
Perth. Jacobite in the Duke of
Perth's regiment. Captured at
Carlisle. Prisoner at Carlisle.
Transported 1747(?)
(P)

MACCONE NEIL
Royalist soldier captured at
Worcester. Transported from
Gravesend to Boston on the
John and Sarah, master John
Greene, 13 May 1652
(NER)

MCCONNELL ALEXANDER
Royalist soldier captured
at Worcester. Transported
from Gravesend to Boston
on the John and Sarah,
master John Greene,
13 May 1652
(NER)

MACCONNELL "CANA"
Royalist soldier captured
at Worcester. Transported
from Gravesend to Boston
on the John and Sarah,
master John Greene,
13 May 1652
(NER)

MACCONNELL DANIEL
Royalist soldier captured
at Worcester. Transported
from Gravesend to Boston
on the John and Sarah,
master John Greene,
13 May 1652
(NER)

MCCONNELL JAMES
Whitelargs of Stratoun.
Thief. Banished to the
Plantations in America
for life, at Ayr 1 May
1717
(JC)

MCCONNELL WILLIAM
Royalist soldier captured
at Worcester. Transported
from Gravesend to Boston
on the John and Sarah,
master John Greene,
13 May 1652
(NER)

MCCONOCHIE DUGAL
Servant to Craiginterve.
Covenanter in Argyll's
rebellion. Captured at
Dunbarton. Banished to
the Plantations 30 July
1685
(PC)

MCCONOCHIE JOHN
Covenanter in Argyll's rebellion
Prisoner in the Laigh Parliament
House, Edinburgh. Banished to
the Plantations 30 July 1685.
Transported from Leith to Jam-
aica by John Ewing August 1685
(PC)

MCCONOCHIE NEIL
Covenanter in Argyll's rebellion
Prisoner in the Laigh Parliament
House, Edinburgh. Banished to
the Plantations 30 July 1685.
Transported from Leith to Jam-
aica by John Ewing August 1685
(PC)

MCCOOK JOHN
Jacobite captured at Preston.
Transported from Liverpool to
Antigua on the Scipio, master
John Scaisbrick, 30 March 1716
(CTB)(SP/C)

MCCORKADALE ARCHIBALD
Transported from Leith to Jam-
aica by John Ewing August 1685
(PC)

MCCORMACK MARK
16, labourer. Moidart. Jacobite.
Prisoner at Carlisle and York.
Transported from Liverpool on the
Veteran, master John Ricky, for
the Leeward Islands. Liberated
by a French privateer and landed
on Martinique June 1747
(P)(RM)

MCCORMACK ROBERT
40, farmer. Clathill, Eigg.
Jacobite in Clanranald's regiment. Prisoner at Inverness,
ship and Tilbury. Transported
from London to Jamaica or Barbados by Samuel Smith
31 March 1747
(P)(RM)

MACCOURTUIE JAMES
Under 15. Servant to
Provost Kirkpatrick of
Kirkcudbright. Thief.
Banished to the Plant-
ations for 14 years, at
Dumfries 9 May 1770.
Transported on the Craw-
ford, master James McLean,
from Port Glasgow. Landed
at Port Oxford, Maryland,
23 July 1771
(SM)(JC)

MACOWIN CATHERINE
Jacobite. Prisoner at
Carlisle. Transported 1747
(P)

MCCOWAN WILLIAM
Jacobite. Prisoner at
Carlisle and Lancaster.
Transported on the Johnson
master William Pemberton,
from Liverpool. Landed at
Port Oxford, Maryland
5 August 1747
(P)(PRO)

MCCOY DANIEL
Jacobite captured at
Preston. Transported from
Liverpool on the Scipio,
master John Scaisbrick,
to Antigua 30 March 1716
(CTB)(SP/C)

MCCOY DANIEL
Jacobite. Prisoner at
York. Transported to
Antigua 8 May 1747
(P)

MCCOY DONALD
Jacobite captured at Pres
ton. Transported from
Liverpool to South Carol-
ina on the Susannah, mas-
ter Thomas Bromhall,
7 May 1716
(SP/C)(CTB)

MCCOY DONALD
Jacobite captured at Preston.
Transported from Liverpool to
South Carolina on the Wakefield
master Thomas Beck 21 April
1716
(CTB)

MCCOY DONALD
Jacobite. Prisoner at Carlisle.
Transported to Antigua 8 May
1747
(P)

MCCOY JOHN
Jacobite captured at Preston.
Transported from Liverpool to
St Kitts on the Hockenhill,
master H. Short 25 June 1716
(SP/C)(CTB)

MCCOY JOHN
Jacobite captured at Preston.
Transported from Liverpool to
South Carolina on the Wakefield
master Thomas Beck, 21 April
1716
(CTB)

MCCOY JOHN
Jacobite captured at Preston.
Transported from Liverpool on
the Two Brothers, master Edward
Rathbone, 26 April 1716. Landed
on Montserrat June 1716
(SP/C)(CTB)(CTP)

MCCOY PATRICK
Jacobite captured at Preston.
Transported from Liverpool on
the Godspeed, master Arthur
Smith, 28 July 1716, for
Virginia. Sold to John Courts
in Maryland 17 October 1716
(SP/C)(CTB)(HM)

MCCOY PAUL
Jacobite captured at
Preston. Transported
from Liverpool to Antigua
on the Scipio, master
John Scaisbrick, 30 March
1716
(CTB)(SP/C)

MCCOY PETER
Bellie, Banffshire. Jac-
obite in the Duke of
Perth's regiment. Pris-
oner at Carlisle and
Chester. Transported on
the Johnson, master
William Pemberton, from
Liverpool 5 May 1747.
Landed at Port Oxford,
Maryland 5 August 1747
(P)(PRO)(JAB)

MACCRAING PETER DOW
Brucklet, Glencoe. Ban-
ished to the Plantations
for 14 years, at Inver-
aray 4 September 1766.
Cattle thief
(SM)

MCCREATH JOHN
Servant to Thomas Gordon
of Aston. Murderer. Pris-
oner in Ayr Tolbooth.
Banished to the Plantat-
ions in America for life,
at Ayr 29 August 1748
(JC)

MCCUBBIN JAMES
Marwhirn. Covenanter.
Banished to the Plantat-
ions 24 October 1684
(PC)

MCCUEAN WALTER
Covenanter. Prisoner in
Leith Tolbooth. Banished
to the Plantations, at
Leith 18 August 1685
(PC)

MCCULLIE JOHN
Covenanter. Prisoner in Edinburgh Tolbooth. Banished to
the Plantations 24 July 1685
(PC)

MCCULLON JOHN
Jacobite captured at Preston.
Transported from Liverpool on
the Elizabeth and Anne, master
Edward Trafford, to Jamaica or
Virginia 29 June 1716
(CTB)(SP/C)

MCCULLOCH MARGARET
Daughter of Godfrey McCulloch.
Carngren, Kirkmarden, Wigton.
Child murder. Banished to the
Plantations in America, at Ayr
1 May 1729
(JC)

MCCULLOCH ROBERT
Jacobite captured at Preston.
Transported from Liverpool on
the Two Brothers, master Edward
Rathbone, for Jamaica 26 April
1716. Landed in Montserrat June
1716
(SP/C)(CTB)(CTP)

MCCUMMING JOHN
Covenanter. Banished to the
Plantations 24 July 1685
(PC)

MCCUREITH ARCHIBALD
Transported from Leith to Jam-
aica by John Ewing August 1685
(PC)

MCCURRIE DONALD
Covenanter in Argyll's rebellion
Prisoner in the Laigh Parliament
House, Edinburgh. Banished to
the Plantations 31 July 1685.
Transported from Leith to Jam-
aica August 1685
(PC)

MCDANELL DANIEL
Jacobite captured at Pres-
ton. Transported from
Liverpool to Antigua on
the Scipio, master John
Scaisbrick, 30 March 1716
(SP/C)

MCDANIEL DANIEL
Perth. Jacobite in Lord
George Murray's regiment.
Captured at Carlisle.
Prisoner at Carlisle and
Liverpool. Transported
from Liverpool on the
Johnson, master William
Pemberton, 5 May 1716.
Lande at Port Oxford,
Maryland 5 August 1747
(P)(PRO)

MCDANIEL JOHN
Jacobite. Transported on
the Johnson, master William
Pemberton, from Liverpool
5 May 1716. Landed at Port
Oxford, Maryland 5 August
1747
(PRO)

MCDANIEL MARY
Jacobite. Transported on
the Johnson, master William
Pemberton, from Liverpool
5 May 1716. Landed at Port
Oxford, Maryland 5 August
1747
(PRO)

MCDARRAN ARCHIBALD
Jacobite. Captured at
Preston. Transported from
Liverpool on the Friendship
master Michael Mankin, to
Maryland 24 May 1716. Sold
to W.Fitzredmond, Maryland,
20 August 1716
(SP/C)(HM)

MCDERMOTT ANGUS
Jacobite captured at Preston.
Transported from Liverpool on
the Two Brothers, master Edward
Rathbone, for Jamaica 26 April
1716. Landed on Montserrat
June 1716
(SP/C)(CTB)(CTP)

MCDERMOTT ANGUS
Jacobite captured at Preston.
Transported from Liverpool on
the Two Brothers, master Edward
Rathbone, for Jamaica 26 April
1716. Landed on Montserrat
June 1716
(SP/C)(CTB)(CTP)

MCDERMOTT ANGUS
Jacobite. Captured at Preston.
Transported from Liverpool on
the Godspeed, master Arthur
Smith, for Virginia 28 July 1716
Sold to John Courts in Maryland
17 October 1716
(SP/C)(CTB)(HM)

MCDERMOTT JOHN
Jacobite captured at Preston.
Transported from Liverpool on
the Scipio,master John Scaisbrick
to Antigua 30 March 1716
(SP/C)

MCDERMOT JOHN alias GAFT
Lochaber. Thief. Banished to
America, at Inverness 1755
(SM)

MCDIARMID JOHN
Son of Patrick McDiarmid, chair-
master in Edinburgh. Housebreaker
Prisoner in Edinburgh Tolbooth.
Banished to the Plantations in
America for 5 years, at Edinburgh
11 August 1764
(JC)

MCDICHMAYE WALTER
Prisoner in Edinburgh
Tolbooth. Transported to
the Plantations from Leith
November 1679
(ETR)

MACDONALD AGNES
Daughter of Agnes MacDonald
Thief. Banished to the
Plantations for life, at
Glasgow 9 May 1775
(SM)

MCDONALD ALEXANDER
30. Cattleherd to Grant
of Corrimony, Inverness
Jacobite in Glengarry's
regiment. Prisoner at
Duddingston, Edinburgh,
Canongate and Carlisle.
Transported, 1747(?)
(P)

MCDONALD ALEXANDER
Jacobite. Transported
from Liverpool on the
Gildart, master Richard
Holmes, 5 May 1747.
Landed at Port North
Potomack, Maryland
5 August 1747
(PRO)

MCDONALD ALEXANDER
60. Farmer. Glenmoriston.
Jacobite in Glengarry's
regiment. Prisoner at
Inverness, ship and Til-
bury. Transported 1747(?)
(P)

MCDONALD ALEXANDER
24. Merchant. Mickle -
Strath, Ross. Jacobite
in Cromarty's regiment.
Prisoner at Inverness,
ships and Medway.
Transported, 1747(?)
(P)

MCDONALD ALEXANDER
38. Farmer. Glenmoriston.
Jacobite in Glengarry's
regiment. Prisoner at Inverness
ship and Tilbury. Transported
from London to Barbados or Jamaica by Samuel Smith 31 March
1747
(P)(RM)

MCDONALD ALEXANDER
30. Farmer. Glenmoriston.
Jacobite in Glengarry's regiment
Prisoner at Inverness, ship and
Tilbury. Transported from London
to Barbados or Jamaica by Samuel
Smith 31 March 1747
(P)(RM)

MCDONALD ALEXANDER
30. Farmer in Glenmoriston. From
Glen Urquhart. Jacobite in Glengarry's regiment. Prisoner at
Inverness, ship and Tilbury.
Transported from London to Jamaica or Barbados by Samuel Smith
31 March 1747
(P)(RM)

MCDONALD ALEXANDER
46. Glen Urquhart. Jacobite in
Glengarry's regiment. Prisoner
at Inverness, ship and Tilbury.
Transported from London to Jamaica or Barbados by Samuel Smith
31 March 1747
(P)(RM)

MCDONALD ALEXANDER
Reay, Caithness. Shipwreck looter
Banished for life 1772. Trans-
ported on the Donald, master
Thomas Ramsay. Landed at Port
James, Upper District, Virginia
13 March 1773
(SM)(JC)

MCDONALD ALLAN
36. Army deserter. Inverness. Jacobite in Cromartys regiment. Prisoner at Inverness, ships and Tilbury Transported from London to Jamaica or Barbados by Samuel Smith 31 March 1747
(P)(RM)

MCDONALD ALLAN or ANGUS
Rioter at Mylnefield. Banished to the Plantations, at Perth 1773
(SM)

MCDONALD ANGUS
20. Farmer. Cromiel, South Uist. Jacobite in Raasay's regiment. Prisoner on ship and at Tilbury. Transported 1747(?)
(P)

MCDONALD ANGUS
Tailor. Kirkton of Raasay. Jacobite in Raasay's regiiment. Prisoner on ship and at Tilbury. Transported 1747(?)
(P)

MCDONALD ANGUS
50. Jacobite in Clanranald's regiment. Prisoner at Inverness, ship and Tilbury. Transported 20 March 1747
(P)

MCDONALD ANGUS
Farmer. Guilen, Eigg. Jacobite in Clanranald's regiment. Prisoner on ship and at Tilbury. Transported 20 March 1747
(P)

MCDONALD ANGUS
50. Rannoch. Jacobite in Keppoch's regiment. Prisoner at Torwood, Stirling, Leith, Edinburgh, Carlisle and York. Transported 1747
(P)

MCDONALD ANGUS
40. Jacobite in Glengarry's regiment. Prisoner at Prestonpans, Edinburgh, Canongate and Carlisle. Transported 1747(?)
(P)

MCDONALD ANGUS
Labourer. Inverness. Jacobite in Glengarry's regiment. Prisoner at Dalkeith, Edinburgh Carlisle and York. Transported to Antigua 8 May 1747
(P)

MCDONALD ANGUS
Jacobite. Transported from Liverpool on the Gildart, master Richard Holmes, 5 May 1747. Landed at Port North Potomac, Maryland 5 August 1747
(PRO)

MCDONALD ANGUS
Transported on the Matty, master Robert Peacock, from Port Glasgow. Landed at Port Oxford, Maryland 17 December 1771
(JC)

MACDONALD ANGUS ROY
Strathmassey, Badenoch. Cattle thief. Banished to the Plantations for life 1773
(SM)

MCDONALD ANN
Widow of James McIntosh, day labourer, Castle Grant, Forres. Thief. Banished to the Plantations for life, at Inverness 9 May 1770. Transported from Glasgow on the Brilliant, master Robert Bennet. Landed at Port Hampton, Virginia 7 October 1772
(SM)(JC)

MACDONALD ANNE
Nairn. Thief. Banished to the Plantations for life, at Inverness 20 May 1775
(SM)

MCDONALD ARCHIBALD
45. Labourer. Inverness.
Jacobite in Keppoch's
regiment. Prisoner at
Duddingston, Edinburgh
and Carlisle. Transported
1747(?)
(P)

MCDONALD ARCHIBALD
25. Farmer's servant.
Kilcreich, Inverness.
Jacobite in McLachlan's
regiment. Prisoner at
Inverness and Tilbury.
Transported 20 March 1747
(P)

MCDONALD ARCHIBALD
42. Farmer. Glenmoriston.
Jacobite in Glengarry's
regiment. Prisoner at
Inverness, ship and Til-
bury. Transported from
Liverpool on the Johnson
master William Pemberton
5 May 1747. Died aboard
ship 4 June 1747
(P)(PRO)

MCDONALD DANIEL
19. Labourer. Lettoch-
beag, Kinloch, Inverness
Jacobite in Atholl Brig-
ade. Captured at Carlisle
Prisoner at Carlisle and
Chester. Transported on
the Veteran, master John
Ricky, for the Leeward
Islands 5 May 1747. Lib-
erated by a French priv-
ateer and landed on
Martinique June 1747
(P)(RM)

MCDONALD DENIS
Jacobite captured at
Preston. Transported
from Liverpool for Jam-
aicaon the Two Brothers
master Edward Rathbone
26 April 1716. Landed
on Montserrat June 1716
(CTB)(CTP)(SP/C)

MCDONALD DONALD
Buchlyvie. Prisoner in Canongate
Tolbooth. Transported from Leith
on the St Michael of Scarborough
master Edward Johnston, to the
Plantations 12 December 1678
(PC)

MCDONALD DONALD
Jacobite captured at Preston.
Transported from Liverpool to
Antigua on the Scipio, master
John Scaisbrick, 30 March 1716
(CTB)

MCDONALD DONALD
22. Inverness. Jacobite in Lovats
regiment. Prisoner at Inverness,
ship and Tilbury. Transported
from London to Jamaica or Barbados by Samuel Smith 31 March
1747
(P)(RM)

MCDONALD DONALD
56. Labourer. Camogren, Rannoch.
Jacobite. Prisoner at Stirling,
Edinburgh, Carlisle and Lincoln.
Transported from Liverpool on
the Gildart, master Richard
Holmes, 5 May 1747. Landed at
Port North Potomac, Maryland,
5 August 1747
(P)(PRO)(RM)

MCDONALD DONALD
25. Glen Urquhart. Jacobite in
Glengarry's regiment. Prisoner
at Inverness, ship and Tilbury.
Transported 20 March 1747
(P)

MCDONALD DONALD
50. Farmer. Glen Urquhart. Jac-
obite in Glengarry's regiment.
Prisoner at Inverness, ship and
Tilbury. Transported from London
to Jamaica or Barbados by Samuel
Smith 31 March 1747
(P)(RM)

MCDONALD DONALD
56. Farmer. Clatil, Eigg.
From Uist. Jacobite serg-
eant in Clanranald's regiment. Prisoner on ship
and at Tilbury. Transported from London to Jamaica
or Barbados by Samuel
Smith 31 March 1747
(P)(RM)

MCDONALD DONALD
Farmer. Fivepenny, Eigg.
From Morven, Argyll.
Jacobite in Clanranald's
regiment. Prisoner on
ship and at Tilbury.
Transported 19 March 1747
(P)

MCDONALD DONALD
58. Servant. Edinburgh.
Jacobite. Transported on
the Veteran, master John
Ricky, from Liverpool for
the Leeward Islands 5 May
1747. Liberated by a
French privateer and landed on Martinique June 1747
(P)(RM)

MCDONALD DONALD
22. Labourer. Inverness.
Jacobite in Glengarry's
regiment. Prisoner at
Carlisle, Lancaster and
York. Transported from
Liverpool on the Veteran,
master John Ricky, 5 May
1747 for the Leeward
Islands. Liberated by a
French privateer and
landed on Martinique
June 1747
(P)(RM)

MCDONALD DUNCAN
21. Servant to Fraser of
Culduthal's brother. In-
verness. Jacobite in
Lovat's regiment. Prison-
er at Inverness, ships
and Medway. Transported
31 March 1747 to Jamaica
or Barbados from London
(P)(RM)

MCDONALD DUI'CAN
45. Farmer. Glenmoriston. Jacobite in Glengarry's regiment.
Prisoner at Inverness, ship and
Tilbury. Transported from London
to Jamaica or Barbados 31 March
1747 by Samuel Smith
(P)(RM)

MCDONALD EWAN
35. Jacobite in Glengarry's
regiment. Prisoner at Inverness
and Tilbury. Transported 1747(?)
(P)

MCDONALD or BADENOCH GEORGE
Moulin, Perthshire. Cattle thief.
Banished to America for life
17 February 1772
(JC)

MCDONALD HUGH
30. Glenmoriston. Jacobite in
Glengarry's regiment. Prisoner
at Inverness and on ship.
Transported 1747(?)
(P)

MCDONALD HUGH
13. Arisaig. Jacobite. Transported from Liverpool on the
Veteran, master John Ricky,
for the Leeward Islands 5 May
1747. Liberated by a French
privateer and landed on
Martinique June 1747
(P)(RM)

MCDONALD JAMES
Jacobite captured at Preston.
Transported from Liverpool to
South Carolina on the Susannah,
master Thomas Bromhall, 7 May
1716
(SP/C)(CTB)

MCDONALD JAMES
20. Banff. Jacobite in Glenbucket's regiment. Prisoner at
Inverness. Transported 20 March
1747
(P)

MCDONALD JAMES
49. Farmer. Glenmoriston.
From Glen Urquhart. Jac-
obite in Glengarry's regiment. Prisoner at Inver-
ness, ship and Tilbury.
Transported 20 March 1747
(P)

MCDONALD JAMES
47. Farmer. Guilen, Eigg.
Jacobite in Clanranald's
regiment. Prisoner at
Tilbury. Transported to
Jamaica or Barbados from
London by Samuel Smith
31 March 1747
(P)(RM)

MCDONALD JOHN
Jacobite captured at
Preston. Transported to
South Carolina from
Liverpool on the Susannah
master Thomas Bromhall
7 May 1716
(CTB)(SP/C)

MCDONALD JOHN
Jacobite captured at
Preston. Transported to
South Carolina from
Liverpool on the Wake-
field, master Thomas
Beck, 21 April 1716
(CTB)

MCDONALD JOHN
Jacobite captured at
Preston. Transported on
the Friendship, master
Michael Mankin, from
Liverpool to Maryland
24 May 1716. Sold to
Robert Grundy, Maryland
20 August 1716
(SP/C)(HM)

MCDONALD JOHN
Jacobite captured at
Preston. Transported on
the Friendship, master
Michael Mankin, from
Liverpool to Maryland
24 May 1716
(SP/C)

MCDONALD JOHN
56. Redorach, Elgin. Jacobite
in Glengarry's regiment.
Prisoner at Inverness and Tilbury. Transported 20 March 1747
(P)

MCDONALD JOHN
40. Cowherd. Dongon, Glengarry.
Jacobite in Glengarry's regiment
Prisoner at Inverness and Tilbury
Transported 20 March 1747
(P)

MCDONALD JOHN
20 Cattleherd. Doune. From Glengarry. Jacobite in Glengarry's
regiment. Prisoner at Inverness
and Tilbury. Transported 20
March 1747
(P)

MCDONALD JOHN
30. Farmer. Glen Urquhart.
Jacobite in Glengarry's regiment
Prisoner at Inverness and Til-
bury. Transported 20 March 1747
(P)

MCDONALD JOHN
40. Labourer. Inverness. Jacobite
in Glengarry's regiment. Prisoner
at Inverness, ships and Medway.
Transported from London to Jamaica or Barbados by Samuel Smith
31 March 1747
(P)(RM)

MCDONALD JOHN
20. Tailor. Inverness. Jacobite
in Glengarry's regiment. Prisoner at Inverness and Tilbury.
Transported from London to Jamaica or Barbados by Samuel Smith
31 March 1747
(P)(RM)

MCDONALD JOHN
56. Tailor. Skye. Jacobite in
Glengarry's regiment. Prisoner
at Inverness, ship and Tilbury
Transported from London to Jamaica or Barbados by Samuel Smith
31 March 1747
(P)(RM)

MCDONALD JOHN
60. Farmer. Glenmoriston.
Jacobite in Glengarry's
regiment. Prisoner at
Inverness, ship and Til-
bury. Transported from
London to Jamaica or
Barbados by Samuel Smith
31 March 1747
(P)(RM)

MCDONALD JOHN
24. Stradoun, Banff.
Jacobite in Glenbucket's
regiment. Prisoner at
Inverness, ship and Til-
bury. Transported from
London to Barbados or
Jamaica by Samuel Smith
31 March 1747
(P)(RM)

MCDONALD or MCDONOUGH JOHN
14. Husbandman. Barra.
From Argyll. Jacobite.
Prisoner at Inverness,
ship and Medway. Trans-
ported 20 March 1747
(P)

MCDONALD JOHN
Jacobite in Keppoch's
regiment. Prisoner at
Linlithgow, Leith,
Edinburgh and Carlisle.
Transported 19 March 1747
(P)

MCDONALD JOHN
Labourer. Badenoch. Jac-
obite in Keppoch's regi-
ment. Prisoner at
Duddingston, Edinburgh
and Carlisle. Transported
19 March 1747
(P)

MCDONALD JOHN
40. Labourer. Perth. Jac-
obite in Lord George Murrays
regiment. Prisoner at York
and Carlisle. Transported
(P)

MCDONALD JOHN
36. Farmer. Glenistill, Eigg.
Jacobite in Clanranald's regi-
ment. Prisoner at Tilbury.
Transported 20 March 1747
(P)

MCDONALD JOHN
58. Farmer. Fivepenny, Eigg.
Jacobite in Clanranald's regi-
ment. Prisoner at Tilbury.
Transported 30 March 1747 to
Barbados or Jamaica from
London by Samuel Smith
(P)(RM)

MCDONALD JOHN
36. Farmer. Howlin, Eigg.
Jacobite in Clanranald's regi-
ment. Prisoner at Tilbury.
Transported 20 March 1747
(P)

MCDONALD JOHN
40. Farmer. Galmistal, Eigg.
From Morar, Inverness. Jacobite in Clanranald's regiment
Prisoner at Tilbury. Transported 20 March 1747
(P)

MCDONALD JOHN
Jacobite. Transported from
Liverpool on the Gildart, master
Richard Holmes, 5 May 1747.
Landed at Port North Potomac,
Maryland 5 August 1747
(PRO)

MCDONALD JOSEPH
27. Weaver or servant. Moray.
Jacobite. Prisoner at Lancaster.
Transported from Liverpool on
the Veteran, master John Ricky,
for the Leeward Islands 5 May
1747. Liberated by a French
privateer and landed on Martinique June 1747
(P)(RM)

MACDONALD KENNETH
alias MACEANOR
Ross-shire. Thief.
Banished, at Inverness
September 1754
(SM)

MCDONALD MARGARET
21. Inverness. Jacobite.
Prisoner at Inverness, ship
and Medway. Transported
1747(?)
(P)

MCDONALD MARGARET
23. Spinner. Perthshire.
Jacobite. Prisoner at Lan-
caster. Transported from
Liverpool on the Veteran,
master John Ricky, for the
Leeward Islands 5 May 1747
Liberated by a French
privateer and landed on
Martinique June 1747
(P)(RM)

MCDONALD MARY
35. Inverness. Jacobite.
Prisoner at Lancaster.
Transported 1747(?)
(P)

MCDONALD OWEN
Jacobite in Glengarry's
regiment. Prisoner at Til-
bury. Transported from
London to Barbados or Jam-
aica by Samuel Smith 20
March 1747
(P)(RM)

MCDONALD OWEN
40. Farmer. Glen Urquhart.
Jacobite in Glengarry's
regiment. Prisoner at
Inverness and Tilbury.
Transported from London
to Jamaica or Barbados by
Samuel Smith 31 March 1747
(P)(RM)

MACDONALD RANALD
Jacobite in Clanranald's regiment
Prisoner at Fort William. Fort
Augustus and Inverness. Trans-
ported 1747(?)
(P)

MCDONALD RANALD
Farmer. Grinlin, Eigg. From
Morven, Argyll. Jacobite in
Clanranald's regiment. Prisoner
at Tilbury. Transported from
London to Jamaica or Barbados
31 March 1747
(P)(RM)

MCDONALD RODERICK
Farmer. Kirkton, Eigg. Jacobite
in Clanranald's regiment. Pris-
oner at Inverness, ship and Til-
bury. Transported from London to
Jamaica or Barbados by Samuel
Smith 31 March 1747
(P)(RM)

MCDONALD RODERICK
22. Husbandman. Sandvegg, Eigg.
From Morven, Argyll. Jacobite in
Clanranald's regiment. Prisoner
at Tilbury. Transported from
London to Jamaica or Barbados by
Samuel Smith 31 March 1747
(P)(RM)

MCDONALD RONALD
Edinburgh City Guardsman. Jacobite
Prisoner at Edinburgh and Carlisle
Transported from Liverpool on the
Gildart, master Richard Holmes,
5 May 1747. Landed at Port North
Potomac, Maryland 5 August 1747
(P)(PRO)

MACDONALD RONALD
Son of Archibald MacDonald of
Barrisdale. Enlisted in French
service. Banished to the Plantations for 7 years, at Edinburgh
13 August 1754. Taken from Edinburgh to Leith for transportation
17 June 1755
(SM)

MCDONALD RORY
Jacobite captured at Preston
Transported from Liverpool
to South Carolina on the
Susannah, master Thomas
Bromhall, 7 May 1716
(SP/C)(CTB)

MACDONALD RORY DOW
Loddie of Slisgarne, Glen-
garry. Thief. Banished at
Inverness 1753
(SM)

MCDONALD SWEEN
18. Beggar. Inverness.
Jacobite in Lovat's regi-
ment. Prisoner at Inver-
ness and Tilbury. Trans-
ported from London to
Jamaica or Barbados 31
March 1747
(P)(RM)

MCDONALD WILLIAM
Jacobite captured at Preston
Transported from Liverpool
on the Two Brothers, master
Edward Rathbone, for Jamaica
26 April 1716. Landed on
Montserrat June 1716
(SP/C)(CTB)(CTP)

MCDONALD WILLIAM
Jacobite captured at Preston.
Transported from Liverpool
to South Carolina on the
Susannah, master Thomas
Bromhall, 7 May 1716
(CTB)(SP/C)

MCDONALD WILLIAM
40. Weaver. Drumnadeeven,
Inverness. Jacobite in
McIntosh's regiment. Prisoner at Inverness, ship
and Medway. Transported
from London to Jamaica or
Barbados by Samuel Smith
31 March 1747
(P)(RM)

MCDONALD WILLIAM
35. Farmer. Glenmoriston. Jac-
obite in Glengarry's regiment.
Prisoner at Inverness and
Tilbury. Transported from London
to Jamaica or Barbados by Samuel
Smith 31 March 1747
(P)(RM)

MCDONALD WILLIAM
60. Farmer. Jacobite. Prisoner
at Carlisle. Transported 1747(?)
(P)

MCDONALD WILLIAM
50. Farmer. Glenmoriston.
Jacobite in Glengarry's regiment
Prisoner at Inverness and Tilbury
Transported from London to Jam-
aica or Barbados by Samuel Smith
31 March 1747
(P)(RM)

MCDONALD WILLIAM
55. Farmer. Glen Urquhart. Jac-
obite in Glengarry's regiment.
Prisoner at Inverness, ship and
Tilbury. Transported from London
to Jamaica or Barbados by Samuel
Smith 31 March 1747
(P)(RM)

MCDONALL DENIS
Jacobite captured at Preston.
Transported from Liverpool on
the Two Brothers, master Edward
Rathbone, for Jamaica 26 April
1716. Landed on Montserrat June
1716
(SP/C)(CTB)(CTP)

MACDONELL JOHN
Royalist soldier captured at
Worcester. Transported on the
John and Sarah, master John
Greene, from Gravesend to
Boston 13 May 1652
(NER)

MACDORTON PHILIP
Jacobite captured at Preston
Transported from Liverpool
on the Two Brothers, master
Edward Rathbone, for Jamaica
26 April 1716. Landed in
Montserrat June 1716
(SP/C)(CTB)(CTP)

MCDOUGALL ALEXANDER
Jacobite captured at Preston
Transported from Liverpool
on the Friendship, master
Michael Mankin, to Maryland
24 May 1716. Sold to Daniel
Sherwood in Maryland 20
August 1716
(SP/C)(HM)

MCDOUGALL ALEXANDER
26. Inverness. Jacobite in
Lovat's regiment. Prisoner
at Inverness and Tilbury.
Transported from London to
Jamaica or Barbados 31
March 1747 by Samuel Smith
(P)(RM)

MCDOUGALL ALLAN
26. Gardener. Strathlach-
lan, Argyll. Jacobite in
McLachlan's regiment. Captured at Falkirk. Prisoner
at Edinburgh, Carlisle and
York. Transported from
Liverpool on the Veteran,
master John Ricky, 5 May
1747 for the Leeward Is-
lands. Liberated by a
French privateer and landed on Martinique June 1747
(P)(RM)

MCDOUGALL CHARLES
Covenanter. Prisoner in
Kirkcudbright Tolbooth.
Banished to the Plantations
11 October 1684, at Kirk-
cudbright
(PC)

MCDOUGALL DUNCAN
Covenanter in Argyll's rebellion
Prisoner in the Laigh Parliament
House, Edinburgh. Banished to the
Plantations 31 July 1685. Trans-
ported from Leith to Jamaica by
John Ewing August 1685
(PC)

MCDOUGAL JOHN
26. Tailor. Bullone, Ross. Jacobite in Cromarty's regiment.
Prisoner at Inverness, ship and
Tilbury. Transported 20 March
1747
(P)

MCDOUGALL JOHN
Pedlar. Galnashel, Eigg. Jacobite
in Clanranald's regiment. Pris-
oner at Inverness, ship and Til-
bury. Transported from London to
Jamaica or Barbados by Samuel
Smith 31 March 1747
(P)(RM)

MCDOUNIE JOHN
Covenanter. Prisoner in the Laigh
Parliament House, Edinburgh. Ban-
ished to the Plantations 31 July
1685. Transported from Leith to
Jamaica by John Ewing August 1685
(PC)

MCDUFF JAMES
Labourer. Ballincreughan, Perth-
shire. Jacobite in Roy Stuart's
regiment. Captured at Carlisle.
Prisoner at Carlisle and Chester.
Transported from Liverpool on the
Johnson, master William Pemberton.
Landed at Port Oxford, Maryland
5 August 1747
(P)(PRO)

MCDUGALL HUGH
Jacobite captured at Preston.
Transported from Liverpool on the
Godspeed, master Arthur Smith, for
Virginia 28 July 1716. Sold to
Robert Hanson in Maryland 17 Oct-
ober 1716
(SP/C)(CTB)(HM)

MCEWAN ANDREW
Thief. Banished August
1774. Transported by shipmaster John Rankine. Landed at Port North Potomack,
Maryland 17 October 1775
(JC)

MCEWAN ARCHIBALD
Transported from Leith to
Jamaica by John Ewing
August 1685
(PC)

MCEWAN DONALD
Prisoner in Edinburgh Tol-
booth. Transported from
Leith to Jamaica by John
Ewing August 1685
(ETR)(PC)

MCEWAN DUNCAN
Covenanter. Prisoner in
Paul's Work, Edinburgh.
Transported from Leith to
East New Jersey by Robert
Barclay of Urie July 1685
(PC)

MCEWAN JOHN
Covenanter. Captured at
Crawfordmuir. Prisoner
at Canongate, Dunnottar,
and Leith. Banished to the
Plantations, at Leith 18
August 1685. Transported
from Leith to East New
Jersey on the Henry and
Francis, master Richard
Hutton, by George Scott
of Pitlochie 5 September
1685
(PC)

MCEWAN JOHN
Jacobite captured at Pres-
ton. Transported from
Liverpool on the Godspeed,
master Arthur Smith, for
Virginia 28 July 1716.
Sold to John Fendall in
Maryland 17 October 1716
(SP/C)(CTB)(HM)

MCEWAN KATHERINE
40. Fort William. Jacobite.
Prisoner at Carlisle and Lancaster. Transported from Liverpool on the Johnson, master
William Pemberton. Landed at
Port Oxford, Maryland 5 August
1747
(P)(PRO)

MCFADZEAN JANET
Wife of John Harper, elder.
Portrack. Covenanter. Prisoner
at Dumfries and Edinburgh. Ban-
ished to the Plantations, at
Dumfries 25 October 1684
(PC)

MCFARLANE ELIZABETH
30. Sewer. Perth. Jacobite.
Captured at Carlisle. Prisoner
at Carlisle and York. Transported
on the Veteran, master John Ricky
from Liverpool 5 May 1747 for the
Leeward Islands. Liberated by a
French privateer and landed on
Martinique June 1747
(P)(RM)

MCFARLANE JANET
Fireraiser. Banished for 7 years,
at Perth September 1750
(SM)

MCFARLANE JOHN
Jacobite captured at Preston.
Transported from Liverpool on the
Two Brothers, master Edward Rath-
bone, for Jamaica 26 April 1716.
Landed on Montserrat June 1716
(SP/C)(CTB)(CTP)

MCFARLANE JOHN alias MACANDREW
Tenant. Southdale, Ross-shire.
Sheepstealer. Banished to
America, at Inverness 1755
(SM)

MCFARLANE ROBERT or BARRON
Tailor. Gartmore. Jacobite
Prisoner at Tough, Stirling
Leith, Canongate and Car-
lisle. Transported 1747(?)
(P)

MCFARQUHAR KENNETH
45. Tenant farmer. Newton
of Redcastle. Jacobite in
Cromarty's regiment.
Prisoner at Inverness,
ship and Tilbury. Trans-
ported from London to
Barbados or Jamaica by
Samuel Smith 31 March 1747
(P)(RM)

MACFEARGHUIS RODERICK
Jacobite in the Duke of
Perth's regiment. Pris-
oner at Carlisle. Trans-
ported 1747(?)
(P)

MCFEE HUGH
30. Labourer. Inverness.
Jacobite. Prisoner at
Lancaster. Transported
from Liverpool on the
Veteran, master John
Ricky, 5 May 1747 for the
Leeward Islands. Liber-
ated by a French priv-
ateer and landed on
Martinique June 1747
(P)(RM)

MACGACHAN CHRISTIAN
Widow of Alexander Banks,
collier, Kilwinning.
Vagrant. Banished at
Glasgow 1754
(SM)

MCGACHIN JAMES
Dalry. Covenanter. Pris-
oner in Canongate Tolbooth
Banished to Carolina 19
June 1684. Transported
from Leith by Robert
Malloch, merchant in Edin-
burgh August 1684
(PC)

MCGIBBON ARCHIBALD
Covenanter. Warded in Edinburgh
Tolbooth 10 July 1685. Banished
to the Plantations 24 July 1685
Transported from Leith to Jam-
aica by John Ewing August 1685
(PC)

MCGIBBON DUNCAN
Jacobite captured at Preston.
Transported from Liverpool on
the Two Brothers, master Edward
Rathbone, for Jamaica 26 April
1716. Landed on Montserrat June
1716
(SP/C)(CTB)(CTP)

MCGIBBON HECTOR
Covenanter. Prisoner in Edin-
burgh Tolbooth. Transported
from Leith to Jamaica by John
Ewing August 1685
(PC)

MCGIBBON JOHN
Glenowkeill, Argyll. Covenanter
in Argyll's rebellion. Prisoner
in Paul's Work, Edinburgh. Ban-
ished to the Plantations 24
July 1685. Transported from
Leith to Jamaica by John Ewing
August 1685
(PC)

MCGIE JEAN
Covenanter. Prisoner at Dunnottar
and Leith. Banished to the Plant-
ations, at Leith 18 August 1685.
Transported from Leith by George
Scott of Pitlochie to East New
Jersey on the Henry and Francis,
master Richard Hutton, 5 Septem-
ber 1685
(PC)

MCGIE JOHN
Transported from Leith to East
New Jersey by George Scott of
Pitlochie on the Henry and Fran-
cis, master Richard Hutton, 5
September 1685
(PC)

MACGILL JAMES
Royalist soldier captured
at Worcester. Transported
on the John and Sarah,
master John Greene, from
Gravesend to Boston 13 May
1652
(NER)

MCGILL JANET
Banished for life. Trans-
ported from Glasgow on
the Brilliant, master
Robert Bennet. Landed at
Port Hampton, Virginia
7 October 1772
(JC)

MCGILL ROBERT
Prisoner in Edinburgh Tol-
booth. Transported from
Leith to Plantations 15
November 1679
(ETR)

MCGILLIVERAY DANIEL
Jacobite captured at Preston
Transported from Liverpool
on the Elizabeth and Anne,
master Edward Trafford, for
Virginia or Jamaica 29 June
1716. Landed in Virginia -
unindentured
(CTB)(SP/C)

MCGILLIVERAY DONALD
Jacobite captured at Preston
Transported from Liverpool
on the Susannah, master
Thomas Bromhall, for South
Carolina 7 May 1716
(CTB)(SP/C)

MCGILLEVERAY FARQUHAR
Jacobite captured at Preston
Transported from Liverpool
on the Friendship, master
Michael Mankin, 24 May 1716,
to Maryland. Sold to Samuel
Young, Maryland 20 August
1716
(SP/C)(HM)

MCGILLIVRAY FERGUS
Jacobite captured at Preston.
Transported from Liverpool to
South Carolina on the Susannah,
master Thomas Bromhall, 7 May
1716
(SP/C)(CTB)

MCGILLIVRAY JAMES
Jacobite captured at Preston.
Transported from Liverpool to
South Carolina on the Wakefield,
master Thomas Beck, 21 April 1716
(CTB)

MCGILVERAY JOHN
Jacobite captured at Preston.
Transported from Liverpool to
Antigua on the Scipio, master
John Scaisbrick, 30 March 1716
(CTB)(SP/C)

MCGILLIVRAY JOHN
Jacobite captured at Preston.
Transported from Liverpool to
South Carolina on the Wakefield,
master Thomas Beck, 21 April 1716
(CTB)

MCGILLIVRAY LOUGHLAN
Jacobite captured at Preston.
Transported from Liverpool to
South Carolina on the Wakefield,
master Thomas Beck, 21 April 1716
(CTB)

MCGILLIVRAY OWEN
Jacobite captured at Preston.
Transported from Liverpool to
South Carolina on the Wakefield,
master Thomas Beck, 21 April 1716
(CTB)

MCGILLIVERAY WILLIAM
Jacobite captured at Preston.
Transported from Liverpool on
the Friendship, master Michael
Mankin, 24 May 1716 for Maryland.
Sold to Thomas Mackell, Maryland
20 August 1716
(SP/C)(HM)

MCGILLIVRAY WILLIAM
Jacobite captured at Preston
Transported from Liverpool
to Virginia or Jamaica on
the Elizabeth and Anne, master Edward Trafford 29 June
1716. Landed in Virginia -
unindentured
(CTB)(SP/C)

MCGILLEVEREY WILLIAM
Jacobite captured at Preston
Transported from Liverpool
to Maryland on the Friendship, master Michael Mankin,
24 May 1716. Sold to Robert
Ungle in Maryland 20 August
1716
(SP/C)(HM)

MCGILLEVRAY WILLIAM or GRANT
Schoolmaster. Buckie. Forger
Prisoner in Edinburgh Tol-
booth. Banished to the
Plantations in America for
life, at Edinburgh 21 March
1758
(JC)

MCGILLICH JOHN
Covenanter in Argyll's reb-
ellion. Prisoner in Canon-
gate Tolbooth. Banished to
the Plantations 30 July 1685
Transported from Leith to
Jamaica August 1685
(PC)

MCGILLIES DANIEL
60. Labourer. Arisaig. Jacobite in Glengarry's regiment. Prisoner at Carlisle
and York. Transported to
Antigua 8 May 1747
(P)

MCGILLIES DANIEL
Son of Daniel McGillies. 12.
Arisaig. Jacobite. Transported
from Liverpool for the Leeward
Islands 5 May 1747 on the
Veteran, master John Ricky
Liberated by a French privateer
and landed on Martinique June
1747
(P)(RM)

MCGILLIS DONALD
18. Labourer. Inverness.
Jacobite in Glengarry's regiment
Prisoner in Carlisle and York.
Transported from Liverpool on
the Veteran, master John Ricky,
for the Leeward Islands 5 May
1747. Liberated by a French
privateer and landed on Martinique June 1747
(P)(RM)

MCGILLIS HECTOR
16. Herd. Inverness. Jacobite
in Glengarry's regiment. Prisoner at Carlisle and York. Trans
ported from Liverpool to the
Leeward Islands on the Veteran,
master John Ricky, 5 May 1747.
Liberated by a French privateer
and landed on Martinique June
1747
(P)(RM)

MCGIVEN ALEXANDER
Jacobite captured at Preston.
Transported from Liverpool to
Virginia on the Godspeed, master
Arthur Smith, 28 July 1716.
Landed in Maryland and escaped
18 October 1716
(SP/C)(CTB)(HM)

MCGOWAN JOHN
Covenanter in Argyll's rebellion
Prisoner in Laigh Parliament House
Banished 30 July 1685. Trans-
ported from Leith to Jamaica by
John Ewing August 1685
(PC)

MCGRAW DONALD
24. Farmer. Clochgolore,
Ross. Jacobite in Crom-
arty's regiment. Prisoner
at Inverness, ship and Til
bury. Transported 20 March
1747 from London to Jamaica
or Barbados by Samuel Smith
(P)(RM)

MCGRAW DONALD
48. Perth. Jacobite in
Lord George Murray's regiment. Prisoner at Inver-
ness and Tilbury. Trans-
ported 1747 (?)
(P)

MCGREGOR CALLUM
Thief. Prisoner in Edin-
burgh Tolbooth. Trans-
ported from Leith to Bar-
bados on the Blossom by
William Johnston, merchant
in Edinburgh 2 August 1680
(ETR)

MCGREGOR DONALD
Thief. Prisoner in Stir-
ling Tolbooth. Transport-
ed from Leith to East New
Jersey by David Toshach
of Monievaird 5 May 1684
(PC)

MCGREGOR DUNCAN
Jacobite captured at Preston. Transported from
Liverpool to South Carol-
ina on the Susannah,mas-
ter Thomas Bromhall
7 May 1716
(SP/C)(CTB)

MCGREGOR DUNCAN
Jacobite. Transported on
the Johnson, master William
Pemberton, from Liverpool
5 May 1747. Landed at Port
Oxford, Maryland 5 August
1747
(PRO)

MCGREGOR DUNCAN
Farmer. Tarland, Aberdeenshire.
Jacobite engign in Farquharson's
regiment. Prisoner at Culloden,
Inverness and London. Transported
from Liverpool on the Gildart,
master Richard Holmes 5 May 1747
Landed at Port North Potomac,
Maryland 5 August 1747
(P)(JAB)(PRO)

MCGREGOR DUNCAN or JOHN DOW GRANT
Horsethief. Banished to the
Plantations, at Perth 5 September
1764
(SM)

MCGREGOR GREGOR
Jacobite captured at Preston.
Transported from Liverpool on
the Anne, master Robert Wallace,
for Virginia 31 July 1716
(CTB)(SP/C)

MCGREGOR ISABEL
Sheepstealer. Banished to the
Plantations for 14 years, at
Aberdeen 30 April 1768
(SM)

MCGREGOR JOHN
Jacobite captured at Preston.
Transported from Liverpool for
Virginia on the Godspeed, master
Arthur Smith, 28 July 1716. Sold
to Richard Eglin in Maryland
17 October 1716
(SP/C)(CTB)(HM)

MCGREGOR JOHN
Labourer. Perthshire. Jacobite
in the Duke of Perth's regiment.
Prisoner at Bridge of Allan,
Stirling, Edinburgh and Carlisle.
Transported from Liverpool on the
Johnson, master William Pemberton,
Landed at Port Oxford, Maryland
5 August 1747
(P)(PRO)

MCGREGOR JOHN
Labourer. Dundurn, Perth-
shire. Jacobite in the
Duke of Perth's regiment.
Captured at Carlisle.
Prisoner at Carlisle and
Chester. Transported from
Liverpool on the Johnson,
master William Pemberton.
Landed at Port Oxford,
Maryland 5 August 1747
(P)(PRO)

MCGREGOR MALCOLM
Jacobite captured at Pres-
ton. Transported from
Liverpool to South Carol-
ina on the Susannah, master
Thomas Bromhall, 7 May 1716
(CTB)(SP/C)

MCGREGOR MARK
24. Cook. Balgowan, Perth.
Jacobite in Baggot's
Hussar's. Prisoner at
Perth, Canongate and Car-
lisle. Transported from
Liverpool on the Gildart,
master Richard Holmes.
Landed at Port North
Potomac, Maryland 5 August
1747
(P)(PRO)

MCGRUTHER WILLIAM
Jacobite captured at Preston
Transported from Liverpool
on the Elizabeth and Anne,
master Edward Trafford, 29
June 1716.Landed in Virginia
- unindentured
(CTB)(SP/C)

MCGUFFOG GRIZZEL
Child murder. Prisoner in
Banff Tolbooth. Banished to
the Plantations in America
for life, at Edinburgh 19
December 1746
(JC)

MCHAFFIE JOHN
Gargerie. Covenanter. Banished to the Plantations
17 October 1684
(PC)

MACHARDY JOHN
Jacobite captured at Preston.
Transported from Liverpool on
the Godspeed, master Arthur
Smith, for Virginia 28 July
1716
(SP/C)(CTB)

MCHATTON NEIL
Covenanter. Captured after
Argyll's rebellion. Prisoner
in Laigh Parliament House, Edin-
burgh. Banished to New England
9 July 1685. Transported from
Leith to New England by William
Arbuckle, merchant in Glasgow,
July 1685
(PC)

MCICHAN JOHN
Covenanter. Banished to the
Plantations 24 July 1685.
Transported from Leith to
Jamaica by John Ewing August
1685
(PC)

MCILBRYDE DUNCAN
Covenanter in Argyll's rebellion
Prisoner in Paul's Work, Edinburgh
Banished to the Plantations 31
August 1685. Transported from
Leith to Jamaica by John Ewing
August 1685
(PC)

MCILBRYDE NEIL
Tenant of McLachlan of Craigin-
tervie. Covenanter in Argyll's
rebellion. Prisoner in Paul's
Work, Edinburgh. Banished to the
Plantations 30 July 1685. Trans
ported from Leith to Jamaica by
John Ewing August 1685
(PC)

MCILMOON DONALD
Covenanter in Argyll's
rebellion. Prisoner in
Canongate Tolbooth. Ban-
ished to the Plantations
30 July 1685. Transported
from Leith to Jamaica by
John Ewing August 1685.
Stigmatised
(PC)

MCILROY GILBERT
Covenanter. Prisoner in
Edinburgh Tolbooth, war-
ded 23 July 1685. Banish
ed to the Plantations 29
July 1685. Stigmatised.
Transported from Leith
to Jamaica by John Ewing
August 1685
(PC)(ETR)

MCILSHALLUM JOHN
Transported from Leith
to Jamaica by John Ewing
August 1685
(PC)

MCILVAY DUNCAN
Prisoner in Canongate
Tolbooth. Transported
from Leith to Carolina
by Robert Malloch, mer-
chant in Edinburgh,
August 1684
(PC)

MCILVORY DUNCAN
Covenanter in Argyll's
rebellion. Prisoner in
Paul's Work, Edinburgh
Banished to the Plant-
ations 30 July 1685.
Transported from Leith
to Jamaica by John Ewing
August 1685
(PC)

MCILVORY JOHN
Cragintyrie. Covenanter
in Argyll's rebellion.
Prisoner in Paul's Work.
Banished to the Plantat-
ions 30 July 1685
(PC)

MCILVAIN ARCHIBALD
Glendaruel. Covenanter in Argyll's
rebellion. Prisoner in Canongate
Tolbooth. Banished to the Plant-
ations 30 July 1685. Stigmatised.
Transported from Leith to Jamaica
by John Ewing August 1685
(PC)

MCILVERRAN DONALD
Covenanter in Argyll's rebellion
Prisoner in Canongate Tolbooth.
Banished to the Plantations 30
July 1685. Transported from Leith
to Jamaica by John Ewing August
1685
(PC)

MCINLAY ELIZABETH
Childmurder. Transported, at Ayr
September 1750
(SM)

MCINLAY NEIL
Transported from Leith to Jamaica
August 1685
(PC)

MCINLIER DUNCAN
Jacobite captured at Preston.
Transported from Liverpool on
the Two Brothers, master Edward
Rathbone, for Jamaica 26 April
1716. Landed on Montserrat June
1716
(SP/C)(CTB)(CTP)

MCINNES ANDREW
27. Grazier. Tray, Morar. Jacobite in Clanranald's regiment.
Prisoner at Inverness, ship and
Tilbury. Transported 30 March
1747
(P)

MCINNES JOHN
Jacobite captured at Preston.
Transported from Liverpool to
South Carolina on the Susannah,
master Thomas Bromhall 7 May 1716
(SP/C)(CTB)

MACINNES JOHN
Sailor. Thief. Banished
to the Plantations for 5
years, at Inverness 20
May 1775
(SM)

MCINNY ALEXANDER
Jacobite. Transported on
the Gildart, master Rich-
ard Holmes, from Liverpool.
Landed at Port North Potomac, Maryland 5 August 1747
(PRO)

MCINTAGGART JOHN
Servant to McAlastair.
Covenanter in Argyll's
rebellion. Prisoner in the
Laigh Parliament House,
Edinburgh. Banished to the
Plantations 30 July 1685.
Transported from Leith to
Jamaica by John Ewing
August 1685
(PC)

MCINTAGGART PATRICK
Jacobite. Prisoner at
Carlisle, Lancaster and
Liverpool. Transported
from Liverpool on the
Johnson, master William
Pemberton. Landed at Port
Oxford, Maryland 5 August
1747
(P)(PRO)

MCINTOSH ALEXANDER
Jacobite captured at
Preston. Transported from
Liverpool to St Kitts on
the Hockenhill, master
H.Short, 25 June 1716
(SP/C)(CTB)

MCINTOSH ALEXANDER
Jacobite captured at Preston
Transported from Liverpool
on the Godspeed, master
Arthur Smith, for Virginia
28 July 1716. Sold to Dan-
iel Stewart in Maryland 17
October 1716
(SP/C)(CTB)(HM)

MCINTOSH ALEXANDER
69. Labourer. Balnabrough, Perth
Jacobite in the Duke of Perth's
regiment. Prisoner at Perth, Canongate and Carlisle. Transported
from Liverpool on the Gildart,
master Richard Holmes. 5 May
1747. Landed at Port North Potomac, Maryland 5 August 1747
(P)(PRO)

MCINTOSH ALEXANDER
20. Servant. Moray. Jacobite in
MacIntosh's regiment. Prisoner
at Inverness, ship and Tilbury.
Transported from London to Jamaica or Barbados by Samuel Smith
31 March 1747
(P)(RM)

MCINTOSH ANGUS
Jacobite captured at Preston.
Transported from Liverpool on
the Two Brothers, master Edward
Rathbone, for Jamaica 26 April
1716. Landed on Montserrat June
1716
(SP/C)(CTB)(CTP)

MCINTOSH ANGUS
26. Labourer. Inverness. Jacobite in Glengarry's regiment.
Captured at Carlisle. Prisoner
at Carlisle and York.Transported
from Liverpool on the Veteran,
master John Ricky, 5 May 1747.
Liberated by a French privateer
and landed on Martinique June
1747
(P)(RM)

MACINTOSH DANIEL
Royalist soldier captured at
Worcester. Transported on the
John and Sarah, master John
Greene, from Gravesend to
Boston 13 May 1652
(NER)

119

MCINTOSH DONALD
Thief. Prisoner in Stirling
Tolbooth. Transported to
East New Jersey by David
Toshach of Monievaird
5 May 1684
(PC)

MCINTOSH DUNCAN
Jacobite captured at
Preston. Transported from
Liverpool to South Carol-
ina on the Wakefield, mas
ter Thomas Beck, 21 April
1716
(CTB)

MCINTOSH DUNCAN
Jacobite captured at
Preston. Transported from
Liverpool to South Carol-
ina on the Susannah, mas-
ter Thomas Bromhall, 7
May 1716
(CTB)(SP/C)

MCINTOSH DUNCAN
60. Carpenter. Inverness
Jacobite in the Duke of
Perth's regiment. Pris-
oner at Carlisle and Lan-
caster. Transported 1747(?)
Returned to Scotland 1748
(P)

MCINTOSH DUNCAN
19. Husbandman. Dyke,
Moray. Jacobite in
McIntosh's regiment.
Prisoner at Inverness,
ship and Medway. Trans-
ported from London to
Jamaica or Barbados by
Samuel Smith 20 March 1747
(P)(RM)

MCINTOSH EWAN
Jacobite captured at Preston. Transported from Liverpool to South Carolina
on the Susannah, master
Thomas Bromhall, 7 May 1716
(CTB)(SP/C)

MCINTOSH ISABEL
Daughter of John McIntosh, farmer,
Potty, Invernessshire. Servant
to George Duguid, merchant in
Edinburgh. Attempted child murder.
Prisoner in Edinburgh Tolbooth.
Banished from Scotland for 14
years, at Edinburgh 22 March 1763
(JC)

MCINTOSH JAMES
Jacobite captured at Preston.
Transported from Liverpool to
South Carolina on the Wakefield,
master Thomas Beck, 21 April 1716
(CTB)

MCINTOSH JAMES
Jacobite captured at Preston.
Transported from Liverpool to
South Carolina on the Susannah,
master Thomas Bromhall, 7 May
1716
(SP/C)(CTB)

MCINTOSH JAMES
Jacobite captured at Preston.
Transported from Liverpool to
Virginia on the Godspeed, master
Arthur Smith, 28 July 1716. Sold
to Robert Hanson in Maryland 17
October 1716
(SP/C)(CTB)(HM)

MCINTOSH JAMES
Jacobite captured at Preston.
Transported from Liverpool to
Virginia or Jamaica 29 June 1716
on the Elizabeth and Anne, master
Edward Trafford. Landed in Vir-
ginia - indentured
(CTB)(SP/C)

MCINTOSH JAMES
Jacobite captured at Preston.
Transported from Liverpool tc
Virginia or Jamaica 29 June 1716
on the Elizabeth and Anne, master
Edward Trafford. Landed in Vir-
ginia - indentured
(CTB)(SP/C)

MCINTOSH JAMES
Jacobite captured at Preston. Transported from Liverpool for Virginia on the
Godspeed, master Arthur
Smith, 28 July 1716. Sold
to Henry H.Hawkins in Maryland 17 October 1716
(SP/C)(CTB)(HM)

MCINTOSH JANE or ANN
20. Knitter. Inverness.
Jacobite captured at
Carlisle. Prisoner at
Carlisle and Lancaster.
Transported from Liverpool
for the Leeward Islands on
the Veteran, master John
Ricky, 5 May 1747. Liber-
ated by a French privateer
and landed on Martinique
June 1747
(P)(RM)

MCINTOSH JOHN
Jacobite captured at Pres-
ton. Transported from
Liverpool to South Carolina
on the Susannah, master
Thomas Bromhall, 7 May 1716
(CTB)(SP/C)

MCINTOSH JOHN
Jacobite captured at Pres-
ton. Transported from
Liverpool to Virginia or
Jamaica on the Elizabeth
and Anne, master Edward
Trafford, 29 June 1716
(CTB)(SP/C)

MCINTOSH JOHN
Jacobite captured at Pres-
ton. Transported from
Liverpool to Virginia or
Jamaica on the Elizabeth
and Anne, master Edward
Trafford, 29 June 1716.
Landed in Virginia -
indentured
(CTB)(SP/C)

MCINTOSH JOHN
Jacobite captured at Preston.
Transported from Liverpool to
South Carolina on the Wakefield,
master Thomas Beck, 21 April 1716
(CTB)

MCINTOSH JOHN
Jacobite captured at Preston.
Transported from Liverpool to
South Carolina on the Susannah,
master Thomas Bromhall, 7 May
1716
(CTB)(SP/C)

MCINTOSH JOHN
Jacobite captured at Preston.
Transported from Liverpool to
South Carolina on the Susannah,
master Thomas Bromhall, 7 May
1716
(CTB)(SP/C)

MCINTOSH JOHN
51. Fiddler. Inverness. Jacobite
in the Duke of Perth's regiment.
Prisoner at Carlisle and Lancaster. Transported from Liverpool for the Leeward Islands on
the Veteran,master John Ricky,
5 May 1747. Liberated by a
French privateer and landed on
Martinique June 1747
(P)(RM)

MCINTOSH JOHN
Sailor. Servant to Captain Smith
of the Freemason of Leith. Thief
Prisoner in Edinburgh Tolbooth.
Banished to the Plantations in
America for life, at Edinburgh
9 July 1764
(JC)

MCINTOSH LACHLAN
Jacobite captured at Preston.
Transported from Liverpool for
Virginia on the Godspeed, master
Arthur Smith, 28 July 1716. Sold
to Henry Miles in Maryland
17 October 1716
(SP/C)(CTB)(HM)

MCINTOSH LACHLAN
Jacobite captured at Preston.
Transported from Liverpool
to Antigua on the Scipio,
master John Scaisbrick 30
March 1716
(CTB)(SP/C)

MCINTOSH LACHLAN
22. Tailor or merchant.
Inverness. Jacobite Lt. Col.
of Lovat's regiment. Prisoner at Culloden, Inverness,
ship and Medway. Transported from London to Barbados
or Jamaica by Samuel Smith
31 March 1747
(P)(RM)

MCINTOSH MALCOLM
Jacobite captured at Preston
Transported from Liverpool
to Antigua on the Scipio,
master John Scaisbrick
30 March 1716
(CTB)(SP/C)

MCINTOSH PETER
34. Labourer. Inverness.
Jacobite in the Duke of
Perth's regiment. Prisoner
at Carlisle and York.
Transported from Liverpool
for the Leeward Islands on
the Veteran, master John
Ricky, 5 May 1747. Liber-
ated by a French privateer
and landed on Martinique
June 1747
(P)(RM)

MCINTOSH THOMAS
Jacobite captured at Preston
Transported from Liverpool
to Virginia or Jamaica on
the Elizabeth and Anne,
master Edward Trafford,
29 June 1716
(CTB)(SP/C)

MACINTOSH WILLIAM
Royalist soldier captured
at Worcester. Transported
on the John and Sarah, master John Greene, from Gravesend to Boston 13 May 1652
(NER)

MCINTOSH WILLIAM
Jacobite captured at Preston.
Transported from Liverpool to
South Carolina on the Susannah,
master Thomas Bromhall, 7 May
1716
(CTB)(SP/C)

MCINTOSH WILLIAM
Jacobite captured at Preston.
Transported from Liverpool to
South Carolina on the Wakefield,
master Thomas Beck, 21 April
1716
(CTB)

MCINTOSH WILLIAM
Jacobite captured at Preston.
Transported from Liverpool to
Antigua on the Scipio, master
John Scaisbrick, 30 March 1716
(CTB)(SP/C)

MCINTOSH WILLIAM
Jacobite captured at Preston.
Transported from Liverpool to
Antigua on the Scipio, master
John Scaisbrick, 30 March 1716
(CTB)(SP/C)

MCINTOSH WILLIAM
Jacobite captured at Preston.
Transported from Liverpool to
Virginia on the Anne, master
Robert Wallace, 31 July 1716
(CTB)(SP/C)

MCINTYRE ANN
20. Argyll. Jacobite. Prisoner
at Carlisle. Transported to
Antigua 8 May 1747
(P)

MCINTYRE ARCHIBALD
Glendaruel. Covenanter in Argyll's
rebellion. Prisoner in Canongate
Tolbooth. Banished to the Plant-
ations 30 July 1685. Transported
from Leith to Jamaica by John Ewing
August 1685
(PC)

MCINTYRE ARCHIBALD
50. Lead miner. Argyll.
Jacobite. Prisoner at
York and Lincoln. Trans-
ported from Liverpool on
the Johnson, master
William Pemberton. Landed
at Port Oxford, Maryland
5 August 1747
(P)(PRO)

MCINTYRE DENIS
Jacobite captured at
Preston. Transported on
the Two Brothers, master
Edward Rathbone, from
Liverpool for Jamaica
26 April 1716. Landed
on Montserrat June 1716
(SP/C)(CTB)(CTP)

MCINTYRE DONALD
56. "Quack doctor".
Argyll. Jacobite. Pris-
oner at Carlisle and
Lancaster. Transported
from Liverpool on the
Johnson, master William
Pemberton, 5 May 1747.
Landed at Port Oxford,
Maryland 5 August 1747
(P)(PRO)

MCINTYRE DUNCAN
42. Brewer. Lochielhead
Jacobite in Ardshiel's
regiment. Prisoner at
Inverness, ship and
Tilbury. Transported
20 March 1747
(P)

MCINTYRE DUNCAN
Killici. Army pensioner.
Horse thief. Banished
to the Plantations for
life, at Inveraray 1773
(SM)

MCINTYRE FINLAY
Jacobite captured at Preston.
Transported from Liverpool to
Virginia on the Godspeed, master
Arthur Smith, 28 July 1716. Sold
to John Penn in Maryland 17 Oct-
ober 1716
(SP/C)(CTB)(HM)

MCINTYRE HUGH
Jacobite captured at Preston.
Transported from Liverpool to
Virginia on the Godspeed, master
Arthur Smith, 28 July 1716. Sold
to John Vincent in Maryland
17 October 1716
(CTB)(SP/C)(HM)

MCINTYRE JOHN
Jacobite captured at Preston.
Transported from Liverpool to
Jamaica on the Two Brothers,
master Edward Rathbone, 26 April
1716. Landed on Montserrat June
1716
(SP/C)(CTB)(CTP)

MACINTYRE JOHN
Jacobite captured at Preston.
Transported from Liverpool on
the Friendship, master Michael
Mankin, 24 May 1716. Sold to
Daniel Sherwood in Maryland
20 August 1716
(HM)

MCINTYRE JOHN
Soldier in General Campbell's
Argyll Fencibles. Thief. Banished to the Plantations for
14 years, at Aberdeen 18 September 1763
(SM)

MCINTYRE MARY
Jacobite captured at Carlisle.
Prisoner at Carlisle. Transported
to Antigua 8 May 1747
(P)

MCISAAK MURDOCH
Machrimore, Kintyre.
Covenanter. Captured at
Dunbarton after Argyll's
rebellion. Prisoner in
Laigh Parliament House,
Edinburgh. Banished to
the Plantations 9 July
1685. Transported from
Leith to New England by
William Arbuckle, merch-
ant in Glasgow, July
1685
(PC)

MCIVAR ANGUS
Glassary. Covenanter.
Captured after Argyll's
rebellion. Prisoner in
the Laigh Parliament
House, Edinburgh. Ban-
ished to New England
9 July 1685. Transported
from Leith to New Eng-
land by William Arbuckle
merchant in Glasgow,
July 1685
(PC)

MCIVAR DONALD
Covenanter in Argyll's
rebellion. Prisoner in
Paul's Work, Edinburgh.
Banished to the Plant-
ations 30 July 1685.
Transported from Leith
to Jamaica by John Ewing
August 1685
(PC)

MCIVAR DUNCAN
Covenanter in Argyll's
rebellion. Prisoner in
Laigh Parliament House
Edinburgh. Banished to
the Plantations 30 July
1685. Transported from
Leith to Jamaica by John
Ewing August 1685
(PC)

MCIVAR JOHN
Tulloch, Argyll. Covenanter in
Argyll's rebellion. Prisoner
in Canongate and Laigh Parliament House, Edinburgh. Banished
to the Plantations 24 July 1685.
Transported from Leith to Jamaica
by John Ewing August 1685
(PC)

MCIVAR MALCOLM
Transported from Leith to Jam-
aica by John Ewing August 1685
(PC)

MACKAIN ALASTAIR
Royalist soldier captured at
Worcester. Transported from
Gravesend to Boston on the
John and Sarah, master John
Greene, 13 May 1652
(NER)

MACKAIN DANIEL
Royalist soldier captured at
Worcester. Transported from
Gravesend to Boston on the
John and Sarah, master John
Greene, 13 May 1652
(NER)

MACKAIN NEIL
Royalist soldier captured at
Worcester. Transported from
Gravesend to Boston on the
John and Sarah, master John
Greene, 13 May 1652
(NER)

MACKAIN SAMUEL
Royalist soldier captured at
Worcester. Transported from
Gravesend to Boston on the
John and Sarah, master John
Greene, 13 May 1652
(NER)

MACKAIN WILLIAM
Royalist soldier captured
at Worcester. Transported
from Gravesend to Boston
on the John and Sarah,
master John Greene, 13
May 1652
(NER)

MCKAIRNE NEIL
Covenanter in Argyll's
rebellion. Prisoner in
Paul's Work, Edinburgh
Banished to the Plant-
ations 30 July 1685.
Transported from Leith
to Jamaica by John Ewing
August 1685
(PC)

MACKANE JOHN
Royalist soldier captured
at Worcester. Transported
from Gravesend to Boston
on the John and Sarah,
master John Greene,
13 May 1652
(NER)

MACKANDY JEAN
Child murder. Banished
to the Plantations for
life, at Aberdeen
3 September 1766
(SM)

MACKAINE ROBERT
Royalist soldier captured
at Worcester. Transported
on the John and Sarah,
master John Greene, from
Gravesend to Boston
13 May 1652
(NER)

MACKANE PATRICK
Royalist soldier captured
at Worcester. Transported
on the John and Sarah,
master John Greene, from
Gravesend to Boston
13 May 1652
(NER)

MACKAY ALEXANDER
Royalist soldier captured at
Worcester. Transported from
Gravesend to Boston on the
John and Sarah, master John
Creene, 13 May 1652
(NER)

MACKAY ANDREW
Jacobite. Transported from
Liverpool on the Johnson,
master William Pemberton.
Died on ship 15 June 1747
(PRO)

MCKAY DONALD
Youngest brother of Alexander
McKay of Achmonie. Achmonie,
Glen Urquhart. Jacobite in
Glengarry's regiment. Prisoner
at Inverness and on ship.
Transported to Barbados.
Planter in Jamaica. Returned
to Scotland
(P)

MCKAY DUNCAN
Skipnish, Kintyre. Covenanter.
Prisoner in Paul's Work, Edin-
burgh. Banished to the Plant-
ations 24 July 1685
(PC)

MCKAY DUNCAN
Labourer. Castle Doune, Perth.
From Inverness. Jacobite in
Ogilvy's regiment. Captured
at Carlisle. Prisoner at
Carlisle, Chester and York.
Transported
(P)

MACKAY HUGH
Royalist soldier captured at
Worcester. Transported from
Gravesend to Boston on the
John and Sarah, master John
Greene, 13 May 1652
(NER)

MACKAY JOHN
Royalist soldier captured
at Worcester. Transported
on the John and Sarah,
master John Greene, from
Gravesend to Boston 13 May
1652
(NER)

MCKAY MARTIN
Transported from Leith
to Jamaica by John Ewing
August 1685
(PC)

MCKAY PETER
Jacobite in Glengarry's
regiment. Prisoner at
Tilbury. Transported
1747(?)
(P)

MCKAY ROBERT
22. Cooper. Fochabers.
From Sutherland. Jacobite
in Lord Lewis Gordon's
regiment. Prisoner at
Inverness, ship and Til-
bury. Transported 1747(?)
(P)

MCKAY ROBERT
26. Nether Clashoer, Elgin
Jacobite sergeant in Cromarty's regiment. Prisoner
at Inverness and Tilbury.
Transported 20 March 1747
(P)

MCKAY ROBERT
20. Dornoch. Jacobite in
Lord Lewis Gordon's regi-
ment. Prisoner at Inver-
ness, ship and Tilbury.
Transported 1747(?)
(P)

MCKAY THOMAS
47. Woodturner. Glenmoriston. From Banff. Jacobite
in Glengarry's regiment.
Prisoner at Inverness,
ship and Tilbury. Trans-
ported 20 March 1747
(P)

MCKECHAN WALTER
Shirgarton. Prisoner in Canongate
Tolbooth. Transported from Leith
to the Plantations on the
St Michael of Scarborough, master
Edward Johnston, 12 December 1678
(PC)

MCKEELS DANIEL
Jacobite captured at Preston.
Transported from Liverpool to
South Carolina on the Susannah,
master Thomas Bromhall, 7 May
1716
(SP/C)(CTB)

MCKEICHAN NEIL
Baranazare, Lorne. Covenanter
in Argyll's rebellion. Prisoner
in Canongate Tolbooth. Banished
to the Plantations 24 July 1685
Transported from Leith to Jamaica
by John Ewing August 1685
(PC)

MACKELL ALASTAIR
Royalist soldier captured at
Worcester. Transported from
Gravesend to Boston on the
John and Sarah, master John
Greene, 13 May 1652

MCKELLAR ANGUS
Covenanter in Argyll's rebellion
Prisoner in the Laigh Parliament
House, Edinburgh. Transported
from Leith to New England July
1685 by William Arbuckle, merc-
hant in Glasgow
(PC)

MCKELLO DONALD
Covenanter in Argyll's rebellion.
Prisoner in Paul's Work, Edinburgh
Banished to the Plantations 30
July 1685. Transported from Leith
to Jamaica by John Ewing August
1685
(PC)

MCKELLO DUGALD
Transported from Leith to
Jamaica by John Ewing
August 1685
(PC)

MCKELLO JOHN
Covenanter in Argyll's
rebellion. Prisoner in
Paul's Work, Edinburgh.
Banished to the Plant-
ations 30 July 1685.
Transported from Leith
to Jamaica by John Ewing
August 1685
(PC)

MCKELLO MARTIN
Covenanter in Argyll's
rebellion. Prisoner in
Paul's Work, Edinburgh
Banished to the Plant-
ations 30 July 1685
(PC)

MACKEN WILLIAM
Royalist soldier captured
at Worcester. Transported
from Gravesend to Boston
on the John and Sarah,
master John Greene,
13 May 1652
(NER)

MCKENNY ALEXANDER
Jacobite captured at
Preston. Transported
from Liverpool to Jam-
aica or Virginia on the
Elizabeth and Anne, mas-
ter Edward Trafford, 29
June 1716. Landed in
Virginia - unindentured
(CTB)(SP/C)

MCKENNY COLIN
Jacobite captured at
Preston. Transported from
Liverpool to Antigua on
the Scipio, master John
Scaisbrick, 30 March 1716
(CTB)

MCKENZIE ALEXANDER
25. Husbandman. Drumhardinich.
Inverness. Jacobite in Lovat's
regiment. Prisoner at Inverness
ship and Medway. Transported
1747(?)
(P)

MCKENZIE ALEXANDER
32. Cromarty. Jacobite in
Cromarty's regiment. Prisoner
at Inverness and ship. Transported from London to Jamaica
or Barbados by Samuel Smith
31 March 1747
(P)(RM)

MCKENZIE ALEXANDER
30. Cromarty. Jacobite in
Cromarty's regiment Prisoner
at Inverness and ship. Transported 31 March 1747 from
London to Barbados or Jamaica
by Samuel Smith
(P)(RM)

MCKENZIE ALEXANDER
28. Snuffseller. Logie, Ross.
Jacobite in Cromarty's regiment
Prisoner at Inverness, ship and
Medway. Transported from London
to Jamaica or Barbados by Samuel
Smith 31 March 1747
(P)(RM)

MCKENZIE ALEXANDER
24. Ross. Jacobite in Cromarty's
regiment. Prisoner at Inverness
and Tilbury. Transported from
London to Jamaica or Barbados
by Samuel Smith 31 March 1747
(P)(RM)

MCKENZIE ALEXANDER
18. Tailor and army deserter.
Argyll. Jacobite in Cromarty's
regiment. Prisoner at Falkirk,
Inverness, ship and Tilbury.
Transported from London to
Jamaica or Barbados by Samuel
Smith 31 March 1747
(P)(RM)

MCKENZIE ALEXANDER
40. Cromarty. Jacobite in
Cromarty's regiment. Prisoner at Inverness, ship
and Tilbury. Transported
from London to Barbados or
Jamaica by Samuel Smith
31 March 1747
(P)(RM)

MCKENZIE ALEXANDER
28. Grieve to Mackenzie
of Balmudathy. From Coull,
Coutrie, Ross. Jacobite
in Cromarty's regiment.
Prisoner at Inverness, ship
and Tilbury. Transported
from London to Barbados or
Jamaica by Samuel Smith
31 March 1747
(P)(RM)

MCKENZIE ALEXANDER
22. Servant to Mackenzie
in Ballacchriche, Ross.
Jacobite in Cromarty's
regiment. Prisoner at
Inverness and Tilbury.
Transported from London
to Barbados or Jamaica by
Samuel Smith 31 March 1747
(P)(RM)

MCKENZIE ALEXANDER
50. Farmer. Achendrein,
Ross. Jacobite in Cromarty's
regiment. Prisoner at Inverness, ship and Tilbury.
Transported from London to
Barbados or Jamaica 31 March
1747
(P)(RM)

MCKENZIE ALEXANDER
23. Servant to Janet McKenzie,
Bracklock. From Ross. Jacobite
in Cromarty's regiment. Prisoner at Inverness, ship and
Tilbury. Transported from
London to Jamaica or Barbados
by Samuel Smith 31 March 1747
(P)(RM)

MCKENZIE ALEXANDER of CORRY
40. Factor to Lord Cromarty.
Thurso. Jacobite lieutenant in
Cromarty's regiment. Prisoner
at Dunrobin, Inverness, Tilbury
and Southwark. Transported from
London to Barbados or Jamaica by
Samuel Smith 31 March 1747
(P)(RM)

MCKENZIE ANN
60. Knitter. Glengarry. Jacobite
captured at Carlisle. Prisoner
at Carlisle and Lancaster. Transported from Liverpool on the ship
Johnson, master William Pemberton.
Landed at Port Oxford, Maryland
5 August 1747
(P)(PRO)

MCKENZIE ARCHIBALD
18. Herd. Jacobite in Glengarry's
regiment. Prisoner at Stirling
and Carlisle. Transported
(P)

MCKENZIE DANIEL
33. Servant to Donald Mair, Curmigh
Inverness. Jacobite in Barisdale's
regiment. Prisoner at Inverness,
ship and Tilbury. Transported
(P)

MCKENZIE DANIEL
Perth. Jacobite in the Duke of
Perth's regiment. Prisoner at
Carlisle and Lancaster. Trans-
ported
(P)

MCKENZIE DONALD
25. Inverness. Jacobite in Lovat's
regiment. Prisoner at Inverness.
Transported 20 March 1747
(P)

MCKENZIE DONALD
30. Jacobite in Barisdale's
regiment. Prisoner at Inverness
and Tilbury. Transported 20 March
1747
(P)

MCKENZIE DONALD
35. Husbandman. Letanoch-
glass, Ross. Jacobite in
Cromarty's regiment. Prisoner at Inverness, ships
and Tilbury. Transported
19 March 1747
(P)

MCKENZIE DONALD
20. Husbandman. Ballene,
Ross. Jacobite in Crom-
arty's regiment. Prison-
er at Inverness, ship
and Medway. Transported
20 March 1747
(P)

MCKENZIE DONALD
36. Jacobite in Cromarty's
regiment. Prisoner at
Inverness, ship and Til-
bury. Transported to Jam-
aica or Barbados from London by Samuel Smith 31
March 1747
(P)(RM)

MCKENZIE DONALD
20. Ross. Jacobite in
Cromarty's regiment. Pri-
soner at Inverness, ship
and Tilbury. Transported
from London to Jamaica
or Barbados by Samuel
Smith 31 March 1747
(P)(RM)

MCKENZIE DONALD
40. Farmer. Ballevloide,
Ross. Jacobite in Crom-
arty's regiment. Prison-
er at Inverness, ship
and Tilbury. Transported
from London to Jamaica
or Barbados by Samuel
Smith 31 March 1747
(F)(RM)

MCKENZIE DONALD
25. Castleleod. Jacobite in
Cromarty's regiment. Prisoner
at Inverness, ship and Tilbury.
Transported from London to
Jamaica or Barbados by Samuel
Smith 31 March 1747
(P)(RM)

MCKENZIE DONALD
40. Farmer. Badrallach, Loch
Broom. Jacobite in Cromarty's
regiment. Prisoner at Inverness
and Tilbury. Transported from
London to Barbados or Jamaica
by Samuel Smith 31 March 1747
(P)(RM)

MCKENZIE DONALD
38. Labourer. Jacobite captured
at Carlisle. Prisoner at Carlisle. Transported 21 July 1748
(P)

MCKENZIE DONALD
Tenant of Ivahanny. Jacobite
captain in Cromarty's regiment.
Prisoner at Edinburgh and London.
Transported, 1747(?)
(P)

MCKENZIE DUNCAN
Tailor. Ferryhouse, Locheil,
Argyll. Jacobite in Lochiel's
regiment. Prisoner at Inverness
ship and Tilbury. Transported.
(P)   1747(?)

MCKENZIE DUNCAN
26. Cromarty. Jacobite in
Cromarty's regiment. Prisoner
at Inverness. Transported, 1747
(P)

MCKENZIE DUNCAN
20. Ross. Jacobite in Cromarty's
regiment. Prisoner at Inverness,
ship and Tilbury. Transported
1747(?)
(P)

129

MCKENZIE DUNCAN
18. Ross. Jacobite in
Cromarty's regiment.
Prisoner at Inverness,
ship and Tilbury. Trans-
ported 1747 (?)
(P)

MCKENZIE DUNCAN
40. Farmer. Braemore, Ross.
Jacobite in Cromarty's
regiment. Prisoner at
Inverness, ship and Tilbury
Transported 20 March 1747
(P)

MCKENZIE DUNCAN
27. Husbandman, Ballone,
Ross. Jacobite in Cromarty's
regiment. Prisoner at
Inverness, ships and
Tilbury. Transported
from London to Jamaica or
Barbados by Samuel Smith
31 March 1747
(P)

MCKENZIE ELIZABETH
Spouse of ... Murchison.
Accomplice to murder.
Banished at Inverness,
October 1749
(SM)

MACKENZIE EWAN BUY
Thief. Transported for
life, at Inverness May 1753
(SM)

MCKENZIE GEORGE
32. Ross. Jacobite in
Cromarty's regiment. Prisoner at Inverness, ship
and Tilbury. Transported
from London to Barbados or
Jamaica by Samuel Smith
31 March 1747
(P)(RM)

MCKENZIE GEORGE
32. Farmer. Coigach, Ross.
Jacobite in Cromarty's regiment
Prisoner at Inverness, ship and
Medway. Transported 1747(?)
(P)

MCKENZIE GEORGE
21. Servant to Thomas Urquhart,
Glasslaw, Ross. Jacobite in
Cromarty's regiment. Prisoner
at Inverness, ship and Tilbury.
Transported 20 March 1747
(P)

MCKENZIE HECTOR
45. Forester to Lord Cromarty.
Lochbroom. Jacobite ensign in
Cromarty's regiment. Prisoner
at Dunrobin, Inverness, ship
and London. Banished to America
13 October 1748
(P)

MCKENZIE JAMES
20. Inverness. Jacobite in
Cromarty's regiment. Prisoner
at Inverness and on ship.
Transported 20 March 1747
(P)

MCKENZIE JAMES
22. Tailor. Oolder Hooste,
Inverness. Prisoner at Inver-
ness, ship and Tilbury. Jac-
obite in McIntosh's regiment.
Transported from London to
Jamaica or Barbados by Samuel
Smith 31 March 1747
(P)(RM)

MCKENZIE JAMES
20. Joiner. Suddie, Ross. Jacobite in Cromarty's regiment.
Prisoner at Inverness, ship
and Medway. Transported from
London to Barbados or Jamaica
by Samuel Smith 31 March 1747
(P)(RM)

MACKENZIE JAMES
Pickpocket. Banished to
the Plantations for life
in 1774
(SM)

MCKENZIE JANE
19. Sewer. Inverness.
Jacobite captured at Car-
lisle. Prisoner at Car-
lisle and York. Transported from Liverpool for the
Leeward Islands 5 May 1747
on the Veteran, master
John Ricky. Liberated by
a French privateer and
landed on Martinique June
1747
(P)(RM)

MCKENZIE JOHN
20. Weaver. Achtonshiel,
Ross. Jacobite in Crom-
arty's regiment. Pris-
oner at Inverness, ship
and Tilbury. Transported
from London to Barbados
or Jamaica by Samuel
Smith 31 March 1747
(P)(RM)

MCKENZIE JOHN
56. Farmer. Dormie, Ross.
Jacobite in Cromarty's
regiment. Prisoner at
Inverness, ship and Til-
bury. Transported from
London to Barbados or
Jamaica by Samuel Smith
31 March 1747
(P)(RM)

MCKENZIE JOHN
28. Achtermead, Ross.
Jacobite in Cromarty's
regiment. Prisoner at
Inverness, ship and Til-
bury. Transported from
London to Barbados or
Jamaica by Samuel Smith
31 March 1747
(P)(RM)

MCKENZIE JOHN
38. Servant to John Stuart.
Ross. Jacobite in Cromarty's
regiment. Prisoner at Inverness
ship and Tilbury. Transported
from London to Jamaica or Barbados by Samuel Smith 31 March
1747
(P)(RM)

MCKENZIE JOHN
20. Servant to Mr Dingwall.
Strathpeffer, Ross. Jacobite in
Cromarty's regiment. Prisoner
at Inverness, ship and Tilbury.
Transported from London to Barbados or Jamaica by Samuel Smith
31 March 1747
(P)(RM)

MCKENZIE JOHN
50. Husbandman. Dingwall. Jac-
obite in Cromarty's regiment.
Prisoner at Inverness, ship and
Tilbury. Transported from London
to Jamaica or Barbados by Samuel
Smith 31 March 1747
(P)(RM)

MCKENZIE JOHN
40. Farmer. Dornoch. Jacobite in
Cromarty's regiment. Prisoner at
Inverness, ship and Tilbury.
Transported from London to Jam-
aica or Barbados by Samuel Smith
31 March 1747
(P)(RM)

MCKENZIE JOHN
32. Gentleman. Ardloch, Assynt.
Jacobite captain in Cromarty's
regiment. Prisoner at Carlisle
and Lancaster. Transported from
Liverpool for the Leeward Islands
on the Veteran, master John Ricky
5 May 1747. Liberated by a French
privateer and landed on Martinique
June 1747
(P)(RM)

MCKENZIE KENNETH
19. Husbandman. Little
Strath, Ross. Jacobite
in Cromarty's regiment.
Prisoner at Inverness.
Transported from London
to Jamaica or Barbados
by Samuel Smith 31
March 1747
(P)(RM)

MCKENZIE JOHN
27. Cromarty. Jacobite
in Cromarty's regiment.
Prisoner at Inverness.
Transported 1747(?)
(P)

MCKENZIE JOHN
18. Servant to Colin
McKenzie. Logie, Ross.
Jacobite in Cromarty's
regiment. Prisoner at
Inverness, ship and
Medway. Transported
20 March 1747
(P)

MCKENZIE JOHN
40. Farmer. Logie, Ross.
Jacobite in Cromarty's
regiment. Prisoner at
Inverness, ship and
Medway. Transported 20
March 1747
(P)

MCKENZIE JOHN
45. Farmer. Auchterdon-
ald, Ross. Jacobite in
Cromarty's regiment.
Prisoner at Inverness,
ship and Medway. Trans-
ported 20 March 1747
(P)

MCKENZIE JOHN
36. Farmer. Ashlet,
Ross. Jacobite in
Cromarty's regiment.
Prisoner at Inverness,
ship and Medway. Trans-
ported 20 March 1747
(P)

MCKENZIE KENNETH
30. Farmer. Aschellach, Ross.
Jacobite in Cromarty's regiment.
Prisoner at Inverness, ship and
Tilbury. Transported 20 March
1747
(P)

MCKENZIE KENNETH
21. Ross. Jacobite in Cromarty's
regiment. Prisoner at Inverness,
ship and Tilbury. Transported
19 March 1747
(P)

MCKENZIE KENNETH
19. Husbandman. Lochmallin, Ross.
Jacobite in Cromarty's regiment.
Prisoner at Inverness, ship and
Medway. Transported 19 March 1747
(P)

MCKENZIE KENNETH
30. Husbandman. Ballon, Ross.
Jacobite in Cromarty's regiment.
Prisoner at Inverness, ships
and Medway. Transported from
London to Jamaica or Barbados
by Samuel Smith 31 March 1747
(P)(RM)

MCKENZIE KENNETH
55. Farmer. Invervaigh, Lochbroom. Jacobite in Cromarty's
regiment. Prisoner at Inverness,
ship and Tilbury. Transported
19 March 1747
(P)

MCKENZIE KENNETH
32. Farmer. Bullon, Ross. Jac-
obite in Cromarty's regiment.
Prisoner at Inverness, ship and
Tilbury. Transported from London
to Jamaica or Barbados by Samuel
Smith 31 March 1747
(P)(RM)

MCKENZIE KENNETH
26. Lochbroom, Ross. Jacobite in
Cromarty's regiment. Prisoner at
Inverness, ship and Tilbury.
Transported from London to Jam-
aica or Barbados by Samuel Smith
31 March 1747
(P)(RM)

MCKENZIE KENNETH
38. Servant to Alexander
Mansel. Ross. Jacobite
in Cromarty's regiment.
Prisoner at Inverness,
ship and Tilbury. Trans-
ported from London to
Jamaica or Barbados by
Samuel Smith 31 March
1747
(P)(RM)

MCKENZIE KENNETH
22. Servant to the
Minister at Contin, Ross.
Jacobite in Barisdale's
regiment. Prisoner at
Inverness, ship and
Medway. Transported to
Jamaica or Barbados from
London by Samuel Smith
31 March 1747
(P)(RM)

MCKENZIE LEWIS
21. Apprentice joiner.
Elgin. Jacobite in Crom-
arty's regiment. Prisoner
at Inverness, ship and
Tilbury. Transported
April 1747
(P)

MCKENZIE MARY
20. Spinner. Lochaber.
Jacobite captured at Car-
lisle. Prisoner at Car-
lisle and Lancaster.
Transported from Liverpool
for the Leeward Islands on
the Veteran, master John
Ricky, 5 May 1747. Liber-
ated by a French privateer
and landed on Martinique
June 1747
(P)(RM)

MCKENZIE MURDOCH
22. Servant to Format
McLeod. Ross. Jacobite
in Cromarty's regiment.
Prisoner at Inverness,
ship and Tilbury. Trans-
ported from London to
Jamaica or Barbados by
Samuel Smith 31 March 1747
(P)(RM)

MCKENZIE MURDOCH
20. Herdsman. Tully, Dingwall.
Jacobite in Cromarty's regiment.
Prisoner at Inverness, ship and
Tilbury. Transported from London
to Jamaica or Barbados by Samuel
Smith 31 March 1747
(P)(RM)

MCKENZIE MURDOCH
40. Farmer. Strathnacalliach,
Ross. Jacobite in Cromarty's
regiment. Prisoner at Inverness.
Transported from London to Jamaica or Barbados by Samuel Smith
31 March 1747
(P)(RM)

MCKENZIE RODERICK or ROGER
56. Husbandman. Logie. Caithness.
Jacobite in Cromarty's regiment.
Prisoner at Inverness, ship and
Medway. Transported from London
to Barbados or Jamaica by Samuel
Smith 31 March 1747
(P)(RM)

MCKENZIE RODERICK or ROGER
26. Servant to the Minister of
Lochbroom. Jacobite in Cromarty's
regiment. Prisoner at Inverness,
ship and Medway. Transported
from London to Jamaica or Barbados
by Samuel Smith 31 March 1747
(P)(RM)

MCKENZIE RODERICK
36. Farmer. Lochbroom. Jacobite
in Cromarty's regiment. Prisoner
at Inverness, ship and Medway.
Transported 20 March 1747
(P)

MCKENZIE RORY
56. Husbandman. Little Strath,
Ross. Jacobite in Cromarty's
regiment. Prisoner at Inverness
and Tilbury. Transported 20 March
1747
(P)

MCKENZIE RORY or RODERICK
23. Husbandman. Strathna-
cailliach, Ross. Jacobite
in Cromarty's regiment.
Prisoner at Inverness,
ship and Medway. Trans-
ported 1747(?)
(P)

MCKENZIE RORY
26. Ross. Jacobite in
Cromarty's regiment.
Prisoner at Inverness,
ship and Tilbury. Trans-
ported 20 March 1747
(P)

MCKENZIE THOMAS
Jacobite captured at
Preston. Transported
from Liverpool to
St Kitts on the Hocken-
hill, master H. Short,
25 June 1716
(CTB)(SP/C)

MCKENZIE WILLIAM
Jacobite captured at
Preston. Transported
from Liverpool to
South Carolina on the
Wakefield, master
Thomas Beck, 21 April
1716
(CTB)(SP/C)

MCKENZIE WILLIAM
21. Ross. Jacobite in
Cromarty's regiment.
Prisoner at Inverness.
Transported 1747(?)
(P)

MCKENZIE WILLIAM
36. Husbandman. Banff.
From Ross. Jacobite in
Cromarty's regiment.
Prisoner at Inverness,
ship and Medway. Trans-
ported 1747(?)
(P)

MACKETH NEIL
Royalist soldier captured at
Worcester. Transported from
Gravesend to Boston on the
John and Sarah, master John
Greene, 13 May 1652
(NER)

MCKETHRICK JOHN
Son of William Mackitterick or
McKethrick, carter in Bridgend
of Dumfries. Rioter in Dumfries.
Banished to the Plantations for
7 years in 1771. Transported on
the Matty, master Robert Peacock,
from Port Glasgow. Landed at
Port Oxford, Maryland, 17 December 1771
(JC)

MACKIE ALEXANDER
Forger. Banished to the Plant-
ations for life, at Glasgow 1773
(SM)

MACKIE DANIEL
18. Labourer. Moray. Jacobite.
Prisoner at Carlisle and York.
Transported from Liverpool to
the Leeward Islands on the
Veteran, master John Ricky,
5 May 1747. Liberated by a
French privateer and landed on
Martinique June 1747
(P)(RM)

MACKIE HILL
Royalist soldier captured at
Worcester. Transported from
Gravesend to Boston on the
John and Sarah, master John Greene
13 May 1652
(NER)

MACKIE JANET
Prisoner in Edinburgh Tolbooth.
Transported from Greenock to
New York 21 October 1682
(ETR)

MACKIE RORY
Royalist soldier captured
at Worcester. Transported
from Gravesend to Boston
on the John and Sarah,
master John Greene,13 May
1652
(NER)

MCKIE TASKEL
60. Former soldier. Inver
ness. Jacobite in Crom-
arty's regiment. Prisoner
at Inverness, ship and
Medway. Transported from
London to Jamaica or Bar
bados by Samuel Smith
31 March 1747
(P)(RM)

MACKIE ROBERT
Ostler. Brechin. Jacob-
ite in Ogilvy's regiment.
Prisoner at Charlestown,
Montrose, Inverness and
Tilbury. Transported
20 March 1747
(P)

MCKILLON DONALD
Glendarvel. Covenanter
in Argyll's rebellion.
Banished to the Plant-
ations 30 July 1685.
Transported from Leith
to Jamaica by John Ewing
August 1685
(PC)

MCKINLAY NEIL
Tenant of McLay. Covenanter
in Argyll's rebellion. Prisoner in the Laigh Parliament
House, Edinburgh. Banished
to the Plantations 31 July
1685. Transported from Leith
to Jamaica by John Ewing
August 1685
(PC)

MCKINNEY DONALD
Jacobite. Transported from
Liverpool on the Gildart.
Landed Port North Potomac,
Maryland 5 August 1747
(PRO)

MCKINNON ALEXANDER
Pipemaker. Formerly in Glasgow
lately in Edinburgh. Slander.
Prisoner in Edinburgh Tolbooth.
Transported from Leith to Bar-
bados on William Johnston's
ship The Blossom, 10 August 1680
(ETR)(PC)

MCKINNON DONALD
40. Skye. Jacobite in Clanranalds
regiment. Prisoner at Inverness
and Tilbury. Transported from
London to Jamaica or Barbados
by Samuel Smith 31 March 1747
(P)(RM)

MCKINNON JOHN
Duppen of Kintyre. Covenanter
in Argyll's rebellion. Prisoner
in Paul's Work, Edinburgh. Banished to the Plantations 24 July
1685. Transported from Leith to
Jamaica by John Ewing August 1685
(PC)

MCKINVINE DUNCAN
Servant to Duncan McIlvra, Beach
in Ross, Argyll. Adulterer and
accomplice to child murder.
Transported to Virginia 2 August
1733
(JC)

MCKIRRECH ARCHIBALD
Covenanter in Argyll's rebellion.
Prisoner in the Laigh Parliament
House, Edinburgh. Banished to the
Plantations 31 July 1685. Trans-
ported from Leith to Jamaica by
John Ewing August 1685
(PC)

MCKISSOCK DUNCAN
60. Jacobite in Clanranald's
regiment. Prisoner at Inverness,
ship and Tilbury. Transported
20 March 1747
(P)

MACKNITH DANIEL
Royalist soldier captured
at Worcester. Transported
from Gravesend to Boston
on the John and Sarah,
master John Greene, 13
May 1652
(NER)

MACKNITH PATRICK
Royalist soldier captured
at Worcester. Transported
from Gravesend to Boston
on the John and Sarah,
master John Greene,
13 May 1652
(NER)

MACKTRETH PATRICK
Royalist soldier captured
at Worcester. Transported
from Gravesend to Boston
on the John and Sarah,
13 May 1652
(NER)

MCLACHLAN ARCHIBALD
Tenant of McLachlan of
Craigintervie. Covenanter
in Argyll's rebellion.
Prisoner in Paul's Work,
Edinburgh. Banished to
the Plantations 30 July
1685
(PC)

MCLACHLAN DONALD
Covenanter in Argyll's
rebellion. Prisoner in
Paul's Work, Edinburgh.
Banished to the Plant-
ations 30 July 1685.
Transported from Leith
to Jamaica by John Ewing
August 1685
(PC)

MCLACHLAN DOUGAL
59. Husbandman. Argyll.
Jacobite in McLachlan's
regiment. Prisoner at
Blackness, Edinburgh
and Carlisle. Transported
1747(?)
(P)

MCLACHLAN JOHN DOW
Achahouse, Argyll. Covenanter
in Argyll's rebellion. Prisoner
in Paul's Work, Edinburgh. Banished to the Plantations 24 July
1685. Transported from Leith to
Jamaica by John Ewing August 1685
(PC)

MCLACHLAN PETER
40. Weaver. Fochabers, Moray.
Jacobite in Glenbucket's regi-
ment. Prisoner at Carlisle and
Chester. Transported from Liver-
pool on the Johnson, master
William Pemberton, 5 May 1747.
Landed at Port Oxford, Maryland
5 August 1747
(P)(PRO)

MCLAREN DANIEL
Jacobite captured at Preston.
Transported from Liverpool to
Antigua on the Scipio, master
John Scaisbrick, 30 March 1716
(CTB)(SP/C)

MCLAREN DUNCAN
Perthshire. Jacobite in the
Atholl Brigade. Prisoner at
Perth and Carlisle. Transported
1747(?)
(P)

MCLAREN JAMES
Jacobite captured at Preston.
Transported from Liverpool to
Virginia on the Godspeed, master
Arthur Smith, 28 July 1716.
Sold to Randall Garland in
Maryland 17 October 1716
(SP/C)(CTB)(HM)

MCLAREN JANET
Adultery. Banished to the Plant-
ations, at Stirling 1752
(SM)

MCLAREN JOHN
Jacobite captured at Preston.
Transported from Liverpool to
Antigua on the Scipio, master
John Scaisbrick, 30 March 1716
(CTB)(SP/C)

MCLAREN JOHN
Jacobite captured at Pres-
ton. Transported from
Liverpool to Antigua on
the Scipio, master John
Scaisbrick, 30 March 1716
(CTB)(SP/C)

MCLAREN JOHN
Jacobite captured at Pres-
ton. Transported from
Liverpool to South Carol-
ina on the Susannah, master
Thomas Bromhall, 7 May 1716
(CTB)(SP/C)

MCLAREN JOHN or MCLEARN
Weaver. Paisley. Thief.
Prisoner in Edinburgh Tol-
booth. Banished to the
Plantations in America for
life, at Edinburgh 15 March
1765
(JC)

MCLAREN PATRICK
Jacobite captured at Pres-
ton. Transported from
Liverpool to South Carol-
ina on the Susannah, master
Thomas Bromhall, 7 May 1716
(CTB)(SP/C)

MCLAREN WALTER
Jacobite captured at Pres-
ton. Transported from
Liverpool to St Kitts on
the Hockenhill, master
H.Short, 25 June 1716
(CTB)(SP/C)

MCLEA DOUGAL
16. Jacobite in McIntosh's
regiment. Prisoner at
Inverness and Tilbury.
Transported 1747(?)
(P)

MCLEA JOHN
Flesher. Glasgow. Thief.
Banished to the Plantat-
ions in the British West
Indies for life, at Glas-
gow 20 September 1775
(SM)

MCLEAN ALEXANDER
Transported from Leith to
Jamaica by John Ewing August
1685
(PC)

MCLEAN ALEXANDER
Jacobite captured at Preston.
Transported from Liverpool to
South Carolina on the Wakefield,
master Thomas Beck, 21 April 1716
(CTB)(SP/C)

MCLEAN ALEXANDER
40. Ross. Jacobite in Cromarty's
regiment. Prisoner at Inverness,
ship and Tilbury. Transported
20 March 1747
(P)

MCLEAN ALEXANDER
Pedlar. Inverness. Jacobite in
the Atholl Brigade. Prisoner at
Winsley, Chester and York.
Transported 1747(?)
(P)

MCLEAN ALLAN
Jacobite captured at Preston,
Transported from Liverpool to
Maryland on the Friendship,
master Michael Mankin, 24 May
1716. Sold to Thomas McNemara
in Maryland 20 August 1716
(CTB)(SP/C)(HM)

MCLEAN ANDREW
Covenanter in Argyll's rebellion.
Prisoner in Edinburgh Tolbooth.
Banished to the Plantations
31 July 1685. Stigmatised. Trans-
ported from Leith to Jamaica by
John Ewing August 1685
(PC)

MCLEAN ANGUS
Prisoner in Edinburgh Tolbooth.
Transported from Leith to Barbados by George Hutchison, merchant in Edinburgh, 7 December
1665
(ETR)

MCLEAN ANGUS
43. Farmer. Eigg. Jacobite
in Clanranald's regiment.
Prisoner at Inverness, ship
and Tilbury. Transported
from London to Barbados or
Jamaica by Samuel Smith
31 March 1747
(P)(RM)

MCLEAN DANIEL
Jacobite captured at Pres-
ton. Transported from
Liverpool to Jamaica on
the Two Brothers, master
Edward Rathbone, 26 April
1716. Landed on Montserrat
June 1716
(SP/C)(CTB)(CTP)

MCLEAN DOUGAL
16. Labourer. Ross. Jac-
obite in McIntosh's regi-
ment. Prisoner at Inver-
ness, ship and Tilbury.
Transported from London
to Barbados or Jamaica
by Samuel Smith 31 March
1747
(P)(RM)

MCLEAN DUNCAN
Covenanter in Argyll's
rebellion. Prisoner in
Paul's Work, Edinburgh.
Banished to the Plant-
ations 30 July 1685
(PC)

MCLEAN DUNCAN
42. Farmer. Dormie, Ross.
Jacobite in Cromarty's
regiment. Prisoner at
Inverness, ship and Til-
bury. Transported from
London to Barbados or
Jamaica by Samuel Smith
31 March 1747
(P)(RM)

MACLEAN DUNCAN
Sailor. Thief. Banished
to the Plantations for
5 years, at Inverness
20 May 1775
(SM)

MCLEAN FARQUHAR
Ross. Jacobite in Cromarty's
regiment. Prisoner at Inverness,
and ship. Transported from
London to Barbados or Jamaica
by Samuel Smith 31 March 1747
(P)(RM)

MCLEAN HECTOR
44. Farmer. Langwell, Ross. Jac-
obite in Cromarty's regiment.
Prisoner at Inverness and Tilbury.
Transported from London to Jamaica
or Barbados by Samuel Smith 31
March 1747
(P)(RM)

MCLEAN HECTOR
40. Cromarty. Jacobite in Crom-
arty's regiment. Prisoner at
Inverness, ship and Tilbury.
Transported 20 March 1747
(P)

MCLEAN HUGH
Covenanter in Argyll's rebellion.
Prisoner in Paul's Work, Edinburgh
Banished to the Plantations 30
July 1685. Transported from London
to Barbados or Jamaica by John
Ewing August 1685
(PC)

MCLEAN JAMES
19. Nailmaker. Stirling. Jacobite
in the Duke of Perth's regiment.
Captured at Carlisle. Prisoner at
Carlisle, York and Lincoln. Transported from Liverpool for the Leeward Islands on the Veteran, master
John Ricky, 5 May 1747. Liberated
by a French privateer and landed
on Martinique June 1747
(P)(RM)

MACLEAN JAMES
Gateside, East Lothian. Burglar.
Banished to the Plantations for
life, at Stirling 28 April 1774
(SM)

MCLEAN JOHN
Covenanter. Prisoner in Edinburgh
Tolbooth. Banished to the Plant-
ations 24 July 1685
(PC)

MCLEAN JOHN
Portindryan. Covenanter
in Argyll's rebellion.
Prisoner at Glasgow,
Edinburgh Tolbooth and
Paul's Work, Edinburgh.
Banished to the Plant-
ations 30 July 1685.
Transported from Leith
to Jamaica by John Ewing
August 1685
(PC)

MCLEAN JOHN
Jacobite captured at
Preston. Transported
from Liverpool to South
Carolina on the Wake-
field, master Thomas
Beck, 21 April 1716
(CTB)(SP/C)

MACLEAN JOHN
Jacobite captured at
Preston. Transported
from Liverpool to Mary-
land on the Friendship,
master Michael Mankin,
24 May 1716. Sold to
Edward Parish in Mary-
land 20 August 1716
(HM)

MACLEAN JOHN
Gardener. Laagg, Eigg.
Jacobite in Clanranald's
regiment. Prisoner at
Tilbury. Transported
1747(?)
(P)

MCLEAN JOHN
16. Labourer. Argyll.
Jacobite in McLachlan's
regiment. Prisoner at
Inverness, ship and
Tilbury. Transported
from London to Jamaica
or Barbados by Samuel
Smith 31 March 1747
(P)(RM)

MCLEAN JOHN
25. Jacobite in Clan-
ranald's regiment.
Prisoner at Inverness
and Tilbury. Transported
1747(?)   (P)

MCLEAN JOHN
Jacobite transported from Liver-
pool on the Gildart, master
Richard Holmes, 5 May 1747.
Landed at Port North Potomac,
Maryland 5 August 1747
(PRO)

MCLEAN MALCOLM
17. Bricklayer. Jacobite.
Prisoner at Carlisle. Transported
from Liverpool on the Gildart,
master Richard Holmes, 5 May 1747
Landed at Port North Potomac,
Maryland 5 August 1747
(P)(PRO)

MCLEAN MARY
Spouse of Archibald McGowan or
McDonald, Argyll. Adultress who
murdered her illegitimate child.
Transported to Virginia 2 August
1733
(JC)

MCLEAN NEIL alias WILLIAM CAMPBELL
Son of Gillian McLean, cottar in
Kilmichael. Banished to America
for life, at Inveraray September
1772. Transported from Port Glas-
gow on the Phoenix, master John
Lamont. Landed at Port Accomack,
Virginia 20 December 1772
(JC)

MCLEAN OWEN
Weaver. Tullohghallan, Strathearn.
Jacobite in Glenbucket's regiment.
Captured at Carlisle. Prisoner at
Carlisle and Chester. Transported
1747(?)
(P)

MCLEAN PETER
Jacobite captured at Preston.
Transported from Liverpool to
Antigua on the Scipio, master
John Scaisbrick, 30 March 1716
(CTB)(SP/C)

MCLEAN PETER
28. Corporal in French
Service. Jacobite
captured at Carlisle.
Prisoner at Carlisle
and York. Transported
1747(?)
(P)

MCLEAN THOMAS
25. Servant to Murdoch
McKenzie of Auchterlin-
tor, Ross. Jacobite in
Cromarty's regiment.
Prisoner at Inverness,
ship and Tilbury. Trans-
ported from London to
Barbados or Jamaica by
Samuel Smith 31 March
1747
(P)(RM)

MCLEAN WILLIAM
Covenanter. Prisoner
in Edinburgh Tolbooth.
Banished to the Plant-
ations 24 July 1685
(PC)

MCLEAN WILLIAM
32. Labourer. Inverness
Jacobite. Prisoner at
Carlisle and York. Trans-
ported from Liverpool to
the Leeward Islands on
the Veteran, master John
Ricky, 5 May 1747. Lib-
erated by a French priv-
ateer and landed on
Martinique June 1747
(P)(RM)

MCLEAN WILLIAM
14. Lochbroom. Jacobite
in Cromarty's regiment.
Prisoner at Inverness,
ship and Tilbury. Trans-
ported 1747(?)
(P)

MCLEAR ALEXANDER
Jacobite captured at Preston.
Transported from Liverpool on
the Two Brothers, master Edward
Rathbone, for Jamaica 26 April
1716. Landed on Montserrat
June 1716
(SP/C)(CTP)

MCLEARINS ALEXANDER
Jacobite captured at Preston.
Transported from Liverpool to
Antigua on the Scipio, master
John Scaisbrick, 30 March 1716
(CTB)(SP/C)

MCLEISH DUNCAN
18. Pedlar. Perthshire. Jacobite
in the Duke of Perth's regiment.
Prisoner at Edinburgh, Carlisle
and Lincoln. Transported from
Liverpool for the Leeward Islands
on the Veteran, master John Ricky
5 May 1747. Liberated by a French
privateer and landed on Martinique June 1747
(P)(RM)

MCLELAN MARGARET
Covenanter. Prisoner at Dumfries,
Dunnottar and Leith. Banished to
the Plantations, at Leith 18 August 1685. Transported from Leith
to East New Jersey by George Scott
of Pitlochie on the Henry and
Francis, master Richard Hutton,
5 September 1685
(PC)

MCLELLAN RODERICK
25. Farmer. Achtascaild, Ross.
Jacobite in Cromarty's regiment.
Prisoner at Inverness and Tilbury.
Transported from London to Jamaica
or Barbados by Samuel Smith 31
March 1747
(P)(RM)

MCLENNAN ANGUS
Farmer. Morar. Jacobite in Glen-
garry's regiment. Prisoner at
Inverness, ship and Tilbury. Trans
ported 20 March 1747
(P)

MCLENNAN ANGUS
33. Farmer. Burblach,
Morar. Jacobite in
Glengarry's regiment.
Prisoner at Inverness,
ship and Tilbury.
Transported from Lon-
don to Barbados or
Jamaica by Samuel
Smith 31 March 1747
(P)(RM)

MCLENNAN DONALD
Farmer. Burblach,
Morar. Jacobite in
Glengarry's regiment.
Prisoner at Inverness
ship and Tilbury.
Transported from
London to Jamaica or
Barbados by Samuel
Smith 31 March 1747
(P)(RM)

MCLENNAN DONALD
Farmer. Kilconan,
Inverness. Jacobite
in Glengarry's regi-
ment. Prisoner at
Inverness, ship and
Tilbury. Transported
20 March 1747
(P)

MCLENNAN DUNCAN
43. Dairyman. Ross.
Jacobite in Cromarty's
regiment. Prisoner at
Inverness, ship and
Tilbury. Transported
20 March 1747 from
London to Barbados
or Jamaica by Samuel
Smith
(P)(RM)

MCLENNAN FARQUHAR
38. Farmer. Burt, Glen-
garry. Jacobite in
Glengarry's regiment.
Prisoner at Tilbury.
Transported 1747(?)
(P)

MCLENNAN JOHN
33. Tailor. Inverness. Jacobite
in Glengarry's regiment. Prisoner at Inverness, ship and
Tilbury. Transported from London
to Jamaica or Barbados by Samuel
Smith 31 March 1747
(P)(RM)

MCLENNAN RODERICK
25. Farmer. Achtascaild, Ross.
Jacobite in Cromarty's regiment.
Prisoner at Inverness and Tilbury
Transported from London to Jam-
aica or Barbados by Samuel Smith
31 March 1747
(P)(RM)

MCLEOD ALEXANDER
19. Labourer. Inverness. Jac-
obite in Glengarry's regiment.
Prisoner at Carlisle and York.
Transported from Liverpool to
the Leeward Islands on the
Veteran, master John Ricky,
5 May 1747. Liberated by a
French privateer and landed on
Martinique June 1747
(P)(RM)

MCLEOD ALEXANDER
40. Ploughman. Lochbroom.
Jacobite in Cromarty's regiment.
Prisoner at Inverness, ship and
Tilbury. Transported 1747(?)
(P)

MCLEOD ALEXANDER
26. Farmer. Kerogarreoch, Lochbroom. Jacobite in Cromarty's
regiment. Prisoner at Inverness,
ship and Tilbury. Transported
from London to Barbados or Jamaica by Samuel Smith 31 March
1747
(P)(RM)

MCLEOD ALEXANDER
50. Husbandman. Dingwall.
Jacobite in Cromarty's
regiment. Prisoner at
Inverness, ship and Til-
bury. Transported 20
March 1747
(P)

MCLEOD ALEXANDER
30. Inverness. Jacobite
in Lochiel's regiment.
Prisoner at Culloden,
Inverness and ship.
Transported 1747(?)
(P)

MCLEOD ALEXANDER
50. Army deserter.
Nithsdale. Jacobite.
Prisoner at Perth,
Stirling, Carlisle,
York and Lancaster.
Transported 1747(?)
(P)

MCLEOD ANGUS
35. Labourer. Inverness.
Jacobite. Prisoner at
Carlisle and York. Trans
ported from Liverpool on
the Johnson, master Will
iam Pemberton. Landed at
Port Oxford, Maryland
5 August 1747
(P)(PRO)

MCLEOD ANGUS
Transported on the Rain-
bow, master William
Gordon, from Greenock.
Landed at Port Hampton,
Virginia 3 May 1775
(JC)

MCLEOD DANIEL
44. Ross. Jacobite in
Cromarty's regiment.
Prisoner at Inverness,
ship and Tilbury. Trans-
ported from London to
Barbados or Jamaica by
Samuel Smith 1747
(P)(RM)

MCLEOD DONALD
44. Farmer. Coigach, Ross.
Jacobite in Cromarty's regiment.
Prisoner at Inverness, ship and
Medway. Transported from London
to Jamaica or Barbados by Samuel
Smith 20 March 1747
(P)(RM)

MCLEOD DONALD
26. Farmer. Crosshill, Ross.
Jacobite in Lovat's regiment.
Prisoner at Inverness, ship and
Medway. Transported from London
to Jamaica or Barbados by Samuel
Smith 31 March 1747
(P)(RM)

MCLEOD DONALD
22. Servant to Alexander McLeod.
Coigach, Ross. Jacobite in Cromarty's regiment. Prisoner at
Inverness, ship and Tilbury.
Transported from London to Jamaica or Barbados by Samuel Smith
31 March 1747
(P)(RM)

MCLEOD DUNCAN
19. Army deserter. Inverness.
Jacobite in Cromarty's regiment.
Prisoner at Inverness, ships and
Tilbury. Transported 31 March
1747
(P)

MCLEOD DUNCAN
24. Cromarty. Jacobite in
Cromarty's regiment. Prisoner
at Inverness and ship. Transported 20 March 1747
(P)

MCLEOD DUNCAN
23. Ross. Jacobite in Cromarty's
regiment. Prisoner at Inverness
and ship. Transported 20 March
1747
(P)

MCLEOD HENRIETTA
Spouse of Angus McLeod.
Transported from Greenock
on the Rainbow, master
William Gordon. Landed
at Port Hampton, Virginia
3 May 1775
(JC)

MCLEOD HUGH alias
        JAMES MCBAIN
Thief. Banished to the
Plantations for life, at
Aberdeen 18 May 1769
(SM)

MACLEOD JOHN
Royalist soldier captured
at Worcester. Transported
from Gravesend to Boston
on the John and Sarah,
master John Greene, 13 May
1652
(NER)

MCLEOD JOHN
Jacobite captured at Preston. Transported from
Liverpool to South Carol-
ina on the Wakefield,
master Thomas Beck,
21 April 1716
(CTB)(SP/C)

MCLEOD JOHN
25. Labourer. Jacobite
in Cromarty's regiment.
Prisoner at Carlisle and
York. Transported from
Liverpool for the Leeward
Islands on the Veteran,
master John Ricky, 5 May
1747. Liberated by a
French privateer and
landed on Martinique
June 1747
(P)(RM)

MCLEOD JOHN
40. Cook. Glenelg. Jacobite.
Prisoner at Inverness, ship
and Tilbury. Transported
from London to Barbados or
Jamaica by Samuel Smith 31
March 1747
(P)(RM)

MCLEOD JOHN
18. Cattleherd. Ross. Jacobite
in Cromarty's regiment.
Prisoner at Inverness, ship
and Tilbury. Transported from
London to Barbados or Jamaica
by Samuel Smith 31 March 1747
(P)(RM)

MCLEOD JOHN
21. Servant to McKenzie of
Langwell, Lochbroom. Jacobite
in Cromarty's regiment. Prisoner at Inverness, ship and
Tilbury. Transported from
London to Jamaica or Barbados
by Samuel Smith 31 March 1747
(P)(RM)

MCLEOD JOHN
57. Farmer. Ullapool, Lochbroom.
Jacobite in Cromarty's regiment.
Prisoner at Inverness, ship and
Tilbury. Transported from London
to Jamaica or Barbados by Samuel
Smith 31 March 1747
(P)(RM)

MCLEOD JOHN
41. Farmer. Dormie, Ross. Jacobite in Cromarty's regiment.
Prisoner at Inverness, ship
and Tilbury. Transported 20
March 1747
(P)

MCLEOD KENNETH
Jacobite. Prisoner at
Edinburgh and Carlisle.
Transported from Liver-
pool on the Gildart,
master Richard Holmes.
Landed at Port North
Potomac, Maryland 5
August 1747
(P)(PRO)

MCLEOD MURDOCH
21. Servant to Duncan
Simpson of Ferintosh,
Ross. Jacobite in
Cromarty's regiment.
Prisoner at Inverness,
ship and Tilbury. Trans-
ported from London to
Jamaica or Barbados by
Samuel Smith 31 March
1747
(P)(RM)

MCLEOD MURDOCH
18. Herdsman to Kenneth
McKenzie of Asson, Ross.
Jacobite in Cromarty's
regiment. Prisoner at
Inverness, ship and Til-
bury. Transported from
London to Barbados or
Jamaica by Samuel Smith
31 March 1747
(P)(RM)

MCLEOD MURDOCH
45. Farmer. Skye. Jacob-
ite in Glengarry's regi-
ment. Prisoner at Inver-
ness, ship and Medway.
Transported from London
to Jamaica or Barbados
by Samuel Smith 31 March
1747
(P)(RM)

MACLEOD 'MURTLE'
Royalist soldier captured
at Worcester. Transported
from Gravesend to Boston
on the John and Sarah,
master John Greene, 13
May 1652
(NER)

MCLEOD NEIL
21. Husbandman. Hillach, Raasay.
Jacobite in Raasay's regiment.
Prisoner at Inverness, ship
and Tilbury. Transported from
London to Barbados or Jamaica
by Samuel Smith 20 March 1747
(P)(RM)

MCLEOD RODERICK
20. Langwell, Ross. Jacobite
in Cromarty's regiment. Prisoner at Inverness, ship and
Tilbury. Transported from
London to Jamaica or Barbados
by Samuel Smith 31 March 1747
(P)(RM)

MCLEOD SAUNDERS
55. Jacobite in Cromarty's
regiment. Prisoner at Inverness
and Tilbury. Transported
31 March 1747
(P)

MCLINE ALEXANDER
Covenanter in Argyll's rebellion.
Prisoner in the Laigh Parliament
House, Edinburgh. Banished to the
Plantations 30 July 1685. Trans-
ported from Leith to Jamaica by
John Ewing August 1685
(PC)

MCLOUGHLIN ARCHIBALD
Jacobite captured at Preston.
Transported from Liverpool to
Virginia or Jamaica on the
Elizabeth and Anne, master
Edward Trafford, 29 June 1716
(SP/C)(CTB)

MCLOUGHLAN JOHN
Jacobite captured at Preston.
Transported from Liverpool to
Maryland or Virginia on the
Friendship, master Michael
Mankin, 24 May 1716
(CTB)(SP/C)

MCMARTIN ANGUS
18. Cowherd. Kirkton,
Eigg. Jacobite in Clan-
ranald's regiment. Pris-
oner at Inverness, ship
and Tilbury. Transported
from London to Jamaica
or Barbados by Samuel
Smith 31 March 1747
(P)(RM)

MCMARTIN ANGUS
20. Jacobite in Clan-
ranald's regiment.
Prisoner at Inverness,
ship and Tilbury. Trans-
ported from London to
Jamaica or Barbados by
Samuel Smith 31 March
1747
(P)(RM)

MCMASTER MALCOLM
60. Husbandman. Fort
William. Jacobite.
Prisoner at Inverness,
ship and Medway. Trans-
ported from London to
Jamaica or Barbados by
Samuel Smith 31 March
1747
(P)(RM)

MCMICHAEL DUNCAN
Islay. Covenanter in
Argyll's rebellion.
Captured at Dumbarton.
Prisoner in Laigh Parl-
iament House, Edinburgh.
Banished to the Plant-
ations 30 July 1685.
Transported from Leith
to Jamaica by John
Ewing August 1685
(PC)

MCMICHAEL ROGER
Dalry, Galloway. Cov-
enanter. Prisoner in
Laigh Parliament House,
Edinburgh. Banished to
the Plantations 31
July 1685. Transported
from Leith to Jamaica
by John Ewing August
1685
(PC)

MCMILLAN ALEXANDER
Covenanter. Galloway. Prisoner
in Canongate Tolbooth. Transported from Leith to the
Plantations in America by
Alexander Fearne and his shipmaster Edward Barnes December
1685
(ETR)

MCMILLAN DONALD
30. Sheuglie, Glenurquhart,
Jacobite in Glengarry's regiment. Prisoner at Inverness
and ship. Transported but
returned to Scotland
(P)

MCMILLAN DUNCAN
Caridale, Kintyre. Covenanter
in Argyll's rebellion. Pris-
oner in Laigh Parliament House,
Edinburgh. Banished to the
Plantations 30 July 1685.
Transported from Leith to
Jamaica by John Ewing
August 1685
(PC)

MCMILLAN JOHN
Covenanter. Prisoner in Laigh
Parliament House, Edinburgh.
In Argyll's rebellion. Trans-
ported from Leith to New Eng-
land by William Arbuckle,
merchant in Glasgow
(PC)

MCMURRAY ALAN
39. Farmer. Galmistal, Eigg.
Jacobite in Clanranald's regiment. Prisoner at Inverness,
ship and Tilbury. Transported
from London to Barbados or
Jamaica by Samuel Smith
31 March 1747
(P)(RM)

MACMURTRY ELIZABETH
Paisley. Child murder. Banished
to the Plantations for life,
at Glasgow 15 October 1774
(SM)

MACNAB JAMES
Royalist soldier captured
at Worcester. Transported
from Gravesend to Boston
on the John and Sarah,
master John Greene,
13 May 1652
(NER)

MCNABB ALEXANDER
Jacobite captured at Pres-
ton. Transported from
Liverpool for Jamaica on
the Two Brothers, master
Edward Rathbone, 26 April
1716. Landed on Montserrat
June 1716
(SP/C)(CTB)(CTP)

MCNABB JOHN
Jacobite captured at Pres-
ton. Transported from
Liverpool for Jamaica on
the Two Brothers, master
Edward Rathbone, 26 April
1716. Landed on Montserrat
June 1716
(SP/C)(CTB)(CTP)

MCNAB JOHN
67. Labourer. Jacobite in
the Atholl Brigade. Pris-
oner at Stirling, Edinburgh
and Carlisle. Transported
from Liverpool on the ship
Johnson, master William
Pemberton, 5 May 1747.
Landed at Port Oxford,
Maryland 5 August 1747
(P)(PRO)

MCNABB THOMAS
Jacobite captured at Pres-
ton. Transported from
Liverpool to Maryland on
the Friendship, master
Michael Mankin, 24 May
1716. Sold to William
Thomas in Maryland
20 August 1716
(SP/C)(CTB)(HM)

MCNAUGHTON DUNCAN
Jacobite captured at Preston.
Transported from Liverpool to
South Carolina on the Susannah,
master Thomas Bromhall, 7 May
1716
(SP/C)(CTB)

MCNAUGHTON MALCOLM
Jacobite captured at Preston.
Transported from Liverpool to
Jamaica or Virginia on the
Elizabeth and Anne, master
Edward Trafford, 29 June 1716.
Lande at York, Virginia -
unindentured
(SP/C)(VSP)

MACNEIL DANIEL
Royalist soldier captured at
Worcester. Transported from
Gravesend to Boston on the
John and Sarah, master John
Greene, 13 May 1652
(NER)

MACNEIL JAMES
Royalist soldier captured at
Worcester. Transported from
Gravesend to Boston on the
John and Sarah, master John
Greene, 13 May 1652
(NER)

MCNEIL ARCHIBALD
Covenanter in Argyll's rebellion.
Prisoner in the Laigh Parliament
House, Edinburgh. Banished to
the Plantations 30 July 1685.
Transported from Leith to Jamaica
by John Ewing August 1685
(PC)

MCNEIL HECTOR
Covenanter in Argyll's rebellion.
Prisoner in the Laigh Parliament
House, Edinburgh. Banished to
the Plantations 31 July 1685.
Transported from Leith to Jamaica
by John Ewing August 1685
(PC)

MCNEIL JOHN
Covenanter in Argyll's rebellion. Prisoner in the Laigh Parliament House, Edinburgh. Banished to the Plantations 30 July 1685. Transported from Leith to Jamaica by John Ewing August 1685
(PC)

MACNEIL JOHN
Cattle thief. Transported for 14 years, at Inveraray 18 May 1764
(SM)

MACNEIL PATRICK
Royalist soldier captured at Worcester. Transported from Gravesend to Boston on the John and Sarah, master John Greene, 13 May 1652
(NER)

MCNEIL ROGER
28. Servant to the laird of Watersay, Barra. Jacobite in Clanranald's regiment. Prisoner at Tilbury. Transported 1747(?)
(P)

MCNICOLL DONALD GLASS
Pedlar in Strathfillan. Cattle thief. Transported to America 18 December 1721
(JC)

MACNICOL JOHN
Barlea, Glencoe. Banished to the Plantations for 14 years, at Inveraray 4 September 1766. Cattle thief
(SM)

MCNORMER DUNCAN
Jacobite captured at Preston. Transported from Liverpool for Jamaica on the Two Brothers, master Edward Rathbone, 26 April 1716. Landed on Montserrat June 1716
(SP/C)(CTB)(CTP)

MCPHAIL DONALD
Soldier in the Argyllshire regiment. Thief. Banished to America for 14 years, at Inveraray 11 May 1763
(SM)

MCPHAILL DONALD DOW
Banished at Inveraray, Argyll for theft. Transported from Port Glasgow on the Dolphin, master George Service. Landed at Port Oxford, Maryland 1 February 1773
(JC)

MCPHAIL DUNCAN
Jacobite captured at Preston. Transported from Liverpool to Virginia or Jamaica on the Elizabeth and Anne, master Edward Trafford, 29 June 1716 Died at sea
(SP/C)(CTB)(VSP)

MCPHAIL MALCOLM alias CAMPBELL
Horsethief. Banished to the Plantations in the British West Indies for 7 years, at Stirling 14 September 1775
(SM)

MCPHEE ANGUS alias MCCRAIG
Cattle thief. Transported for life, at Inverness 1752
(SM)

MCPHEE EWAN
28. Servant to Donald
Cameron of Cluny. From
Locharchaig. Jacobite
in Lochiel's regiment.
Prisoner at Inverness,
ship and Tilbury. Trans
ported from London to
Barbados or Jamaica by
Samuel Smith 31 March
1747
(P)(RM)

MCPHEE MURDOCH
43. Farmer. Sandvegg,
Eigg. From Morven in
Argyll. Jacobite in
Clanranald's regiment.
Transported from Lon-
don to Barbados or
Jamaica by Samuel
Smith 31 March 1747
(P)(RM)

MCPHERSON ALEXANDER
Jacobite captured at
Preston. Transported
from Liverpool to
South Carolina on the
Wakefield, master
Thomas Beck, 21 April
1716
(CTB)(SP/C)

MCPHERSON ALEXANDER
Jacobite captured at
Preston. Transported
from Liverpool for
Jamaica on the Two
Brothers, master
Edward Rathbone, 26
April 1716. Landed
on Montserrat June
1716
(SP/C)(CTB)(CTP)

MCPHERSON ALEXANDER
alias MCGILLERVARY
Thief. Prisoner in
Aberdeen Tolbooth.
Banished to the
Plantations for life,
at Aberdeen May 1726
(JC)

MCPHERSON ANGUS
Jacobite captured at Preston.
Transported from Liverpool to
South Carolina on the Susannah,
master Thomas Bromhall, 7 May
1716
(SP/C)(CTB)

MCPHERSON ARCHIBALD
16. Cowherd. Skye. Jacobite in
Clanranald's regiment. Captured
at Carlisle. Prisoner at Carlisle
York and Lincoln. Transported
from Liverpool for the Leeward
Islands on the Veteran, master
John Ricky, 5 May 1747. Liberated by a French privateer and
landed on Martinique June 1747
(P)(RM)

MCPHERSON DANIEL
Jacobite captured at Preston.
Transported from Liverpool to
Antigua on the Scipio, master
John Scaisbrick, 30 March 1716
(CTB)

MCPHERSON DONALD
Jacobite captured at Preston.
Transported from Liverpool to
St Kitts on the Hockenhill,
master H. Short, 25 June 1716
(SP/C)(CTB)

MCPHERSON DONALD
Jacobite captured at Preston.
Transported from Liverpool to
South Carolina on the Wakefield,
master Thomas Beck, 21 April 1716
(SP/C)(CTB)

MCPHERSON DONALD
Jacobite captured at Preston.
Transported from Liverpool to
South Carolina on the Susannah,
master Thomas Bromhall, 7 May
1716
(CTB)(SP/C)

MCPHERSON DUNCAN
Tenant to Archibald Campbell of
Inverawe. Cattle thief. Trans-
ported to America 17 October 1722
(JC)

MCPHERSON DUNCAN
Jacobite captured at Pres-
ton. Transported from
Liverpool to South Carol-
ina on the Susannah, mas-
ter Thomas Bromnall, 7
May 1716
(SP/C)(CTB)

MCPHERSON DUNCAN
36. Labourer. Inverness.
Jacobite in Glenbucket's
regiment. Prisoner at
Carlisle and York. Trans
ported from Liverpool to
the Leeward Islands on
the Veteran, master John
Ricky, 5 May 1747. Lib-
erated by a French priv-
ateer and landed on
Martinique June 1747
(P)(RM)

MCPHERSON JAMES
22. Labourer. Aberdeen
Jacobite in McIntosh's
regiment. Prisoner at
Carlisle and York.
Transported from Liver-
pool to the Leeward
Islands on the Veteran,
master John Ricky, 5
May 1747. Liberated
by a French privateer
and landed on Martin-
ique June 1747
(P)(RM)

MCPHERSON JEAN
Child murder. Banished,
at Inverness October 1749
(SM)

MACPHERSON JOHN
Royalist soldier
captured at Worcester.
Transported from Graves-
end to Boston on the John
and Sarah, master John
Ricky, 13 May 1652
(NER)

MCPHERSON JOHN
Jacobite captured at Preston.
Transported from Liverpool to
South Carolina on the Susannah,
master Thomas Bromhall, 7 May
1716
(CTB)(SP/C)

MCPHERSON JOHN
43. Servant. Inverness. Jacobite
in McIntosh's regiment. Prisoner
at Inverness, ship and Tilbury.
Transported from London to
Jamaica or Barbados by Samuel
Smith 31 March 1747
(P)(RM)

MCPHERSON JOHN
15. Glengarry. Jacobite in Glengarry's regiment. Transported
from Liverpool on the Gildart,
master Richard Holmes. Landed
at Port North Potomac, Maryland
5 August 1747
(P)(PRO)

MCPHERSON 'ORIGLAIS'
Royalist soldier captured at
Worcester. Transported from
Gravesend to Boston on the
John and Sarah, master John
Greene, 13 May 1652
(NER)

MCPHERSON OWEN
Jacobite captured at Preston.
Transported from Liverpool for
Virginia or Jamaica on the
Elizabeth and Anne, master Edward
Trafford, 29 June 1716. Landed
in Virginia - indentured at York
(CTB)(SP/C)(VSP)

MACPHERSON ROBERT
Royalist soldier captured at
Worcester. Transported from
Gravesend to Boston on the
John and Sarah, master John
Greene, 13 May 1652
(NER)

MCPHERSON WILLIAM
Jacobite captured at Pres-
ton. Transported from
Liverpool to Virginia on
the Godspeed, master
Arthur Smith, 28 July 1716
Sold to Michael Martin in
Maryland 17 October 1716
(SP/C)(CTB)(HM)

MCPHIE PETER
Servant to McLeod of
Waterstyne, Skye. Murder.
Banished to the Plantat-
ions for life, at Perth
1773
(SM)

MCQUARRY ALEXANDER
37. Farmer. Fivepenny,
Eigg. From Morven. Jacob-
ite in Clanranald's regi-
ment. Prisoner at Inver-
ness, ship and Tilbury.
Transported 20 March 1747
(P)

MCQUARRY DONALD
Eigg. Jacobite in Clan-
ranald's regiment. Pris-
oner at Tilbury. Trans-
ported from London to
Barbados or Jamaica by
Samuel Smith 31 March
1747
(P)(RM)

MCQUARRY JOHN
Farmer. Galmistal, Eigg.
Jacobite in Clanranald's
regiment. Prisoner at
Inverness, ship and Til-
bury. Transported from
London to Barbados or
Jamaica by Samuel Smith
31 March 1747
(P)(RM)

MCQUARRY JOHN
40. Eigg. Jacobite in
Clanranald's regiment.
Prisoner at Inverness
and on ship. Transported
1747(?)
(P)

MCQUEEN ALEXANDER
Jacobite captured at Preston.
Transported from Liverpool to
South Carolina on the Wakefield,
master Thomas Beck, 21 April 1716
(CTB)(SP/C)

MCQUEEN ALEXANDER
Jacobite captured at Preston.
Transported from Liverpool to
South Carolina on the Wakefield,
master Thomas Beck, 21 April 1716
(CTB)(SP/C)

MCQUEEN ALEXANDER
Jacobite captured at Preston.
Transported from Liverpool to
Maryland on the Friendship,
master Michael Mankin, 24 May
1716. Sold to Daniel Sherwood
in Maryland 20 August 1716
(SP/C)(HM)

MCQUEEN DANIEL
Jacobite captured at Preston.
Transported from Liverpool to
Antigua on the Scipio, master
John Scaisbrick, 30 March 1716
(CTB)

MCQUEEN DAVID
Jacobite captured at Preston.
Transported from Liverpool to
South Carolina on the Wakefield,
master Thomas Beck, 21 April
1716
(CTB)(SP/C)

MCQUEEN DAVID
Jacobite captured at Preston.
Transported from Liverpool to
Maryland on the Friendship,
master Michael Mankin, 24 May
1716. Sold to Daniel Sherwood
in Maryland 20 August 1716
(SP/C)(CTB)(HM)

MCQUEEN DUGALL
Jacobite captured at Preston.
Transported from Liverpool to
Maryland on the Friendship,
master Michael Mankin, 24 May
1716. Sold to William Holland Esq.
in Maryland 20 August 1716
(SP/C)(CTB)(HM)

MCQUEEN DUNCAN
Covenanter in Argyll's
rebellion. Prisoner in
the Laigh Parliament
House, Edinburgh. Ban-
ished to the Plantations
31 July 1685. Transported
from Leith to Jamaica by
John Ewing August 1685
(PC)

MCQUEEN DUNCAN
Jacobite captured at
Preston. Transported from
Liverpool to South Carol-
ina on the Wakefield, mas-
ter Thomas Beck, 21 April
1716
(CTB)(SP/C)

MCQUEEN HECTOR
Jacobite captured at
Preston. Transported from
Liverpool to Maryland on
the Friendship, master
Michael Mankin, 24 May
1716. Sold to Aaron Raw-
lings in Maryland
20 August 1716
(SP/C)(CTB)(HM)

MCQUEEN HUGH
Covenanter in Argyll's
rebellion. Prisoner in
Paul's Work, Edinburgh.
Banished to the Plant-
ations 30 July 1685.
Transported from Leith to
Jamaica by John Ewing
August 1685
(PC)

MCQUEEN JANET
Covenanter. Prisoner in
Canongate Tolbooth. Ban-
ished to the Plantations
28 July 1685. Stigmatised
Transported from Leith to
Jamaica by John Ewing
August 1685
(PC)

MCQUEEN JOHN
Jacobite captured at Preston.
Transported from Liverpool to
South Carolina on the Wakefield,
master Thomas Beck, 21 April
1716
(SP/C)(CTB)

MCQUEEN WALTER
Transported from Leith to East
New Jersey by George Scott of
Pitlochie on the Henry and Francis
master Richard Hutton, 5 September
1685
(PC)

MCQUEIN ROBERT
Nithsdale. Covenanter. Prisoner
in Canongate and Leith. Transported from Leith to East New
Jersey by George Scott of Pitlochie on the Henry and Francis,
master Richard Hutton, 5 September 1685
(PC)

MCQUERRIST JOHN
Jacobite. Prisoner at Carlisle
and Liverpool. Transported from
Liverpool on the Johnson, master
William Pemberton, 5 May 1747.
Landed at Port Oxford, Maryland
5 August 1747
(P)(PRO)

MCQUERRIST RODERICK
Jacobite. Prisoner at Carlisle
and Liverpool. Transported from
Liverpool on the Johnson, master
William Pemberton, 5 May 1747.
Landed at Port Oxford, Maryland
5 August 1747
(P)(PRO)

MACQUILLAN DANIEL
Royalist captured at Worcester.
Transported from Gravesend to
Boston on the John and Sarah,
master John Greene, 13 May 1652
(NER)

MACQUILLAN JOHN
Royalist captured at
Worcester. Transported
from Gravesend to Boston
on the John and Sarah,
master John Greene,
13 May 1652
(NER)

MCQUIN ALEXANDER
Jacobite captured at
Preston. Transported
from Liverpool to South
Carolina on the Wakefield,
master Thomas Beck, 21
April 1716
(CTB)(SP/C)

MCQUINN DANIEL
Jacobite captured at
Preston. Transported
from Liverpool to Ant-
igua on the Scipio, mas-
ter John Scaisbrick,
30 March 1716
(SP/C)(CTP)

MCQUIN DUNCAN or DANIEL
Jacobite captured at
Preston. Transported
from Liverpool to Jam-
aica or Virginia on the
Elizabeth and Anne, mas-
ter Edward Trafford, 29
June 1716. Landed at
York, Virginia -
unindentured
(CTB)(SP/C)(VSP)

MCQUIN FLORA
10. Highlands. Jacobite
Prisoner at Lancaster.
Transported from Liver-
pool on the Johnson,
master William Pember-
ton, 5 May 1747. Land-
ed at Port Oxford,
Maryland 5 August 1747
(P)(PRO)

MCQUIN JOHN
Jacobite captured at Preston.
Transported from Liverpool to
South Carolina on the Susannah,
master Thomas Bromhill, 7 May
1716
(SP/C)(CTB)

MCRAE DONALD
Lochbroom. Jacobite in Glen-
garry's regiment. Prisoner at
Tilbury. Transported 1747(?)
(P)

MCRAE JOHN
Servant to Archibald Ogilvie
of Inchmartine. Prisoner in
Edinburgh Tolbooth. Thief.
Banished to America for 7 years
9 March 1767
(SM)(JC)

MCREADY JOHN
Rathay. Covenanter. Prisoner
in Edinburgh Tolbooth. Transported to the Plantations in
the Indies 1 August 1678
(PC)

MCRANALD DONALD
60. Jacobite in Clanranald's
regiment. Prisoner at Inverness
and Tilbury. Transported 1747(?)
(P)

MCRITCHIE JOHN
70. Herd to Lord Lovat. Jacobite
in Lovat's regiment. Prisoner
at Inverness and on ship. Transported 1747(?)
(P)

MCRORY ALASTAIR
Royalist soldier captured at
Worcester. Transported from
Gravesend to Boston on the
John and Sarah, master John
Greene, 13 May 1652
(NER)

MCROSS DONALD
24. Sutherland. Jacobite
in Cromarty's regiment.
Prisoner at Inverness and
on ship. Transported 1747
(P)

MCTAILLIOR DONALD
Covenanter in Argyll's
rebellion. Tenant of
Campbell of Fordie.
Prisoner in Canongate
Tolbooth. Banished to
the Plantations 30 July
1685. Transported from
Leith to Jamaica by
John Ewing August 1685
(PC)

MACTHOMAS ALASTAIR
Royalist soldier capt-
ured at Worcester.
Transported from Graves
end to Boston on the
John and Sarah, master
John Greene, 13 May
1652
(NER)

MCUILLAN WILLIAM
Servant. Borrowstoun,
Caithness. Thief and
housebreaker. Banished
for life in 1772.
Transported on the ship
Donald, master Thomas
Ramsay. Landed at Port
James, Upper District,
Virginia 13 March 1773
(JC)

MCURICH ARCHIBALD
Herd on McLay's land.
Covenanter in Argyll's
rebellion. Prisoner in
Laigh Parliament House,
Edinburgh. Transported
from Leith to New Eng-
land by William Arbuckle
merchant in Glasgow,
July 1685
(PC)

MCVANE JOHN
Jacobite captured at Preston.
Transported from Liverpool to
South Carolina on the Susannah,
master Thomas Bromhall, 7 May
1716
(CTB)(SP/C)

MCVANE MALCOLM
Jacobite captured at Preston.
Transported from Liverpool to
South Carolina on the Susannah,
master Thomas Bromhall, 7 May
1716
(SP/C)(CTB)

MCVERRAN ARCHIBALD
Transported from Leith to
Jamaica by John Ewing August 1685
(PC)

MCVEY DONALD
Covenanter. Prisoner at Canongate
and Dunnottar. Banished to the
Plantations 20 May 1685
(PC)

MCVICAR DONALD
Inveraray. Covenanter in Argyll's
rebellion. Prisoner at Glasgow
and the Laigh Parliament House,
Edinburgh. Transported from Leith
to New England by William Arbuckle
merchant in Glasgow, July 1685
(PC)

MCVICAR DUNCAN
17. Son of the Baillie of Camp-
belltown. Covenanter. Prisoner
in the Laigh Parliament House,
Edinburgh. Transported from
Leith to New England by William
Arbuckle, merchant in Glasgow,
6 July 1685
(PC)

MCVIG DUNCAN
Covenanter. Banished to the
Plantations 24 July 1685. Trans-
ported from Leith to Jamaica by
John Ewing August 1685
(PC)

MCVORICH MALCOLM
Thief. Prisoner in Stirling
Tolbooth. Transported to
East New Jersey by David
Toshach of Monievaird
5 May 1684
(PC)

MCWARISH ROBERT
42. Labourer. Jacobite.
Prisoner at Carlisle.
Transported 1747(?)
(P)

MCWARISH JOHN
28. Labourer. Jacobite.
Prisoner at Carlisle.
Transported 1747(?)
(P)

MCWHIDDIE ALLAN
Covenanter in Argyll's
rebellion. Prisoner in
the Laigh Parliament
House, Edinburgh. Ban-
ished to the Plantations
31 July 1685. Transported
from Leith to Jamaica by
John Ewing August 1685
(PC)

MACWILLIAM DONALD
Cattle thief. Transported
for life, at Inverness
1752
(SM)

MCWILLIAM 'GELLUST'
Royalist soldier captured
at Worcester. Transported
from Gravesend to Boston
on the John and Sarah,
master John Greene,
13 May 1652
(NER)

MACWILLIAM KENNETH
Cattle thief. Transported
for life, at Inverness
1752
(SM)

MCWILLIE JOHN
Covenanter. Prisoner in Edin-
burgh Tolbooth. Banished to
the Plantations 29 July 1685.
Transported from Leith to
Jamaica by John Ewing August
1685
(ETR)(PC)

MACHANE MATTHEW
Eaglesham. Prisoner in Glasgow
Tolbooth. Banished to the
Plantations, at Glasgow June
1684. Transported from the
Clyde to America on the ship
Pelican, by Walter Gibson
merchant in Glasgow, June 1684
(PC)

MACK JAMES
Prisoner in Canongate Tolbooth.
Banished to the Plantations in
America December 1685. Trans-
ported from Leith to America
by Alexander Fearne and his
ship master Edward Barnes
December 1685
(ETR)(PC)

MAIN JOHN
22. Fisherman. Futtie, Aberdeen
Jacobite in Lord Lewis Gordon's
regiment. Prisoner at Aberdeen
Canongate and Carlisle. Transported 1747(?)
(P)

MAIR WILLIAM
Prisoner in Stirling Tolbooth.
Transported from Leith to East
New Jersey by George Scott of
Pitlochie on the Henry and
Francis, master Richard Hutton,
5 September 1685
(PC)

MAITLAND JOHN
Prisoner at Canongate Tolbooth.
Banished to the Plantations in
America - to be transported by
Walter Gibson, 21 May 1684
(PC)

MALCOLM JAMES
Jacobite captured at
Preston. Transported
from Liverpool to
Jamaica or Virginia
on the Elizabeth and
Anne, master Edward
Trafford, 29 June 1716
Landed at York, Virginia
- unindentured
(SP/C)(CTB)(VSP)

MALLONE JAMES
Jacobite captured at
Preston. Transported
from Liverpool to
Virginia on the God-
speed,master Arthur
Smith, 28 July 1716.
Sold to Charles Digges
in Maryland 17 October
1716
(SP/C)(CTB)(HM)

MANN ALEXANDER
33. Butcher. Jacobite
in Roy Stuart's regi-
ment. Prisoner at Car-
lisle. Transported
1747(?)
(P)

MANN DANIEL
Royalist soldier capt-
ured at Worcester. Trans-
ported from Gravesend to
Boston on the John and
Sarah, master John Greene
13 May 1652
(NER)

MANN JAMES
20. Baker. Dunkeld. Jac-
obite in Roy Stuart's
regiment. Captured at
Carlisle. Prisoner at
Carlisle, York and Lin-
coln. Transported from
Liverpool for the Lee-
ward Islands on the
Veteran, master John
Ricky, 5 May 1747.
Liberated by a French
privateer and landed
on Martinique June 1747
(P)(RM)

MANN JOHN
Royalist soldier captured at
Worcester. Transported from
Gravesend to Boston on the
John and Sarah, master John
Greene, 13 May 1652
(NER)

MANN PATRICK
Royalist soldier captured at
Worcester. Transported from
Gravesend to Boston on the
John and Sarah, master John
Greene, 13 May 1652
(NER)

MANN WILLIAM
Jacobite captured at Preston.
Transported from Liverpool to
Maryland on the Friendship,
master Michael Mankin, 24 May
1716. Sold to Daniel Sherwood
in Maryland 20 August 1716
(SP/C)(CTB)(HM)

MANN WILLIAM
Banished for life. Transported
from Glasgow on the Brilliant,
master Robert Bennet. Landed
at Port Hampton, Virginia
7 October 1772
(JC)

MANSON ALEXANDER
Prisoner in Edinburgh Tolbooth.
Banished to the Plantations
31 July 1685. Stigmatised 4
August 1685. Transported from
Leith to Jamaica by John Ewing
August 1685
(PC)(ETR)

MARJORYBANKS GEORGE
Jacobite captured at Preston.
Transported from Liverpool to
Virginia or Jamaica on the
Elizabeth and Anne, master
Edward Trafford, 29 June 1716.
Landed at York, Virginia -
unindentured
(SP/C)(CTB)(VSP)

MARJORYBANKS JAMES
Forger. Banished for life,
at Dumfries 1753
(SM)

MARNOCH ALEXANDER
26. Shoemaker. Aberdeen.
Jacobite. Prisoner at
York. Transported from
Liverpool for the Lee-
ward Islands on the
Veteran, master John
Ricky, 5 May 1747.
Liberated by a French
privateer and landed
on Martinique June 1747
(P)(JAB)(RM)

MARNOCK GILBERT
Chapman. Covenanter.
Banished to the Plant-
ations in the Indies
1 August 1678. Trans-
ported from Leith on the
St Michael of Scarborough
master Edward Johnston,
12 December 1678
(PC)

MARR ALEXANDER
Jacobite in Glenbucket's
regiment. Captured at
Carlisle. Prisoner at
Carlisle. Transported
from Liverpool on the
Johnson, master William
Pemberton, 5 May 1747.
Landed at Port Oxford,
Maryland 5 August 1747
(P)(PRO)

MARR ANN
Transported on the Boyd,
master William Dunlop.
Landed at Norfolk,
Virginia 24 August 1764
(JC)

MARSHALL AGNES
Servant to Robert Marshall.
Darnest, Paisley Abbey
Parish. Child murder.
Banished to the Plantat-
ions for life, at Glasgow
16 May 1770
(SM)

MARSHALL ALEXANDER
Covenanter. Prisoner in Thieves'
hole, Edinburgh. Banished to
the Plantations 24 July 1685
(PC)

MARSHALL JANET
Cowgate, Edinburgh. Thief.
Prisoner in Edinburgh Tolbooth.
Banished to the Plantations
in America for 14 years, at
Edinburgh 19 January 1767
(JC)

MARSHALL JOHN
Smith. Glasgow. Covenanter.
Banished to the Plantations
in the Indies 13 June 1678
(PC)

MARSHALL JOHN
Shotts. Covenanter. Prisoner
in Glasgow Tolbooth. Banished
to the Plantations, at Glasgow
June 1684. Transported from
the Clyde to America on the
Pelican by Walter Gibson,
merchant in Glasgow, June 1684
(PC)

MARSHALL MICHAEL
Straven. Prisoner in Thieveshole
Edinburgh. Banished to the
Plantations 11 August 1685.
Stigmatised 4 August 1685.
Transported from Leith to East
New Jersey by George Scott of
Pitlochie on the Henry and
Francis, master Richard Hutton,
5 September 1685
(PC)

MARSHALL THOMAS
Shotts. Covenanter. Prisoner
in Glasgow Tolbooth. Banished
to the Plantations, at Glasgow
June 1684. Transported from
the Clyde to America on the
Pelican, by Walter Gibson,
merchant in Glasgow, June 1684
(PC)

156

MARSHALL WILLIAM
Prisoner at Edinburgh,
Canongate and Leith.
Transported from Leith
to East New Jersey by
George Scott of Pit-
lochie on the Henry
and Francis, master
Richard Hutton,
5 September 1685
(PC)

MARTIN ALEXANDER
Thief. Banished to the
Plantations for life,
at Aberdeen May 1753
(SM)

MARTIN COLIN
Former soldier in
Drumlanrig's regiment.
Vagrant. Banished, at
Glasgow 1754
(SM)

MARTIN DANIEL
Royalist soldier capt-
ured at Worcester.
Transported from Graves-
end to Boston on the
John and Sarah, master
John Greene, 13 May 1652
(NER)

MARTIN JOHN the elder
Prisoner in Canongate
Tolbooth. Banished to the
Plantations in America
21 May 1684. Transported
from Leith by Walter
Gibson
(PC)

MARTIN JOHN the younger
Prisoner in Canongate
Tolbooth. Banished to the
Plantations in America
21 May 1684. Transported
from Leith by Walter
Gibson
(PC)

MARTIN JOHN
Kirkmichael, Kintyre. Covenanter
in Argyll's rebellion. Prisoner
in the Laigh Parliament House,
Edinburgh. Banished to the
Plantations 31 July 1685.
Transported from Leith to
Jamaica by John Ewing August
1685
(PC)

MARTIN JOHN
42. Stocking weaver. Stonehaven.
Jacobite in Drummond's regiment.
Prisoner at Inverness, ship and
Tilbury. Transported from London
to Jamaica or Barbados by Samuel
Smith 31 March 1747
(P)(RM)

MARTIN JOHN
Cupar. Rioter at Mylnefield.
Banished to the Plantations
for life, at Perth 1773
(SM)

MARTIN WILLIAM
Jacobite captured at Preston.
Transported from Liverpool to
Virginia or Jamaica on the
Elizabeth and Anne, master
Edward Trafford, 29 June 1716.
Landed at York, Virginia -
unindentured
(CTB)(SP/C)(VSP)

MARTIN WILLIAM
Transported on the Boyd, master
William Dunlop. Landed at
Norfolk, Virginia 24 August 1764
(JC)

MARTISON JOHN
Jacobite captured at Preston.
Transported from Liverpool to
Maryland on the Friendship,
master Michael Mankin, 24 May
1716. Sold to Peter Anderson
in Maryland 20 August 1716
(SP/C)(CTB)(HM)

MASON JAMES
58 or 49. Moray. Jacobite
in Lord Lewis Gordon's
regiment. Prisoner at
Inverness, ships and Til-
bury. Transported from
London to Barbados or
Jamaica by Samuel Smith
20 March 1747
(P)(RM)

MASON JOHN
48. Wright. Aberdeen.
Jacobite in Crighton's
regiment. Prisoner at
Inverness, ship and
Tilbury. Transported
20 March 1747
(JAB)(P)

MASON JOHN
18. Barber. Aberdeen.
Jacobite. Transported
from Liverpool for the
Leeward Islands on the
Veteran, master John
Ricky, 5 May 1747.
Liberated by a French
privateer and landed
on Martinique June 1747
(P)(JAB)(RM)

MATHER DAVID the elder
Bridgeness. Covenanter.
Banished to the Plant-
ations in America
16 August 1670
(PC)

MATTHEW ANDREW
32. Maltster. Perthshire
Jacobite in the Duke of
Perth's regiment. Pris-
oner at Carlisle, Lin-
coln and York. Trans-
ported from Liverpool
for the Leeward Islands
on the Veteran, master
John Ricky, 5 May 1747.
Liberated by a French
privateer and landed
on Martinique June 1747
(P)(RM)

MATTHEW ANDREW
56. Angus. Jacobite in Ogilvy's
regiment. Prisoner at Inverness
and on ships. Transported
8 May 1747
(P)

MATTHEWSON JOHN
Jacobite captured at Preston.
Transported from Liverpool to
South Carolina on the Susannah,
master Thomas Bromhall, 7 May
1716
(CTB)(SP/C)

MATTHIESON GLASHAN
Thief. Prisoner in Edinburgh
Tolbooth. Servant to James
Riddell, merchant in Leith.
Transported to the Plantations
by William Johnston, merchant
in Edinburgh 2 August 1680
(ETR)

MATTHIESON JOHN
Closeburn. Covenanter. Prisoner
in Canongate Tolbooth. Banished
to Carolina 19 June 1684. Transported from Leith by Robert
Malloch, merchant in Edinburgh
(PC)

MATHIESON KENNETH
26. Servant to his brother
Finlay. Strathpeffer, Ross.
Jacobite in Cromarty's regiment.
Prisoner at Inverness and Tilbury.
Transported from London to Jam-
aica or Barbados by Samuel Smith
31 March 1747
(P)(RM)

MATHIESON WALTER
Servant to Isaac Grant W.S. House
breaker. Banished to America for
7 years, 21 January 1772. Transported from Port Glasgow on the
Matty, master Robert Peacock.
Landed at Port Oxford, Maryland
16 May 1772
(JC)

MAVOR ALEXANDER
Portioner of Urquhart,
Inverness-shire. Cov-
enanter. Banished to
the Plantations 4 March
1685, at Elgin
(PC)

MAVOR MARK
Son of Alexander Mavor.
Urquhart, Inverness.
Covenanter. Banished
to the Plantations
4 March 1685, at Elgin
(PC)

MAXTON JAMES
Clerk to Thomas Fairholm
junior, merchant in Edin
burgh. Forger. Prisoner
in Edinburgh Tolbooth.
Banished to the Plant-
ations in America for
life, at Edinburgh
19 January 1767
(JC)

MAXWELL ADAM
17. Labourer. Jacobite
in Roy Stuart's regiment
Prisoner at Carlisle.
Transported 22 April 1747
(P)

MAXWELL CHARLES
Netherkeir. Covenanter.
Banished to the Plant-
ations 24 October 1684
(PC)

MAXWELL DANIEL
Royalist soldier captured
at Worcester. Transported
on the John and Sarah,
master John Greene, from
Gravesend to Boston,
13 May 1652
(NER)

MAXWELL JAMES
Maltman. Glasgow. Covenanter.
Banished to the Plantations
in the Indies 13 June 1678
(PC)

MAXWELL JAMES
Cathcart. Covenanter. Prisoner
in Edinburgh Tolbooth. Banished
to the Plantations in the Indies
7 November 1678. Transported
from Leith on the St Michael
of Scarborough, master Edward
Johnston, 12 December 1678
(PC)

MAXWELL JAMES the younger
Cathcart. Covenanter. Prisoner
in Edinburgh Tolbooth. Transported from Leith on the
St Michael of Scarborough,
master Edward Johnston, 12
December 1678. Banished to
the Plantations in the Indies
7 November 1678
(PC)

MAXWELL ROBERT
Cathcart. Covenanter. Prisoner
in Edinburgh Tolbooth. Banished
to the Plantations in the Indies
7 November 1678. Transported
from Leith on the St Michael
of Scarborough, master Edward
Johnston, 12 December 1678
(PC)

MAXWELL WILLIAM
Jacobite captured at Preston.
Transported from Liverpool to
Virginia or Jamaica on the
Elizabeth and Anne, master
Edward Trafford, 29 June 1716.
Landed at York, Virginia -
unindentured
(CTB)(SP/C)(VSP)

MAXWELL WILLIAM
Prisoner in Glasgow Tolbooth.
Assault. Banished from Scotland
for 7 years, at Glasgow May 1725
(JC)

MECHLANE ELIZABETH
Covenanter. Banished to
the Plantations in
America 11 October 1684
(PC)

MEIKLE MR ROBERT
Chaplain to Sir James
Stewart. Covenanter.
Prisoner in Edinburgh
Tolbooth. Transported
from Leith on the
St Michael of Scarborough
master Edward Johnston,
12 December 1678
(PC)

MEIKLE ROBERT
Transported from Port Glas-
gow on the Matty, master
Robert Peacock. Landed at
Port Oxford, Maryland
16 May 1772
(JC)

MEIKLE ROBERT
Transported from Port Glas-
gow on the Polly, master
James McArthur. Landed at
Port Oxford, Maryland
16 September 1771
(JC)

MEIKLEJOHN JOHN
31. Deserter from the
Royal Scots. Stirling.
Jacobite. Prisoner at
Inverness, ships and
Medway. Transported
from London to Jamaica
or Barbados by Samuel
Smith 31 March 1747
(P)(RM)

MEIN ALEXANDER
Covenanter. Prisoner at
Kirkcudbright, Dumfries,
and Canongate. Banished
to the Plantations, at
Kirkcudbright 13 October
1684
(PC)

MEIRN ELIZABETH
Spouse of George Tod, Aberdeen.
Thief. Banished for life 1773
(SM)

MELDRUM OF CROMBIE MR GEORGE
Minister. Aberchirdor, Banff.
Prisoner at Elgin and Edinburgh
Banished to the Plantations,
at Elgin 4 February 1685
(PC)

MELDRUM GEORGE
Jacobite captured at Preston.
Transported from Liverpool to
Antigua on the Scipio, master
John Scaisbrick, 30 March 1716
(SP/C)(CTB)

MELVILLE JOHN
Tinker. Husband of Mary Wilson
Thief. Banished for life in 1772
(SM)

MELVILLE WILLIAM
Miner, servant to George
Forbes, merchant in Aberdeen.
Jacobite in Stonywood's regi-
ment. Prisoner at Aberdeen,
Canongate and Carlisle. Trans-
ported from Liverpool on the
Johnson, master William Pemberton
5 May 1747. Landed at Port
Oxford, Maryland 5 August 1747
(P)(JAB)(PRO)

MENZIES ARCHIBALD
Jacobite captured at Preston.
Transported from Liverpool to
Virginia or Jamaica on the
Elizabeth and Anne, master
Edward Trafford, 29 June 1716.
Landed at York, Virginia -
indentured
(CTB)(SP/C)(VSP)

MENZIES ROBERT
Jacobite captured at Preston.
Transported from Liverpool to
Virginia or Jamaica on the
Elizabeth and Anne, master
Edward Trafford, 29 June 1716.
Landed at York, Virginia -
unindentured
(CTB)(SP/C)(VSP)

SCOTS BANISHED TO THE AMERICAN PLANTATIONS

MENZIES WALTER
18. Flaxdresser. Atholl.
Jacobite in Ogilvy's
regiment. Captured at
Carlisle. Transported
from Liverpool for the
Leeward Islands on the
Veteran, master John
Ricky, 5 May 1747.
Liberated by a French
privateer and landed on
Martinique June 1747
(P)(OR)(RM)

MICHEY JOHN
Jacobite captured at
Preston. Transported from
Liverpool for Virginia or
Jamaica on the Elizabeth
and Anne, master Edward
Trafford, 29 June 1716.
Landed at York, Virginia
- unindentured
(SP/C)(VSP)

MIDDLEMISS JAMES
          the younger
Tenant in Southcoat.
Banished from Scotland
for life, at Jedburgh
10 May 1726
(JC)

MIDDLEMISS JAMES
          the elder
Tenant in Southcoat.
Banished from Scotland
for life, at Jedburgh
10 May 1726
(JC)

MIDDLETON ALEXANDER
41. Servant. Edinburgh
or Aberdeen. Jacobite
in the Duke of Perth's
regiment. Captured at
Carlisle, Transported
from Liverpool to the
Leeward Islands on the
Veteran, master John
Ricky, 5 May 1747.
Liberated by a French
privateer and landed
on Martinique June 1747
(P)(RM)

MIDDLETON JAMES
Thief. Banished to the Plant-
ations for life, at Aberdeen
May 1753
(SM)

MILDRAIN GEORGE
Jacobite captured at Preston.
Transported from Liverpool to
Antigua on the Scipiu, master
John Scaisbrick, 30 March 1716
(CTB)

MILL ANDREW
17. Tailor. Banffshire. Jacobite.
Prisoner at Carlisle, York and
Lincoln. Transported from Liverpool for the Leeward Islands on
the Veteran, master John Ricky,
5 May 1747. Liberated by a French
privateer and landed on Martinique
June 1747
(P)(JAB)(RM)

MILL ANDREW
Thief. Banished to America for
life, at Aberdeen 1752
(SM)

MILL DAVID
Jacobite captured at Preston.
Transported from Liverpool to
Maryland on the Friendship,
master Michael Mankin, 24 May
1716. Sold to Evan Jones in
Maryland 20 August 1716
(SP/C)(CTB)(HM)

MILL WILLIAM
Thief. Banished to the Plantations for life, at Perth
5 May 1775
(SM)

MILLER ALEXANDER
Royalist soldier captured at
Worcester. Transported from
Gravesend to Boston on the
John and Sarah, master John
Greene, 13 May 1652
(NER)

161

MILLER ANDREW
Prisoner in Edinburgh
Tolbooth. Transported
from Greenock to New
York, 21 October 1682
(ETR)

MILLER ANNE
Thief. Banished to the
Plantations for 7 years,
at Ayr May 1749
(SM)

MILLER DAVID
Tinker. Thief. Trans-
ported to America, at
Edinburgh 1752
(SM)

MILLER FARQUHAR
50. Gardener. Edinburgh.
Jacobite in the Duke of
Perth's regiment. Pris-
oner at Kippen, Stirling
and Carlisle. Transported
from Liverpool on the
Gildart, master Richard
Holmes, 5 May 1747.
Landed at Port North
Potomac, Maryland
5 August 1747
(P)(PRO)

MILLER JAMES
Kirkcaldy. Covenanter.
Prisoner in Edinburgh
Tolbooth. Banished to
the Plantations in the
Indies 1 August 1678.
Transported from Leith
on the St Michael of
Scarborough, master
Edward Johnston. 12
December 1678
(PC)

MILLER KATHERINE
Servant to James Burt,
vintner in Perth.
Banished to the Plant-
ations for 10 years in
1767
(SM)

MILLER MARGARET
Covenanter. Prisoner at Dunnottar
and Leith. Banished to the
Plantations, at Leith 18 August
1685. Transported from Leith
to East New Jersey by George
Scott of Pitlochie on the
Henry and Francis, master
Richard Hutton, 5 September 1685
(PC)

MILLER ROBERT
Thief. Transported from Ayr to
Barbados 1653
(JC)

MILLER ROBERT
Prisoner in Edinburgh Tolbooth.
Transported from Leith to the
Plantations 15 November 1679
(ETR)

MILLER THOMAS
Soldier in Colonel Alexander's
company. Thief. Transported to
Barbados 27 February 1668
(PC)

MILLER THOMAS
Prisoner in Edinburgh Tolbooth.
Transported from Leith to the
Plantations 15 November 1679
(ETR)

MILLER WILLIAM
Thief and vagabond. Banished
to the Plantations in America,
at Jedburgh 2 May 1731
(JC)

MILLIGAN LILIAN
Servant to James Clark, merchant
in Dumfries. Child murder. Banished to the Plantations for
life, at Dumfries 14 September
1774. Transported from Greenock
on the Rainbow, master William
Gordon. Landed at Port Hampton,
Virginia 3 May 1775
(JC)

MILLIGAN MARGARET
Wife of William Milligan.
Covenanter. Banished to
the Plantations, at Dum-
fries 3 October 1684
(PC)

MILLIGAN WILLIAM
Weaver. Rioter in Dum-
fries. Banished to the
Plantations for 3 years
in 1771. Transported on
the Matty, master Robert
Peacock, from Port Glas-
gow. Landed at Port
Oxford, Maryland
17 December 1771
(SM)(JC)

MILLESON ALEXANDER
Royalist captured at
Worcester. Transported
from Gravesend to Boston
on the John and Sarah,
master John Greene,
13 May 1652
(NER)

MILLS WILLIAM
22. Servant. Aberdeen.
Jacobite. Transported
from Liverpool for the
Leeward Islands 5 May
1747 on the Veteran,
master John Ricky.
Liberated by a French
privateer and landed
on Martinique June 1747
(P)(RM)

MILNE DAVID
Prisoner in Edinburgh
Tolbooth. Transported
from Greenock to New
York 21 October 1682
(ETR)

MILNE JAMES
Servant. Alderstounmuir.
Thief. Prisoner in
Edinburgh Tolbooth.
Banished to the Plant-
ations in America for
life, at Edinburgh
14 March 1758
(JC)

MILWARD DAVID
Royalist soldier captured at
Worcester. Transported from
Gravesend to Boston on the
John and Sarah, master John
Greene, 13 May 1652
(NER)

MILWARD JAMES
Royalist soldier captured at
Worcester. Transported from
Gravesend to Boston on the
John and Sarah, master John
Greene, 13 May 1652
(NER)

MITCHELL AGNES
Daughter of William Mitchell,
deceased, wright in Linlithgow.
Child murder. Prisoner in
Edinburgh Tolbooth. Banished
to the Plantations in America
for life, at Edinburgh
31 July 1738
(JC)

MITCHELL ALEXANDER
28. Servant to Boag Stewart,
Chamberlain to the Duke of
Perth. Jacobite in Lord Lewis
Gordon's regiment. Prisoner at
Inverness, ship and Tilbury.
Transported from London to
Jamaica or Barbados by Samuel
Smith 31 March 1747
(P)(RM)

MITCHELL ALEXANDER
Servant to Robert Dundas of
Arniston. Prisoner in Edinburgh
Tolbooth. Thief. Banished to
the Plantations in America for
14 years, at Edinburgh 20
December 1765
(JC)

MITCHELL DAVID
Jacobite captured at Preston.
Transported from Liverpool to
Virginia or Jamaica on the
Elizabeth and Anne, master
Edward Trafford, 29 June 1716.
Landed at York, Virginia -
unindentured
(SP/C)(CTB)(VSP)

163

MITCHELL GEORGE
Jacobite captured at Preston. Transported from Liverpool to St Kitts on the Hockenhill, master H.Short, 21 April 1716 (CTB)

MITCHELL GEORGE
Old Machar, Aberdeenshire. Jacobite in Ogilvy's regiment. Prisoner at Aberdeen Canongate and Carlisle, Transported from Liverpool on the Gildart, master Richard Holmes, 5 May 1747. Landed at Port North Potomac, Maryland 5 August 1747 (P)(OR)(JAB)(PRO)

MITCHELL JAMES
Royalist soldier captured at Worcester. Transported from Gravesend to Boston on the John and Sarah, master John Greene, 13 May 1652 (NER)

MITCHELL JAMES
Jacobite captured at Preston. Transported from Liverpool to Maryland on the Friendship, master Michael Mankin, 24 May 1716. Sold to Benjamin Tasker in Maryland 20 August 1716 (SP/C)(CTB)(HM)

MITCHELL JOHN
Transported from Leith to Jamaica by John Ewing August 1685 (PC)

MITCHELL JOHN
Gardener in Colonsay. Thief. Transported to America 24 December 1718 (JC)

MITCHELL JOHN
48. Alehouse keeper. Edinburgh. Jacobite in Glengarry's regiment Prisoner at Inverness and Tilbury. Transported 20 March 1747 (P)

MITCHELL WALTER
Farmer's son from King Edward, Aberdeenshire. Student at Aberdeen University in 1745 aged 17. Jacobite ensign and adjutant in the Duke of Perth's regiment. Banished to America September 1748 (P)(JAB)

MOFFAT JAMES
Prisoner in Edinburgh or Canongate Tolbooth. Banished to the Plantations in Carolina - to be transported by Robert Malloch, August 1684 (PC)

MOFFAT JEAN
Covenanter. Prisoner in Leith and Dunnottar. Banished to the Plantations, at Leith 18 August 1685. Transported from Leith to East New Jersey by George Scott of Pitlochie on the ship Henry and Francis, master Richard Hutton, 5 September 1685 (PC)

MOIR HENRY
Surgeon. Brother of Robert Moir. Kelso. Jacobite in Balmerino's Life Guards. Prisoner at Inverness and Southwark. Transported September 1748 (P)

MOIR ROBERT
Kelso. Jacobite in Balmerino's Life Guards. Prisoner at Inverness and London. Transported to America September 1748 (P)

MONDELL JOHN
Jacobite captured at Pres-
ton. Transported from
Liverpool to Virginia or
Jamaica on the Elizabeth
and Anne, master Edward
Trafford, 29 June 1716.
Landed at York, Virginia
- unindentured
(CTB)(SP/C)(VSP)

MONORGAN GILBERT
Covenanter in Argyll's
rebellion. Prisoner in
Canongate Tolbooth. Ban-
ished to the Plantations
26 August 1685. Trans-
ported from Leith to
East New Jersey by George
Scott of Pitlochie on the
Henry and Francis, master
Richard Hutton, 5 Sept-
ember 1685
(PC)

MONRO ALLAN
28. Farmer. Glenmoriston.
Jacobite in Glengarry's
regiment. Prisoner at
Inverness, ship and Til-
bury. Transported from
London to Barbados or
Jamaica by Samuel Smith
31 March 1747
(P)(RM)

MONRO DUNCAN
19. Labourer. Inverness.
Jacobite in Glenbucket's
regiment. Prisoner at
Carlisle and York. Trans-
ported from Liverpool to
the Leeward Islands on the
Veteran, master John Ricky
5 May 1747. Liberated by a
French privateer and landed on Martinique June 1747
(P)(RM)

MONRO HECTOR
31. Army deserter - a drummer
in Loudoun's regiment. Jacobite
Prisoner at Inverness and on
ship. Transported from London
to Barbados or Jamaica by
Samuel Smith 31 March 1747
(P)(RM)

MONRO HUGH
Royalist soldier captured at
Worcester. Transported from
Gravesend to Boston on the
John and Sarah, master John
Greene, 13 May 1652
(NER)

MUNRO HUGH
Prisoner in Edinburgh Tolbooth.
Transported from Leith by
Alexander Fearne to the Plant-
ations in America December 1685
(ETR)

MONRO JANET
Edinburgh. Thief. Banished to
the Plantations, at Glasgow
16 May 1770
(SM)

MONRO JOHN
Royalist soldier captured at
Worcester. Transported from
Gravesend to Boston on the
John and Sarah, master John
Greene, 13 May 1652
(NER)

MONRO ROBERT
Royalist soldier captured at
Worcester. Transported from
Gravesend to Boston on the
John and Sarah, master John
Greene, 13 May 1652
(NER)

MONTGOMERY ALEXANDER
Linlithgow. Covenanter.
Prisoner in Edinburgh
Tolbooth. Banished to the
Plantations in America 27
May 1684. Transported
from Leith to Carolina by
Robert Malloch, merchant
in Edinburgh June 1684
(PC)

MONTGOMERY NICHOLAS
Jacobite captured at
Preston. Transported
from Liverpool to Jam-
aica or Virginia on the
Elizabeth and Anne, master
Edward Trafford, 29 June
1716
(CTB)(SP/C)

MONTROSE LAUGHLAN
Royalist soldier capt-
ured at Worcester. Trans-
ported from Gravesend to
Boston on the John and
Sarah, master John Greene,
13 May 1652
(NER)

MONWILLIAM DANIEL
Royalist captured at
Worcester. Transported
from Gravesend to
Boston on the John and
Sarah, master John
Greene, 13 May 1652
(NER)

MONWILLIAM DAVID
Royalist soldier capt-
ured at Worcester.
Transported from
Gravesend to Boston on
the John and Sarah,
master John Greene, 13
May 1652
(NER)

MOODIE ELISABETH
Vagabond. Banished to
the Plantations for life,
at Aberdeen 11 May 1717
(JC)

MOODY GEORGE
Jacobite captured at Preston.
Transported from Liverpool for
Jamaica on the Two Brothers,
master Edward Rathbone, 26
April 1716. Landed on Montserrat
June 1716
(SP/C)(CTB)(CTP)

MOORE COLIN
'Beddyvaughan'. Jacobite in
Glenbucket's regiment. Prisoner
at Carlisle and Chester.
Transported 1747(?)
(P)

MOORE DONALD
Covenanter in Argyll's rebellion
Prisoner in Paul's Work, Edin-
burgh. Banished to the Plant-
ations 30 July 1685. Transported
from Leith to Jamaica by John
Ewing August 1685
(PC)

MOORE GEORGE
Covenanter. Prisoner at Leith.
Transported from Leith to East
New Jersey by George Scott of
Pitlochie on the Henry and
Francis, master Richard Hutton,
5 September 1685
(PC)

MOORE ROBERT
Transported from Leith to
Jamaica by John Ewing August
1685
(PC)

MOOR WILLIAM
Prisoner in Stirling Tolbooth.
Released to go to the Plant-
ations in America 24 March
1685
(PC)

MOORE DONALD
Covenanter. Prisoner in
Paul's Work, Edinburgh.
Transported from Leith
to East New Jersey by
Robert Barclay of Urie
31 July 1685
(PC)

MOORE JAMES
Royalist soldier capt-
ured at Worcester. Trans-
ported from Gravesend to
Boston on the John and
Sarah, master John Greene
13 May 1652
(NER)

MORE JOHN
Royalist soldier capt-
ured at Worcester. Trans-
ported from Gravesend to
Boston on the John and
Sarah, master John Greene
13 May 1652
(NER)

MORGAN ALLAN
25. Jacobite in Raasay's
regiment. Prisoner at
Inverness and Tilbury.
Transported from London
to Barbados or Jamaica
by Samuel Smith 31 March
1747
(P)(RM)

MORGAN CHARLES
18. Barber. Elgin. Jac-
obite in Glenbucket's
regiment. Prisoner at
Carlisle and York.
Transported from Liver-
pool for the Leeward
Islands on the Veteran,
master John Ricky, 5
May 1747. Liberated by
a French privateer and
landed on Martinique
June 1747
(P)(RM)

MORGAN PETER or PATRICK
Foginell, Aberdeenshire.
Jacobite in Roy Stuart's regi-
ment. Prisoner at Chester.
Transported from Liverpool on
the Johnson, master William
Pemberton, 5 May 1747.
Landed at Port Oxford, Maryland
5 August 1747
(P)(JAB)(PRO)

MORRISON ALEXANDER
50. Distiller on Mull. From
Lewis. Jacobite in McLachlan's
regiment. Prisoner at Inverness
ships and Medway. Transported
from London to Barbados or
Jamaica by Samuel Smith 31
March 1747
(P)(RM)

MORRISON ANDREW
Banished for robbery 15 February
1773. Transported from Port
Glasgow on the Thomas of Glasgow
master John Robertson. Landed at
James River, Upper District,
Virginia 5 June 1773
(JC)

MORISON DONALD
Covenanter in Argyll's rebellion.
Prisoner in Paul's Work, Edinburgh
Banished to the Plantations 30
July 1685. Transported from Leith
to Jamaica by John Ewing August
1685
(PC)

MORRISON JAMES
Jacobite captured at Preston.
Transported from Liverpool to
Antigua on the Scipio, master
John Scaisbrick, 30 March 1716
(CTB)(SP/C)

MORISON JANET
Prisoner in Edinburgh Tolbooth.
Transported from Greenock to
New York 21 October 1682
(ETR)

MORISON JOHN
Erickstaines. Covenanter.
Banished to the Plant-
ations in America, at
Glasgow 17 October 1684
(PC)

MORTIMER ALEXANDER
Jacobite captured at Pres-
ton. Transported from
Liverpool to Maryland on
the Friendship, master
Michael Mankin, 24 May
1716. Sold to Henry
Ernallse, Maryland
20 August 1716
(SP/C)(CTB)(HM)

MORTIMER GEORGE
Jacobite captured at
Preston. Transported from
Liverpool for Jamaica on
the Two Brothers, master
Edward Rathbone, 26 April
1716. Landed on Montserrat
June 1716
(SP/C)(CTB)(CTP)

MORTIMER ISABEL
Child murder. Banished to
America, at Aberdeen June
1758
(SM)

MORTON PATRICK
Royalist soldier captured
at Worcester. Transported
from Gravesend to Boston
on the John and Sarah,
master John Greene,
13 May 1652
(NER)

MORTON WILLIAM
Craigieknow. Portioner of
Gattonside. Hamesucken.
Banished to the Plantations
for 7 years, at Jedburgh
16 September 1763
(SM)

MOSSMAN OF MOUNT JAMES
Covenanter. Banished to the
Plantations. Transported
from Leith on the St Michael
of Scarborough, master
Edward Johnston, 12 December
1678
(PC)

MOUBRAY THOMAS
Kirkliston. Covenanter.
Prisoner in Edinburgh Tolbooth
Banished to the Plantations in
the Indies 1 August 1678.
Transported from Leith on the
St Michael of Scarborough,
master Edward Johnston,
12 December 1678
(PC)

MOUBRAY WILLIAM
Jacobite captured at Preston.
Transported from Liverpool
to Maryland on the Friendship,
master Michael Mankin, 24 May
1716. Sold to Henry Tripp in
Maryland 20 August 1716
(SP/C)(CTB)(HM)

MUCKLE ROBERT
60. Labourer. Duns. Jacobite.
Prisoner at Cockermouth, Whitehaven and Carlisle. Transported
1747(?)
(P)

MUIR ADAM
Covenanter. Prisoner in Edinburgh Tolbooth. Banished to
the Plantations 24 July 1685
(PC)

MUIR GEORGE
Covenanter. Prisoner at Glas-
gow, Dunnottar and Leith.
Banished to the Plantations,
at Leith 18 August 1685
(PC)

MUIR JAMES
Lesmahowgow. Covenanter.
Prisoner in Edinburgh
Tolbooth. Banished to the
Plantations 5 May 1684.
Transported from Leith by
George Lockhart, merchant
in New York, James Glen,
stationer burgess of
Edinburgh, and Thomas
Gordon, burgess of Edin-
burgh, 16 May 1684
(PC)

MUIR JAMES
Banished to the Plantations
Transported from Greenock
on the Rainbow, master
William Gordon. Landed at
Port Hampton, Virginia
3 May 1775
(JC)

MUIR ROBERT
Covenanter. Prisoner in
Laigh Parliament house,
Edinburgh. Transported
from Leith to East New
Jersey by George Scott
of Pitlochie on the
Henry and Francis, mas-
ter Richard Hutton,
5 September 1685
(PC)

MUIR ROBERT
Thief. Prisoner in
Stirling Tolbooth.
Banished, at Stirling
20 May 1731
(JC)

MUIR WILLIAM
Thief. Banished for life,
at Dumfries 1753
(SM)

MUIRHEAD JAMES
Prisoner in Edinburgh or
Canongate Tolbooth. Ban-
ished to Carolina with
Robert Malloch August 1684
(PC)

MUIRHEAD GAVIN
Cambusnethan. Covenanter.
Banished to the Plantations
5 May 1684. Prisoner in Edinburgh Tolbooth. Transported
from Leith by George Lockhart,
merchant in New York, James
Glen, stationer burgess of
Edinburgh, and Thomas Gordon,
burgess of Edinburgh, 16 May 1684
(PC)

MUIRHEAD JAMES
Covenanter. Prisoner at Leith,
Canongate and Dunnottar. Banished to the Plantations, at
Leith 18 August 1685. Transported from Leith to East New
Jersey by George Scott of Pitlochie on the Henry and Francis,
master Richard Hutton, 5 September 1685
(PC)

MUIRHEAD JOHN
Covenanter. Prisoner in Edin-
burgh Tolbooth. Banished to
East New Jersey 21 August 1685
Transported from Leith to East
New Jersey by George Scott of
Pitlochie on the Henry and
Francis, master Richard Hutton,
5 September 1685
(PC)(ETR)

MUIRHEAD MARGARET
Prisoner in Edinburgh or Canon-
gate Tolbooths. Banished to
Carolina with Robert Malloch
August 1684
(PC)

MUN ARCHIBALD
Weaver. Thief. Banished for
life, at Glasgow 1752
(SM)

MUNDILL JOHN
Covenanter. Prisoner at
Edinburgh and Leith. Ban-
ished to the Plantations
31 July 1685. Stigmatised
Transported from Leith to
East New Jersey by George
Scott of Pitlochie on the
Henry and Francis, master
Richard Hutton, 5 Septem-
ber 1685
(PC)(ETR)

MURDOCH WILLIAM
40. Wool merchant. Call-
ander, Perthshire. Jac-
obite ensign. Prisoner
at Canongate and Carlisle
Transported from Liver-
pool on the Johnson,
master William Pemberton.
Landed at Port Oxford,
Maryland 5 August 1747
(P)(PRO)

MURRAY ALEXANDER
Jacobite captured at Pres-
ton. Transported from
Liverpool to Virginia on
the Anne, master Robert
Wallace, 31 July 1716
(CTB)(SP/C)

MURRAY ALEXANDER
Jacobite captured at Pres-
ton. Transported from
Liverpool to Virginia on
the Anne, master Robert
Wallace, 31 July 1716
(CTB)(SP/C)

MURRAY ANNA
Child murder. Prisoner in
Edinburgh Tolbooth. Ban-
ished to the Plantations
31 July 1685. Transported
from Leith to Jamaica by
John Ewing August 1685
(ETR)(PC)

MURRAY DAVID
Jacobite captured at Pres-
ton. Transported from
Liverpool to Virginia on
the Anne, master Robert
Wallace, 31 July 1716
(CTB)(SP/C)

MURRAY HENRY
Jacobite captured at Preston.
Transported from Liverpool to
Antigua on the Scipio, master
John Scaisbrick, 30 March 1716
(CTB)(SP/C)

MURRAY HENRY
Jacobite captured at Preston.
Transported from Liverpool to
Maryland on the Friendship,
master Michael Mankin, 24 May
1716. Sold to William Holland
Esq. in Maryland 20 August 1716
(SP/C)(CTB)(HM)

MURRAY JAMES
Royalist captured at Worcester.
Transported from Gravesend to
Boston on the John and Sarah,
master John Greene, 13 May 1652
(NER)

MURRAY JAMES
Covenanter in Argyll's rebellion.
Prisoner at Canongate. Banished
to the Plantations 30 July 1685.
Stigmatised 4 August 1685. Transported from Leith to East New
Jersey by George Scott of Pitlochie on the Henry and Francis,
master Richard Hutton, 4 August
1685
(PC)

MURRAY JAMES
Jacobite captured at Preston.
Transported from Liverpool to
Virginia or Jamaica on the
Elizabeth and Anne, master
Edward Trafford, 29 June 1716.
Landed at York, Virginia -
unindentured
(CTB)(SP/C)(VSP)

MURRAY JOHN
Royalist soldier captured at
Worcester. Transported from
Gravesend to Boston on the
John and Sarah, master John
Greene, 13 May 1652
(NER)

MURRAY JOHN
30. Weaver. Annandale.
Jacobite in Glenbucket's
regiment. Captured at
Carlisle. Prisoner at
Carlisle and York.Trans-
ported from Liverpool
for the Leeward Islands
on the Veteran, master
John Ricky, 5 May 1747.
Liberated by a French
privateer and landed on
Martinique June 1747
(P)(RM)

MURRAY JOHN
Paisley. Prisoner in
Edinburgh Tolbooth.
Attempted murder. Ban-
ished to America for 7
years, 20 July 1767
(JC)

MURRAY JONAS
Royalist soldier capt-
ured at Worcester.
Transported from Gra-
vesend to Boston on the
John and Sarah, master
John Greene, 13 May
1652
(NER)

MURRAY NEIL
Royalist soldier capt-
ured at Worcester.
Transported from Gra-
vesend to Boston on the
John and Sarah, master
John Greene, 13 May
1652
(NER)

MURRAY PATRICK
Jacobite captured at
Preston. Transported
from Liverpool to St
Kitts on the Hocken-
hill, master H. Short,
25 June 1716
(CTB)(SP/C)

MURRAY PATRICK or MCGREGOR
Farmer. Perthshire. Jacobite
in Glengyle's regiment.
Prisoner at Aberdeen, Canongate
and Carlisle. Transported from
Liverpool on the Johnson, master
William Pemberton. Landed at
Port Oxford, Maryland 5 August
1747
(P)(PRO)

MURRAY WILLIAM
Jacobite captured at Preston.
Transported from Liverpool to
St Kitts on the Hockenhill,
master H. Short, 25 June 1716
(CTB)(SP/C)

NAIRN THOMAS
35. Chapman. Strathdon, Aberdeenshire. Jacobite in Glenbucket's regiment. Prisoner
at Inverness, ship and Southwark. Transported 19 March 1747
(P)

NAISMITH JOHN
18. Wool weaver. Dundee.
Jacobite in Ogilvy's regiment.
Prisoner at Stirling, Carlisle
and Liverpool. Transported
from Liverpool on the Johnson,
master William Pemberton.
Landed at Port Oxford, Maryland
5 August 1747
(P)(OR)(PRO)

NEAVE ALEXANDER
Jacobite captured at Preston.
Transported from Liverpool to
Maryland on the Friendship,
master Michael Mankin, 24 May
1716. Sold to Thomas Broadhurst
in Maryland 20 August 1716
(SP/C)(CTB)(HM)

NEILSON GEORGE
Jacobite captured at Preston.
Transported from Liverpool to
Virginia on the Godspeed, master
Arthur Smith, 28 July 1716. Sold
to Charles Digges in Maryland
18 October 1716
(SP/C)(CTB)(HM)

NEILSON JAMES
26. Labourer. Aberdeen.
Jacobite. Prisoner at
York. Transportedfrom
Liverpool to the Leeward
Islands on the Veteran,
master John Ricky, 5 May
1747. Liberated by a
French privateer and
landed on Martinique
June 1747
(P)(RM)

NEVERY JAMES
Jacobite captured at
Preston. Transported
from Liverpool to
Maryland on the ship
Friendship, master
Michael Mankin, 24 May
1716. Sold to William
Holland Esq. in Mary-
land 20 August 1716
(SP/C)(CTB)(HM)

NEWBIGGING ANDREW
Prisoner in Edinburgh
Tolbooth. Transported
from Leith to the
Plantations November
1679
(ETR)

NEWTON JOHN
England. Jacobite.
Transported from Liver-
pool on the Johnson,
master William Pember-
ton. Landed at Port
Oxford, Maryland
5 August 1747
(P)(PRO)

NEWTON JOHN
Schoolmaster. Haddington.
Fraud. Prisoner in Edin-
burgh Tolbooth. Banished
to the Plantations in
America for life, at
Edinburgh 4 March 1762
(JC)

NEWTON JOHNATHAN
Jacobite captured at Preston.
Transported from Liverpool to
South Carolina on the Susannah,
master Thomas Bromhill, 7 May
1716
(SP/C)(CTB)

NICHOLL GEORGE
26. Weaver. Aberdeen. Jacobite
captured at Carlisle. Prisoner
at Carlisle and York. Transported
from Liverpool for the Leeward
Islands on the Veteran, master
John Ricky, 5 May 1747. Liberated by a French privateer and
landed on Martinique June 1747
(P)(RM)

NICHOLL JAMES
24. Brechin. Jacobite in Ogilvy's
regiment. Prisoner at Inverness
and Tilbury. Transported from
London to Barbados or Jamaica by
Samuel Smith 20 March 1747
(P)(RM)

NICHOLSON JOHN
Jacobite captured at Preston.
Transported from Liverpool to
South Carolina on the Wakefield,
master Thomas Beck, 21 April 1716
(CTB)(SP/C)

NICHOLSON JOHN
Jacobite captured at Preston.
Transported from Liverpool to
Antigua on the Scipio, master
John Scaisbrick, 30 March 1716
(SP/C)(CTB)

NICOL BARBARA
Daughter of Norman Nicol, in
Bennyhillock, Aberdeen. Banished
from Scotland for life, at Aber-
deen May 1727
(JC)

NICOLL JOHN
Transported from Leith to
Jamaica by John Ewing
August 1685
(PC)

NICOLSON ISABEL
Fireraiser and thief.
Prisoner in Edinburgh Tol-
booth. Banished to the
Plantations for life, at
Edinburgh 6 August 1711
(JC)

NICOLSON JOHN
Bridgend, Liberton.
Adulterer. Warded in
Edinburgh Tolbooth 10
March 1684. Transported
from Leith to East New
Jersey by Thomas Gordon
4 May 1684
(ETR)(Lib.KSR)

NIMMO JAMES
Jacobite captured at Pres-
ton. Transported from
Liverpool to Antigua on
the Scipio, master John
Scaisbrick, 30 March 1716
(CTB)(SP/C)

NINIAN GRIZEL
Banished for life. Trans-
ported from Glasgow on the
Brilliant, master Robert
Bennet. Landed at Port
Hampton, Virginia
7 October 1772
(JC)

NISBET GILES
Duns, Berwickshire. Cattle
thief. Banished to the
Plantations in 1768
(SM)

NISBET JANET
Duns, Berwickshire. Cattle
thief. Banished to the
Plantations in 1768
(SM)

NISBET JAMES
Jacobite captured at Preston.
Transported from Liverpool to
Virginia or Jamaica on the
Elizabeth and Anne, master
Edward Trafford, 29 September
1716. Landed in Virginia at
York - indentured
(SP/C)(CTB)(VSP)

NISBET JOHN
Woolfiner. Glasgow. Covenanter.
Prisoner in Glasgow Tolbooth.
Banished at Glasgow June 1684.
Transported from the Clyde to
America on the Pelican by Walter
Gibson, merchant in Glasgow
(PC)

NISBET JOHN
21. Tutor. Falkirk. Jacobite
in Lord John Drummond's regiment
Prisoner at Inverness and on
ships. Transported 1747(?)
(P)

NISBET MR WILLIAM
Minister in Orkney. Adulterer.
Banished to the Plantations
for life, at Aberdeen 24 May
1766
(SM)

NIVEN WILLIAM
Cathcart. Prisoner at Edinburgh
and Canongate. Banished to the
Plantations 9 October 1684.
Transported from Leith on the
St Michael of Scarborough, master
Edward Johnston, 12 December 1678
(PC)

NIVEN WILLIAM
Labourer. Ayr. Pickpocket.
Banished to the Plantations
for life, at Ayr 24 May 1775
(SM)

NIVEN WILLIAM
Tenant of Maxwell of Pol-
lock. Covenanter. Prison-
er at Canongate and Leith.
Banished to the Plantations
9 October 1684. Transported
from Leith to East New
Jersey by George Scott of
Pitlochie on the ship
Henry and Francis, master
Richard Hutton, 5 Septem-
ber 1685
(PC)

NOBLE WILLIAM
Jacobite captured at Pres-
ton. Transported from
Liverpool to Virginia or
Jamaica on the Elizabeth
and Anne, master Edward
Trafford, 29 September
1716. Landed at York in
Virginia - unindentured
(SP/C)(CTB)(VSP)

NORVIL ADAM
Jacobite. Transported
from Liverpool on the
Johnson, master William
Pemberton. Landed at
Port Oxford, Maryland
5 August 1747
(PRO)

OCHILTREE DAVID
Covenanter in Argyll's
rebellion. Prisoner in
Canongate Tolbooth.
Banished to the Plant-
ations 30 July 1685.
Transported from Leith
to Jamaica by John Ewing
August 1685
(PC)

OCKFORD JANET
Prisoner in Edinburgh
Tolbooth. Transported
to Barbados by George
Hutchison, merchant in
Edinburgh 7 December
1665
(ETR)

OGILVIE ALEXANDER
Brother of Captain Thomas
Ogilvie of Eastmilne. Bigamy.
Prisoner in Edinburgh Tolbooth
Banished, at Edinburgh
4 August 1766
(JC)

OGILVY HENRY
Jacobite captured at Preston.
Transported from Liverpool to
St Kitts on the Hockenhill,
master H. Short, 25 June 1716
(CTB)

OGILVIE ISOBEL
Child murder. Banished, at
Aberdeen May 1749
(SM)

OGILVY JAMES
Thief. Prisoner in Edinburgh
Tolbooth. Transported from
Leith to Virginia on the ship
Phoenix of Leith, master James
Gibson, by Robert Learmonth,
merchant in Edinburgh
4 May 1666
(ETR)

OGILVY JOHN
Jacobite captured at Preston.
Transported from Liverpool to
Jamaica or Virginia on the
Elizabeth and Anne, master
Edward Trafford, 29 June 1716.
Landed at York, Virginia -
unindentured
(CTB)(SP/C)(VSP)

OGILVIE JOHN
Servant to Captain Alexander
Kinloch. 25. Jacobite in Ogilvy's
regiment. Prisoner at Carlisle
and Canongate. Transported from
Liverpool on the Gildart, master
Richard Holmes. Landed Port North
Potomac, Maryland 5 August 1747
(P)(OR)(PRO)

OGILVY JOHN
Quiech, Angus. Attempted
murder of Robert Skinner
landwaiter, Aberdeen.
Banished to America
9 March 1756
(SM)

OGLEBY HENRY
Jacobite captured at Pres-
ton. Transported from
Liverpool to St Kitts on
the Hockenhill, master
H.Short, 25 June 1716
(SP/C)

OLIPHANT CHARLES
Excise officer, Aberdeen
and Inverness. Jacobite
lieutenant in Lord John
Drummond's regiment.
Convicted of High Treason
20 December 1746.
Reprieved 12 February
1746. Banished to America
September 1748
(JAB)

OLIPHANT LAWRENCE
Jacobite captured at Pres-
ton. Transported from
Liverpool to St Kitts on
the Hockenhill, master
H.Short, 25 June 1716
(SP/C)(CTB)

OLIPHANT WILLIAM
Covenanter. Prisoner at
Edinburgh, Burntisland,
Dunnottar and Leith. Ban-
ished to the Plantations,
at Leith 18 August 1685.
Transported from Leith
to East New Jersey by
George Scott of Pitlochie
on the Henry and Francis,
master Richard Hutton,
5 September 1685
(ETR)(PC)

OLIVER JAMES
Jedburgh Forest. Covenanter.
Prisoner at Edinburgh and
Canongate Tolbooths. Banished
to the Plantations 24 July
1685. Transported from Leith
to Jamaica by John Ewing
August 1685
(ETR)(PC)

O'NEIL DANIEL
Royalist soldier captured at
Worcester. Transported from
Gravesend to Boston on the
John and Sarah, master John
Greene, 13 May 1652
(NER)

ORR DUNCAN
14. Weaver. Perthshire. Jacobite soldier. Prisoner at
Lancaster. Transported from
Liverpool for the Leeward
Islands on the Veteran, master
John Ricky, 5 May 1747. Liberated by a French privateer
and landed on Martinique June
1747
(P)(RM)

ORR DUNCAN
41. Labourer. Perthshire. Jacobite. Prisoner at Lancaster.
Transported from Liverpool for
the Leeward Islands on the
Veteran, master John Ricky,
5 May 1747. Liberated by a
French privateer and landed
on Martinique June 1747
(P)(PRO)

ORR ROBERT
Milnbank. Covenanter. Banished
to the Plantations in America
16 August 1670
(PC)

ORROCK ALEXANDER
Jacobite captured at Preston.
Transported from Liverpool to
Virginia on the Godspeed, master
Arthur Smith, 28 July 1716.
Sold to Henry Wharton in Mary-
land 18 October 1716
(SP/C)(CTB)(HM)

OSWALD JOSEPH
Jacobite captured at Preston. Transported from Liverpool to Antigua on the Scipio, master John Scaisbrick, 30 March 1716 (CTB)(SP/C)

OSWALD JOHN
Petty thief. Banished for life 1773 (SM)

PADDY JOHN
Jacobite. Transported from Liverpool on the Gildart, master Richard Holmes. Landed at Port North Potomac, Maryland 5 August 1747 (PRO)

PALMER JOHN
Thief. Prisoner in Jedburgh Tolbooth. Banished to the Plantations in America, at Jedburgh 11 May 1726 (JC)

PANTON ROBERT
Dalmeny. Prisoner in Edinburgh Tolbooth. Banished to the Plantations 7 November 1678. Transported from Leith on the St Michael of Scarborough master Edward Johnston, 12 December 1678 (PC)

PARK JOHN
Weaver. Lanark. Covenanter. Prisoner in Edinburgh Tolbooth. Transported from Leith to America by Alexander Fearne and his shipmaster Edward Barnes December 1685 (ETR)(PC)

PARK THOMAS
Jacobite captured at Preston. Transported from Liverpool to Maryland on the Friendship, master Michael Mankin, 24 May 1716. Sold to Philip Dowell in Maryland 20 August 1716 (SP/C)(CTB)(HM)

PARKER WILLIAM
Soldier in Rich's Regiment of Foot. Forger. Banished to New England June 1751 (SM)

PATERSON ANDREW
Hamilton. Prisoner at Leith. Transported from Leith to East New Jersey by George Scott of Pitlochie on the Henry and Francis, master Richard Hutton, 5 September 1685 (PC)

PATTERSON DAVID
Royalist soldier captured at Worcester. Transported from Gravesend to Boston on the John and Sarah, master John Greene, 13 May 1652 (NER)

PATERSON DAVID
Eaglesham. Covenanter. Prisoner in Edinburgh Tolbooth. Banished to the Plantations 26 November 1685. Transported from Leith to America by Alexander Fearne and his shipmaster Edward Barnes 17 December 1685 (ETR)(PC)

PATTERSON JAMES
Royalist soldier captured at Worcester. Transported from Gravesend to Boston on the John and Sarah, master John Greene, 13 May 1652 (NER)

PATERSON JAMES
Prisoner in Canongate or
Edinburgh Tolbooths.
Transported from Leith to
Carolina by Robert Malloch
merchant in Edinburgh,
August 1684
(PC)

PATTERSON JAMES
Jacobite captured at Pres-
ton. Transported on the
Elizabeth and Anne, master
Edward Trafford, from
Liverpool for Jamaica or
Virginia 29 June 1716.
Landed at York, Virginia
- unindentured
(SP/C)(CTB)(VSP)

PATERSON JEAN
Banished for 7 years. Trans-
ported from Glasgow on the
Brilliant, master Robert
Bennet. Landed at Port
Hampton, Virginia
7 October 1772
(JC)

PATERSON MARGARET
Prisoner in the Correction
House, Edinburgh. Trans-
ported to the Plantations
by James Montgomerie
14 November 1694
(EBE)

PATERSON MRS MARY
Widow of William Ainsly,
Dumfries. Fireraiser. Ban-
ished to the Plantations
for life in 1767
(SM)

PATERSON NINIAN
Prisoner in Glasgow Tolbooth
Transported to East New Jersey by Walter Gibson, merchant in Glasgow 21 February
1684
(PC)

PATERSON ROBERT
19. Hosier. Aberdeen. Jacobite
in Glenbucket's regiment.
Captured at Carlisle. Prisoner
at Carlisle. Transported from
Liverpool for the Leeward Islands
on the Veteran, master John
Ricky, 5 May 1747. Liberated
by a French privateer and landed
on Martinique June 1747
(P)(JAB)(RM)

PATERSON STEPHEN
Clerk of the Carron Company.
Prisoner in Edinburgh Tolbooth
Forger. Banished to the Plant-
ations in America for 10 years,
at Edinburgh 15 February 1765
(JC)

PATON GEORGE
20. Brewer's servant. Dirleton
East Lothian. Jacobite in the
Duke of Perth's regiment.
Prisoner at Torwood, Stirling
and Carlisle. Transported
1747(?)
(P)

PATON JOHN
Monkland. Prisoner in Glasgow
Tolbooth. Banished at Glasgow
June 1684. Transported from
the Clyde to America on the
Pelican by Walter Gibson,
merchant in Glasgow, June 1684
(PC)

PATON JOHN
Jacobite. Transported from
Liverpool on the Gildart, master
Richard Holmes. Landed at Port
North Potomac, Maryland 5 August
1747
(PRO)

PATRICK JAMES
Kilmarnock. Covenanter. Prisoner
in Canongate Tolbooth. Banished
to the Plantations 10 December
1685. Transported from Leith by
Alexander Fearne to America
December 1685
(ETR)(PC)

PATTULLO JAMES or JOHN
Jacobite captured at Pres-
ton. Transported from
Liverpool to Virginia or
Jamaica on the Elizabeth
and Anne, master Edward
Trafford, 29 June 1716.
Landed at York, Virginia
- unindentured
(SP/C)(CTB)(VSP)

PEACOCK JAMES
Assault. Banished for
life, at Ayr 1753
(SM)

PEARSON ELSPETH
Spouse of John Martin,
Cupar. Rioter at Mylne
field. Banished to the
Plantations for life,
at Perth 1773
(SM)

PEDDIE JOHN
42. Merchant. Arbroath.
Jacobite. Prisoner at
Arbroath, Dundee, Can-
ongate and Carlisle.
Transported from Liver-
pool on the Gildart,
master Richard Holmes.
Landed at Port North
Potomack, Maryland
5 August 1747
(P)(PRO)

PEDDIN ALEXANDER
Prisoner in Edinburgh
Tolbooth. Banished to the
Plantations 12 December
1678
(PC)

PERRY GEORGE
Royalist soldier captured
at Worcester. Transported
from Gravesend to Boston
on the John and Sarah,
master John Greene,
13 May 1652
(NER)

PETER ANNE
Kintore. Child murder. Banished
for life, at Aberdeen 12 September 1776
(SM)

PETER JAMES
Jacobite captured at Preston.
Transported from Liverpool to
Jamaica or Virginia on the
Elizabeth and Anne, master
Edward Trafford, 29 June 1716.
Landed at York, Virginia -
unindentured
(CTB)(SP/C)(VSP)

PETER JOHN
Jacobite captured at Preston.
Transported from Liverpool to
Maryland on the Friendship,
master Michael Mankin, 24 May
1716. Sold to William Holland
Esq. in Maryland 20 August 1716
(SP/C)(CTB)(VSP)

PETER JOHN
Jacobite captured at Preston.
Transported from Liverpool to
Virginia or Jamaica on the
Elizabeth and Anne, master
Edward Trafford, 29 June 1716.
Landed at York, Virginia -
unindentured
(CTB)(SP/C)(VSP)

PETRIE JAMES
20. Labourer. Angus. Jacobite
in Ogilvy's regiment. Captured
at Carlisle, prisoner there.
Transported from Liverpool for
the Leeward Islands on the
Veteran, master John Ricky, 5
May 1747. Liberated by a French
privateer and landed on Martinique June 1747
(P)(OR)(RM)

PETTY JOHN
Covenanter. Prisoner in Edinburgh
Tolbooth. Banished to the
Plantations 24 July 1685
(PC)

PHILP GEORGE
Doctor. Huntly. Illegal
abortionist. Banished,
at Aberdeen 1771. Trans-
ported on the Betsy, master
James Ramsay. Landed at
Port of James River, Upper
District 29 April 1772
(SM)(JC)

PIGGOTT ALEXANDER
26. Bridgend, Kingoldrum,
Angus. Jacobite in Ogilvy's
regiment. Prisoner at Inver
ness, ship and Tilbury.
Transported from London to
Barbados or Jamaica by
Samuel Smith 31 March 1747
(P)(RM)

PINMURRAY ALICE
Jacobite captured at Car-
lisle. Prisoner at Car-
lisle and Lancaster. Transported from Liverpool on
the Johnson, master William
Pemberton. Landed at Port
Oxford, Maryland 5 August
1747
(P)(PRO)

PIRIE JOSEPH
Pickpocket. Banished for
7 years, at Ayr 27 Sept-
ember 1775
(SM)

POLLOCK JOHN
Covenanter. Prisoner at
Glasgow, Dunnottar and
Leith. Banished to the
Plantations, at Leith
18 August 1685. Trans-
ported from Leith to East
New Jersey by George Scott
of Pitlochie on the ship
Henry and Francis, master
Richard Hutton, 5 September
1685
(PC)

POLLOCK WILLIAM
Horsehirer and brandy dealer.
Glasgow. Murder. Prisoner in
Edinburgh Tolbooth. Banished
to the Plantations in America
for 7 years, at Edinburgh
15 January 1763
(JC)

PORTEOUS ....
Servitour to John Telfer,
painter in Edinburgh. Rioter.
Transported to Virginia or
Barbados 13 September 1666
(PC)

PORTEOUS JOHN
Jacobite captured at Preston.
Transported from Liverpool
for Virginia or Jamaica on
the Elizabeth and Anne,
master Edward Trafford, 29
June 1716
(CTB)(SP/C)

PORTEOUS ROBERT
Servant to Mrs Scott-Nisbet
of Craigintinny. Thief.
Banished to America for life.
1 August 1768
(JC)

PORTEOUS STEVEN
Tailor. Canongate. Prisoner
in Edinburgh Tolbooth. Banished to the Plantations.
Transported from Leith on the
St Michael of Scarborough,
master Edward Johnston,
12 December 1678
(PC)

PORTER WILLIAM
Son of William Porter, deceased,
shopkeeper in Glasgow. Pickpocket. Prisoner in Edinburgh
Tolbooth. Banished to the
Plantations in America for 14
years, at Edinburgh 4 August
1766
(JC)

POTT ANTHONY alias
              HEIDSHOIP
Prisoner from Jedburgh
Tolbooth. Transported
to Barbados 17 April
1666
(ETR)

POTTS THOMAS
Jacobite captured at
Preston. Transported
from Liverpool to Mary-
land on the Friendship,
master Michael Mankin,
24 May 1716. Sold to
William Bladen Esq. in
Maryland 20 August 1716
(CTB)(SP/C)(HM)

POUSTIE JOHN
Tailor. Edinburgh. Jac-
obite in Roy Stuart's
regiment. Prisoner at
Edinburgh and Carlisle.
Transported 9 November
1748
(P)

PRICE RALPH
34. Miller. Jacobite.
Prisoner at Carlisle and
Whitehaven. Transported
from Liverpool on the
Gildart, master Richard
Holmes. Landed at Port
North Potomac, Maryland
5 August 1747
(P)(PRO)

PRINGLE JOHN
Pickpocket. Prisoner in
Edinburgh Tolbooth,
warded there 6 May 1720.
Released for transport-
ation 15 December 1720
(ETR)

PRINGLE THOMAS
Prisoner in Edinburgh
Tolbooth. Transported
from Leith to the
Plantations November
1679
(ETR)

PROCTOR JOSEPH
Jacobite captured at Preston.
Transported from Liverpool to
Antigua on the Scipio, master
John Scaisbrick, 30 March 1716
(CTB)(SP/C)

PROCTOR WILLIAM
Wright. Elgin. Thief. Prisoner
in Edinburgh Tolbooth. Banished
to the Plantations in America
for life, at Edinburgh January
1767
(SM)(JC)

PROPHET SYLVESTER
Jacobite captured at Preston.
Transported from Liverpool for
Jamaica or Virginia on the
Elizabeth and Anne, master
Edward Trafford, 29 June 1716.
Landed at York, Virginia -
unindentured
(SP/C)(CTB)(VSP)

PROVAN ROBERT
Banished for shopbreaking 15
February 1773. Transported
from Port Glasgow on the ship
Thomas of Glasgow, master John
Robertson. Landed at James
River, Upper District, Virginia
5 June 1773
(JC)

PRYDE JAMES
Weaver. Strathmiglo, Fife.
Covenanter. Prisoner in Canongate Tolbooth. Transported to
the Plantations from Leith
12 December 1678
(PC)

PYE JOHN
Thief. Banished to the Plantations for 14 years, at Perth
5 May 1775
(SM)

QUEEN GEORGE
Royalist soldier captured
at Worcester. Transported
from Gravesend to Boston
on the John and Sarah,
master John Greene,
13 May 1652
(NER)

RAE JAMES
Uddingston. Covenanter.
Prisoner in Edinburgh
Tolbooth. Banished to
the Plantations 26 Nov-
ember 1685. Transported
from Leith by Alexander
Fearne and his shipmaster
Edward Barnes December
1685
(ETR)(PC)

RAE JAMES
Tenant of David Lumsden
of Cushnie, Aberdeenshire
Jacobite captured at Pres
ton. Transported from
Liverpool to Virginia or
Jamaica on the Elizabeth
and Anne, master Edward
Trafford, 29 June 1716.
Landed at York, Virginia
- unindentured
(JAB)(SP/C)(CTB)(VSP)

RAE JOHN
Tailor. Falkirk. Prisoner
in Canongate Tolbooth.
Transported from Leith on
St Michael of Scarborough,
master Edward Johnston,
12 December 1678
(PC)

RAE JOHN
Jacobite captured at Pres-
ton. Transported from
Liverpool to South Carol-
ina on the Susannah, master
Thomas Bromhall, 7 May 1716
(CTB)(SP/C)

RAE WILLIAM
Weaver. Glasgow. Prisoner in
Canongate Tolbooth. Transported
from Leith to the Plantations
on the St Michael of Scarborough,
master Edward Johnston,
12 December 1678
(PC)

RAMSAY ANDREW
Jacobite captured at Preston.
Transported from Liverpool to
St Kitts on the Hockenhill,
master H.Short, 25 June 1716
(CTB)(SP/C)

RAMSAY GEORGE
Tenant farmer. Strathbogie,
Aberdeenshire. Jacobite
ensign in the Duke of Perth's
regiment. Prisoner at Carlisle
and Southwark. Transported
21 July 1748
(P)

RAMSAY JOHN
Jacobite captured at Preston.
Transported from Liverpool to
Maryland on the Friendship,
master Michael Mankin, 24 May
1716. Sold to William Bladen
Esq. in Maryland 20 August 1716
(SP/C)(CTB)(HM)

RAMSAY WILLIAM
Jacobite captured at Preston.
Transported from Liverpool to
St Kitts on the Hockenhill,
master H.Short, 25 June 1716
(CTB)(SP/C)

RANALD FRANCIS
16. Herd. Strathbogie, Aberdeen-
shire. Jacobite in Lord Lewis
Gordon's regiment. Prisoner at
Inverness, ship and Tilbury.
Transported from London to
Jamaica or Barbados by Samuel
Smith 31 March 1747
(P)(RM)

RANKIN JOHN
Bonhardpans. Covenanter.
Banished to the Plantations
in America 16 August 1670
(PC)

RANKEN JOHN
Jacobite captured at Preston. Transported from
Liverpool to South Carol-
ina on the Wakefield, master Thomas Beck, 21 April
1716
(CTB)(SP/C)

RANNIE WILLIAM
Carter. In Herman St Ter-
mants(?). Prisoner in
Edinburgh Tolbooth. Thief.
Banished to America for 7
years, 9 March 1767
(SM)(JC)

RANNOLDSON JAMES
25. Weaver. Fettercairn.
Jacobite in Bannerman's
regiment. Prisoner at
Inverness, ship and Til-
bury. Transported from
London to Jamaica or Bar-
bados by Samuel Smith
31 March 1747
(P)(RM)

RASH JAMES
Jacobite captured at Preston. Transported from
Liverpool to South Carol-
ina on the Wakefield,
master Thomas Beck,
21 April 1716
(CTB)(SP/C)

RATTRAY ANN
Murderer. Prisoner in
Aberdeen Tolbooth. Banished
to the Plantations for life
at Aberdeen May 1726. Trans
ported from Glasgow on the
Concord of Glasgow, master
James Butchart. Landed at
Charles County, Maryland
24 May 1728. Sold there by
David Cochrane, merchant in
Maryland
(JC)

REID ALEXANDER
Jacobite captured at Preston.
Transported from Liverpool to
Antigua on the Scipio, master
John Scaisbrick, 30 March 1716
(CTB)(SP/C)

REID ANDREW
Covenanter in Argyll's rebellion.
Prisoner in Edinburgh Tolbooth.
Banished to the Plantations 24
July 1685. Stigmatised 4 August
1685. Transported from Leith to
Jamaica by John Ewing August 1685
(ETR)(PC)

REID DAVID
Myrend, Kingoldrum, Angus.
Jacobite in Ogilvy's regiment.
Prisoner at Carlisle and Chester.
Transported 1747(?)
(P)

REID GEORGE
30. Labourer. Banff. Jacobite
in the Duke of Perth's regiment.
Captured at Carlisle. Prisoner
at Carlisle and Chester. Transported from Liverpool for the
Leeward Islands on the Veteran,
master John Ricky, 5 May 1747.
Liberated by a French privateer
and landed on Martinique June 1747
(P)(JAB)(RM)

REID JAMES
18. Labourer. Angus or Aberdeenshire. Jacobite in Ogilvy's
regiment. Captured at Carlisle.
Prisoner at Carlisle. Transported
from Liverpool for the Leeward
Islands 5 May 1747. Liberated by
a French privateer and landed on
Martinique June 1747
(P)(OR)(RM)

REID MALCOLM
Jacobite captured at Preston.
Transported from Liverpool to
South Carolina on the Susannah,
master Thomas Bromhall, 7 May
1716
(CTB)(SP/C)

REID MARGARET
Forfar. Oxen thief.
Banished for life,
at Perth 1753
(SM)

REID ROBERT
Weaver. Langside. Pris-
oner in Canongate Tol-
booth. Banished to the
Plantations in the Indies
13 June 1678. Transported
from Leith on the ship
St Michael of Scarborough,
master Edward Johnston,
12 December 1678
(PC)

REID ROBERT
Cathcart. Prisoner in
Edinburgh Tolbooth. Trans-
ported from Leith on the
St Michael of Scarborough,
master Edward Johnston,
12 December 1678
(PC)

REID of MID CLOVA, ROBERT
Tenant of David Lumsden of
Cushnie, Aberdeenshire.
Jacobite captured at Pres-
ton. Transported from
Liverpool to Virginia or
Jamaica on the Elizabeth
and Anne, master Edward
Trafford, 29 June 1716
(JAB)(SP/C)(CTB)

RENNIE JOHN
Covenanter. Prisoner at
Dunnottar and Leith. Ban-
ished to the Plantations,
at Leith 18 August 1685.
Transported from Leith to
East New Jersey by George
Scott of Pitlochie on the
Henry and Francis, master
Richard Hutton, 5 Septem-
ber 1685
(PC)

RENNIE MARION
Covenanter. Prisoner in Leith.
Banished to the Plantations,
at Leith 18 August 1685. Trans
ported from Leith to East New
Jersey by George Scott of Pitlochie on the Henry and Francis,
master Richard Hutton, 5 September 1685
(PC)

RENTON JAMES
Jacobite captured at Preston.
Transported from Liverpool for
Virginia on the Godspeed, master
Arthur Smith, 28 July 1716.
Unsold initially on landing in
Maryland 18 October 1716
(SP/C)(CTB)(HM)

RENWICK JOHN
Barnselloch. Covenanter.
Prisoner in Kirkcudbright
Tolbooth. Banished to the
Plantations, at Kirkcudbright
13 October 1684. Transferred
to Edinburgh
(PC)

RESTON JAMES
Covenanter. Prisoner at Leith.
Transported from Leith to East
New Jersey by George Scott of
Pitlochie on the Henry and
Francis, master Richard Hutton,
5 September 1685
(PC)

REYLEY DAVID
20. Tenant farmer of the laird
of Latheron, Caithness. Jacobite
in Cromarty's regiment. Transported from London to Jamaica
or Barbados by Samuel Smith
30 March 1747
(P)(RM)

RHIND ALEXANDER
Jacobite captured at Pres-
ton. Transported from
Liverpool to Maryland on
the Friendship, master
Michael Mankin, 24 May
1716. Sold to William
Bladen Esq. in Maryland
20 August 1716
(SP/C)(CTB)(HM)

RICHARD THOMAS
Covenanter. Greenock
Mains, Muirkirk. Pris-
oner in Edinburgh Tol-
booth. Banished to the
Plantations 29 July 1685
Stigmatised. Transported
from Leith to Jamaica by
John Ewing August 1685
(ETR)(PC)

RICHARDSON JOHN
Jacobite captured at Preston. Transported from Liver
pool to South Carolina on
the Wakefield, master
Thomas Beck, 21 April 1716
(SP/C)(CTB)

RICHARDSON ROBERT
Jacobite captured at Preston. Transported from Liver
pool to South Carolina on
the Wakefield, master
Thomas Beck, 21 April 1716
(SP/C)(CTB)

RICHARDSON WILLIAM
Transported to the Plant-
ations on The Crown 17
November 1679.
(William volunteered to
act as a substitute for
his brother John, tenant
to Lord Ross, to allow
him to look after his
family.)
(PC)

RIDDELL MR ARCHIBALD
Covenanter. Prisoner on the
Bass Rock. Transported from
Leith to East New Jersey by
George Scott of Pitlochie on
the Henry and Francis, master
Richard Hutton, 5 September
1685. Settled in Woodbridge,
New Jersey. Returned to Scotland
(PC)

RIDDELL HUGH
Covenanter. Prisoner in Edinburgh
Tolbooth. Transported to New
York 1683
(PC)

RIDDLE MARGARET
Thief. Prisoner in Edinburgh
Tolbooth. Banished to the
Plantations for life, at Edin-
burgh 7 February 1775
(JC)

RIDDOCH PETER
26. Slater. Doune, Stirlingshire.
Jacobite in Kilmarnock's Horse.
Prisoner at Doune and Stirling.
Transported from Liverpool on
the Johnson, master William
Pemberton. Landed at Port
Oxford, Maryland 5 August 1747
(P)(PRO)

RIDLEY ALEXANDER
Jacobite captured at Preston.
Transported from Liverpool to
Antigua on the Scipio, master
John Scaisbrick, 30 March 1716
(SP/C)(CTB)

RIDLEY JOHN
Jacobite captured at Preston.
Transported from Liverpool to
Antigua on the Scipio, master
John Scaisbrick, 30 March 1716
(SP/C)(CTB)

RIDLEY JOHN
Jacobite captured at Preston.
Transported from Liverpool to
St Kitts on the Hockenhill, mas-
ter H.Short, 25 June 1716
(CTB)

RIDPATH JOHN
Tinker. Adulterer. Prisoner
in Edinburgh Tolbooth.
Whipped, stigmatised and
banished 8 December 1662
(ETR)

RITCHIE ALEXANDER
Arbroath. Jacobite in
Ogilvy's regiment. Pris
oner at Arbroath, Dundee,
Canongate and Carlisle.
Transported 1747(?)
(P)

RITCHIE ALEXANDER
Butcher. Kirkcudbright.
Thief. Banished to the
Plantations for life, at
Dumfries 9 May 1770
(SM)

RITCHIE JOHN
Kirkcaldy. Deserter from
Colonel McKay's Dutch regiment. Jacobite in Lord John
Drummond's regiment. Prisoner at Huntingtower, Perth
and Stirling. Transported
1747(?)
(P)

RITCHIE JOHN
16. Son of Alexander Ritchie,
butcher in Kirkcudbright.
Thief. Banished to the Plantations for 14 years, at Dumfries 9 May 1770. Transported
from Port Glasgow on the
Crawford, master James
McLean. Landed at Port Oxford
Maryland 23 July 1771
(SM)(JC)

RITCHIE JOSEPH
Jacobite captured at Preston
Transported from Liverpool
to Antigua on the Scipio,
master John Scaisbrick,
30 March 1716
(CTB)(SP/C)

RITCHIE WILLIAM
18. Inverness-shire. Jacobite
in the Duke of Perth's regiment.
Prisoner on ships and at Tilbury.
Transported from London to Jamaica or Barbados by Samuel Smith
30 March 1747
(P)(RM)

ROBERTSON ALEXANDER
Jacobite captured at Preston.
Transported from Liverpool to
Antigua on the Scipio, master
John Scaisbrick, 30 March 1716
(CTB)(SP/C)

ROBB ELIZABETH
35. Knitter. Aberdeen. Jacobite.
Captured at Carlisle. Prisoner
at Carlisle and York. Transported
from Liverpool for the Leeward
Islands on the Veteran, master
John Ricky, 5 May 1747. Liberated by a French privateer and
landed on Martinique June 1747
(P)(JAB)(RM)

ROBB JAMES
Jacobite captured at Preston.
Transported from Liverpool to
South Carolina on the Susannah,
master Thomas Bromhall, 7 May
1716
(SP/C)(CTB)

ROBB JOHN
Jacobite captured at Preston.
Transported from Liverpool to
South Carolina on the Susannah,
master Thomas Bromhall, 7 May
1716
(SP/C)(CTB)

ROBB THOMAS
Jacobite captured at Preston.
Transported from Liverpool to
South Carolina on the Susannah,
master Thomas Bromhall, 7 May
1716
(CTB)(SP/C)

ROBERTSON ALEXANDER
Jacobite captured at Pres-
ton. Transported from
Liverpool to Antigua on
the Scipio, master John
Scaisbrick, 30 March 1716
(CTB)(SP/C)

ROBERTSON ALEXANDER
40 Labourer. Tenant to
Robertson of Struan.
Jacobite. Prisoner at
Monklands, Stirling and
Carlisle. Transported
from Liverpool to the
Leeward Islands on the
Veteran, master John
Ricky, 5 May 1747. Lib-
erated by a French priv-
ateer and landed on
Martinique June 1747
(P)(RM)

ROBERTSON DANIEL
Jacobite captured at Pres-
ton. Transported from
Liverpool to Antigua on
the Scipio, master John
Scaisbrick, 30 March 1716
(CTB)(SP/C)

ROBERTSON DANIEL
Jacobite captured at Pres-
ton. Transported from
Liverpool to Jamaica on
the Two Brothers, master
Edward Rathbone, 26 April
1716. Landed on Montserrat
June 1716
(SP/C)(CTB)(CTP)

ROBERTSON DONALD
Jacobite captured at Pres-
ton. Transported from
Liverpool to South Carol-
ina on the Susannah, mas-
ter Thomas Bromhall, 7
May 1716
(CTB)(SP/C)

ROBERTSON DONALD
Jacobite captured at Preston.
Transported from Liverpool to
Maryland on the Friendship,
master Michael Mankin, 24 May
1716. Sold to Thomas Robbins
in Maryland 20 August 1716
(SP/C)(CTB)(HM)

ROBERTSON DUNCAN
Jacobite captured at Preston.
Transported from Liverpool to
Antigua on the Scipio, master
John Scaisbrick, 30 March 1716
(CTB)(SP/C)

ROBERTSON DUNCAN
Jacobite captured at Preston.
Transported from Liverpool to
Jamaica on the Two Brothers,
master Edward Rathbone, 26
April 1716. Landed on Montserrat
June 1716
(SP/C)(CTB)(CTP)

ROBERTSON EUPHAME alias
          ELIZABETH THOMSON
Shopbreaker. Banished for life,
at Ayr September 1754
(SM)

ROBERTSON FRANCIS
Jacobite captured at Preston.
Transported from Liverpool to
Antigua on the Scipio, master
John Scaisbrick, 30 March 1716
(CTB)(SP/C)

ROBERTSON GEORGE
21. Weaver's apprentice.
Logginish, Perth. Jacobite in
Lord George Murray's regiment.
Prisoner at Inverness and Tilbury
Transported from London to Jam-
aica or Barbados by Samuel Smith
31 March 1747
(P)(RM)

ROBERTSON JAMES
Jacobite captured at Preston.
Transported from Liverpool to
Antigua on the Scipio, master
John Scaisbrick, 30 March 1716
(CTB)(SP/C)

ROBERTSON JAMES
Jacobite captured at Pres-
ton. Transported from
Liverpool to Jamaica on
the Two Brothers, master
Edward Rathbone, 26 April
1716. Landed on Montserrat
June 1716
(SP/C)(CTB)(CTP)

ROBERTSON JAMES
Jacobite captured at Preston. Transported from
Liverpool to South Carol-
ina on the Susannah, mas-
ter Thomas Bromhall,
7 May 1716
(CTB)(SP/C)

ROBERTSON JAMES
Jacobite captured at Pres-
ton. Transported from
Liverpool to Maryland on
the Friendship, master
Michael Mankin, 24 May
1716. Sold to Joseph
Hopkins in Maryland
20 August 1716
(SP/C)(CTB)(HM)

ROBERTSON JEAN
Widow of Angus Byers,
sailor. Thief. Prisoner
in Edinburgh Tolbooth.
Banished to the Plant-
ations in America for
14 years, at Edinburgh
19 January 1767
(JC)

ROBERTSON JOHN
Jacobite captured at Pres-
ton. Transported from
Liverpool to Antigua on
the Scipio, master John
Scaisbrick, 30 March 1716
(CTB)(SP/C)

ROBERTSON JOHN
Jacobite captured at Preston.
Transported from Liverpool to
Jamaica on the Two Brothers,
master Edward Rathbone, 26
April 1716. Landed on Montserrat
June 1716
(SP/C)(CTB)(CTP)

ROBERTSON JOHN
Jacobite captured at Preston.
Transported from Liverpool to
Maryland on the Friendship,
master Michael Mankin, 24 May
1716. Sold to Thomas McNemara
in Maryland 20 August 1716
(SP/C)(HM)

ROBERTSON JOHN
19. Labourer. Inverness. Jacobite
Prisoner at Inverness. Transported from Liverpool to the Leeward
Islands on the Veteran, master
John Ricky, 5 May 1747. Liberated
by a French privateer and landed
on Martinique June 1747
(P)(RM)

ROBERTSON JOHN
Stratherrol. Jacobite captain
in Ogilvy's regiment. Prisoner
at Stratherrol, Dundee, Carlisle
and Chester. Transported 1747(?)
(P)

ROBERTSON JOHN
Postman. Thief. Banished to the
West Indies for life, at Glasgow
17 May 1776
(SM)

ROBERTSON LEONARD
Jacobite captured at Preston.
Transported from Liverpool to
Maryland on the Friendship,
master Michael Mankin, 24 May
1716. Sold to Thomas Doccora
in Maryland 20 August 1716
(SP/C)(CTB)(HM)

ROBERTSON MALCOLM
Jacobite. Transported
from Liverpool on the
Johnson, master William
PembertonLanded at Port
Oxford. Maryland
5 August 1747
(PRO)

ROBERTSON MARGARET
Gypsy. Prisoner in Edin-
burgh Tolbooth. Trans-
ported from Greenock to
New York 21 October 1682
(ETR)

ROBERTSON MARY
Gypsy. Prisoner in Jed-
burgh Tolbooth. Banished
at Jedburgh 30 November
1714. Transported from
Glasgow on a Greenock
ship, master James Watson,
by merchants Robert Bun-
tine of Airdoch, James
Lees and Charles Crau-
ford, to Virginia
1 January 1715
(GR)

ROBERTSON NEIL
Cordwainer. Logerait,
Perthshire. Jacobite
in Lord George Murray's
regiment. Prisoner at
Carlisle and Chester.
Transported 1747(?)
(P)

ROBERTSON PATRICK
Royalist soldier captured
at Worcester. Transported
from Gravesend to Boston
on the John and Sarah,
master John Greene,
13 May 1652
(NER)

ROBERTSON PATRICK
Jacobite captured at Preston.
Transported from Liverpool
to Maryland or Virginia on
the Friendship, master Michael
Mankin, 24 May 1716
(SP/C)(CTB)

ROBERTSON RICHARD
Banished. Transported from
Port Glasgow on the Thomas of
Glasgow, master John Robertson.
Landed at James River Upper
District, Virginia 5 June 1773
(JC)

ROBERTSON ROBERT
Journeyman wright. Edinburgh.
Housebreaker. Prisoner in
Edinburgh Tolbooth. Banished
to the Plantations for life,
at Edinburgh 22 December 1774
(JC)

ROBERTSON ROWLAND
Jacobite captured at Preston.
Transported from Liverpool to
Virginia on the Godspeed, master
Arthur Smith, 28 July 1716.
Sold to Thomas Jameson in
Maryland 18 October 1716
(SP/C)(CTB)(HM)

ROBERTSON THOMAS
Farmer. Windyedge, Aberdargie,
Perthshire. Jacobite captain.
Prisoner at Canongate and
Carlisle. Transported 1747(?)
(P)

ROBERTSON WILLIAM
20. Weaver. Spinei, Morayshire.
Jacobite in Lord Lewis Gordon's
regiment. Prisoner at Inverness
and Tilbury. Transported from
Liverpool for the Leeward Islands
on the Veteran, master John Ricky,
5 May 1747. Liberated by a French
privateer and landed on Martinique June 1747
(P)(RM)

ROBERTSON WILLIAM
17. Labourer. Perth.
Jacobite in the Duke of
Perth's regiment. Capt-
ured at Carlisle. Pris-
oner at Carlisle and
York. Transported from
Liverpool for the Lee-
ward Islands on the
Veteran, master John
Ricky, 5 May 1747.
Liberated by a French
privateer and landed
on Martinique June 1747
(P)(RM)

ROBERTSON WILLIAM
14. Pickpocket. Banished
to the Plantations for 7
years, at Perth 5 May 1775
(SM)

ROBINSON ALASTAIR
Royalist soldier captured
at Worcester. Transported
from Gravesend to Boston
on the John and Sarah,
master John Greene,
13 May 1652
(NER)

ROBINSON ALEXANDER
35. Angus. Jacobite in
Ogilvy's regiment. Pris-
oner at Inverness, ship
and Tilbury. Transported
1747(?)
(P)

ROBINSON CHARLES
Royalist soldier captured
at Worcester. Transported
from Gravesend to Boston
on the John and Sarah,
master John Greene,
13 May 1652
(NER)

ROBINSON DANIEL
Royalist soldier captured
at Worcester. Transported
from Gravesend to Boston
on the John and Sarah,
master John Greene,
13 May 1652
(NER)

ROBINSON DANIEL or DONALD
Jacobite. Prisoner at Stirling
and Carlisle. Transported
from Liverpool on the Gildart
master Richard Holmes. Landed
at Port North Potomac, Maryland
5 August 1747
(P)(PRO)

ROBINSON DAVID
70. Labourer. Jacobite.
Prisoner in Carlisle.
Transported 1747(?)
(P)

ROBINSON DUNCAN
Jacobite captured at Preston.
Transported from Liverpool
to South Carolina on the
Susannah, master Thomas
Bromhall, 7 May 1716
(CTB)(SP/C)

ROBINSON JAMES
Royalist soldier captured at
Worcester. Transported from
Gravesend to Boston on the
John and Sarah, master John
Greene, 13 May 1652
(NER)

ROBINSON JAMES
Jacobite captured at Preston.
Transported from Liverpool to
Jamaica or Virginia on the
Elizabeth and Anne, master
Edward Trafford, 29 June 1716
Landed at York, Virginia -
unindentured
(SP/C)(CTB)(VSP)

ROBINSON JOHN
Royalist soldier captured at
Worcester. Transported from
Gravesend to Boston on the
John and Sarah, master John
Greene, 13 May 1652
(NER)

ROBINSON JOHN
Jacobite captured at Pres-
ton. Transported from
Liverpool to St Kitts on
the Hockenhill, master
H.Short, 25 June 1716
(SP/C)(CTB)

ROBINSON JOHN
Jacobite captured at Pres-
ton. Transported from
Liverpool to Virginia or
Jamaica on the Elizabeth
and Anne, master Edward
Trafford, 29 June 1716.
Landed at York, Virginia
- indentured
(SP/C)(CTB)(VSP)

ROBINSON JOHN
Jacobite captured at Preston. Transported from
Liverpool to South Carol-
ina on the Susannah, mas-
ter Thomas Bromhall,
7 May 1716
(CTB)(SP/C)

ROBINSON ROBERT
Jacobite captured at Pres-
ton. Transported from
Liverpool to Virginia or
Jamaica on the Elizabeth
and Anne, master Edward
Trafford, 29 June 1716.
Landed at York, Virginia
- unindentured
(CTB)(SP/C)(VSP)

ROBINSON THOMAS
Jacobite. Prisoner at
Carlisle. Transported
1747(?)
(P)

ROBISON ANDREW
Prisoner in Edinburgh
Tolbooth. Transported
to New England 8 April
1668
(PC)

ROBISON JOHN
Thief. Banished to the Plant-
ations in the West Indies, at
Dumfries 1 May 1728
(JC)

ROME MR GEORGE
Covenanter. Prisoner in Canon-
gate or Edinburgh Tolbooths.
Transported to Carolina by
Robert Malloch 1684

ROSE ALEXANDER
18. Jacobite in Lord George
Murray's regiment. Prisoner
at Inverness, ship and Tilbury
Transported from London to
Jamaica or Barbados by Samuel
Smith 31 March 1747
(P)(RM)

ROSE ALEXANDER
18. Husbandman. Nairn. From
Moray. Jacobite in Lord Lewis
Gordon's regiment. Prisoner
at Inverness, ship and Tilbury
Transported 31 March 1747
(P)

ROSE JAMES
Exciseman. Muthill. Forger.
Banished to America 4 February
1757
(ETR)

ROSS ALASTAIR
Royalist soldier captured at
Worcester. Transported from
Gravesend to Boston on the
John and Sarah, master John
Greene, 13 May 1652
(NER)

ROSS ALEXANDER
20. Servant to Gordon of Carroll.
Sutherland. Jacobite in the
Atholl Brigade. Prisoner at
Inverness, ship, Tilbury and
Southwark. Transported 1747(?)
(P)

ROSS ALEXANDER
18. Nairn. Jacobite in
Lord Lewis Gordon's
regiment. Prisoner at
Inverness, ship and
Tilbury. Transported
1747(?)
(P)

ROSS ALEXANDER
50. Farmer. Kirkton of
Lochbroom. Jacobite in
Cromarty's regiment.
Prisoner at Inverness,
ship and Tilbury. Trans-
ported from London to
Jamaica or Barbados by
Samuel Smith 31 March
1747
(P)(RM)

ROSS CHARLES
Jacobite captured at
Preston. Transported
from Liverpool to South
Carolina on the Wakefield,
master Thomas Beck, 21
April 1716
(CTB)(SP/C)

ROSS CHARLES
Soldier. Robber. Prisoner
in Edinburgh Tolbooth.
Banished to the Plant-
ations in America for
life, at Edinburgh 3
March 1747
(JC)

ROSS CHRISTINE
Rosekien, Ross-shire.
Thief. Banished for 14
years in 1773
(SM)

ROSS DANIEL
Royalist soldier capt-
ured at Worcester.
Transported from Graves-
end to Boston on the
John and Sarah, master
John Greene, 13 May
1652
(NER)

ROSS DANIEL
40. Servant. Ross-shire.
Jacobite. Prisoner at York.
Transported from Liverpool for
the Leeward Islands on the
Veteran, master John Ricky,
5 May 1747. Liberated by a
French privateer and landed
on Martinique June 1747
(P)(RM)

ROSS DAVID
Royalist soldier captured at
Worcester. Transported from
Gravesend to Boston on the
John and Sarah, master John
Greene, 13 May 1652
(NER)

ROSS DONALD
24. Servant to Joseph Stewart
of Cromar, Inverness. Jacobite
in Roy Stuart's regiment.
Transported 20 March 1747.
Prisoner at Inverness, ship
and Tilbury
(P)

ROSS DONALD
20. Jacobite in Cromarty's
regiment. Prisoner at Inverness and Tilbury. Transported
20 March 1747
(P)

ROSS DONALD
56. Jacobite in Cromarty's
regiment. Prisoner at Inverness and Tilbury. Transported
from London to Barbados or
Jamaica by Samuel Smith
31 March 1747
(P)(RM)

ROSS DUNCAN
30. Farmer. Auchenarvier, Ross.
Jacobite in Cromarty's regiment. Prisoner at Inverness,
ship and Tilbury. Transported
from London to Barbados or
Jamaica by Samuel Smith
31 March 1747
(P)(RM)

ROSS ELIZABETH
Child murder. Transported
to America, at Edinburgh
1752
(SM)

ROSS GEORGE
Ross-shire. Cattle thief.
Transported for 7 years,
at Inverness 1752
(SM)

ROSS HUGH
Jacobite captured at
Preston. Transported
from Liverpool to Antigua
on the Scipio, master John
Scaisbrick, 30 March 1716
(CTB)(SP/C)

ROSS ISABEL
Rosekien, Ross-shire.
Thief. Banished for 14
years in 1773
(SM)

ROSS JAMES
Royalist soldier captured
at Worcester. Transported
from Gravesend to Boston
on the John and Sarah,
master John Greene,
13 May 1652

ROSS JAMES
20. Carpenter. Edinburgh.
Jacobite in the Duke of
Perth's regiment. Pris-
oner at York and Lincoln.
Transported from Liverpool
for the Leeward Islands
5 May 1747. Liberated by
a French privateer and
landed on Martinique
June 1747
(P)(RM)

ROSS JEAN
Gypsy. Prisoner in Jed-
burgh Tolbooth. Banished
at Jedburgh 30 November
1714. Transported from
Glasgow to Virginia by
Robert Buntine, James Lees
and Charles Crauford
January 1, 1715
(GR)

ROSS JOHN
Royalist soldier captured at
Worcester. Transported from
Gravesend to Boston on the
John and Sarah, master John
Greene, 13 May 1652
(NER)

ROSS JOHN
Royalist soldier captured at
Worcester. Transported from
Gravesend to Boston on the
John and Sarah, master John
Greene, 13 May 1652
(NER)

ROSS JOHN
Forger. Prisoner in Edinburgh
Tolbooth. Banished to the
Plantations 3 February 1670.
Transported from Leith to
Virginia by James Johnston,
James Currie and Patrick
Fyffe, merchants in Edinburgh,
on the Ewe and Lamb, master
James Guthrie
(PC)

ROSS JOHN
Jacobite captured at Preston.
Transported from Liverpool to
Maryland on the Friendship,
master Michael Mankin, 24 May
1716. Sold to Edgar Webb in
Maryland 20 August 1716
(SP/C)(CTB)(HM)

ROSS JOHN
17. Miller in Forbloch, Ross.
Jacobite in Glengarry's regiment
Prisoner at Inverness, ships
and Medway. Transported from
London to Barbados or Jamaica
by Samuel Smith 31 March 1747
(P)(RM)

ROSS JONAS
Royalist soldier captured at
Worcester. Transported from
Gravesend to Boston on the
John and Sarah, master John
Greene, 13 May 1652
(NER)

SCOTS BANISHED TO THE AMERICAN PLANTATIONS

ROSS RANALD
18. Husbandman. Milton
of Ord, Ross. Jacobite
in Cromarty's regiment
Prisoner at Inverness,
ship and Tilbury. Trans
ported from London to
Barbados or Jamaica by
Samuel Smith 31 March
1747
(P)(RM)

ROSS ROBERT
Glover. Perth. Prisoner
in Edinburgh Tolbooth.
Forger. Banished to
America for life,18
December 1767
(JC)

ROSS THOMAS
Jacobite captured at
Preston. Transported
from Liverpool to South
Carolina on the Susanah,
master Thomas Bromhall,
7 May 1716
(CTB)(SP/C)

ROSS THOMAS
63. Labourer. Aberdeen.
Jacobite. Prisoner at
Carlisle and York. Trans-
ported from Liverpool on
the Johnson, master Will-
iam Pemberton, May 1747
Landed at Port Oxford,
Maryland 5 August 1747
(P)(JAB)(PRO)

ROSS WILLIAM
36. Sailor. Aberdeenshire.
Jacobite captured at Car-
lisle. Prisoner at York,
Carlisle and Lincoln.
Transported from Liver-
pool for the Leeward
Islands on the Veteran,
master John Ricky, 5 May
1747. Liberated by a
French privateer and
landed on Martinique
June 1747
(P)(JAB)(RM)

ROWAN JOHN
Thief. Banished for life, at
Glasgow 1753
(SM)

ROY DONALD
Royalist soldier captured
at Worcester. Transported on
the John and Sarah, master
John Greene, from Gravesend
to Boston 13 May 1652
(NER)

RUGG DONALD
Tenant in Freswick, Caithness.
Housebreaking and theft.
Banished to the Plantations
for life in 1768
(SM)

RUSSELL DAVID
20. Glover. Aberdeen. Jacobite
in Stonywood's regiment.
Prisoner at Aberdeen, Canongate
and Carlisle. Transported from
Liverpool on the Johnson, master
William Pemberton. Landed at
Port Oxford, Maryland 5 August
1747
(P)(PRO)

RUSSELL GAVIN
Covenanter. Prisoner in Edinburgh
Tolbooth. Banished to the Plant-
ations 24 July 1685
(PC)(ETR)

RUSSELL JAMES
Covenanter. Banished to the
Plantations in America
11 October 1684
(PC)

RUSSELL JOHN
Covenanter. Banished to the
Plantations in America
11 October 1684
(PC)

RUSSELL JOHN
24. Sail weaver. Backmyre,
Barry, Angus. Jacobite in
Ogilvy's regiment. Prisoner
at Barry, Arbroath, Dundee,
Canongate and Carlisle.
Transported from Liverpool
on the Gildart, master
Richard Holmes.Landed at
Port North Potomack, Mary-
land 5 August 1747
(P)(OR)(PRO)

RUSSELL PETER
Covenanter. Prisoner at
Burntisland, Dunnottar
and Leith. Banished to the
Plantations, at Leith 18
August 1685. Transported
from Leith to East New
Jersey by George Scott of
Pitlochie on the Henry and
Francis, master Richard
Hutton, 5 September 1685
(PC)

RUSSELL ROBERT
Transported from Leith to
the Plantations November
1679
(ETR)

RUSSELL SIMON
Royalist soldier captured
at Worcester. Transported
from Gravesend to Boston
on the John and Sarah,
master John Greene,
13 May 1652
(NER)

RUSSELL THOMAS
Covenanter. Prisoner in
Thieveshole and Leith.
Transported from Leith
to East New Jersey by
George Scott of Pitlochie
on the Henry and Francis,
master Richard Hutton,
5 September 1685
(PC)

RUTHERFORD GEORGE
Jacobite captured at Preston.
Transported from Liverpool to
Virginia or Jamaica on the
Elizabeth and Anne, master
Edward Trafford, 29 June 1716
(CTB)(SP/C)

RUTHERFORD JAMES
Jacobite captured at Preston.
Transported from Liverpool to
Virginia on the Godspeed,
master Arthur Smith , 28 July
1716. Sold to Arthur Smith
in Maryland 18 October 1716
(SP/C)(CTB)(HM)

RUTHERFORD JOHN
Jacobite captured at Preston.
Transported from Liverpool to
Virginia or Jamaica on the
Elizabeth and Anne, master
Edward Trafford, 29 June 1716
(CTB)(SP/C)(VSP)

RUTHERFORD JOHN
Jacobite captured at Preston.
Transported from Liverpool to
Virginia or Jamaica on the
Elizabeth and Anne, master
Edward Trafford, 29 June 1716.
Landed at York, Virginia -
unindentured
(CTB)(SP/C)(VSP)

SAMUEL GEORGE
18. Bookbinder. Edinburgh.
Jacobite in the Duke of Perth's
regiment. Prisoner at Carlisle
and Lincoln. Transported from
Liverpool for the Leeward
Islands on the Veteran, master
John Ricky, 5 May 1747.
Liberated by a French privateer
and landed on Martinique June
1716
(P)(PRO)

SANDERSON DANIEL
Former servant to James
Strang, minister of
Tyningham. Vagabond.
Prisoner in Dunbar Tol-
booth. Transported from
Leith to Virginia on
the Convertin, Captain
Lightfoot, September
1668
(PC)

SCHAW JOHN
Soldier in Captain
Goulstone's company,
General Skelton's regi-
ment of Foot. Horsethief.
Prisoner in Edinburgh
Tolbooth. Banished to the
Plantations in America
for life, at Edinburgh
3 March 1747
(JC)

SCOTT ANDREW
Covenanter. Teviotdale.
Prisoner at Edinburgh and
Canongate Tolbooths. Ban-
ished to the Plantations
24 July 1685
(ETR)(PC)

SCOTT CHRISTIAN
Covenanter. Prisoner at
Dunnottar and Leith. Ban-
ished to the Plantations,
at Leith 18 August 1685.
Transported from Leith to
East New Jersey by George
Scott of Pitlochie on the
Henry and Francis, master
Richard Hutton,
5 September 1685
(PC)

SCOTT CHRISTIAN
Daughter of James Scott,
weaver in Kirkcaldy,
servant to John Hay, school
doctor, Kirkcaldy. Child
murder. Prisoner in Edin-
burgh Tolbooth. Banished
to the Plantations in
America for life, at
Edinburgh 6 August 1762
(JC)

SCOTT DAVID
Tailor. Arbroath. Jacobite
in Ogilvy's regiment. Pris-
oner at Montrose and Stirling.
Transported from Liverpool
on the Gildart, master
Richard Holmes. Landed at
Port North Potomac, Maryland
5 August 1747
(P)(OR)(PRO)

SCOTT JOHN
Royalist soldier captured at
Worcester. Transported from
Gravesend to Boston on the
John and Sarah, master John
Greene, 13 May 1652
(NER)

SCOTT JOHN
Prisoner in Edinburgh Tolbooth
Transported from Leith to the
Plantations November 1679
(ETR)

SCOTT JOHN
Jacobite captured at Preston.
Transported from Liverpool
for Jamaica on the Two Brothers,
master Edward Rathbone, 26
April 1716. Landed on Montserrat
June 1716
(CTB)(SP/C)(CTP)

SCOTT JOHN
17. Herd. Atholl. Jacobite in
Roy Stuart's regiment. Capt-
ured at Carlisle. Prisoner at
Carlisle and York. Transported
from Liverpool for the Leeward
Islands on the Veteran, master
John Ricky, 5 May 1747. Lib-
erated by a French privateer
and landed on Martinique
June 1747
(P)(RM)

SHAW DONALD
Jacobite captured at Pres-
ton. Transported from
Liverpool to Jamaica or
Virginia on the Elizabeth
and Anne, master Edward
Trafford, 29 June 1716.
Landed at York, Virginia
- indentured
(SP/C)(VSP)

SHAW DONALD
Jacobite captured at Preston. Transported from
Liverpool to South Carol-
ina on the Susannah, mas-
ter Thomas Bromhall,
7 May 1716
(CTB)(SP/C)

SHAW EWAN
Jacobite captured at Preston. Transported from
Liverpool to South Carol-
ina on the Susannah, mas-
ter Thomas Bromhall,
7 May 1716
(CTB)(SP/C)

SHAW JAMES
Jacobite captured at Pres-
ton. Transported from
Liverpool to Virginia or
Maryland on the Friendship,
master Michael Mankin,
24 May 1716
(CTB)(SP/C)

SHAW JAMES
Jacobite captured at Pres-
ton. Transported from
Liverpool to Virginia on
the Godspeed, master
Arthur Smith, 28 July 1716.
Sold to John Donaldson in
Maryland 17 October 1716
(SP/C)(CTB)(HM)

SHAW JOHN
Jacobite captured at Preston.
Transported from Liverpool to
Jamaica or Virginia on the
Elizabeth and Anne, master
Edward Trafford, 29 June 1716.
Landed at York, Virginia -
unindentured
(CTB)(SP/C)(VSP)

SHAW JOHN
Jacobite captured at Preston.
Transported from Liverpool to
Antigua on the Scipio, master
John Scaisbrick, 30 March 1716
(CTB)(SP/C)

SHAW JOHN
Jacobite captured at Preston.
Transported from Liverpool to
South Carolina on the Wakefield,
master Thomas Beck, 21 April
1716
(CTB)(SP/C)

SHAW JOHN
Jacobite captured at Preston.
Transported from Liverpool to
South Carolina on the Wakefield,
master Thomas Beck, 21 April
1716
(CTB)(SP/C)

SHAW JOHN
Jacobite captured at Preston.
Transported from Liverpool to
South Carolina on the Susannah,
master Thomas Bromhall, 7 May
1716
(CTB)(SP/C)

SHAW MARGARET
15. Spinner. Perthshire. Jac-
obite. Prisoner at Carlisle and
Lancaster. Transported from
Liverpool on the Johnson, master
William Pemberton. Landed at
Port Oxford, Maryland 5 August
1747
(P)(PRO)

SHAW MARY
40. Iverness. Jacobite.
Prisoner at Carlisle,
and Lancaster. Trans-
ported from Liverpool
on the Johnson, master
William Pemberton.
Landed at Port Oxford,
Maryland 5 August 1747
(P)(PRO)

SHAW PETER
Jacobite captured at Preston. Transported from
Liverpool to South Carol-
ina on the Susannah, mas-
ter Thomas Bromhall,
7 May 1716
(CTB)(SP/C)

SHAW THOMAS
Jacobite captured at Pres-
ton. Transported from
Liverpool to Virginia on
the Godspeed, master
Arthur Smith, 28 July 1716.
Sold to Michael Martin in
Maryland 17 October 1716
(SP/C)(CTB)(HM)

SHAW WILLIAM
Jacobite captured at Preston. Transported from
Liverpool to South Carol-
ina on the Susannah, mas
ter Thomas Bromhall,
7 May 1715
(CTB)(SP/C)

SHAW WILLIAM
Jacobite captured at Pres-
ton. Transported from
Liverpool to Virginia on
the Godspeed, master
Arthur Smith, 28 July 1716.
Sold to John Hawkins in
Maryland 17 October 1716
(SP/C)(CTB)(HM)

SHEARER JAMES
Barber. Rape. Banished to
the Plantations for 14
years, at Ayr 3 May 1764
(SM)

SHEARER JAMES
Elgin. Ex soldier, thief.
Prisoner in Edinburgh Tolbooth.
Banished to the Plantations in
America for life, at Edinburgh
January 1757
(JC)(SM)

SHEDDON CHARLES
70. Servant. Ayr. Jacobite.
Prisoner in York. Transported
1747(?)
(P)

SHEDDEN ROBERT
Travelling chapman. Pickpocket.
Banished to the Plantations in
the British West Indies for
life, at Glasgow 20 September
1775
(SM)

SHEPHERD JOHN
20. Servant to Mr Watson, inn-
keeper, Arbroath. From Ferryden,
Montrose. Jacobite in Ogilvy's
regiment. Prisoner at Stirling,
Leith, Canongate and Carlisle.
Transported from Liverpool on
the Gildart, master Richard
Holmes. Landed at Port North
Potomac, Maryland 5 August 1747
(P)(PRO)(OR)

SHERIDAN THOMAS
Soldier in the 17th regiment
of Foot. Thief. Banished to
America for life, 25 February
1772. Transported from Port
Glasgow on the Matty, master
Robert Peacock. Landed at Port
Oxford, Maryland 16 May 1772
(JC)

SHIELD GEORGE
Prisoner in Edinburgh Tolbooth.
Transported from Leith or Buck-
haven to Barbados on Edward
Baird's ship 22 December 1665
(ETR)

SHIELDS JAMES
Prisoner in Edinburgh Tolbooth. Transported to
Virginia on the Phoenix
of Leith, master James
Gibson, by Robert Lear-
month and partners,
merchants in Edinburgh,
24 April 1666
(ETR)

SHIELDS JOHN
Jacobite captured at Pres-
ton. Transported from
Liverpool to Antigua on
the Scipio, master John
Scaisbrick, 30 March 1716
(CTB)(SP/C)

SHIELS or WILSON JOHN
Gardener. Edinburgh.
Sheep stealer. Banished
to America for life
25 July 1769
(JC)

SHILESTON THOMAS
Covenanter. Hillend,
Dunspurn Parish. Covenanter
Prisoner at Dumfries, Dunn-
ottar and Leith. Banished
to the Plantations, at
Leith 18 August 1685.
Transported from Leith to
East New Jersey by
George Scott of Pitlochie
on the Henry and Francis,
master Richard Hutton,
5 September 1685
(PC)

SHISH JAMES
Bo'ness. Covenanter.
Transported to America
16 August 1670
(PC)

SHORT GEORGE
Cordiner. Glasgow. Forger.
Banished from Scotland for
5 years, at Edinburgh
18 March 1766
(JC)

SHONGER or SWINGER ALEXANDER
Jacobite captured at Preston.
Transported from Liverpool to
Virginia or Maryland on the
Friendship, master Michael
Mankin, 24 May 1716. Sold to
Phil. Sherwood in Maryland
20 August 1716
(SP/C)(CTB)(HM)

SHORTER DUNCAN
Jacobite captured at Preston.
Transported from Liverpool for
Jamaica on the Two Brothers,
master Edward Rathbone, 26
April 1716. Landed on Montserrat
June 1716
(SP/C)(CTB)(CTP)

SHUTTARD BERNARD
Jacobite captured at Preston.
Transported from Liverpool to
South Carolina on the Susannah,
master Thomas Bromhall, 7 May
1716
(CTB)(SP/C)

SILVER ANDREW
Thief. Banished for 7 years,
at Aberdeen May 1750
(SM)

SIMM WILLIAM
Jacobite captured at Preston.
Transported from Liverpool to
Maryland on the Friendship,
master Michael Mankin, 24 May
1716. Sold to William
Nicholson in Maryland 20 August
1716
(SP/C)(CTB)(HM)

SIMPSON ALASTAIR
Royalist soldier captured at
Worcester. Transported from
Gravesend to Boston on the
John and Sarah, master John
Greene, 13 May 1652
(NER)

SIMPSON DANIEL
Royalist soldier captured
at Worcester. Transported
from Gravesend to Boston
on the John and Sarah,
master John Greene, 13
May 1652
(NER)

SIMSON DAVID
Royalist soldier captured
at Worcester. Transported
from Gravesend to Boston
on the John and Sarah,
master John Greene,
13 May 1652
(NER)

SIMPSON DAVID
56. Linen weaver. Auldbar,
Angus. Jacobite in Ogilvy's
regiment. Prisoner at
Auldbar, Dundee, Canongate
and Carlisle. Transported
1747(?)
(P)

SIMPSON ELIZABETH
Thief. Banished to the
Plantations in the West
Indies, at Dumfries
1 May 1728
(JC)

SIMSON JAMES
Jacobite captured at Preston. Transported from
Liverpool to South Carol-
ina on the Susannah, mas-
ter Thomas Bromhall
7 May 1716
(CTB)(SP/C)

SIMPSON JAMES
20. Shoemaker. Arbroath.
Jacobite in Ogilvy's
regiment. Prisoner at
Arbroath, Dundee, Canon-
gate and Carlisle. Trans-
ported from Liverpool on
the Johnson, master Will-
iam Pemberton. Landed at
Port Oxford, Maryland
5 August 1747
(P)(OR)(PRO)

SIMPSON JOHN
Prisoner in Edinburgh Tolbooth.
Warded by order of the Privy
Council 22 July 1685. Banished
to the Plantations 31 July 1685.
Stigmatised 4 August 1685.
Transported from Leith to Jam-
aica by John Ewing August 1685
(ETR)(PC)

SIMPSON MARGARET
33. Haddington. "Lady Hamilton's
woman". Jacobite. Prisoner at
York. Transported 1747(?)
(P)

SIMPSON WILLIAM
Jacobite captured at Preston.
Transported from Liverpool to
Virginia on the Godspeed, master
Arthur Smith, 28 July 1716.
Sold to John Rogers in Maryland
17 October 1716
(SP/C)(CTB)(HM)

SINCLAIR DUNCAN
Covenanter in Argyll's rebellion.
Prisoner in the Laigh Parliament
House, Edinburgh. Banished to
the Plantations 31 July 1685.
Transported from Leith to Jam-
aica by John Ewing August 1685
(PC)

SINCLAIR JAMES
Jacobite captured at Preston.
Transported from Liverpool to
Virginia on the Godspeed, mas-
ter Arthur Smith, 28 July 1716.
Sold to Henry Whort in Maryland
17 October 1716
(SP/C)(CTB)(HM)

SINCLAIR JAMES
19. Husbandman. Dunbeith, Caithness. Jacobite in Cromarty's
regiment. Prisoner in Inverness
and ships. Transported from
London to Jamaica or Barbados
by Samuel Smith 31 March 1747
(P)(RM)

SINCLAIR JOHN
Son of William Sinclair,
Parish of Dunnet, Caith-
ness. Prisoner in Edin-
burgh Tolbooth. Trans-
ported from Leith to the
Plantations in America
on the Blossom by William
Johnston, merchant in
Edinburgh August 1680
(ETR)

SINCLAIR PATRICK
Jacobite captured at Preston. Transported from
Liverpool to South Carol-
ina on the Wakefield, master Thomas Beck 21 April
1716
(CTB)(SP/C)

SINCLAIR SOLOMON
Royalist soldier captured
at Worcester. Transported
from Gravesend to Boston
on the John and Sarah,
master John Greene,
13 May 1652
(NER)

SINCLAIR WILLIAM
Jacobite captured at Pres-
ton. Transported from
Liverpool to Virginia on
the Anne, master Robert
Wallace, 31 July 1716
(CTB)(SP/C)

SLOSS ROBERT
Ayr. Covenanter. Banished
to the Plantations
5 February 1685
(PC)

SLOWAN GEORGE
Prisoner in Dumfries Tol-
booth. Banished from
Scotland for 3 years, at
Dumfries 3 May 1726
(JC)

SMALL JAMES
Jacobite captured at Preston.
Transported from Liverpool to
Maryland on the Friendship,
master Michael Mankin, 24 May
1716. Sold to Sam. Peele in
Maryland 20 August 1716
(CTB)(SP/C)(HM)

SMEALL ELIZABETH
Servant to Robert Meikle, carter
St Cuthbert's parish, Edinburgh.
Prisoner in Edinburgh Tolbooth.
Child murder. Banished for life
16 March 1768
(JC)

SMISON PATRICK
Royalist soldier captured at
Worcester. Transported from
Gravesend to Boston on the
John and Sarah, master John
Greene, 13 May 1652
(NER)

SMITH ALEXANDER
Jacobite captured at Preston.
Transported from Liverpool to
Jamaica on the Two Brothers,
master Edward Rathbone, 26
April 1716. Landed on Montserrat
June 1716
(SP/C)(CTB)(CTP)

SMITH ALEXANDER
Jacobite captured at Preston.
Transported from Liverpool to
Maryland on the Friendship,
master Michael Mankin, 24 May
1716. Sold to Samuel Chew in
Maryland 20 August 1716
(SP/C)(CTB)(HM)

SMITH ALEXANDER
20. Jacobite in the Duke of
Perth's regiment. Prisoner at
Edinburgh and Canongate. Trans-
ported from Liverpool on the
Johnson, master William Pemberton
Landed at Port Oxford, Maryland
5 August 1747
(P)(PRO)

SMITH ANDREW
21. Husbandman near Old
Meldrum, Aberdeenshire.
Jacobite in Crighton's
regiment. Prisoner at
Edinburgh and on ships
at Tilbury. Transported
from London to Jamaica
or Barbados by Samuel
Smith 31 March 1747
(P)(JAB)(RM)

SMITH ANDREW
18. Weaver. Edinburgh.
Jacobite in Roy Stuart's
regiment. Prisoner at
Wigan, Carlisle and
Chester. Transported
from Liverpool on the
Gildart, master Richard
Holmes. Landed at Port
North Potomac, Maryland
5 August 1747
(P)(PRO)

SMITH ANDREW JUNIOR
Inveramsay, Aberdeenshire.
Son of Patrick Smith and
his wife Elizabeth Kerr.
Husbandman near Meldrum,
Aberdeenshire. 31. Jacobite
in Crighton's regiment.
Prisoner at Edinburgh and
on ships. Transported from
Liverpool on the Gildart,
master Richard Holmes, 31
March 1747. Landed at
Port North Potomac, Mary-
land 5 August 1747
(P)(JAB)(PRO)

SMITH CHARLES
Jacobite captured at Pres-
ton. Transported from
Liverpool to Virginia or
Jamaica on the Elizabeth
and Anne, master Edward
Trafford, 29 June 1716
(CTB)(SP/C)

SMITH CHARLES
Drummer. Robber. Prisoner
in Edinburgh Tolbooth.
Banished to the Plantations
in America, at Edinburgh
3 March 1747
(JC)

SMITH DANIEL
Jacobite captured at Preston.
Transported from Liverpool for
Jamaica on the Two Brothers,
master Edward Rathbone, 26
April 1716. Landed on Mont-
serrat June 1716
(SP/C)(CTB)(CTP)

SMITH DAVID
Jacobite captured at Preston.
Transported from Liverpool to
South Carolina on the Susannah,
master Thomas Bromhall, 7 May
1716
(CTB)(SP/C)

SMITH DONALD
Jacobite captured at Preston.
Transported from Liverpool to
South Carolina on the Wakefield,
master Thomas Beck, 21 April
1716
(CTB)(SP/C)

SMITH DONALD
Jacobite captured at Preston.
Transported from Liverpool to
South Carolina on the Susannah,
master Thomas Bromhall, 7 May
1716
(CTB)(SP/C)

SMITH DONALD
50. Glen Urquhart. Jacobite
in Glengarry's regiment.
Prisoner at Inverness, ship
and Tilbury. Transported from
London to Barbados or Jamaica
by Samuel Smith 31 March 1747
(P)(RM)

SMITH GEORGE
Evendale. Covenanter. Prisoner
in Glasgow Tolbooth. Banished
to the Plantations, at Glasgow
June 1684. Transported from
the Clyde to America on the
Pelican by Walter Gibson,
merchant in Glasgow, June 1684
(PC)

SMITH GEORGE
24. Husbandman. Cairnbulg,
Aberdeenshire. Jacobite in
Kilmarnock's Horse. Prison-
er at Inverness, ship and
Tilbury. Transported from
London to Barbados or Jam-
aica by Samuel Smith,
31 March 1747
(P)(RM)

SMITH GEORGE
Thief. Banished to the
British West Indies or
America for life, at Perth
September 1775
(SM)

SMITH HENRY
Royalist soldier captured
at Worcester. Transported
from Gravesend to Boston
on the John and Sarah,
master John Greene,
13 May 1652
(NER)

SMITH JAMES
Strathspey. Jacobite in
MacPherson's regiment.
Prisoner at Wigan and
Chester. Transported from
Liverpool on the Gildart,
master Richard Holmes.
Landed at Port North Pot-
omac, Maryland 5 August
1747
(P)(PRO)

SMITH JAMES
59. Workman. Loanhead,
Old Machar, Aberdeen.
Jacobite in Crighton's
regiment. Prisoner at
Culloden,Inverness,
ships and Tilbury.
Transported from London
to Barbados or Jamaica
by Samuel Smith
31 March 1747
(P)(JAB)(RM)

SMITH JAMES
Craigends. Thief. Banished for
life, at Ayr 1752
(SM)

SMITH JAMES
Weaver. Banished for life.
Transported from Glasgow on
the Brilliant, master Robert
Bennet.Landed at Port Hampton,
Virginia 7 October 1772
(JC)

SMITH JOHN
Hamilton. Prisoner in Edinburgh
Tolbooth. Transported from
Leith to Carolina by Walter
Gibson, 21 May 1684
(PC)

SMITH JOHN
Kirkintilloch. Covenanter.
Prisoner at Glasgow, Dunnottar
and Leith. Banished to the
Plantations, at Leith 18 August
1685. Transported from Leith
to East New Jersey by George
Scott of Pitlochie on the
Henry and Francis, master
Richard Hutton, 5 September
1685
(PC)

SMITH JOHN
Transported from Glasgow to
South Carolina on the brigantine
John and Robert, master Thomas
Clark, 22 July 1730. Bail bond
by Robert Paterson 2 October
1728
(JC)

SMITH JOHN
Former Deacon of the Weavers
Craft of Dumfries. Rioter in
Dumfries 1759. Prisoner in
Edinburgh Tolbooth. Transported
to the Plantations for life
1760. Banished at Edinburgn
15 December 1760
(SM)(JC)

SMITH JOHN
21. Goldsmith. Aberdeen.
Jacobite in the Duke of
Perth's regiment.
Captured at Carlisle.
Prisoner at Carlisle and
York. Transported from
Liverpool for the Lee-
ward Islands on the
Veteran, master John
Ricky, 5 May 1747.
Liberated by a French
privateer and landed
on Martinique June 1747
(P)(JAB)(RM)

SMITH PATRICK
Jacobite captured at
Preston. Transported
from Liverpool to South
Carolina on the Susannah,
master Thomas Bromhall,
7 May 1716
(CTB)(SP/C)

SMITH PATRICK
Jacobite captured at
Preston. Transported
from Liverpool for
Virginia on the Godspeed,
master Arthur Smith,
27 July 1716. Sold to
Gustavus Brown in Mary-
land 18 October 1716
(SP/C)(CTB)(HM)

SMITH ROBERT
Jacobite captured at
Preston. Transported
from Liverpool to
Jamaica or Virginia on
the Elizabeth and Anne,
master Edward Trafford,
29 June 1716. Landed at
York, Virginia - indent-
ured
(CTB)(SP/C)(VSP)

SMITH THOMAS
Former soldier. Previously
banished to Barbados by
Cromwell. Thief. Prisoner
in Edinburgh Tolbooth.
Banished 23 September 1662
(ETR)

SMITH THOMAS
Jacobite captured at Preston.
Transported from Liverpool to
Maryland on the Friendship,
master Michael Mankin, 24 May
1716. Sold to Joseph Bullock
in Maryland 20 August 1716
(SP/C)(CTB)(HM)

SMITH WILLIAM
Carmunnock. Covenanter. Pris-
oner in Glasgow Tolbooth.
Banished at Glasgow June 1684.
Transported from the Clyde to
America on the Pelican by
Walter Gibson, merchant in
Glasgow June 1684
(PC)

SMITH WILLIAM
Cambusnethan. Covenanter.
Banished to the Plantations
1685. Prisoner in Canongate
Tolbooth. Transported from
Leith to East New Jersey by
George Scott of Pitlochie on
the Henry and Francis, master
Richard Hutton, 5 September
1685
(PC)

SMITH WILLIAM
Jacobite. Transported from
Liverpool on the Gildart,
master Richard Holmes.
Landed at Port North Potomac,
Maryland 5 August 1747
(PRO)

SOMERVILLE JAMES
Fermourer. Cambusnethan.
Covenanter. Prisoner in Edinburgh Tolbooth. Transported
from Leith to the Plantations
in America by Alexander Fearne,
merchant, and his shipmaster
Edward Barnes, December 1685
(ETR)(PC)

SOMERVILLE JAMES
Jacobite captured at
Preston. Transported
from Liverpool for
Virginia on the Godspeed,
master Arthur Smith,
28 July 1716. Landed
in Maryland and escaped
18 October 1716
(SP/C)(CTB)(HM)

SOMERVILLE PATRICK
Tailor. Canongate.
Covenanter. Prisoner in
Edinburgh Tolbooth.
Transported from Leith
to the Plantations 1678
(PC)

SOMERVILLE PETER
15. Shoemaker. Angus or
Lothian. Jacobite
drummerboy in Ogilvy's
regiment. Captured at
Carlisle. Prisoner at
Carlisle and Lincoln.
Transported from Liver-
pool for the Leeward
Islands on the Veteran,
master John Ricky,
5 May 1747. Liberated
by a French privateer
and landed on Martinique
June 1747
(P)(OR)(RM)

SOMERVILLE WILLIAM
Cambusnethan(?). Coven-
anter. Brother of James
Somerville. Prisoner in
Edinburgh Tolbooth.
Transported from Leith
to the Plantations by
Alexander Fearne, merchant,
and his shipmaster Edward
Barnes, December 1685
(ETR)(PC)

SONGSTER ANDREW
Jacobite captured at
Preston. Transported
from Liverpool to South
Carolina on the Wakefield,
master Thomas Beck,
21 April 1716
(CTB)(SP/C)

SOUTAR JOHN
Joiner. Ellon. Jacobite in
Grant's regiment. Prisoner at
Carlisle and Chester. Trans-
ported from Liverpool on the
Johnson, master William
Pemberton. Landed at Port
Oxford, Maryland 5 August 1747
(P)(PRO)

SOUTHLAND ADAM
Jacobite. Prisoner at Lincoln.
Transported from Liverpool by
Samuel Smith May 1747
(P)(RM)

SPALDING ALEXANDER
Jacobite captured at Preston.
Transported from Liverpool to
Maryland on the Friendship,
master Michael Mankin, 24 May
1716. Sold to William Nicholson
in Maryland 20 August 1716
(SP/C)(CTB)(HM)

SPEED WILLIAM
Jacobite. Transported from
Liverpool on the Gildart,
master Richard Holmes. Landed
at Port North Potomac, Maryland
5 August 1747
(PRO)

SPENCE ROBERT
Merchant in Kirkcaldy, Fife.
Forger. Banished to America
for 7 years, 25 July 1769
(JC)

SPROTT JOHN
Thief. Banished to the Plant-
ations for 14 years in 1769
(SM)

SPROUT WILLIAM
Clontarch(?). Covenanter.
Prisoner at Edinburgh, Dunnottar
and Leith. Banished to the
Plantations, at Leith 18 August
1685. Transported from Leith
to East New Jersey by George
Scott of Pitlochie on the
Henry and Francis, master
Richard Hutton, 5 September 1685
(PC)

STALKER DUNCAN BUIE
Lubea, Glencoe. Cattle
thief. Banished to the
Plantations for life,
at Inveraray 4 September 1766
(SM)

STARK DONALD the younger
Olrigg, Caithness.
Housebreaker. Banished
to America for life
25 July 1769
(JC)

STARK JOHN
Thief. Banished at Stir-
ling 1754
(SM)

STEEL ALEXANDER
Forger. Prisoner in
Edinburgh Tolbooth.
Banished to the Plant-
ations 3 February 1670.
Transported from Leith
to Virginia by James
Johnston, James Currie
and Patrick Fyffe,
merchants in Edinburgh
on the Ewe and Lamb,
master James Guthrie
(PC)

STEEL JOHN
Apprentice tailor.
Lanark. Attempted
murder. Banished to the
Plantations for life in
1767
(SM)

STEEL MICHAEL
Labourer. Logie Almond.
Jacobite in Atholl Brig-
ade. Prisoner in Perth
and Canongate. Trans-
ported from Liverpool
on the Johnson, master
William Pemberton.
Landed at Port Oxford
Maryland 5 August 1747
(P)(PRO)

STEPHEN JAMES
25. Mearns. Jacobite in Banner-
man's regiment. Prisoner at
Inverness, ship and Tilbury.
Transported from London to
Jamaica or Barbados by Samuel
Smith 31 March 1747
(P)(RM)

STEPHEN WILLIAM
Student of Divinity. Fireraiser.
Transported to the Plantations
for 7 years, at Stirling
25 May 1764
(SM)

STEVEN WILLIAM
Glasgow. Covenanter. Prisoner
at Edinburgh Tolbooth. Trans-
ported from Leith to the
Plantations on the St Michael
of Scarborough, master Edward
Johnston, 12 December 1678
(PC)

STEVENSON OF DYKES WILLIAM JR.
Forger. Transported to
America 1747. Retransported
1750
(SM)

STEWART AGNES
Daughter of William Stewart
a former soldier. Hilltown,
Dundee. Housebreaker. Banished
to the Plantations for life,
at Perth April 1773
(SM)

STEWART ALEXANDER
Kirkliston. Covenanter. Pris-
oner in Edinburgh Tolbooth.
Transported from Leith to the
Plantations on the St Michael
of Scarborough, master Edward
Johnston, 12 December 1678
(PC)

STEWART ALEXANDER
Jacobite captured at
Preston. Transported
from Liverpool to
Antigua on the Scipio,
master John Scaisbrick,
30 March 1716
(CTB)(SP/C)

STEWART ALEXANDER
Jacobite captured at
Preston. Transported
from Liverpool to South
Carolina on the Susannah
master Thomas Bromhall,
7 May 1716
(CTB)(SP/C)

STEWART ALEXANDER
Jacobite captured at
Preston. Transported
from Liverpool to
Virginia or Jamaica on
the Elizabeth and Anne,
master Edward Trafford,
29 June 1716. Landed
at York, Virginia -
unindentured
(CTB)(SP/C)(VSP)

STEWART ALEXANDER
Jacobite captured at
Preston. Transported
from Liverpool to
Virginia or Jamaica on
the Elizabeth and Anne,
master Edward Trafford,
29 June 1716. Landed
at York, Virginia -
unindentured
(CTB)(SP/C)(VSP)

STEWART ALEXANDER
23. Mariner. Strathspey,
Moray. Jacobite. Pris-
oner at Perth and Car-
lisle. Transported from
Liverpool on the Gildart
master Richard Holmes.
Landed at Port North
Potomac, Maryland
5 August 1747
(P)(PRO)

STEWART ALEXANDER
Footman to Prince Charles.
Former servant to Mrs Murray
of Broughton. 34. Perthshire.
Jacobite. Prisoner at Perth,
Falkland, Canongate, Carlisle,
Penrith, Kendal, Lancaster,
Preston and Liverpool. Trans-
ported from Liverpool for
Wicomica, Maryland., 14 May
1747. Landed at Port North
Potomac, Maryland 5 August 1747
(Escaped and returned to Scot-
land 1748)
(P)(PRO)

STEWART AUSTIN
Royalist soldier captured at
Worcester. Transported from
Gravesend to Boston on the
John and Sarah, master John
Greene, 13 May 1652
(NER)

STEWART CHARLES
Royalist soldier captured at
Worcester. Transported from
Gravesend to Boston on the
John and Sarah, master John
Greene, 13 May 1652
(NER)

STEWART CHARLES
Jacobite captured at Preston.
Transported from Liverpool to
Antigua on the Scipio, master
John Scaisbrick, 30 March 1716
(CTB)(SP/C)

STEWART CHARLES
Cromdale, Inverness-shire.
Cattlethief. Banished to the
Plantations for 14 years, at
Inverness 10 May 1768
(SM)

STEWART CHARLES
Son of James Stewart, horner
or spoonmaker. Newton of Glamis
Angus. Housebreaker. Banished
to the Plantations for life,
at Perth April 1773
(SM)

STEWART DANIEL
Jacobite captured at Pres-
ton. Transported from
Liverpool to Antigua on
the Scipio, master John
Scaisbrick, 30 March 1716
(CTB)(SP/C)

STEWART DANIEL
Jacobite captured at Pres-
ton. Transported from
Liverpool toAntigua on
the Scipio, master John
Scaisbrick, 30 March 1716
(CTB)(SP/C)

STEWART DANIEL
Jacobite captured at Pres-
ton. Transported from
Liverpool to Antigua on
the Scipio, master John
Scaisbrick, 30 March 1716
(CTB)(SP/C)

STEWART DANIEL
Jacobite captured at Pres-
ton. Transported from
Liverpool for Virginia on
the Godspeed, master
Arthur Smith, 28 July 1716.
Sold to Richard Eglin in
Maryland 17 October 1716
(SP/C)(CTB)(HM)

STEWART DAVID
Jacobite captured at Pres-
ton. Transported from
Liverpool to Maryland on
the Friendship, master
Michael Mankin, 24 May
1716. Sold to Jacob
Henderson in Maryland
20 August 1716
(SP/C)(CTB)(HM)

STEWART DAVID
40. Banff. Jacobite in
Lord Lewis Gordon's
regiment. Prisoner at
Carlisle. Transported
1747(?)
(P)

STUART DAVID
50. Ross. Jacobite in Stonywood's
regiment. Prisoner at Inverness
and Tilbury. Transported
20 March 1747
(P)

STEWART DONALD
Jacobite captured at Preston.
Transported from Liverpool to
South Carolina on the Wakefield,
master Thomas Beck, 21 April
1716
(CTB)(SP/C)

STEWART DONALD
Jacobite captured at Preston.
Transported from Liverpool to
Virginia or Jamaica on the
Elizabeth and Anne, master
Edward Trafford, 29 June 1716.
Landed at York, Virginia -
unindentured
(CTB)(SP/C)(VSP)

STEWART DONALD
Strathie, Deeside. Horsethief.
Banished to the Plantations
for life, at Perth 28 April
1773. Transported from
Greenock on the Rainbow,
master William Gordon. Landed
at Port Hampton, Virginia
3 May 1775
(JC)

STEWART DUNCAN
Jacobite captured at Preston.
Transported from Liverpool
to South Carolina on the
Susannah, master Thomas
Bromhall, 7 May 1716
(CTB)(SP/C)

STEWART DUNCAN
Jacobite captured at Pres-
ton. Transported from
Liverpool for Jamaica on
the Two Brothers, master
Edward Rathbone, 26 April
1716. Landed on Montserrat
June 1716
(CTB)(SP/C)(CTP)

STEWART DUNCAN
21. Cattleherd. Breadal-
bane. Jacobite in Roy
Stuart's regiment.
Prisoner at Inverness
and on ship. Transported
1747(?)
(P)

STEWART DUNCAN
21. Argyll. Jacobite in
Ardshiel's regiment.
Prisoner at Inverness,
ships and Tilbury. Trans-
ported from London to
Barbados or Jamaica by
Samuel Smith 31 March
1747
(P)(RM)

STEWART GABRIEL or GILBERT
Blacksmith. Servant to
John Richardson, smith in
Calton. Thief. Prisoner
in Edinburgh Tolbooth.
Banished to the Plant-
ations in America for 14
years, at Edinburgh
19 January 1767
(JC)

STEWART GRIZEL
Child murder. Transported
to America, at Edinburgh
1752
(SM)

STEWART HUGH
Jacobite captured at Preston. Transported from
Liverpool to South Carol-
ina on the Susannah, mas-
ter Thomas Bromhall,
7 May 1716
(CTB)(SP/C)

STUART HUGH
58. Inverness. Jacobite in
Glengarry's regiment. Prisoner
at Inverness, ship and Tilbury.
Transported from London to
Barbados or Jamaica by Samuel
Smith 31 March 1747
(P)(RM)

STEWART JAMES
Covenanter. Prisoner at Glasgow,
Stirling, Edinburgh and Canon-
gate Tolbooths. Banished to the
Plantations, at Glasgow 11
October 1684. Transported
from Leith to East New Jersey
by Robert Barclay of Urie
30 July 1685
(PC)

STEWART JAMES
Jacobite captured at Preston.
Transported from Liverpool to
Virginia or Jamaica on the
Elizabeth and Anne, master
Edward Trafford, 29 June 1716
Landed at York, Virginia -
unindentured
(CTB)(SP/C)(VSP)

STEWART JAMES
Natural brother of Ardshiel.
Quartermaster of Ardshiel's
regiment. Jacobite. Prisoner
at Southwark. Transported
1747(?)
(P)

STEWART JANET
Sewing mistress. Corstorphine.
Child murder. Banished to
America for life 25 February
1771. Transported from Port
Glasgow on the Crawford,
master James McLean. Landed
at Port Oxford, Maryland
23 July 1771
(JC)

STEWART or HUNTER JEAN
Servant to William Spence,
tailor in Edinburgh. Thief.
Banished at Perth 14 Oct-
ober 1772. Transported
from Port Glasgow on the
Phoenix, master John
Lamont. Landed at Port
Accomack, Virginia
20 December 1773
(JC)

STEWART MR JOHN
Covenanter. Banished to
the Plantations
2 March 1685
(PC)

STEWART JOHN
Jacobite captured at Pres-
ton. Transported from
Liverpool to Antigua on
the Scipio, master John
Scaisbrick, 30 March 1716
(CTB)(SP/C)

STEWART JOHN
Jacobite captured at Pres-
ton. Transported from
Liverpool to Antigua on
the Scipio, master John
Scaisbrick, 30 March 1716
(CTB)(SP/C)

STEWART JOHN
Jacobite captured at Pres-
ton. Transported from
Liverpool to Virginia or
Jamaica on the Elizabeth
and Anne, master Edward
Trafford, 29 June 1716.
Landed at York, Virginia
- unindentured
(CTB)(SP/C)(VSP)

STEWART JOHN
Jacobite captured at Pres-
ton. Transported from
Liverpool for Jamaica on
the Two Brothers, master
Edward Rathbone, 26 April
1716. Landed on Montserrat
June 1716
(SP/C)(CTB)(CTP)

STEWART JOHN
Jacobite captured at Preston.
Transported from Liverpool to
Virginia or Jamaica on the
Elizabeth and Anne, master
Edward Trafford, 29 June 1716.
Landed at York, Virginia -
indentured
(CTB)(SP/C)(VSP)

STEWART JOHN
Jacobite captured at Preston.
Transported from Liverpool to
Virginia or Jamaica on the
Elizabeth and Anne, master
Edward Trafford, 29 June 1716.
Landed at York, Virginia -
indentured
(CTB)(SP/C)(VSP)

STEWART JOHN
Jacobite captured at Preston.
Transported from Liverpool to
Virginia or Jamaica on the
Elizabeth and Anne, master
Edward Trafford, 29 June 1716.
Landed at York, Virginia -
indentured
(CTB)(SP/C)(VSP)

STEWART JOHN
Jacobite captured at Preston.
Transported from Liverpool to
Jamaica on the Two Brothers,
master Edward Rathbone, 26
April 1716. Landed on Montserrat
June 1716
(CTB)(SP/C)(CTP)

STEWART JOHN
Jacobite captured at Preston.
Transported from Liverpool to
South Carolina on the Susannah,
master Thomas Bromhall, 7 May
1716.
(CTB)

STEWART JOHN
Jacobite captured at Preston.
Transported from Liverpool to
Antigua on the Scipio, master
John Scaisbrick, 30 March 1716
(CTB)(SP/C)

STEWART JOHN
Jacobite captured at Preston. Transported from
Liverpool to Virginia on
the Godspeed, master
Arthur Smith, 28 July
1716. Sold to John
Middleton in Maryland
17 October 1716
(SP/C)(CTB)(HM)

STEWART JOHN
14. Jacobite in Glengarry's regiment. Prisoner at Inverness and
Tilbury. Transported
from London to Jamaica
or Barbados by Samuel
Smith 31 March 1747
(P)(RM)

STEWART JOHN
17. Labourer. Perthshire.
Jacobite. Prisoner in
Lancaster. Transported
from Liverpool for the
Leeward Islands on the
Veteran, master John
Ricky, 5 May 1747. Liberated by a French privateer and landed on
Martinique June 1747
(P)(RM)

STEWART JOHN
18. Labourer. Aberdeen.
Jacobite in Glenbucket's
regiment. Captured at
Carlisle. Prisoner at
Carlisle and York. Transported from Liverpool for
the Leeward Islands on the
Veteran, master John
Ricky, 5 May 1747. Liberated by a French privateer
and landed on Martinique
June 1747
(P)(JAB)(RM)

STEWART JOHN
Thief. Banished, at Ayr
1752
(SM)

STEWART JOSEPH
Thief. Banished, at Ayr 1752
(SM)

STEWART MALCOLM
Jacobite captured at Preston.
Transported from Liverpool to
Virginia or Jamaica on the
Elizabeth and Anne, master
Edward Trafford, 29 June 1716.
Landed at York, Virginia -
indentured
(VSP)(CTB)(SP/C)

STEWART MARGARET
Wife of William Wilson, tinker.
Spittal. Thief and pickpocket.
Banished to the Plantations
for 7 years, at Jedburgh
24 September 1766
(SM)

STEWART NEIL
Royalist soldier captured at
Worcester. Transported from
Gravesend to Boston on the
John and Sarah, master John
Greene, 13 May 1652
(NER)

STEWART NEIL
Jacobite captured at Preston.
Transported from Liverpool to
South Carolina on the Susannah,
master Thomas Bromhall, 7 May
1716
(CTB)(SP/C)

STEWART NEIL
Jacobite captured at Preston.
Transported from Liverpool to
South Carolina on the Susannah,
master Thomas Bromhall, 7 May
1716
(CTB)(SP/C)

STEWART PATRICK
Covenanter in Argyll's
rebellion. Prisoner in
the Canongate. Banished
to the Plantations 30
July 1685. Transported
from Leith to Jamaica
by John Ewing August
1685
(PC)

STEWART PATRICK
Jacobite captured at
Preston. Transported
from Liverpool to South
Carolina on the Susannah
master Thomas Bromhall,
7 May 1716
(CTB)(SP/C)

STEWART PATRICK
Jacobite captured at
Preston. Transported
from Liverpool to Jamaica
or Virginia on the ship
Elizabeth and Anne, mas-
ter Edward Trafford, 29
June 1716. Landed at
York, Virginia - unind-
entured
(CTB)(SP/C)(VSP)

STEWART PETER
Thief. Banished at Ayr
1752
(SM)

STEWART ROBERT
Royalist soldier captured
at Worcester. Transported
from Gravesend to Boston
on the John and Sarah,
master John Greene,
13 May 1652
(NER)

STEWART ROBERT
Royalist soldier captured
at Worcester. Transported
from Gravesend to Boston
on the John and Sarah,
master John Greene,
13 May 1652
(NER)

STEWART ROBERT
Jacobite captured at Preston.
Transported from Liverpool to
Jamaica or Virginia on the
Elizabeth and Anne, master
Edward Trafford, 29 June 1716.
Landed at York, Virginia -
indentured
(VSP)(CTB)(SP/C)

STEWART ROBERT
Jacobite captured at Preston.
Transported from Liverpool to
Virginia or Jamaica on the
Elizabeth and Anne, master
Edward Trafford, 29 June 1716.
Landed at York, Virginia -
indentured. (A document at the
Scottish Record Office dated
17 October 1716 certifies that
the above was to continue as
servant to Captain Edward
Trafford for seven years,
signed at Williamsburg,
Virginia)
(SP/C)(CTB)(VSP)

STEWART THOMAS
Jacobite in the Duke of Perth's
regiment. Prisoner at Lancaster.
Transported 1747(?)
(P)

STEWART WALTER
Jacobite captured at Preston.
Transported from Liverpool to
St Kitts on the Hockenhill,
master H. Short, 25 June 1716
(CTB)(SP/C)

STEWART WILLIAM
Royalist soldier captured at
Worcester. Transported from
Gravesend to Boston on the
John and Sarah, master John
Greene, 13 May 1652
(NER)

STEWART WILLIAM
Jacobite captured at
Preston. Transported
from Liverpool to
Antigua on the Scipio,
master John Scaisbrick,
30 March 1716
(CTB)(SP/C)

STEWART WILLIAM
Cousin of Stewart of
Ardshiel. Jacobite
lieutenant. Prisoner
at Edinburgh and Carlisle.
Transported from Liverpool
on the Johnson, master
William Pemberton. Landed
at Port Oxford, Maryland
5 August 1747
(P)(PRO)

STEWART WILLIAM
Weaver. Paisley. Rioter.
Banished for 14 years,
at Glasgow 1752
(SM)

STEWART WILLIAM
        alias JAMES SMITH
Cattle thief. Banished
to the Plantations for
life, at Edinburgh
25 March 1767
(SM)

STEWART WILLIAM
Soldier in 14th regiment
of Foot. Hilltown, Dundee.
Housebreaker. Banished to
the Plantations for life,
at Perth April 1773
(SM)

STIRLING DAVID
Royalist soldier captured
at Worcester. Transported
from Gravesend to Boston
on the John and Sarah,
master John Greene,
13 May 1652
(NER)

STIRLING JOHN
Royalist soldier captured at
Worcester. Transported from
Gravesend to Boston on the
John and Sarah, master John
Greene, 13 May 1652
(NER)

STIRLING MABEL
Gypsy. Prisoner in Jedburgh
Tolbooth. Banished at Jedburgh
30 November 1714. Transported
from Glasgow to Virginia on
a Greenock ship, master James
Watson, by merchants Robert
Buntine of Airdoch, James Lees
and Charles Crauford,1 January
1715
(GR)

STITT EDWARD
Covenanter. Durisdeer(?).
Prisoner in Edinburgh Tolbooth
Banished to the Plantations
28 July 1685. Stigmatised.
Transported from Leith to
Jamaica by John Ewing August
1685
(ETR)(PC)

STOBIE ADAM
Lascar. Covenanter. Prisoner
in Edinburgh Tolbooth. Trans-
ported from Leith to the
Plantations on the St Michael
of Scarborough, master Edward
Johnston, 12 December 1678
(PC)

STONYER WILLIAM
Grenadier in Wolfe's Regiment
of Foot. Thief. Banished at
Inverness September 1754
(SM)

STORIE JAMES
Prisoner in Edinburgh Tolbooth
Transported by Walter Gibson
to Carolina 21 May 1684
(PC)

STRACHAN ALEXANDER
Petty thief. Banished for
life 1773
(SM)

STRACHAN CHARLES
Jacobite captured at Preston. Transported from
Liverpool to South Carol-
ina on the Wakefield, master Thomas Beck, 21 April
1716
(CTB)(SP/C)

STRACHAN JAMES
19. Aberdeen university
student. Mearns. Jacobite
in the Duke of Perth's
regiment. Prisoner at
Stirling, Leith, Canon-
gate and Carlisle. Trans-
ported from Liverpool on
the Gildart, master
Richard Holmes. Landed at
Port North Potomac, Mary-
land 5 August 1747.
Employed as a tutor to a
settler's family there
(P)(PRO)(JAB)

STRANG CHRISTOPHER
Kilkryde. Covenanter.
Prisoner at Glasgow,
Dunnottar and Leith. Ban-
ished to the Plantations,
at Leith 18 August 1685.
Transported from Leith to
East New Jersey by George
Scott of Pitlochie on the
Henry and Francis, master
Richard Hutton, 5 September
1685
(PC)

STRANGE MR DAVID
Minister at Cabrach.
Prisoner in Edinburgh
Tolbooth. Clandestine
marriage. Banished to the
Plantations in America for
life, at Edinburgh
9 December 1738
(JC)

STRATTON JAMES
75. Mason. Moray. Jacobite.
Prisoner at Lancaster.
Transported from Liverpool
on the Johnson, master
William Pemberton. Landed at
Port Oxford, Maryland
5 August 1747
(P)(PRO)

STROAK(STURROCK?)WILLIAM
Jacobite captured at Preston.
Transported from Liverpool
to Virginia or Jamaica on the
Elizabeth and Anne, master
Edward Trafford, 29 June 1716.
Landed at York, Virginia -
unindentured
(CTB)(SP/C)(VSP)

STROCK (STURROCK?) JAMES
Jacobite captured at Preston.
Transported from Liverpool
to Antigua on the Scipio,
master John Scaisbrick,
30 March 1716
(SP/C)(CTB)

STUART ROBERT
Jacobite captured at Preston.
Transported from Liverpool
on the Elizabeth and Anne,
master Edward Trafford, 29
June 1716. Landed at York,
Virginia
(A document at the Scottish
Record Office, signed at
York, Virginia stating that
Robert Stuart, formerly in
Glenbeath, who had been
assigned to William Gordon
had been sent by him on
business to Scotland 3 May
1717)
(SP/C)(VSP)

STUBBS ROBERT
Jacobite captured at
Preston. Transported
from Liverpool on the
Friendship, master
Michael Mankin, to Mary-
land 24 May 1716
Sold to John Valliant
in Maryland 20 August
1716
(SP/C)(CTB)(HM)

SUTHERLAND ADAM
Grange, Prestonpans.
Housebreaker. Prisoner
in Edinburgh Tolbooth.
Banished to the Plant-
ations in America for
life, at Edinburgh
31 July 1745
(JC)

SUTHERLAND ADAM
Jacobite transported
from Liverpool on the
Johnson, master William
Pemberton. Landed at
Port Oxford, Maryland
5 August 1747
(PRO)

SUTHERLAND ADAM
56. Labourer. Suther-
landshire. Jacobite in
Glenbucket's regiment.
Captured at Carlisle.
Prisoner at Carlisle,
York and Lincoln.
Transported from Liver-
pool for the Leeward
Islands on the Veteran,
master John Ricky, 5
May 1747. Liberated by
a French privateer and
landed on Martinique
June 1747
(P)(RM)

SUTHERLAND ALAN
19. Jacobite in Cromarty's
regiment. Prisoner at
Inverness, ship and Til-
bury. Transported 1747(?)
(P)

SUTHERLAND ALEXANDER
19. Husbandman. Ballyhaldrie,
Sutherland. Jacobite in
Cromarty's regiment. Prisoner
at Inverness, ship and Medway.
Transported from London to
Barbados or Jamaica by Samuel
Smith 31 March 1747
(P)(RM)

SUTHERLAND ALEXANDER
34. Caithness. Jacobite in
Bannerman's regiment. Prisoner
at Inverness, ship and Tilbury.
Transported from London to
Jamaica or Barbados by Samuel
Smith 30 March 1747
(P)(RM)

SUTHERLAND ALEXANDER
Housebreaker and thief. Banished
to the Plantations for 5 years,
at Inverness 17 September 1763
(SM)

SUTHERLAND ANSEL
Royalist soldier captured at
Worcester. Transported from
Gravesend to Boston on the
John and Sarah, master John
Greene, 13 May 1652
(NER)

SUTHERLAND DANIEL
Pickpocket. Banished 1772.
Transported on the Donald,
master Thomas Ramsay. Landed
at Port James, Upper District,
Virginia 13 March 1773
(SM)(JC)

SUTHERLAND JOHN
Jacobite captured at Preston.
Transported from Liverpool to
Antigua on the Scipio, master
John Scaisbrick, 30 March 1716
(CTB)(SP/C)

SUTHERLAND JOHN
22. Husbandman. Dunbeath,
Caithness. Jacobite in
Cromarty's regiment.
Prisoner at Inverness,
ships and Medway. Trans-
ported from London to
Barbados or Jamaica
31 March 1747
(P)(RM)

SUTHERLAND NEIL
35. Army deserter. Caith-
ness. Jacobite in Crom-
arty's regiment. Prisoner
at Inverness, ship and
Tilbury. Transported
from London to Barbados
or Jamaica by Samuel
Smith 31 March 1747
(P)(RM)

SUTHERLAND PATRICK
Royalist soldier captured
at Worcester. Transported
from Gravesend to Boston
on the John and Sarah,
master John Greene,
13 May 1652
(NER)

SUTHERLAND WILLIAM
10. Son of Neil Sutherland.
Caithness. Jacobite in
Cromarty's regiment. Prisoner at Inverness, ships
and Tilbury. Transported
from London to Barbados
or Jamaica by Samuel Smith
31 March 1747
(P)(RM)

SUTHERLAND WILLIAM
30. Husbandman. Dunbeath,
Caithness. Jacobite in
Cromarty's regiment.
Prisoner at Inverness,
ships and Medway. Trans-
ported from London to
Barbados or Jamaica by
Samuel Smith 31 March
1747
(P)(RM)

SWAN JOHN
Covenanter. Prisoner in
Canongate Tolbooth. Banished
to the Plantations 24 July
1685. Transported from Leith
to East New Jersey by Robert
Barclay of Urie 30 July 1685
(PC)

SWANSTON JOHN
Chelsea pensioner. Caithness.
Thief and housebreaker.
Banished to the Plantations
for life in 1768
(SM)

SWANSTON CHARLES
Servant to Mrs Ann Sinclair in
Thirdistoft. Housebreaker.
Banished to America for life
25 July 1769
(SM)(JC)

SWINHOE JAMES
Jacobite captured at Preston.
Transported from Liverpool to
South Carolina on the Susannah,
master Thomas Bromhall, 7 May
1716
(CTB)(SP/C)

SWINTOUN JOHN
Covenanter. Teviotdale.
Prisoner at Canongate, Dunnottar
and Leith. Banished to the
Plantations, at Leith 18
August 1685. Transported from
Leith to East New Jersey by
George Scott of Pitlochie on
the Henry and Francis, master
Richard Hutton, 5 September
1685
(PC)

SWORD HUMPHREY
Jacobite captured at Preston.
Transported from Liverpool for
Virginia on the Godspeed, master
Arthur Smith, 29 July 1716.
Landed in Maryland and
escaped 18 October 1716
(SP/C)(CTB)(HM)

SWORD JOHN
Jacobite captured at Pres-
ton. Transported from
Liverpool to St Kitts on
the Hockenhill, master
H.Short, 25 June 1716
(CTB)(SP/C)

SYME HUGH
Eaglesham. Covenanter.
Prisoner in Glasgow Tol-
booth. Banished at Glas-
gow June 1684. Transported
from the Clyde to America
on the Pelican by Walter
Gibson, merchant in Glas-
gow June 1684
(PC)

SYME PATRICK
Prisoner in Edinburgh
Tolbooth. Transported to
Barbados by George Hutch-
ison, merchant in Edin-
burgh, 7 December 1665
(ETR)(PC)

SYME WILLIAM
Eaglesham. Covenanter.
Prisoner in Glasgow Tol-
booth. Banished at Glas-
gow June 1684. Transported
from the Clyde to America
on the Pelican by Walter
Gibson, merchant in Glas-
gow June 1684
(PC)

TAGGART JOHN
Roaderheuk, Annandale(?).
Covenanter. Prisoner at
Leith. Banished to the
Plantations, at Leith
18 August 1685. Trans-
ported from Leith to East
New Jersey by George Scott
of Pitlochie on the
Henry and Francis, master
Richard Hutton, 5 Septem-
ber 1685
(PC)

TAIT WILLIAM
Gypsy and thief. Prisoner in
Dumfries Tolbooth. Banished
to the Plantations in America
for life, at Dumfries 1 May 1739
(JC)

TAIT JOHN
Camphill, Dumfries. Covenanter.
Banished to the Plantations,
at Dumfries 25 October 1684
(PC)

TAIT MARY
Gypsy and thief. Prisoner in
Dumfries Tolbooth. Banished
to the Plantations in America
for life, at Dumfries 1 May 1739
(JC)

TAIT THOMAS
Jacobite captured at Preston.
Transported from Liverpool to
Antigua on the Scipio, master
John Scaisbrick, 30 March 1716
(CTB)(SP/C)

TANKARD WALTER
Jacobite captured at Preston.
Transported from Liverpool
to Jamaica or Virginia on the
Elizabeth and Anne, master
Edward Trafford, 29 June 1716.
Landed at York, Virginia -
indentured
(CTB)(SP/C)

TANNIS AGNES
Covenanter. Prisoner in Leith.
Transported from Leith to East
New Jersey by George Scott of
Pitlochie on the Henry and
Francis, master Richard Hutton,
5 September 1685
(PC)

TAYLOR AGNES
Thief. Banished for life,
at Aberdeen 1753
(SM)

TAYLOR AGNES
Paisley. Thief. Banished
to the Plantations, at
Glasgow 16 May 1770
(SM)

TAYLOR ALEXANDER
38. Labourer. Edinburgh.
Jacobite. Prisoner at
Edinburgh and Carlisle.
Transported from Liver-
pool on the Johnson,
master William Pemberton.
Landed at Port Oxford,
Maryland 5 August 1747
(P)(PRO)

TAYLOR JAMES
Jacobite captured at
Preston. Transported
from Liverpool to
Antigua on the Scipio,
master John Scaisbrick,
30 March 1716
(CTB)(SP/C)

TAYLOR JAMES
Smith and nailer. The
Folley, near Redheugh,
Parish of Cockpen, near
Edinburgh. Housebreaker.
Prisoner in Edinburgh
Tolbooth. Banished to the
Plantations in America
for life, at Edinburgh
11 August 1775
(JC)

TAYLOR JOHN
Servant to Leith of Bohern.
28. Moray. Jacobite in Lord
Lewis Gordon's regiment.
Prisoner at Inverness. Trans-
ported from Liverpool on the
Johnson, master William Pem-
berton. Landed at Port
Oxford, Maryland 5 August
1747
(P)(PRO)

TAYLOR ROBERT
Robber. Banished to America
for life 30 November 1770.
Transported from Port Glasgow
on the Crawford, master James
McLean. Landed at Port Oxford,
Maryland 23 July 1771
(JC)

TAYLOR WILLIAM
Royalist captured at Worcester.
Transported from Gravesend to
Boston on the John and Sarah,
master John Greene, 13 May 1652
(NER)

TEMPLE WILLIAM
Linton. Prisoner in Edinburgh
Tolbooth. Transported from
Leith to the Plantations on
the St Michael of Scarborough,
master Edward Johnston,
12 December 1678
(PC)

TEMPLETON ISOBEL
Banished for life. Transported
from Glasgow on the Brilliant,
master Robert Bennet. Landed
at Port Hampton, Virginia
7 October 1772
(JC)

TENNANT JAMES
Covenanter. Prisoner in Edinburgh
or Canongate. Banished to
Carolina 6 August 1684. Transported by Robert Malloch,
merchant in Edinburgh
(PC)

THOM ROBERT
16. Labourer. Angus. Jacobite in
Ogilvy's regiment. Transported
from Liverpool for the Leeward
Islands on the Veteran, master
John Ricky, 5 May 1747. Liberated by a French privateer and
landed on Martinique June 1747
(P)(OR)(RM)

THOMPSON ALEXANDER
Royalist prisoner capt-
ured at Worcester.
Transported from Graves-
end to Boston on the
John and Sarah, master
John Greene, 13 May 1652
(NER)

THOMSON ANNE
Servant at Struthers.
Banished to the Plant-
ations, at Perth 5 Sept-
ember 1764. Child murder
(SM)

THOMSON ARCHIBALD
Covenanter. Prisoner in
Canongate Tolbooth. Ban-
ished to the Plantat-
ions 24 July 1685. Trans
ported from Leith to Jam-
aica by John Ewing August
1685

(PC)

THOMPSON DANIEL
Jacobite captured at
Preston. Transported
from Liverpool to Jam-
aica or Virginia on
the Elizabeth and Anne
master Edward Trafford
29 June 1716. Landed
at York, Virginia -
indentured
(CTB)(SP/C)(VSP)

THOMSON DONALD
Covenanter. Prisoner
in Laigh Parliament
House, Edinburgh.
In Argyll's rebellion.
Transported from Leith
to New England by
William Arbuckle, mer-
chant in Glasgow July
1685
(PC)

THOMSON DUNCAN
Covenanter in Argyll's rebellion
Prisoner in Paul's Work, Edin-
burgh. Banished to the Plant-
ations 30 July 1685. Transported
from Leith to Jamaica by John
Ewing August 1685
(PC)

THOMSON GABRIEL
Merchant in Glasgow. Prisoner
in Canongate Tolbooth. Transported from Leith or Newhaven
to the Plantations on the
St Michael of Scarborough,
master Edward Johnston,
12 December 1678
(PC)

THOMPSON GEORGE
Jacobite captured at Preston.
Transported from Liverpool to
Maryland on the Friendship,
master Michael Mankin, 24 May
1716. Sold to William Bladen
Esq. in Maryland 20 August 1716
(SP/C)(CTB)(HM)

THOMPSON JAMES
21. Gardener to Sir David
Threipland of Fingask. Fingask,
Kinnaird, Perthshire. Jacobite
sergeant in the Duke of Perth's
regiment. Prisoner at Auchterarder, Stirling, Carlisle and
Lincoln. Transported from Liverpool for the Leeward Islands on
the Veteran, master John Ricky
5 May 1747. Liberated by a
French privateer and landed on
Martinique June 1747
(P)(RM)

THOMSON JOHN
Covenanter in Argyll's rebellion.
Prisoner in Laigh Parliament
House, Edinburgh. Transported
from Leith to New England by
William Arbuckle, merchant in
Glasgow 6 July 1685
(PC)

THOMPSON JOHN
18. Banff. Jacobite in
Lord Lewis Gordon's
regiment. Captured at
Carlisle. Prisoner at
Carlisle, York and
Whitehave. Transported
1747(?)

THOMSON MARY
Child murder. Banished
for life in 1773
(SM)

THOMSON NEIL
Covenanter in Argyll's
rebellion. Prisoner in
Paul's Work, Edinburgh
Banished to the Plant-
ations 30 July 1685.
Transported from Leith
to Jamaica by John
Ewing August 1685
(PC)

THOMSON PATRICK
Shoemaker. Dundee. Jac-
obite in Ogilvy's regi-
ment. Prisoner at
Arbroath, Stirling and
Carlisle. Transported
to Antigua 8 May 1747
(P)

THOMSON WILLIAM
Covenanter. Prisoner
in Paul's Work, Edin-
burgh. Banished to the
Plantations. Transported
from Leith to East New
Jersey by Robert
Barclay of Urie,
31 July 1685
(PC)

THOMSON WILLIAM
17. Tailor. Glasgow. Jac-
obite. Prisoner at Perth,
Canongate and Carlisle.
Transported from Liverpool
on the Gildart, master
Richard Holmes. Landed at
Port North Potomac
5 August 1747
(P)(PRO)

THOMPSON WILLIAM
40. Labourer. Little Kenny,
Kingoldrum, Angus. Jacobite
in Ogilvy's regiment. Prisoner
at Carlisle, York and Lincoln.
Transported from Liverpool for
the Leeward Islands on the
Veteran, master John Ricky,
5 May 1747. Liberated by a
French privateer and landed
on Martinique June 1747
(P)(OR)(RM)

THORBURN WILLIAM
Jacobite captured at Preston.
Transported from Liverpool to
Antigua on the Scipio, master
John Scaisbrick, 30 March 1747
(CTB)(SP/C)

TILLERY ANDREW
42. Horsehirer. Old Machar,
Aberdeen. Jacobite. Prisoner
at Canongate and Carlisle.
Transported from Liverpool
on the Johnson, master William
Pemberton.Landed at Port
Oxford, Maryland 5 August 1747
(P)(JAB)(PRO)

TOD GEORGE
Aberdeen. Thief. Banished
for life 1773
(SM)

TODD JOHN
Jacobite captured at Preston.
Transported from Liverpool to
Antigua on the Scipio, master
John Scaisbrick, 30 March 1716
(CTB)(SP/C)

TODSHALL JOHN
Prisoner in Edinburgh Tolbooth
Transported from Leith or Buck-
haven to Barbados by Edward
Baird 22 December 1665
(ETR)

TORK ISOBEL
Banished to the Plantations
in America 11 October 1684
(PC)

TOSH DAVID
Travelling chapman. Son of
John Tosh, farmer in
Easter Ordy, Oathlaw,
Angus. Horse thief. Banish-
ed to the Plantations for
life in 1767
(SM)

TOSHACH KATHERINE
Child murder. Prisoner in
Perth Tolbooth. Banished
to the Plantations in
America for life, at
Perth 21 May 1728
(JC)

TOWER PATRICK
Royalist soldier captured
at Worcester. Transported
from Gravesend to Boston
on the John and Sarah,
master John Greene,
13 May 1652
(NER)

TROOP JOHN
20. Gardener. Stirling.
Jacobite artilleryman.
Captured at Carlisle.
Prisoner at Carlisle and
Lincoln, Transported from
Liverpool to the Leeward
Islands on the Veteran,
master John Ricky, 5 May
1747. Liberated by a French
privateer and landed on
Martinique June 1747
(P)(RM)

TRUMBALL MICHAEL
Jacobite captured at Pres-
ton. Transported from
Liverpool for Jamaica on
the Two Brothers, master
Edward Rathbone, 26 April
1716. Landed on Montserrat
June 1716
(SP/C)(CTB)(CTP)

TURNBULL THOMAS
Covenanter in Argyll's rebellion
Prisoner in Edinburgh Tolbooth.
Banished to the Plantations
31 July 1685. Stigmatised.
Transported from Leith to
Jamaica by John Ewing August
1685
(ETR)(PC)

TURNBULL WILLIAM
Covenanter. Prisoner in Leith
Tolbooth. Transported from
Leith to East New Jersey by
George Scott of Pitlochie on
the Henry and Francis, master
Richard Hutton, 5 September
1685
(PC)

TURNBULL WILLIAM
Brother to Bieuly(?).Prisoner
in Edinburgh Tolbooth. Transported from Leith or Newhaven
to the Plantations on the
St Michael of Scarborough,
master Edward Johnston,
12 December 1678
(PC)

TURNER JOHN
Thief. Banished to the
Plantations for life, at
Glasgow 1753
(SM)

TURNER WILLIAM
Jacobite captured at Preston.
Transported from Liverpool to
Jamaica or Barbados on the
Elizabeth and Anne, master
Edward Trafford, 29 June 1716.
Landed at York, Virginia -
indentured
(CTB)(VSP)(SP/C)

TURPNEY JOHN
Covenanter. Prisoner at Leith.
Transported from Leith to East
New Jersey by George Scott of
Pitlochie on the Henry and
Francis, master Richard Hutton,
5 September 1685
(PC)

TWEEDIE JANET
Child murder. Trans-
ported, at Jedburgh
19 May 1764
(SM)

URIE JOHN
Blairgorts. Covenanter.
Prisoner in Canongate
Tolbooth. Transported
from Leith to the Plant-
ations on the St Michael
of Scarborough, master
Edward Johnston,
12 December 1678
(PC)

URIE JOHN
Covenanter. Prisoner at
Glasgow, Dunnottar and
Leith. Transported from
Leith to East New Jersey
by George Scott of Pit-
lochie on the Henry and
Francis, master Richard
Hutton, 5 September 1685
(PC)

URIE PATRICK
Covenanter. Prisoner at
Dunnottar and Leith.
Transported from Leith
to East New Jersey by
George Scott of Pitlochie
on the Henry and Francis,
master Richard Hutton,
5 September 1685
(PC)

URIE ROBERT
Little Goven. Weaver.
Prisoner in Glasgow Tol-
booth. Banished at Glas-
gow June 1684. Transport-
ed from the Clyde to
America on the Pelican
by Walter Gibson, mer-
chant in Glasgow June
1684
(PC)

URIE WILLIAM
Cathcart. Covenanter. Pris-
oner in Edinburgh Tolbooth.
Banished to the Plantations
in the Indies 13 June 1678.
Transported from Leith on the
St Michael of Scarborough,
master Edward Johnston,
12 December 1678
(PC)

URQUHART DONALD
50. Blacksmith. Glen Urquhart.
Jacobite in Glengarry's regiment. Prisoner at Inverness
and Tilbury. Transported
20 March 1747
(P)

URQUHART HECTOR
47. Farmer. Achterneed, Strathpeffer. Jacobite in Cromarty's
regiment. Prisoner at Inverness, ship and Tilbury. Transported 20 March 1747
(P)

URQUHART MR JAMES
Covenanter. Banished to the
Plantations 2 March 1685
(PC)

URQUHART JAMES
Jacobite captured at Preston.
Transported from Liverpool to
Jamaica or Virginia on the
Elizabeth and Anne, master
Edward Trafford, 29 June 1716.
Landed at York, Virginia -
unindentured. Deposition
2 November 1716
(CTB)(SP/C)(VSP)

URQUHART JAMES
18. Labourer. Aberdeenshire.
Jacobite in Glenbucket's regiment. Captured at Carlisle.
Prisoner at Carlisle and Lincoln. Transported from Liverpool for the Leeward Islands
5 May 1747. Liberated by a
French privateer and landed on
Martinique June 1747
(P)(JAB)(RM)

VALLANCE ALEXANDER
Covenanter. Banished to
the Plantations 5 Feb-
ruary 1685
(PC)

VALLANCE ROBERT
Banished to America.
Transported from Glas-
gow on the Concord of
Glasgow, master James
Butchart. Landed at
Charles County, Mary-
land 24 May 1728.
Sold there by David
Cochrane, merchant
in Maryland
(JC)

WADDELL JAMES
Prisoner in Edinburgh
Tolbooth. Transported
from Leith to the
Plantations November
1679
(ETR)

WALKER AGNES
Crossmichael Parish.
Child murder. Banished
to the Plantations, at
Dumfries 30 September
1763
(SM)

WALKER ALEXANDER
21. Servant. Bervie,
Kincardineshire.
Jacobite. Prisoner at
Canongate and Carlisle.
Transported from Liver-
pool on the Johnson,
master William Pember-
ton. Landed at Port
Oxford, Maryland,
5 August 1747
(P)(PRO)

WALKER DONALD
In Otter. Tenant of the
laird of Gallachallie.
Covenanter in Argyll's
rebellion. Prisoner in
Edinburgh Tolbooth.
Transported from Leith
to Jamaica by John Ewing
August 1685
(ETR)(PC)

WALKER DUNCAN
Covenanter in Argyll's rebellion.
Prisoner in the Laigh Parliament
House, Edinburgh. Banished to
the Plantations 31 July 1685.
Transported from Leith to Jam-
aica by John Ewing August 1685
(PC)

WALKER ISOBEL
Daughter of William Walker,
deceased, in Cluden, Parish
of Irongray, Kirkcudbrightshire.
Murder. Prisoner in Dumfries
Tolbooth. Banished at Dumfries
14 June 1738
(JC)

WALKER PATRICK
18. Covenanter. Prisoner in
Edinburgh Tolbooth. Banished
to Carolina 24 July 1684.
Transported from Leith by
Robert Malloch, merchant in
Edinburgh
(PC)

WALKER PATRICK
Covenanter. Prisoner in Leith.
Transported from Leith to East
New Jersey by George Scott of
Pitlochie on the Henry and
Francis, master Richard Hutton,
5 September 1685
(PC)

WALLACE ANDREW
Prisoner in Edinburgh Tolbooth.
Transported from Leith to the
Plantations November 1679
(ETR)

WALLACE GEORGE
16. Fisherman. Jacobite.
Prisoner at Carlisle. Trans-
ported from Liverpool on the
Gildart, master Richard Holmes.
Landed at Port North Potomac,
Maryland 5 August 1747
(P)(PRO)

WALLACE JANET
Child murder. Prisoner
in Edinburgh Tolbooth.
Banished to the Plant-
ations 30 July 1685.
Stigmatised. Transported
from Leith to Jamaica by
John Ewing August 1685
(ETR)(PC)

WALLACE NICHOLAS
Royalist soldier capt-
ured at Worcester.
Transported from Grav-
esend to Boston on the
John and Sarah, master
John Greene, 13 May 1652
(NER)

WALLACE ROBERT
Jacobite captured at
Preston. Transported
from Liverpool to Jam-
aica on the Two Brothers,
master Edward Rathbone,
26 April 1716. Landed
on Montserrat June 1716
(SP/C)(CTB)(CTP)

WALLET JOHN
Covenanter. Prisoner in
Edinburgh Tolbooth, Dunn-
ottar Castle, and Leith
Tolbooth. Banished to the
Plantations 20 May 1685.
Transported
(PC)

WALLS HERBERT
Lawriddings, Dumfries.
Covenanter. Prisoner at
Dumfries, Canongate and
Dunnottar. Banished to
the Plantations, at
Dumfries 24 October 1684
(PC)

WARDEN EBENEZER
Journeyman wright, Leith
Mills. Housebreaker and
thief. Banished to
America for life, 13 Aug-
ust 1771. Transported
from Port Glasgow on the
Matty, master Robert Pea-
cock. Landed Port Oxford
17 December 1771
(JC)

WARNOCK ROBERT
Banished to the Plantations
in America 11 October 1684
(PC)

WARREN ROBERT
20. Weaver. Aberdeenshire or
Banffshire. Jacobite in Glenbucket's regiment. Captured
at Carlisle. Prisoner at
Carlisle, York and Lincoln.
Transported from Liverpool to
the Leeward Islands on the
Veteran, master John Ricky,
5 May 1747. Liberated by a
French privateer and landed
on Martinique June 1747
(P)(JAB)(RM)

WARRIOR JOHN
England. Jacobite. Transported
from Liverpool on the Johnson,
master William Pemberton.
Landed at Port Oxford, Maryland 5 August 1747
(PRO)

WATSON GEORGE
Labourer. Banff. Jacobite.
Prisoner at Carlisle and
Chester. Transported from
Liverpool on the Johnson,
master William Pemberton.
Landed at Port Oxford,
Maryland 5 August 1747
(P)(JAB)(PRO)

WATSON JAMES
Accessory to a riot against
a minister. Transported to
the Plantations in America
on Sir George Maxwell's
ship 16 June 1670
(PC)

WATSON JAMES
Jacobite captured at Preston.
Transported from Liverpool
to Virginia or Maryland on the
Elizabeth and Anne, master
Edward Trafford, 29 June 1716.
Landed at York, Virginia -
unindentured
(CTB)(SP/C)(VSP)

WATSON JAMES
Jacobite captured at
Preston. Transported
from Liverpool to Jam-
aica or Virginia on the
Elizabeth and Anne, mas-
ter Edward Trafford,
29 June 1716. Landed at
York, Virginia - unind-
entured
(CTB)(SP/C)(VSP)

WATSON JAMES
Prisoner in Edinburgh
Tolbooth. Transported
to America by Charles
Roberton, merchant in
Glasgow, and Allan
Colquhoun, writer in
Edinburgh, 25 January
1728
(JC)

WATSON JOHN
Innkeeper and brewer.
Arbroath. Jacobite in
the Duke of Perth's
regiment. Prisoner at
Stirling, Leith,Canon-
gate and Carlisle.
Transported 1747(?)
(P)

WATSON JOHN
Parkstile of Tillyfont.
Thief. Banished to the
Plantations, at Aber-
deen September 1749
(SM)

WATSON PETER
Jacobite captured at
Preston. Transported
from Liverpool to
Antigua on the Scipio,
master John Scaisbrick,
30 March 1716
(CTB)

WATSON SAMUEL
Son of Alexander Watson.
Minigaff. Thief. Pris-
oner in Dumfries Tol-
booth. Banished to the
Indies for life, at
Dumfries 1 May 1719
(JC)

WATSON WILLIAM
Islay. Covenanter. Prisoner
in Thieveshole, Edinburgh.
Banished to the Plantations
24 July 1685. Transported
from Leith to Jamaica by
John Ewing August 1685
(PC)

WATSON WILLIAM
Jacobite captured at Preston.
Transported from Liverpool
to Antigua on the Scipio,
master John Scaisbrick,
30 March 1716
(CTB)(SP/C)

WATSON WILLIAM
Jacobite captured at Preston.
Transported from Liverpool to
Antigua on the Scipio, master
John Scaisbrick, 30 March 1716
(CTB)(SP/C)

WATT ALEXANDER
Jacobite captured at Preston.
Transported from Liverpool to
Virginia or Jamaica on the
Elizabeth and Anne, master
Edward Trafford, 29 June 1716
Landed at York, Virginia -
unindentured
(VSP)(CTB)(SP/C)

WATT JOHN
Transported from Leith to East
New Jersey by George Scott of
Pitlochie on the Henry and
Francis, master Richard Hutton,
5 September 1685
(PC)

WATT JOHN
22. Fisherman. Gamry, Banff.
Jacobite. Prisoner at Canongate
and Carlisle. Transported from
Liverpool on the Johnson, master
William Pemberton. Landed at
Port Oxford, Maryland
5 August 1747
(P)(JAB)(PRO)

WATTIE JOHN
Parish of Towie.
Murderer. Banished
to the Plantations,
at Aberdeen
22 September 1759
(SM)

WEBSTER ELIZABETH
Prisoner in Edinburgh
Tolbooth. Transported
to Barbados by George
Hutchison, merchant
in Edinburgh, 7 Dec-
ember 1665
(ETR)(PC)

WEBSTER JAMES
Jacobite captured at
Preston. Transported
from Liverpool on the
Friendship, master
Michael Mankin, 24 May
1716. Sold to Stephen
Warman in Maryland
20 August 1716
(SP/C)(CTB)(HM)

WEIR ELIZABETH
Child murder. Banished,
at Ayr September 1749
(SM)

WEIR JOHN
Transported from Leith
to Jamaica by John Ewing
August 1685
(PC)

WEIR THOMAS
Lesmahowgow. Covenanter.
Prisoner in Canongate
Tolbooth. Banished to
the Plantations 24 July
1685. Transported from
Leith to Jamaica by John
Ewing August 1685
(PC)

WHARRY JAMES
Covenanter. Banished to
the Plantations in the
Indies. Transported by
a Leith skipper 11 Oct-
ober 1681
(PC)

WHITE ALEXANDER
Jacobite captured at Preston.
Transported from Liverpool to
Jamaica or Virginia on the
Elizabeth and Anne, master
Edward Trafford, 29 June 1716.
Landed at York, Virginia -
unindentured
(VSP)(CTB)(SP/C)

WHITE HECTOR
Jacobite captured at Preston.
Transported from Liverpool to
Virginia on the Godspeed, master
Arthur Smith, 28 July 1716
(CTB)(SP/C)

WHITE JAMES
Douglas. Covenanter. Prisoner
in Edinburgh Tolbooth. Transported to America by Mr George
Lockhart, merchant in New York
1684
(PC)

WHITE JAMES
Jacobite captured at Preston.
Transported on the Friendship,
master Michael Mankin, from
Liverpool to Maryland 24 May
1716. Sold to Benjamin Dufour
in Maryland 20 August 1716
(SP/C)(CTB)(HM)

WHYTE JOHN
Prisoner in Edinburgh Tolbooth.
Transported from Leith to the
Plantations by Mr Johnston
3 September 1685
(ETR)

WHITE JOHN
Jacobite captured at Preston.
Transported from Liverpool to
Virginia or Jamaica on the
Elizabeth and Anne, master
Edward Trafford, 29 June 1716.
Landed at York, Virginia -
unindentured
(SP/C)(CTB)(VSP)

WHYTE MALCOLM
Transported from Leith
to Jamaica by John Ewing
August 1685
(PC)

WHITE ROBERT
Gardener. Linktoun of
Arnot, Fife. Jacobite
artilleryman. Captured
at Carlisle. Prisoner
at Carlisle. Trans-
ported 1747(?)
(P)

WHITE ROBERT
28. Painter. Glasgow.
Jacobite in the Duke
of Perth's regiment.
Prisoner at Canongate
and Carlisle. Trans-
ported 1747(?)
(P)

WHITE ROBERT
Jacobite. Transported
on the Gildart, master
Richard Holmes. Landed
at Port North Potomac,
Maryland 5 August 1747
(PRO)

WHYTE WILLIAM
Thief. Banished for life,
at Jedburgh 1753
(SM)

WHITELAW ELIZABETH
Covenanter. Prisoner at
Dunnottar and Leith.
Transported from Leith
to East New Jersey by
George Scott of Pit-
lochie on the Henry and
Francis, master Richard
Hutton, 5 September 1685
(PC)

WILKIE JAMES
Jacobite. Transported
from Liverpool to South
Carolina on the Wakefield
master Thomas Beck, 21
April 1716
(SP/C)

WILL LAUCHLAN or MCLEAN
Thief. Banished 1772. Trans-
ported on the Donald, master
Thomas Ramsay. Landed at
Port James, Upper District,
Virginia 13 March 1773
(SM)(JC)

WILLIAMSON ALEXANDER
Glover. Elgin. Thief. Transported. Banished to the Plantations in America for life,
at Edinburgh January 1767
(SM)(JC)

WILLIAMSON JOHN
Angus. Jacobite in Ogilvy's
regiment. Prisoner at Carlisle
and Lancaster. Transported
to Antigua 8 May 1747
(P)

WILLIAMSON THOMAS
Prisoner in Edinburgh Tolbooth
Transported from Leith to the
Plantations November 1679
(ETR)

WILLIAMSON THOMAS
24. Clerk to Adam Fairholme.
Edinburgh. Jacobite in Elcho's
Life Guards. Prisoner at
Inverness, ship and Tilbury.
Transported from London to
Barbados or Jamaica by
Samuel Smith 31 March 1747
(P)(RM)

WILSON ANDREW
Royalist soldier captured at
Worcester. Transported from
Gravesend to Boston on the
John and Sarah, master John
Greene, 13 May 1652
(NER)

WILSON ANDREW
Founder. Aberfoyle, Ferth-
shire. Thief. Banished to
the Plantations for life,
at Perth May 1770. Trans-
ported from Port Glasgow
on the Crawford, master
James McLean. Landed at
Port Oxford, Maryland
23 July 1771

WILSON ANDREW
Tailor. Rioter in Dum-
fries. Banished to the
Plantations for 7 years.
Transported from Port
Glasgow on the Matty,
master Robert Peacock.
Landed at Port Oxford,
Maryland 17 December 1771
(SM)(JC)

WILSON ANNE
Sister of William Wilson,
tinker. Thief and pick-
pocket. Banished to the
Plantations for 7 years,
at Jedburgh 24 September
1766
(SM)

WILSON CHRISTOPHER
Royalist soldier captured
at Worcester. Transported
on the John and Sarah,
master John Greene, from
Gravesend to Boston,
13 May 1652
(NER)

WILSON HELEN
Didrigg, Midcalder. Child
murder. Prisoner in Edin-
burgh Tolbooth. Banished
to the Plantations in
America for life, at Edinburgh 23 February 1747
(JC)

WILSON HENRY
Jacobite captured at Pres-
ton. Transported from
Liverpool to Maryland on
the Friendship, master
Michael Mankin, 24 May 1716
Sold to John Gresham in
Maryland 20 August 1716
(SP/C)(CTB)(HM)

WILSON JAMES
Jacobite captured at Preston.
Transported from Liverpool to
South Carolina on the Wakefield,
master Thomas Beck, 21 April 1716
(SP/C)

WILSON JEAN
Child murder. Banished, at
Ayr 1752
(SM)

WILSON JOHN
Royalist soldier captured at
Worcester. Transported from
Gravesend to Boston, on the
John and Sarah, master John
Greene, 13 May 1652
(NER)

WILSON or MACDONALD MARGARET
Daughter of George Wilson,
soldier in Handasyde's regiment.
Vagrant. Banished at Glasgow
1754
(SM)

WILSON MARY
Wife of John Melville, tinker.
Thief. Banished for life 1772.
Transported from Port Glasgow
on the Polly, master James
McArthur. Landed at Port
Oxford, Maryland 16 September
1772
(SM)(JC)

WILSON PATRICK
Writer in Edinburgh. Banished
for illegally effecting a
marriage. Transported from
Leith to the Plantations in
America by Robert Barbour
15 June 1671
(PC)

WILSON PATRICK
Prisoner in Edinburgh Tolbooth.
Transported from Leith to the
Plantations November 1679
(ETR)

WILSON PETER
Schoolmaster. Edinburgh.
Banished for life for
illegally carrying out
a clandestine marriage.
18 March 1768
(JC)

WILSON WILLIAM
Galloway. Covenanter.
Prisoner in Leith Tol-
booth. Transported from
Leith to East New Jersey
by George Scott of Pit-
lochie on the Henry and
Francis, master Richard
Hutton, 5 September 1685.
Banished to the Plant-
ations 18 August 1685
(PC)

WILSON WILLIAM
Tinker. Spittal. Thief
and pickpocket. Banished
to the Plantations for 7
years, at Jedburgh
24 September 1766
(SM)

WILSON WILLIAM
Hattonslap. Thief. Ban-
ished to America or the
British West Indies for
life, at Aberdeen
September 1775
(SM)

WILSON WILLIAM
Horsethief. Banished to
the Plantations in the
British West Indies for
life, at Glasgow
20 September 1775
(SM)

WINTER EDWARD
Prisoner in Edinburgh
Tolbooth. Transported
from Leith to America by
Alexander Fearne
17 December 1685
(ETR)(PC)

WISE NINIAN
33. Labourer. Jacobite. Prisoner
at Carlisle. Transported from
Liverpool on the Johnson, master
William Pemberton. Landed at
Port Oxford, Maryland
5 August 1747
(P)(PRO)

WISHART ALEXANDER
20. Servant to Thomas Webster.
Montrose, Angus. Jacobite in
Ogilvy's regiment. Prisoner
at Inverness, ships, Tilbury
and Southwark. Transported
19 March 1747
(P)

WISHART ROBERT
40. Labourer. Jacobite.
Prisoner at Canongate and
Carlisle. Transported 1747(?)
(P)

WISHART MR WILLIAM
Covenanter. Prisoner in
Edinburgh or Canongate Tolbooth.
Transported from Leith to
Carolina by Robert Malloch
1684
(PC)

WITHERINGTON RICHARD
Jacobite captured at Preston.
Transported from Liverpool for
Virginia on the Godspeed, master
Arthur Smith, 28 July 1716.
Sold to Randall Garland in
Maryland 18 October 1716
(SP/C)(CTB)(HM)

WOOD DAVID
48. Labourer. Kinneff. Jacobite
in Ogilvy's regiment. Prisoner
at Whistlebury, Montrose, Dundee,
Canongate and Carlisle. Transport
ed from Liverpool on the Gildart,
master Richard Holmes. Landed at
Port North Potomac, Maryland
5 August 1747
(P)(OR)(PRO)

WOOD JAMES
Jacobite captured at Pres-
ton. Transported from
Liverpool to Virginia or
Jamaica on the Elizabeth
and Anne, master Edward
Trafford, 29 June 1716.
Landed at York, Virginia
- unindentured
(VSP)(CTB)(SP/C)

WOOD JOHN
Prisoner in Edinburgh
Tolbooth. Transported
to Barbados by George
Hutcheson, merchant in
Edinburgh 7 December 1665
(ETR)(PC)

WOODELL JOHN
Royalist soldier captured
at Worcester. Transported
from Gravesend to Boston
on the John and Sarah,
master John Greene,
13 May 1652
(NER)

WOOLFE WILLIAM
Jacobite captured at Pres-
ton. Transported from
Liverpool to Antigua on
the Scipio, master John
Scaisbrick, 30 March 1716
(CTB)(SP/C)

WOTHERSPOON GRIZZELL
Covenanter. Prisoner at
Dunnottar and Leith. Ban-
ished to the Plantations,
at Leith 18 August 1685.
Transported from Leith to
East New Jersey by George
Scott of Pitlochie on the
Henry and Francis, master
Richard Hutton, 5 September
1685
(PC)

WRIGHT DUNCAN
40. Farmer. Appin, Argyll.
Jacobite in Roy Stuart's
regiment. Prisoner at Inver-
ness, ships and Medway.
Transported from London to
Jamaica or Barbados by
Samuel Smith 31 March 1747
(P)(RM)

WRIGHT JOHN
Covenanter. Prisoner in
Edinburgh Tolbooth. Banished
to Virginia 4 August 1668.
Transported from Leith to
Virginia on the Convertin,
Captain Lightfoot, September
1668
(PC)

WRIGHT WILLIAM
Jacobite captured at Preston.
Transported from Liverpool
to Jamaica or Virginia on the
Elizabeth and Anne, master
Edward Trafford, 29 June 1716.
Landed at York, Virginia -
unindentured
(CTB)(SP/C)(VSP)

WRIGHT WILLIAM
Banished for theft August
1774. Transported by shipmaster John Rankine and
landed at POrt North Potomac
Maryland 17 October 1775
(JC)

WYLLIE THOMAS
Covenanter. Prisoner in Edinburgh and Canongate Tolbooths
Banished to the Plantations
3 December 1685. Transported
from Leith to the Plantations
in America by Alexander Fearne,
merchant, on the John and
Nicholas, master Edward Barnes
December 1685
(ETR)(PC)

YATES FRANCIS
Fochabers, Morayshire.
Jacobite in Glenbucket's
regiment. Captured at
Carlisle. Prisoner at
Carlisle and Chester.
Transported from Liver-
pool on the Gildart,
master Richard Holmes.
Landed at Port North
Potomac, Maryland
5 August 1747
(P)(PRO)

YEAMAN FRANCIS
Jacobite captured at
Preston. Transported
from Liverpool for South
Carolina on the Susannah,
master Thomas Bromhall,
7 May 1716
(CTB)(SP/C)

YEAMAN JOHN
Covenanter. Prisoner in
Edinburgh Tolbooth.
Banished to the Plant-
ations. Transported from
Leith to the Plantations
on the St Michael of Scar-
borough, master Edward
Johnston, 12 December 1678
(PC)

YEAMAN WILLIAM
Covenanter. Prisoner in
Edinburgh Tolbooth. Ban-
ished to the Plantations.
Transported from Leith on
the St Michael of Scarborough, master Edward John-
ston, 12 December 1685
(PC)

YEATES WILLIAM
Weaver. Clunybeg, Banff.
Jacobite in Glenbucket's
regiment. Captured at
Carlisle. Prisoner at
Carlisle, and Chester.
Transported from Liver-
pool on the Johnson,
master William Pemberton.
Landed at Port North
Potomac, Maryland
5 August 1747
(P)(JAB)(PRO)

YORSTOUN JANET
Gypsy. Prisoner in Jedburgh
Tolbooth. Banished at Jedburgh
30 November 1714. Transported
from Glasgow to Virginia on a
Greenock ship, master James
Watson, by merchants Robert
Buntine of Airdoch, James Lees
and Charles Crauford, 1 January
1715
(GR)

YOUNG GEORGE
Covenanter. Teviotdale. Prisoner at Edinburgh and Canongate Tolbooths. Banished to
the Plantations 24 July 1685.
Transported from Leith to East
New Jersey by Robert Barclay
of Urie August 1685
(PC)

YOUNG JAMES
Covenanter. Netherfield, Aven-
dale. In Argyll's rebellion.
Prisoner in Edinburgh Tolbooth.
Transported from Leith to
Jamaica by John Ewing August
1685
(ETR)(PC)

YOUNG JOHN
Thief. Prisoner in Edinburgh
Tolbooth. Transported from
Leith to the Plantations by
James Curry, baillie of
Edinburgh 5 August 1668
(PC)

YOUNG JOHN
Eaglesham Kirk. Covenanter.
Prisoner in Glasgow Tolbooth.
Banished at Glasgow June 1684
Transported from the Clyde to
America by Walter Gibson,
merchant in Glasgow, on the
Pelican June 1684
(PC)

YOUNG JOHN
Formerly a soldier in
Fraser's Marines. Thief.
Banished, at Jedburgh
October 1749
(SM)

YOUNG MAGNUS
55. Husbandman. Aberdeen.
From Ross. Jacobite in
Farquharson's regiment.
Prisoner at Inverness
and on ships. Transported
from London to Barbados
or Jamaica by Samuel
Smith 31 March 1747
(P)(RM)

YOUNG MARGARET
Wife of John Young.
Thief. Banished, at
Jedburgh October 1749
(SM)

YOUNG MARK
Barnhills. Covenanter.
Brother of George, James
and Robert Young in
Bedrule, Covenanters.
Prisoner in Jedburgh
and Edinburgh. Banished
to the Plantations, at
Jedburgh 16 October 1684
(PC)

YOUNG ROBERT
Prisoner in Edinburgh
Tolbooth. Transported
from Leith to the
Plantations November
1679
(ETR)

YOUNG ROBERT
Covenanter. Goodsburn,
Avendale(?). Prisoner at
Glasgow and Leith. Trans-
ported from Leith to East
New Jersey by George Scott
of Pitlochie on the
Henry and Francis, master
Richard Hutton, 5 September
1685
(PC)

YOUNG ROBERT
Jacobite captured at Preston.
Transported from Liverpool to
South Carolina on the Wakefield,
master Thomas Beck, 21 April
1716
(SP/C)

YOUNG THOMAS
22. Martin, Ross. Jacobite in
Cromarty's regiment. Prisoner
at Inverness, ship and Tilbury.
Transported from London to
Jamaica or Barbados by Samuel
Smith 31 March 1747
(P)(RM)

YOUNG THOMAS
Tidewaiter. Bo'ness. Stabbed
a convict. Banished to America
for life, 8 July 1771. Transported on the St Vincent Hunter,
master George Young. Landed on
St Vincent 4 February 1772
(SM)(JC)

YOUNG WILLIAM
Prisoner in Edinburgh Tolbooth.
Transported from Leith to the
Plantations November 1679
(ETR)

YOUNG WILLIAM
Jacobite captured at Preston.
Transported from Liverpool to
Antigua on the Scipio, master
John Scaisbrick, 30 March 1716
(CTB)(SP/C)

YOUNG WILLIAM
Jacobite captured at Preston.
Transported from Liverpool for
Virginia on the Anne master
Robert Wallace 31 July 1716
(CTB)(SP/C)

YOUNGER JOHN
Thief. Banished to Barbados.
Transported from Ayr 1653
(JC)

ADDENDUM

BAIN WILLIAM
Jacobite captured at
Preston. Transported
from Liverpool to
Maryland on the
Friendship, master
Michael Mankin,
24 May 1716
(CTB)(SP/C)

BANES WILLIAM
Royalist soldier capt-
ured at Worcester.
Transported from
Gravesend to Boston on
the John and Sarah,
master John Greene,
13 May 1652
(NER)

BANNATYNE JOHN
Craigmuir. Covenanter.
Banished to the Plant-
ations in America
24 December 1684
(PC)

BANNERMAN MARK
Jacobite captured at
Preston. Transported
from Liverpool to
St Kitts on the ship
Hockenhill, master
H.Short, 26 June 1716
Escaped to France(?)
(CTB)(SP/C)

BEAMES WILLIAM
Royalist soldier capt-
ured at Worcester.
Transported from Graves-
end to Boston on the
John and Sarah, master
John Greene, 13 May 1652
(NER)

BEAN KENNEDY
Jacobite captured at Pres-
ton. Transported from
Liverpool to St Kitts on
the Hockenhill, master
H.Short, 25 June 1716
(SP/C)(CTB)

BIRD GEORGE
Jacobite captured at Preston.
Transported from Liverpool to
Antigua on the Scipio, master
John Scaisbrick, 30 March 1716
(CTB)(SP/C)

BROW JOHN
Royalist soldier captured at
Worcester. Transported from
Gravesend to Boston on the
John and Sarah, master John
Greene, 13 May 1652
(NER)

BURTON JOSEPH
Jacobite prisoner captured at
Preston. Transported from
Liverpool to Antigua on the
Scipio, master John Scaisbrick
30 March 1716
(SP/C)(CTB)

CAMERON DONALD
Jacobite captured at Preston.
Transported from Liverpool to
South Carolina on the Susannah,
master Thomas Bromhall, 7 May
1716
(SP/C)(CTB)

CAMERON DUNCAN or DONALD
Jacobite captured at Preston.
Transported from Liverpool to
St Kitts on the Hockenhill,
master H.Short, 25 June 1716
(SP/C)(CTB)

CAMERON JOHN
Jacobite captured at Preston.
Transported from Liverpool to
South Carolina on the Susannah,
master Thomas Bromhall, 7 May
1716
(CTB)(SP/C)

CAMPBELL JOHN
Jacobite captured at Preston.
Transported from Liverpool to
South Carolina on the Susannah,
master Thomas Bromhall, 7 May
1716
(CTB)(SP/C)

232

CAMPBELL NEIL
Transported from Leith
to Jamaica by John Ewing
August 1685
(PC)

CHAMBERS JOSEPH
Jacobite captured at
Preston. Transported
from Liverpool to South
Carolina on the Susannah,
master Thomas Bromhall,
7 May 1716
(CTB)(SP/C)

CHARTERIS LAWRENCE
Jacobite captured at Pres-
ton. Transported from
Liverpool to St Kitts on
the Hockenhill, master
H.Short, 25 June 1716
(SP/C)(CTB)

CHRISTIE ARCHIBALD
Jacobite captured at Pres-
ton. Transported from
Liverpool to St Kitts on
the Hockenhill, master
H.Short, 25 June 1716
(SP/C)(CTB)

CLARK HUGH
Jacobite captured at Preston. Transported from
Liverpool to South Carol-
ina on the Susannah, mas-
ter Thomas Bromhall,
7 May 1716
(SP/C)(CTB)

CLARK JAMES
Jacobite captured at Preston. Transported from
Liverpool to South Carol-
ina on the Wakefield, master Thomas Beck, 21 April
1716
(SP/C)(CTB)

CLARK THOMAS
Jacobite captured at Preston. Transported from
Liverpool to South Carol-
ina on the Wakefield, master Thomas Beck, 21 April
1716
(SP/C)(CTB)

CONGLETON JAMES
Jacobite captured at Preston.
Transported from Liverpool to
St Kitts on the Hockenhill,
master H.Short, 25 June 1716
(CTB)(SP/C)

CONNELL JOHN
Royalist soldier captured at
Worcester. Transported from
Gravesend to Boston on the
John and Sarah, master John
Greene, 13 May 1652
(NER)

CORNELL GEORGE
Jacobite captured at Preston.
Transported from Liverpool to
South Carolina on the Susannah,
master Thomas Bromhall,
7 May 1716
(CTB)(SP/C)

CORSAN JAMES
Prisoner in Edinburgh Tolbooth
Transported from Leith to the
Plantations November 1679
(ETR)

CORSON LAURENCE
Glencairn. Banished to the
Plantations 25 October 1684
(PC)

CORSBIE JAMES
Transported from Leith to
Jamaica by John Ewing August
1685
(PC)

COUSINS JOHN
Jacobite captured at Preston.
Transported from Liverpool to
South Carolina on the Susannah,
master Thomas Bromhall,
7 May 1716
(CTB)(SP/C)

COUTE JOSEPH
Jacobite captured at Pres-
ton. Transported from
Liverpool to Antigua on
the Scipio, master John
Scaisbrick, 30 March 1716
(SP/C)

COWAN JOHN
Royalist soldier captured
at Worcester. Transported
from Gravesend to Boston
on the John and Sarah,
master John Greene,
13 May 1652
(NER)

COWSON WILLIAM
Jacobite captured at Preston. Transported from
Liverpool to South Carol-
ina on the Wakefield, master Thomas Beck, 21 April
1716
(CTB)(SP/C)

COWTIE DAVID
Jacobite captured at Pres-
ton. Transported from
Liverpool to Antigua on
the Scipio, master John
Scaisbrick, 30 March 1716
(SP/C)(CTB)

CRAGON JOHN
Royalist soldier captured
at Worcester. Transported
from Gravesend to Boston
on the John and Sarah,
master John Greene,
13 May 1652
(NER)

CRAIG JOHN
Royalist soldier captured
at Worcester. Transported
from Gravesend to Boston
on the John and Sarah,
master John Greene,
13 May 1652
(NER)

CREIGHTON JAMES
Jacobite captured at Preston.
Transported from Liverpool to
South Carolina on the Susannah,
master Thomas Bromhall,
7 May 1716
(CTB)(SP/C)

CRESSWELL ROBERT
Jacobite captured at Preston.
Transported from Liverpool to
St Kitts on the Hockenhill,
master H.Short, 25 June 1716
(CTB)(SP/C)

CRIGHTON THOMAS
Prisoner in Edinburgh Tolbooth
Transported from Leith to the
Plantations November 1679
(ETR)

CROCKETT JOHN
Jacobite captured at Preston.
Transported from Liverpool to
South Carolina on the Susannah,
master Thomas Bromhall,
7 May 1716
(CTB)(SP/C)

CROCKFORD JAMES
Royalist soldier captured at
Worcester. Transported from
Gravesend to Boston on the
John and Sarah, master John
Greene, 13 May 1652
(NER)

CROFT DAVID
Jacobite captured at Preston.
Transported from Liverpool to
South Carolina on the Wakefield,
master Thomas Beck 21 April
1716
CTB)(SP/C)

CROOME JOHN
Royalist soldier captured at
Worcester. Transported from
Gravesend to Boston on the John
and Sarah, master John Greene
13 May 1652
(NER)

CUNNINGHAM DAVID
Prisoner in Edinburgh Tol-
booth. Transported from
Leith to the Plantations
November 1679
(ETR)

CUNNINGHAM GEORGE
Covenanter. Prisoner in
Edinburgh Tolbooth.
Banished to the Plant-
ations 24 July 1685
(PC)

CUNNINGHAM GEORGE
Jacobite captured at Preston. Transported from
Liverpool to South Carol-
ina on the Wakefield,
master Thomas Beck,
21 April 1716
(CTB)(SP/C)

CUNNINGHAM JAMES
Prisoner in Edinburgh
Tolbooth. Banished to the
Plantations in America.
Transported from Leith in
the John and Nicholas,
by Alexander Fearne
December 1685
(ETR)

CURRIE JAMES
Jacobite captured at Pres-
ton. Transported from
Liverpool to St Kitts on
the Hockenhill, master
H.Short. 25 June 1716
(CTB)(SP/C)

DALGETTY ALEXANDER
Jacobite captured at Preston. Transported from
Liverpool to South Carol-
ina on the Susannah, mas-
ter Thomas Bromhall,
7 May 1716
(CTB)(SP/C)

DALMAHOY THOMAS
Jacobite captured at Preston.
Transported from Liverpool to
St Kitts on the Hockenhill,
master H.Short, 25 June 1716
(CTB)(SP/C)

DALZIEL WILLIAM
Jacobite captured at Preston.
Transported from Liverpool to
South Carolina on the Susannah,
master Thomas Bromhall,
7 May 1716
(CTB)(SP/C)

DAVIDSON DONALD
Jacobite captured at Preston.
Transported from Liverpool to
South Carolina on the Susannah,
master Thomas Bromhall,
7 May 1716
(CTB)(SP/C)

DERRITT PETER
Jacobite captured at Preston.
Transported from Liverpool to
Antigua on the Scipio, master
John Scaisbrick, 30 March 1716
(CTB)(SP/C)

DOCTOR DAVID
Jacobite captured at Preston.
Transported from Liverpool to
South Carolina on the Susannah,
master Thomas Bromhall,
7 May 1716
(CTB)(SP/C)

DUFF ALEXANDER
Jacobite captured at Preston.
Transported from Liverpool to
Antigua on the Scipio, master
John Scaisbrick, 30 March 1716
(CTB)(SP/C)

DUFF THOMAS
Jacobite captured at Preston. Transported from Liverpool to South Carolina on the Susannah, master, Thomas Bromhall, 7 May 1716
(CTB)(SP/C)

DUFFUS DANIEL
Jacobite captured at Preston. Transported from Liverpool to Antigua on the Scipio, master John Scaisbrick 30 March 1716
(SP/C)

DUNCAN JOHN
Jacobite captured at Preston. Transported from Liverpool to St Kitts on the Scipio, master John Scaisbrick 30 March 1716
(CTB)(SP/C)

DUNLOP JAMES
Jacobite captured at Preston. Transported from Liverpool to South Carolina on the Wakefield, master Thomas Beck
21 April 1716
(CTB)(SP/C)

DYSART GEORGE
Jacobite captured at Preston. Transported from Liverpool to South Carolina on the Wakefield, master Thomas Beck
21 April 1716
(CTB)(SP/C)

EGGOE JOHN
Jacobite captured at Preston. Transported from Liverpool to South Carolina on the Susannah, master Thomas Bromhall
7 May 1716
(CTB)(SP/C)

EGGOE WILLIAM
Jacobite captured at Preston. Transported from Liverpool to South Carolina on the Susannah, master Thomas Bromhall
7 May 1716
(CTB)(SP/C)

ERWINN CHARLES
Jacobite prisoner captured at Preston. Transported from Liverpool to Antigua on the Scipio, master John Scaisbrick,
30 March 1716
(CTB)(SP/C)

FARQUHARSON JAMES
Royalist soldier captured at Worcester. Transported from Gravesend to Boston on the John and Sarah, master John Greene 13 May 1652
(NER)

FERGUSON AGNES
Transported from Leith to Jamaica by John Ewing August 1685
(PC)

FERGUSON ANGUS
Transported from Leith to Jamaica by John Ewing August 1685
(PC)

FERGUSON FINLAY
Jacobite captured at Preston. Transported from Liverpool to South Carolina on the Wakefield, master Thomas Beck 21 May 1716
(CTB)(SP/C)

FERGUSON ROBERT
Jacobite captured at Preston. Transported from Liverpool to Virginia on the Anne, master Robert Wallace 31 July 1716
(CTB)(SP/C)

FLINT JAMES
Jacobite captured at Preston. Transported from
Liverpool to South Carolina on the Wakefield, master Thomas Beck
21 May 1716

FORBES GEORGE
Jacobite captured at Preston. Transported from
Liverpool to South Carolina on the Susannah, master Thomas Bromhall
7 May 1716
(CTB)(SP/C)

FORSYTH HUGH
Jacobite captured at Preston. Transported from
Liverpool to Antigua on the Scipio, master John
Scaisbrick, 30 March 1716
(CTB)(SP/C)

FOTHERINGHAM JOHN
Jacobite captured at Preston. Transported from
Liverpool to South Carolina on the Susannah, master Thomas Bromhall,
7 May 1716
(CTB)(SP/C)

FRAZER DUNCAN
Jacobite captured at Preston. Transported from
Liverpool to South Carolina on the Susannah, master Thomas Bromhall
7 May 1716
(CTB)(SP/C)

FRAZER HUGH
Jacobite captured at Preston. Transported from
Liverpool to South Carolina on the Susannah, master Thomas Bromhall
7 May 1716
(CTB)(SP/C)

FRASER JOHN
Jacobite captured at Preston. Transported from Liverpool to
South Carolina on the Wakefield, master Thomas Beck, 21 May 1716
(CTB)(SP/C)

GALBRAITH JOHN
Banished to the Plantations
11 August 1685
(PC)

GARNER JAMES
Royalist soldier captured at Worcester. Transported from
Gravesend to Boston on the John and Sarah, master John
Greene 13 May 1652
(NER)

GORDON LACHLAN
Royalist soldier captured at Worcester. Transported from
Gravesend to Boston on the John and Sarah, master John
Greene 13 May 1652
(NER)

GOWER GEORGE
Workman. Alyth. Jacobite in Ogilvy's regiment. Prisoner
at Carlisle. Transported 1747(?)
(P)

GRANT JAMES
Royalist soldier captured at Worcester. Transported from
Gravesend to Boston on the John and Sarah, master John
Greene 13 May 1652
(NER)

GUTHRIE JOHN
Jacobite soldier captured at Preston. Transported from Liverpool to South Carolina on the
Wakefield, master Thomas Beck
21 May 1716
(CTB)

INGLIS JAMES
Royalist soldier captured
at Worcester. Transported
from Gravesend to Boston
on the John and Sarah,
master John Greene,
13 May 1652
(NER)

LAING WILLIAM
Royalist soldier captured
at Worcester. Transported
from Gravesend to Boston
on the John and Sarah,
master John Greene,
13 May 1652
(NER)

MACCOE DANIEL
Royalist soldier captured
at Worcester. Transported
from Gravesend to Boston
on the John and Sarah,
master John Greene,
13 May 1652
(NER)

MACCONN SENLY
Royalist soldier captured
at Worcester. Transported
from Gravesend to Boston
on the John and Sarah,
master John Greene,
13 May 1652
(NER)

MCCOY HUGH
Royalist soldier captured
at Worcester. Transported
from Gravesend to Boston
on the John and Sarah,
master John Greene,
13 May 1652
(NER)

MCDONALD COLL
Jacobite captured at Preston. Transported from
Liverpool to South Carol-
ina on the Wakefield, master Thomas Beck
21 April 1716
(CTB)(SP/C)

MCDONALD DONALD
Jacobite captured at Preston.
Transported from Liverpool to
South Carolina on the Wakefield,
master Thomas Beck 21 April 1716
(CTB)(SP/C)

MCGILLIVRAY ALEXANDER
Jacobite captured at Preston.
Transported from Liverpool to
South Carolina on the Wakefield,
master Thomas Beck, 21 April 1716
(CTB)(SP/C)

MCGILLIVRAY WILLIAM
Jacobite captured at Preston.
Transported from Liverpool to
South Carolina on the Wakefield,
master Thomas Beck 21 April 1716
(CTB)(SP/C)

MCINTOSH ALEXANDER
Jacobite captured at Preston.
Transported from Liverpool to
South Carolina on the Wakefield,
master Thomas Beck 21 April 1716
(CTB)(SP/C)

MCINTOSH DONALD
Jacobite captured at Preston.
Transported from Liverpool to
South Carolina on the Wakefield,
master Thomas Beck 21 April 1716
(CTB)(SP/C)

MCINTOSH JOHN
Jacobite captured at Preston.
Transported from Liverpool to
South Carolina on the Wakefield,
master Thomas Beck 21 April 1716
(CTB)(SP/C)

MACLEAN .....
Royalist soldier captured at
Worcester. Transported from
Gravesend to Boston on the
John and Sarah, master John
Greene 13 May 1652
(NER)

MCNEIL ALASTAIR
Royalist soldier captured
at Worcester. Transported
from Gravesend to Boston
on the John and Sarah,
master John Greene,
13 May 1652
(NER)

MACPHERSON .....
Royalist soldier captured
at Worcester. Transported
from Gravesend to Boston
on the John and Sarah,
master John Greene,
13 May 1652
(NER)

MARSHALL JOHN
Transported from Leith
to East New Jersey on the
Henry and Francis, master
Richard Hutton, by George
Scott of Pitlochie
5 September 1685
(PC)

MONRO DANIEL
Royalist soldier captured
at Worcester. Transported
from Gravesend to Boston
on the John and Sarah,
master John Greene,
13 May 1652
(NER)

MOOR MILES
Jacobite soldier captured
at Preston. Transported
from Liverpool to South
Carolina on the Wakefield,
master Thomas Beck.
21 April 1716
(SP/C)

MUCKSTORE NEIL
Royalist soldier captured
at Worcester. Transported
from Gravesend to Boston
on the John and Sarah,
master John Greene,
13 May 1652
(NER)

ROBINSON JOHN
Royalist soldier captured at
Worcester. Transported from
Gravesend to Boston on the
John and Sarah, master John
Greene 13 May 1652
(NER)

TAYLOR EWAN
Royalist soldier captured at
Worcester. Transported from
Gravesend to Boston on the
John and Sarah,master John
Greene 13 May 1652
(NER)

WALKER WILLIAM
Transported from Leith to
Jamaica by John Ewing
August 1685
(PC)